NINE
WOMEN

NINE WOMEN

Portraits from the American Radical Tradition

JUDITH NIES

UNIVERSITY OF CALIFORNIA PRESS
Berkeley · Los Angeles · London

FOR CRISTINA

University of California Press
Berkeley and Los Angeles, California

University of California Press, Ltd.
London, England

© Judith Nies, 1977, 2002

Library of Congress Cataloging-in-Publication Data

Nies, Judith, 1941–
    Nine women : portraits from the American radical tradition / Judith Nies.
        p.   cm.
    Expanded ed. of: Seven women. c1977.
    Includes bibliographical references and index.
    ISBN 0-520-22965-7 (alk. paper)
        1. Women—United States—Biography.   2. Radicalism—United States.
    3. Women social reformers—United States—Biography.   I. Nies, Judith,
    1941–Seven women.   II. Title.

HQ1412.N53   2002
305.4'092'273—dc21
[B]   2002018704

Manufactured in the United States of America

10   09   08   07   06   05   04   03   02
    10   9   8   7   6   5   4   3   2   1

CONTENTS

(v)

ACKNOWLEDGMENTS

The task of expanding a book after twenty-five years is a very different project from the original conception. For helping me think through the initial ideas and how an updated book might fit into contemporary thinking about women, thanks must go to Jane Holtz Kay, Anita Teeter, Edith Barrett, and Alison Parker. For being available to read early drafts and for pointing me towards firmer stylistic and structural ground I must thank Emily Hiestand, Dr. Susan Fisher, Marilyn Mays, Sarah Flynn, Claire Walker, and Mona Harrington. For ideas about the importance of women as environmental activists many thanks to Dorothy Cole, Maria Van Dusen, Susan Indrisano, and Betsy Wormser, all of whom gave me both the benefit of their own experience as environmental activists and the names of women who had most influenced them. Mary Joy Breton's *Women Pioneers for the Environment* (Northeastern Press, 1998) was also especially helpful. Bella Abzug's friends and family and colleagues were extraordinarily generous with their time and insights: Among them, Gloria Steinem, Liz Abzug, Amy Swerdlow, Mim Kelber, Harold Holzer, and June Zeitlin. And once again I felt a certain continuity with the path of radical women when I found that one of my immediate work colleagues was Fannie Lou Hamer's niece. She generously shared some of her experience of growing up in Mississippi and her childhood visits with Aunt Fannie. Laurie Carter Noble in Boston and Martha Blue in Flagstaff, Arizona, also added depth and detail. Charlene Woodcock has been a superb editor with a wonderful combination of creative ideas and a light hand. Profound thanks to her suggestion that I attend the conference on 20th Century Women's Activism at Smith College in the fall of 2000, her editorial guidance, and her willingness to give me the room to make difficult choices. Thanks also to David Gill and the many other staff at the University of California Press who have efficiently helped in the production of this new edition.

Judith Nies
Cambridge, Mass.
March 2002

There are many people who helped in the formation and execution of this book. First were the men and women who took part in the Vietnam anti-war movement, and who made me aware of my ignorance about the tradition of radicalism in America. Second were the splendid women of the peace movement, particularly the Women's International League for Peace and Freedom, who convinced me that despite my years of university history courses I knew nothing about women in the American past (not even the American women who had been Nobel Peace Prize recipients).

And then there were those who helped me to give outward form to an inner perception: Erwin Knoll, editor of *The Progressive*, who reviewed my first outline and suggested that the world could do without another doctoral dissertation; Aaron Asher, whose idea it was that biography has its most direct impact on young readers; George Nicholson, who has endured and encouraged this book for over five years; and editors Ava Dolgoff and Olga Litowinsky, who at various stages have taught me how to clarify my thinking and, I hope, my writing. I must also thank the manuscript librarians at the Library of Congress, Catholic University, Howard University, the Boston Public Library and the Schlesinger Library at Radcliffe, without whose help much of the necessary material for this book could not have been located.

Among those who helped by their criticism, information, loan of materials or willingness to share their experience in the Catholic Worker movement or radical politics I wish to thank the following: Stanley Vichnewski, Walter Kerrell, Michael Cullen, Colman McCarthy, Francine du Plessix Gray, Abigail McCarthy, Dwight Macdonald, Ida Pruitt, Dorothy Day, and the late Jenny Moore.

I am indebted to a number of people who read chapters, but particularly to Dr. Mical Schneider for her sensitive approach to history as a process, and to David Nies for his critical reactions on psychological motivation. The historians of B Deck in the Library of Congress assisted me more than they know.

Finally, I must thank the couple at the Catholic Worker Farm in Tivoli, New York, who, in 1972, sold me a book on Sylvester Graham's theories of nutrition. Since Graham had been an influence on Sarah Grimke's lifestyle in the 1840s, it crystalized my certainty that there are links which run through the lives of all these women and that a radical sensibility survives the limits of time and place.

Marblehead, Massachusetts
September 1976

J.N.

PREFACE TO
THE 2002 EDITION

———————◆—◆◆—◆———————

Twenty-five years after publication of the first edition of *Seven Women*, I was energized to update the book to include women of the modern feminist, civil rights, and environmental movements because current conservative theory is rearranging the historical reality of the past three decades. A new generation of women is being taught an updated version of the historical passive voice.

Today's conservative theorists explain women's participation at all levels of American society—sports, economics, politics, corporations—as due not to any direct action or agency on the part of women but to large impersonal trends. America's tectonic shift from an industrial to an information economy, say these theorists, brought about women's move out of the family into the paid workforce. The new economy valued women's nimble computer fingers over men's industrial muscle. Conservative historians see the feminist movement of the 1970s as irrelevant. Or as cultural critic Louis Menand commented in the *New Yorker*, "It means . . . that the literature of the women's movement is, in effect, epiphenomenal, a by-product of changes in underlying conditions that were going to happen whether Gloria Steinem published a magazine or not."

When I first conceived of this book, it was 1970 and I was working as a speechwriter in the U.S. Congress. (Speechwriters are like lawyers, always looking for precedents.) The modern women's movement was in its infancy. What motivated me was the experience of seeing with my own eyes how the many women who led the peace movement and gave it voice and effectiveness had been virtually extinguished when the media began covering the anti–Vietnam War demonstrations. All public recognition went to men because authority in America required male spokespeople. Women could do many things, but they could not claim credit or recognition for having done them. My goal was to discover for myself the women activists who had been leaders in previous periods of transformational change, such as the abolitionist period, the labor movement, and the suffrage and civil rights movements—great social and political movements that significantly expanded America's sense of human rights and mitigated some of the worst excesses of capitalism.

Like most women of my generation, I had learned little women's history. Our history books mentioned women only in the temperance and suffrage movements, always in the passive voice. We learned that women "were given" the vote in 1920 because of their contributions to the war effort in World War I. No mention of the specific details that composed the historic reality: ninety years of activism by successive generations of women who raised millions of dollars in pennies and nickels to finance and organize 56 different campaigns for state referenda, 480 campaigns to urge legislatures to put woman's suffrage on the ballot, 47 campaigns for state constitutional conventions, 30 campaigns to urge presidential party platforms to include woman's suffrage as a plank, 19 lobbying efforts with nineteen successive Congresses before the Nineteenth Amendment was ratified. On August 26, 1920, American women gained political citizenship and with it the tools to open doors to education and economic independence.

Today's conservatives—whose lineage goes back to Catherine Beecher and the Protestant clergy educating women to be "good, Christian wives"—tell us that women have achieved equality with men in the American economy (no need for affirmative action). They do not tell us that equity in income levels between men and women exist only within a six-year time frame, during the ages 27 to 33, before choices have to be made about raising children or caring for elderly parents. The tradition of women's activism is being subsumed within a new corporate history where trends are all that matter. A more accurate approach is to understand the intersection of individual activism with larger social patterns. The perceived need for the conscious rearranging of entire systems that many people take for granted is the work of a radical vision.

When Bella Abzug ran for Congress in 1970, for example, she was one of only 9 women out of 435 members of Congress. She was also a practicing lawyer at a time when women made up less than 3 percent of the legal profession. Many law schools in America did not admit women, and those that did had female quotas. The courts saw few women judges; domestic violence was not a crime; children had few rights. Abzug was instrumental in enforcing the laws that made it illegal for educational institutions receiving federal money to discriminate on the basis of gender. She also introduced some of the very first laws defining domestic violence. And she made it difficult for parents to forfeit their children's civil rights. At the same time she called upon women to take their place in Congress, in state legislatures, and on governmental policy-making commissions, including the United Nations. She also publicized what changes were required in institutional mechanisms to allow women's participation. Today, at a historical juncture where America's leaders are calling for respect for women's rights to be included in foreign policy, particularly in Islamic countries, it is significant that many of those same leaders have no idea how change was actually accomplished in America.

Fannie Lou Hamer was the twentieth child of a sharecropper family in Mississippi. Though she was beaten nearly to death after attending a voter registration workshop, she went on to inspire thousands of ordinary people—hair dressers, postal clerks, small store owners, tenant farmers, and share croppers—to join the Mississippi Freedom Democratic Party and to work for political citizenship in the South. Why did President Lyndon Johnson call a press conference in the middle of Fannie Lou Hamer's testimony at the 1964 Democratic Convention? Because after she reached a national television audience, the violence of segregation in Mississippi could no longer be dismissed as a local matter. With Fannie Lou Hamer's entrance on to the national stage the Mississippi political structure was never the same, nor, for that matter, was the national Democratic Party. But it was not the computer revolution that moved Hamer out of the cotton fields of Mississippi to demand economic justice and civil rights for African Americans.

One of the unique political elements that make America different from other countries is the tradition of an empowered citizenry, the belief that ordinary citizens can ask questions of experts, can learn complicated issues, can organize and educate other citizens, and can eventually gain significant redress. Throughout America's history women have conceived and led those movements for change. We have much to learn from women's individual histories and the tradition of radical activism they represent. Today the disproportionate power of corporations in American political life makes knowledge of that activist tradition more important than ever.

Nowhere has women's leadership been more significant than in the environmental movement. Yet how many people know that America's first important environmental organization, the Audubon Society, was established in 1896 by Harriet Hemenway, who refused to condone the slaughter of millions of birds and organized women to stop wearing feathered hats and to protect lands that composed bird habitats? The tradition of understanding the natural environment and human society's interaction with it has been carried on by many women, Rachel Carson, Marjorie Stoneman Douglas, and Roberta Blackgoat, to name only a few. Many people believe that today's environmental movement is the modern-day equivalent of the labor movement at the turn of the twentieth century. When John D. Rockefeller Jr. called Mother Jones "the most dangerous woman in America," it was not only because she was leading strikes, it was because she was educating people about how corporate economics really worked.

Women encounter great resistance to inclusion in the national American narrative of uplift and progress. Yet without the tradition of our female ancestors we have a greatly distorted history. "Tradition means giving the vote to our ancestors," wrote G. K. Chesterton. "Tradition refuses to submit to the small and arrogant oligarchy of those who are walking about."

The theme of this book is that the absence of women in recorded American history results in great distortions, and those distortions in turn create an unreliable narrative of the sequence and dynamic in human events. My goal in this new edition is to bring the historical narrative up to date with American women from the modern civil rights movement, the feminist movement and, probably the most significant movement of the twenty-first century, the environmental movement.

INTRODUCTION

The Tradition of
American Radical Women

For many people the word "radical" brings up images of agitation, angry crowds, and stirring public speeches. It also evokes dedication, commitment, and a struggle against overwhelming odds. The word "women" calls forth mental pictures of the home—privacy, nurture of children, charity, and church work. The two words do not sit together easily: "radical women" is an unfamiliar combination.

From the seventeenth century on there have been women in America who have confronted the Church, the State, the military, big industry, political parties—and demanded radical change. Anne Hutchinson was one of these: a self-taught woman who shook the elders of the Massachusetts Bay Colony to the tips of their square-toed shoes with her assertion of the right of the individual to interpret religious doctrine.

Radicals are in many ways social artists. They restate the hidden truths of society through working with people and social movements rather than color or line. Like the few genuine artists of any age, they teach people to see with fresh vision. They go to the roots (Latin: *radices*) of social beliefs and reexamine tired slogans and lifeless symbols. They are a source of great vitality and energy for any society.

Since American social mythology portrays women as a conservative force, woman are rarely, if ever, analyzed as radicals. Women seem to fall into two historical groups—saints or wives of famous men. There have been, however, many women who were actors on the public stage, tampering with society's most cherished institutions and laying bare the full absurdities of treasured hypocrisies. From the abolitionists to the Vietnam peace movement, to the struggle for an Equal Rights Amendment, women have played an organic role in social and political change.

Today's women claim they have been cut off from their own traditions. They are right. The only tradition for women that most of us know is that of the suffrage movement. But that is not the tradition of Harriet Tubman, Mother Jones, or Dorothy Day. Theirs is the tradition of radical action on behalf of the slaves, the workers, the poor. Tradition means process. It is the means by which one generation passes its ideas and beliefs on to the next. There has been little sense of the tradition of American radical women because there has been little understanding of women as a political force.

Harriet Tubman conducted guerrilla operations in the South for ten years before the Civil War. Working on the Underground Railroad she freed over three hundred slaves, personally conducting them to Canada when it was no longer safe in the North. It was a feat matched by no other person. During the Civil War she worked as an agent for the Union Army, organizing raids against the plantations in the South.

Mother Jones was one of the most effective labor organizers of the early twentieth century, famous throughout the labor movement for her ability to call workers out on strike and keep them out when no one else could. To some she was a "foul-mouthed old bitch" and to others "the Joan of Arc of the coal fields."

Dorothy Day still leads the Catholic Worker movement, a loosely allied group of people who believe in communal sharing, giving to the poor, and total pacifism. Over the past twenty years she has been in jail countless times for civil disobedience—resistance to the draft in World War II, air raid drills in the 1950s, the war in Vietnam in the 1960s. In the Catholic Worker house on the Bowery of New York she has fed and clothed an army of the hungry and the homeless since she began in 1933. Yet when I said to a friend of hers that she really was a militant radical, they said no, of course not, she's a saint. She may well be, but saints are people apart, people whose life bears little resemblance to one's own. It is always difficult to identify with a saint, and very few public men are ever called saints.

Throughout America's history women have fought for the basic freedoms for which the country was founded—free religion, free speech, the right to assemble, the right to petition the government for the redress of grievances. Yet women were not given the basic right of citizenship—that of the vote—until 1920.

The tradition of radical women who have acted on behalf of the most downtrodden elements of American society has been obscured, buried in historical myths about apolitical women. Even the radical origins of the woman's movement have been lost. Sarah Grimké is remembered chiefly, if at all, as the sister of Angelina Grimké. Together they were the first women to speak in public. They spoke on the abolition of slavery, but it was Sarah Grimké who introduced the unheard-of subject called woman's rights. In 1837 she proposed the political, economic, educational, and religious equality of women. It was a time when the subordinate sphere of women was viewed to have been decreed by God. In 1837 Sarah Grimké published *Letters on the Equality of the Sexes*, the first systematic analysis of the role of women in American society. She dealt not only with white women; she was the first to describe the sexual abuse of black women in slavery and drew a powerful parallel between the position of blacks and women in a patriarchal society (a parallel it took a hundred years to confirm in the work of the Swedish sociologist Gunnar Myrdal). Angelina is a "more appropriate" feminist model, since she married, had children, and stopped all public activity after marriage. Sarah never married. Angelina appealed to the women of the South, asking them to influence the men who make the laws. Sarah Grimké proposed that women begin to make the laws themselves. Conventional history can accommodate Angelina, but it cannot take account of Sarah.

One of the young women influenced by Sarah Grimké's writing was Elizabeth Cady Stanton. She had a far more radical life than her reputation as the first person to call for woman's suffrage has allowed her.

In the early 1850s she was one of the very first women to wear pants, "bloomers," and to encourage women to leave the prison of corsets and petticoats. In 1866 she was the first woman to run for Congress. For years she was the only woman who would mention the word "divorce," and talked about it publicly as an individual right. She believed that women had to be economically self-sufficient and not dependent on men and marriage as the only means to economic survival. She believed the vote was always a tool, a means to an end, and grew impatient with male reformers who refused to see that there could be no fundamental changes in American society as long as the family structure remained conservative and constricting. Women, like men, had to be able to have both public and private lives.

Women who would act in public have had to redefine their politics and their personal lives. They had to be political *and* social radicals. No matter how radical their ideas or acts, radical men have often been able to live bourgeois domestic lives. This is not true for women; excruciating personal choices were involved.

Charlotte Perkins Gilman, for example, violated some of society's most rigidly held taboos in order to act in a way that was in harmony with her ideas. Although Charlotte Perkins Gilman described herself as a sociologist rather than as a feminist, in 1898 she attacked two of American society's most cherished institutions, the home and motherhood. She said that the technological age had made the isolated home archaic and that motherhood alone was a primitive way to define a person's identity. She proposed that women become full, functioning members of society rather than occupy the status of half-child, half-adult, which kept them uneducated, untrained for real work, and a vehicle for displaying the wealth of their husbands. She was a successor to Elizabeth Cady Stanton, whom she greatly admired. At the turn of the century, Gilman was a conspicuous critic of American materialism and woman as "the priestess of the temple of consumption." To learn of Charlotte Gilman's life is to see American society as an integrated system in which many of the changes advocated in politics and economics cannot come about without changing the basic institutions of American life—home, marriage, child rearing. Ideas we are discovering in the 1970s about the quality of life in a consumer society have their roots in the turn of the century.

Social forms as the building blocks of political change was the subject which fascinated Anna Louise Strong. A specialist in social revolution, she lived for almost thirty years in the Soviet Union and for fourteen in China. She is one of a handful of Westerners to have known and written about the leaders of the Russian and the Chinese revolutions. A unique link with the traditions of the East, her life makes a transition between the American view of the world and the modern history of Russia and China. She had a journalist's skill for spotting an important story, but she also caught details that other journalists never picked up—the politicization of the Moslem women of Russia, the organization of the "bobbed-haired girls" of China. Her most famous story is the "paper tiger" interview with Mao Tse-tung, in which he declared all imperialists to be paper tigers. An exceptional interviewer, she published some of the first interviews with Stalin, Ho Chi Minh, and other major figures of Asia. Even though she is almost unknown to the general American public, her newsletters from Peking were read in the State Department and the CIA and by journalists assigned to write about China. When she died in Peking in 1970, she was honored by the leaders of China, including Mao Tse-tung and Chou En-lai. She believed that to survive in the modern age one must be able to transcend the limitations of national identity, and her life was proof that it could be done.

Discovering the tradition of American radical women has two important effects. One is that it provides new and important insights into old and incomplete interpretations of the past—the politics of the abolitionist movement, for example, and the two-dimensional interpretations of slavery. The other is that it gives a coherence to the lives of women who have traditionally been portrayed as lone strugglers, isolated voices speaking to an empty audience. Many of these women were aware of one another, asked similar questions about American society, and built on what others had done before them. They were sustained by knowing that there were a few others like them—somewhere.

One of the reasons that every speech Mother Jones ever gave was a history lesson in the labor struggle was that it gave working men and women a sense that they were not acting alone, that they were part of a tradition of struggle, and that their acts were not isolated. In many ways it is awareness of tradition that allows people to overcome personal despair. Without a sense of tradition people act without consciousness or form. Tradition provides connections, and connections give courage. Courage was one trait all these women had in common.

The choice of the seven women who make up this book was made with great difficulty and with the hope that each of them represented a specific problem in the interpretation of women as radicals. When a complete history of American radical women is written it will include many women that I have had to leave out—Lucretia Mott, Sojourner Truth, Elizabeth Gurley Flynn, Kate Richards O'Hare, Ida Tarbell, Emma Goldman, to name only a few. I have tried to focus on women who had captured something unique of the American experience, and I have tried to give a broad outline rather than a detailed picture.

Conventional definitions of the radical do not apply to women. In some ways the real subject of this book is successful rebellion. It is a story of women who were survivors, who learned how to go to the roots of the institutional relationships that dominated their lives and to change them. It is impossible to read accounts of life in slavery or of the treatment of immigrant laborers or the use of children in factories without thinking that the way we approvingly use the phrases "well-adjusted," "politically sophisticated," or "necessary compromise" are ways to shield ourselves from reality. The difference between radicals and other people is that radicals *see* differently, and once having seen a new reality—whether it be for men and women in slavery, bums on the Bowery, laborers in mining towns, oppressed women, peasants in Asia—they cannot rest until they act.

Considering the abuse, public vilification, and physical danger that often accompanied their work, it is often difficult to even guess at what kept them going. But it is clear from their writings, personal interviews, and statements about themselves that they knew they were messengers to the future.

SARAH MOORE GRIMKÉ

——◆·▶◀·◆——

BORN: NOVEMBER 26, 1792, CHARLESTON, SOUTH CAROLINA.
DIED: DECEMBER 23, 1873, BOSTON, MASSACHUSETTS. FATHER:
JOHN FAUCHERAUD GRIMKÉ; MOTHER: MARY SMITH; SISTER: AN-
GELINA GRIMKÉ WELD (1805–79). UNMARRIED.

AUTHOR OF FIRST TRACT ON WOMEN'S RIGHTS IN AMERICA,
*Letters on the Equality of the Sexes and the Condition of
Woman*, 1837.

Women are bought and sold in our slave markets to gratify the brutal lust of those who bear the name of Christians. . . . If [a black] woman desires to preserve her virtue unsullied, she is either bribed or whipped into compliance, or if she dares resist her seducer, her life by the laws of some of the slave states may be, and has actually been, sacrificed to the fury of disappointed passion. . . .

Can any American woman look at these scenes of shocking licentiousness and cruelty, and fold her hands in apathy, and say, "I have nothing to do with slavery"? SHE CANNOT AND BE GUILTLESS.

SARAH MOORE GRIMKÉ IN
*Letters on the Equality of the
Sexes and the Condition of
Woman,* 1837

In June of 1837 a crowd of over a thousand people turned out in the factory town of Lynn, Massachusetts, for an abolitionist meeting. The passionate interest of the crowd had less to do with the subject of abolishing slavery than with their curiosity about the speakers. The antislavery lecturers who were to appear in Lynn were Southerners from South Carolina, agents of the American Anti-Slavery Society. They had once been slaveholders; they carried the name of a well-known aristocratic family. And they were women.

It was that last factor which put a frantic edge on the curiosity of the men in the crowd. There were no other women speakers in the antislavery movement, or in any other reform movement for that matter. The only female in anyone's memory who was known to have appeared before a public audience was a Scotswoman, Fanny Wright. A reformer, she spoke on education for women, a ten-hour workday, racial equality, and birth control; she was principally remembered as the "Monster Female"—as she had been dubbed by the press—or as the "Great Red Harlot of Infidelity"—as she was described by the clergy. Women in the early nineteenth century did not speak in public. Most people believed women to be constitutionally unable to speak in a voice loud enough to be heard. Men and women alike believed that a woman who displayed herself on a public platform before an audience of both sexes committed an act of religious heresy and betrayed a total lack of shame. The Congregational ministers in the crowd were frozen in horror at the prospect of a woman lecturer, for they believed in and fervently preached St. Paul's teachings: "Let your women keep silence . . . I suffer not a woman to teach, nor to usurp authority over the man, but to be in silence."

However, the women in the crowd were not the wives of the clergy. They were workers in Lynn's textile mills and shoe factories. Many of them had been recruited from the rural areas of New Hampshire and Vermont and transported to the city in slavers, as the millowners' wagons were called. Many believed that their lives could not be far different from those of slaves. The Lynn workers had been the first in the country to organize a Factory Girls Association, and their eagerness to hear the speakers had less to do with an interest in antislavery than with curiosity about the strange subject of woman's rights, which these antislavery agents supposedly brought into their talks.

The crowd continued to grow until it overflowed the hall. The aisles were full. Men sat in windows. Some brought stepladders and propped them outside the windows so they could look in. People came and stayed even when it was clear they could not gain entrance. The speakers took their places on the platform. The crowd of over a thousand people strained to see.

What they saw would hardly remind the public imagination of Fanny Wright. They saw two women on the platform, dressed in the simple gray dress and white bonnet of Quaker women. They looked as much like members of a religious order as antislavery agents. They wore no jewelry or any ornament that revealed a personal sense of fashion. They were plain in facial appearance, although the younger of the two had pretty features. There seemed to be a large difference in their ages.

In a moment the president of the local antislavery society called the meeting to order and introduced the two speakers, Sarah and Angelina Grimké. He explained that the two sisters had left their home in South Carolina because of their anguish over slavery. They had moved to Philadelphia, converted to the Quaker faith, and had become active in the abolitionist cause out of a conviction of Christian duty. Even though they were women, he acknowledged, they believed it was their religious duty to share their knowledge of the despicable institution of slavery. Sarah Grimké, the elder of the two, had written *An Epistle to the Clergy of the Southern States*, an attack on the interpretations of the Bible that were used to support slavery. Angelina Grimké was known for a tract called *An Appeal to the Christian Women of the South*, which urged the women of the Southern states to speak out against slavery and to influence their husbands, fathers, sons, and brothers to change the barbarous laws. Both sisters were under threat of arrest if they returned to the South.

Angelina was the first to speak. When she began her speech, her clear, warm voice reached the farthest corners of the hall. The total conviction in her message held people spellbound, and when someone made a noise, another would impatiently shush him. She described the life of a slave, the work in the fields, the long days of back-breaking labor. She told of the breaking up of families—children torn from their parents at the age of five and sold to work farms, where they were held until they could be sold at top prices as adults. She gave vivid detail to the reality of the workhouse and the punishments meted out to blacks who failed to obey the arbitrary authority exercised by nonblacks. With what Wendell Phillips, one of the great orators of the day, would later call "eloquence such as never then had been heard from a woman," Angelina Grimké gave the lie to the prevailing idea that slavery was essentially a benevolent institution taking care of a childlike race of people.

She spoke for an hour, and when she finished there was sustained applause. Then Sarah Grimké came forward. She was forty-four years old, thirteen years older than Angelina, and no one could have guessed that she originally came on the lecture circuit solely as a chaperone and companion for Angelina.

Her method of speaking was different from her sister's. Direct, forceful, matter of fact, she delivered her material in much the way a lawyer presented a case before a jury. She used no oratorical flourishes and drew on no emotionally charged stories. Instead, she explained the historical basis of slavery, the false interpretations of the Bible used to justify it, the twists and turns of the law that upheld an institution which had no legal basis. She presented a clear, compelling case for destroying a corrupt system and told her audience that failure to act to abolish slavery was in effect an act of support. She did not talk specifically about women and their role in the antislavery struggle, but she did suggest that society was a system and that to change the status of one group meant changing the status of all.

The meeting in Lynn was so successful that the local abolitionist leader arranged to have another meeting the following night so that those who had been crowded out of the hall would have an opportunity to hear the Grimké sisters. In the general excitement about the exceptional success of the assembly, it went unnoticed that this was the first time that the two women had addressed a mixed audience, or "promiscuous assembly" as the clergy would later call it. Up to that point they had addressed mainly women and a few curiosity-driven men who had slipped into their audiences; they had gained little publicity. The meeting in Lynn was to prove the turning point.

Within a month the Congregational Clergy of New England had denounced the sisters, who "masqueraded as public lecturers," in an official document known as the *Pastoral Letter*. Written by Nehe-

miah Adams, a Congregational minister with strong pro-South
sentiments, the *Pastoral Letter* was issued by the official body of
Congregational Clergy and was read from the pulpit of every Congregational Church in the State. It warned that

> [woman] depends on the weakness which God has given her
> for her protection. . . . But when she assumes the place and tone
> of man as a public reformer, our care and protection of her
> seem unnecessary . . . and her character becomes unnatural. If
> the vine whose strength and beauty is to lean upon the trellis-
> work, and half conceal its clusters, thinks to assume the inde-
> pendence and the overshadowing nature of the elm, it will not
> only cease to bear fruit, but will fall in shame and dishonor
> into the dust.

Sarah, who had begun publishing a series of articles on women's
rights in a Boston religious newspaper, The *Spectator*, responded,
"Ah! How many of my sex feel . . . that what they have leaned upon
has proved a broken reed at best, and oft a spear." She also had the
boldness to compare the clergy responsible for the *Pastoral Letter*
with the judges at the Salem witch trials, who "solemnly condemned nineteen persons and one dog to death for witchcraft." The
predictable result was that the Congregational clergy forbade members of their congregations to see or hear the Grimkés. Public opinion turned sharply against them. Town meetings refused the use of
town halls for their lectures. The Quaker Meeting of New England
closed all meeting houses to them. Posters announcing their anti-
slavery lectures were defaced or torn down. As Sarah Grimké's articles on woman's rights gained circulation, threats of violence
against them increased. Verbal abuse became explicitly sexual. A
minister stated publicly that he wouldn't be surprised to see Sarah
Grimké walking naked through the streets. The *Boston Post* ran an
editorial, which asked, "Why are all the old hens abolitionists?
Because not being able to obtain husbands they think they may
stand some chance for a Negro, if they can only make amalgama-
tion [integration] possible."

Despite the disapproval of husbands and fathers the women of
New England continued to walk six and eight miles to the meetings,
which were often held in barns, for want of another gathering place.
They came for more than a speech on antislavery. They came to

learn about themselves, to hear someone put into words for the first time the sense of disappointment, betrayal, and loss they felt in their own lives.

If a woman was married to a violent drunk, the law upheld the man's right to beat his wife, limiting only the width of the rod. If she had come to the marriage with some property of her own, the husband had the right to sell it, gamble it away, or dispose of it as he pleased. If she worked, the husband had the right to keep all his wife's earnings.

It was Sarah Grimké who first offered a functional definition of slavery: no means of legal recourse to right wrongs and injustices, no access to education in order to learn to defend oneself, no way to earn a living or maintain an independent income, no possibility of controlling the basic decisions of one's life.

Sarah Grimké vividly impressed upon her audiences the similarity between laws which prevailed for people who were female and people who were in slavery. She quoted from Blackstone's book on law, the prevailing legal code: "A woman's personal property by marriage becomes absolutely her husband's, which at his death, he may leave entirely away from her." She also quoted from the Louisiana slave codes: "All that a slave possesses belongs to his master; he possesses nothing of his own, except what his master chooses he should possess."

According to Angelina, Sarah preached these ideas "nobly and fearlessly," and their "New England sisters" were responsive to the "strange doctrines" about women, which were not only an attack on the similarity of the place that nonmales and nonwhites occupied in American society but were also a proposal for a new social order where women could be preachers, lawyers, teachers.

Sarah described slavery in a way that few male abolitionists ever did. She concentrated on the women, and she discussed slavery not in political terms but in sexual terms.

How could one reconcile the idea that women were constitutionally weak and fragile with the reality of black women working side by side with black men in the fields? If modesty and delicacy were the qualities which women brought to civilization, why were black women stripped naked and whipped with the same ferocity as men? And if women who had sexual relations outside of marriage were supposedly to end either in suicide or madness, why were black women able to become pregnant—often by white men—work, give birth, and return to work? And where, she asked, was the benevolence or nobility of an institution which put black women at the sexual mercy of any white man who chose to have her?

The danger in Sarah Grimké's analysis of the sexual base of slavery lay not so much in her portrayal of sexual oppression as in the question of responsibility she posed to her white female audience: "Can any American woman look at these scenes of shocking licentiousness and cruelty and fold her hands in apathy and say, 'I have nothing to do with slavery'?"

Such a question challenged an elaborate invention of myths concerning woman's sexuality, the code of civilized behavior, and the very nature of nineteenth-century understanding of male-female relations. "Woman," Sarah wrote, "has no political existence.... She is only counted like the slaves of the South, to swell the number of lawmakers...."

Sarah Grimké was not alone in knowing the reality that lay beneath the genial, gracious facade of Southern "gentility." Although historical mythology has given us the smiling, passive, innocent Southern belle, the diaries of Southern women reveal that they knew far more about politics, economics, and sex than history has attributed to them. They were not all ironing their ruffles and pinching in their waists. It is important to know that Sarah Grimké had company in her perceptions of the sexual basis of slavery. The unhappiness of Southern women who spent their lives trying to supervise the servants their husbands were sleeping with was poured into diaries. Fannie Bumpas wrote in 1843: "We contemplate removing to a free state. There we hope to be relieved of . . . the evils of slavery, for slaves are . . . a source of trouble to housewives more than all other things, vexing them and causing much sin." Laura Comer wrote in 1862: "I cannot, nor will not, spend all these precious days of my life following after and watching Negroes. It is a terrible state of life." And Mary Chestnut, also of South Carolina, wrote one of the most powerful indictments of the corruptions of slavery:

> Under slavery we live surrounded by prostitutes, yet an abandoned woman is sent out of any decent house. Who thinks any worse of a Negro or mulatto woman for being a thing we can't

name? God forgive us, but ours is a monstrous system, a wrong and an inequity! Like the patriarchs of old, our men live all in one house with their wives and their concubines; and the mulattoes one sees in every family partly resemble the white children. Any lady is ready to tell you who is the father of all the mulatto children in everybody's household but her own. Those, she seems to think, drop from the clouds. My disgust sometimes is boiling over. Thank God for my country women, but alas for the men!

Yet none of these women could visualize an alternative life outside the society in which they were reared. Nor could they even act in their own society to change the institution they so despised. Had there not been a series of rather unusual circumstances in Sarah Grimké's life, she too may have left us only a diary revealing a lifetime of discontent and subversive observations.

Sarah Grimké's strange journey from Charleston, South Carolina, to Lynn, Massachusetts, began in childhood with her first awareness that there was something sinister about the way nonwhite people were treated. When she was five years old she accidentally witnessed the whipping of a domestic servant. She was found on a wharf in Charleston asking a sea captain to take her some place where such things were not done. "Slavery," she later said, "marred my comfort from the time I can remember myself." Her favorite activity was riding her horse Hiram, because Hiram was neither a slave nor a slaveowner, and therefore he was "free." The childhood perception that under the system of slavery one could only be a victim or victimizer stayed with her all her life.

The Grimké family was probably no more cruel to servants than most upper-class families in the South, and they were possibly more just. The need for total obedience from slaves and the absolute authority of the master encouraged random violence and mindless brutality in every family that held slaves.

When Sarah was eight, she began teaching in the slave children's Sunday school. Black children were not allowed to learn to read, so Sarah was allowed to give only oral instruction. She tried to let the children look at the catechism, to learn the same way she had, but the older teachers sternly reprimanded her. As a result, she took "an almost malicious satisfaction" in teaching her black maid to read. The servant, Kitty, was the same age as Sarah, and while lying before the fire at night, Sarah taught her to read instead of having the child brush Sarah's hair. When Sarah was discovered, her father wasted no words in describing the criminal nature of her activity. He told her that she was disobeying the laws of South Carolina, which forbade teaching reading or writing to slaves, and that she could be punished by imprisonment and fines of large sums of money. It was not easy for an eight-year-old to understand that she had committed crimes against the state.

Some time later Kitty became ill and died. Sarah refused to take another servant. No one was able to understand her strange attitude, but by the age of ten Sarah knew in her heart that, regardless of skin color, human beings were not interchangeable.

Sarah's closest friend and confidant while she was growing up was an older brother. Thomas Grimké was six years older, but he seemed to have an unusual interest in the intellectual precocity of his young sister. He guided her reading, helped her with her studies, and encouraged her to join his lessons in Latin, Greek, mathematics, and geography. Not only her brother but her father too was impressed by her intelligence, and allowed her to join in during his debates with Thomas on points of law and interpretations of court decisions. John Grimké, the chief judge of the Supreme Court of the state of South Carolina, was said to have told his daughter that if she had not been a woman she would have made the greatest jurist in the land. Quite naturally she saw no difference in her aptitude and that of her brother's, and she began making plans to become a lawyer and "stand at the bar with Thomas." At night she studied legal codes and prepared to go off to college, just as Thomas was doing. She might as well have decided she was going to become a prostitute in New Orleans.

When her parents discovered what she was doing, they were horrified. A college for women simply did not exist in 1804. (Emma Willard's Female Seminary, the first school of higher education for women, did not open until 1821.) The prospect of a woman lawyer was not even a glimmer in people's minds. There was no work or profession for women. A role for women apart from wife and mother was unimaginable. Thirty years later, when the Englishwoman Harriet Martineau visited the South, things had not changed much. "A more hopeless state of degradation can hardly be conceived of," she wrote, "however they may ride and play the harp, and sing Italian, and teach their slaves what they call religion."

John and Mary Grimké told Sarah that she had "unwomanly aspirations"; forbade her from picking up a book on Latin, Greek, or law ever again; and told her to banish all thoughts of education from her mind. From then on her schooling followed the typical pattern for a well-bred Southern girl: a little French, watercolor techniques, harpsichord lessons, white-on-white embroidery. To the end of her life her most bitter disappointment was being deprived of an education. In her articles on the equality of the sexes she wrote: "Man has done all he could to debase and enslave [woman's] mind; and now he looks triumphantly on the ruin he has wrought, and says [she] . . . is his inferior."

The emphasis on Sarah's "unwomanly" aspirations undoubtedly had a great deal to do with her insistence on becoming godmother to the last Grimké child, her baby sister, Angelina. Her parents tried to talk her out of the bizarre plan, but finally decided it was potentially less dangerous than desiring to be a woman lawyer. Sarah was thirteen when Angelina was born, the fourteenth and last Grimké baby. (One child had died in infancy. There were thirteen siblings over a span of eighteen years.) For the next thirty years Angelina would refer to Sarah as Mother. Sarah functioned as a parent for Angelina, taking responsibility for her development, inventing new games, challenging her with new ideas. She helped to create a secure, independent, imaginative, emotionally stable young woman who would play a crucial role in her own growth and involvement in the antislavery movement.

Sarah resented that being a girl condemned her to be "a doll, a coquette, a fashionable fool," and wondered why it had to be. She had glimpsed a world of the mind, a world where ideas were important, and it bore no relationship to the world she was expected to function in. In her teens she threw herself into parties and Charleston social life. She was extremely vain and took great pains with her appearance, making the rounds of balls and parties, attending the festivities of race week in Charleston. But something kept her an outsider. "Night after night," she wrote, "I glittered now in this gay scene, now in that, my soul has been disturbed by the query 'Where are the talents committed to thy charge?'" Often she returned home "sick of the frivolous beings I had been with, mortified at my own folly, and weary of the ball-rooms. . . ."

An eighteen-year-old Southern girl in 1810 was not supposed to worry about her talents. Her principal concern in life was securing a home, rearing children, and maintaining the constant visiting with brothers, sisters, cousins, which formed the core of Southern social life. The upper-class Southern woman was queen of the home. The only self-expression she was allowed was religious devotion if she were serious or a luxurious style if she were not.

While Sarah knew that she was not suited for the life expected of her, she had no alternatives. She had to live with her family. She had no opportunities to work or even travel. It was not until she was twenty-eight years old that she decided she had to leave South Carolina and move to Philadelphia. The move was looked upon like a voyage to a foreign country, and she dared to attempt it only after the death of her father.

John Faucheraud Grimké was an American of French Huguenot origin and had been educated in law at Oxford in England. He had begun to practice law in London, but with the outbreak of the American Revolution he returned to South Carolina and served as a colonel in the Revolutionary army. He married Mary Smith, a young woman who came from one of the wealthiest families of the state and was related through marriage to state governors, church elders, judges, and many of the white men who made up the governing plutocracy. John Grimké fathered fourteen children, owned hundreds of slaves, was a brilliant lawyer and, as already noted, a chief judge on the South Carolina Supreme Court. He owned a fashionable town house in Charleston and many properties, including a large plantation on the coast near Beaufort.

In many ways John Grimké was the epitome of a Southern patriarch, a male figure of "just and righteous authority" in the words of George Fitzhugh, the South's leading propagandist for slavery. Fitzhugh's patriarch was the biblical Abraham, a man who "loved and protected all. His wives and his children, his men servants and his maid servants . . . were all equally his property. . . . Who would not desire to have been a slave of that old Patriarch?" Not accidentally, Fitzhugh was also a leading proponent of the subservience of women. "So long as she is nervous, fickle, capricious, delicate, diffident and dependent," Fitzhugh wrote, "man will worship and adore her. . . . Woman, like children, has but one right and that is the right to protection. The right to protection also involves the obligation to obey. A husband, a lord and master designed for every woman." Judge Grimké was a husband, lord, master, and a powerful patriarchal figure.

When Judge Grimké became ill with a disease that no one could diagnose, he decided to go to Philadelphia to consult a well-known specialist, Dr. Physic. In what can only be viewed as a most bizarre decision, he refused to be accompanied on this significant journey by any of his sons or any of his servants. Instead, for his only traveling companion he chose his twenty-six-year-old unmarried daughter who had never set foot outside South Carolina.

Why he did this can only be guessed at, but it is possible he knew he was dying. In the stark immediacy of death perhaps he did not want to be burdened with putting up the courageous bravura for his sons and servants the patriarchal myth demanded. With Sarah, who by that time had been through several religious conversions—she rotated between a gay social life and a life of religious devotion, finding herself equally unfulfilled in both—John Grimké could face death without wearing a mask.

Her father's illness and death marked a turning point in Sarah's life. She described this period in a strange city, acting as the lone nurse to a dying man, as "the greatest blessing next to my conversion that I ever received from God."

She was the sole witness to her father's long illness and final feeble death, and she was the sole mourner at his funeral. He was buried in a tiny town on the New Jersey shore where Dr. Physic had sent him for an ocean cure. Instead of a grand Episcopalian funeral procession with weeping slaves in full uniform and hundreds of mourners from all over the state, Sarah Grimké saw a plain wooden coffin lowered into the ground of a Methodist cemetery. There were no institutional trappings to soften the blatant fact that a life had ended. Sarah Grimké realized—perhaps for the first time—the human frailty and ultimate fragility of the person who had been the single most important source of order and authority in her life. In effect she witnessed the death of the patriarch.

At the same moment she saw the possibilities for a different life. Even though the streets were unpaved and pigs ran in the streets, Philadelphia in 1818 had the bustle and energy and vitality of America's major city, which it was. Sarah realized that the limits of the world were far grander than the narrow corridor she followed around the circumference of Charleston.

Dr. Physic had put her in touch with a Quaker family. Boarding with them, she had her first brush with radical religious ideas, such as the doctrine of "inner light," which allowed that women were spiritually equal with men. Not only was a woman spiritually equal, but if she were gifted in expressing her religious thoughts, she could be a preacher. Quakers were the only religious sect in the country which permitted women preachers, and in most places Quakers, or Friends, were considered quite strange. However, Pennsylvania had been founded by Quakers, and Philadelphia was a Quaker community, the center of the Society of Friends. On the boat returning to Charleston she made the acquaintance of a few Quakers, who not only gave her more information on the Quaker faith but offered to correspond with her. One of them, Israel Morris, became her one link to a different world.

Within months of her return to Charleston, Sarah had a breakdown of such severity that she was unable to do anything except sit and stare into space. She became so morbid that she believed that "every door of hope was closed and that I was given over unto death." Her emotional state was so disturbing that her mother finally sent her off to relatives in North Carolina. There she began to read about the Quaker faith, and her conversion, as she called it, began.

Her previous religious experiences had not been lasting because they allowed her no real expression of her spiritual and intellectual longings. "I fed the hungry, clothed the naked, visited the sick and afflicted, and vainly hoped these outside works would purify a heart defiled with the pride of life."

In the doctrines of the Quaker faith Sarah saw that her own religious impulses had been described by others—men and women alike. She became convinced that she had a "gift in the ministry" and that God had commanded her to move North. As she later told a friend, she received "an unmistakable call, not to be disregarded, to go forth from that land, and her work would be shown her."

But even a call from God was hardly enough to justify the moving of a young lady from her class, her family, her place of birth, to live

with strangers in a strange city. Only hopeless scandal or insanity—
or perhaps both—could explain such a move in the age in which
Sarah Grimké lived. An unmarried woman could live only with a
member of her family. To undertake a journey in 1821 to a city
where there were no relatives was unthinkable. The only precedent
Sarah could find for such a radical uprooting of one's life was in the
Bible.

Her behavior has been attributed by some scholars to her home-
liness, her spinsterish disposition, and her failure to find anyone to
marry her. A spinster was considered a wasted person because the
only functions society valued for women were managing a home
and bearing children. Sarah Grimké's reasons for refusing to marry
were quite a bit more complicated than not being saleable on the
marriage market.

She was not especially unattractive. Looks are largely a matter of
style and emphasizing the best features in one's appearance. Sarah
Grimké had no major physical deformity, spent a lot of time on her
looks, and would probably have stood out as pleasant-looking in her
high school yearbook, had she gone to high school. Although Angelina was supposed to have been the beauty, photographs taken of
the two during the 1860s make them look equally grim. Second, her
family's position and wealth were a guarantee of marriage because
property and family connection were the basis of the marriage contract in the nineteenth-century South. Third, if being a "spinster
type" is a euphemism for fear of sex, Sarah Grimké was not a natural spinster.

Women in the early nineteenth century were not so ignorant of
the physical aspects of love and sex as historians have made out. For
one thing, even with servants to help them, they spent inordinate
amounts of time in the sickroom—caring for children and relatives,
attending at childbirths, and mopping up after miscarriages. There
was hardly a year in which various members of the family were not
laid low by one of the illnesses or epidemics that took over their
lives without warning. In brief, the human body was no mystery to
women. And when a "pure and good man" was code for meaning
free from venereal disease, women were simply not able to be innocent about sex.

Sarah did have at least two proposals of marriage. Her brother
talked her out of one when she was nineteen. The other was when

she was thirty and living in Philadelphia. She had an intense relationship with Israel Morris, the prominent Quaker she had met on the boat. When his wife died he asked Sarah to marry him. From her letters it is clear that she reciprocated his affection but doubted her suitability for bringing up his eight children in the austere Quaker life of Philadelphia. She struggled with herself for a long period—"I struggle against feelings and temptations I blush to think of," she wrote in her diary before definitely refusing the marriage offer. It was an act of considerable courage. Sarah Grimké's whole life up to that point had been an effort to find another role for women besides wife and mother. If she had married Israel Morris, she would have had to give up the meager independence and self-identity she had achieved at such terrible cost. The choice between having someone with whom to share her life and the need to maintain her own identity was painful. She always circled the date of his proposal on her calendar and in times of great emotional stress, such as the unexpected death of her brother Thomas, she turned to him for support.

Her rejection was based on a real not imaginary fear of what she would have to give up to become Mrs. Israel Morris. That she was not a sexual prude or bitter about marriage is evident in her letter congratulating her lifelong friend Sarah Douglass, the first black woman to be appointed a public school teacher in Philadelphia, on her engagement to be married.

I am glad you can reciprocate Mr. D's affection, and that you have told him so. Oh Sarah, how earnestly I hope you may find in him a husband in spirit and in truth. I do not wonder you shrink from sexual intercourse, yet, I suppose in married life, it is as much the natural expression of affection as the warm embrace and ardent kiss—time will familiarize you with the idea, and the more intimate your union with Mr. D. the less you will turn from it.

For the next fifteen years she lived in Philadelphia with Catherine Morris, Israel Morris's sister, and followed the path of a dedicated orthodox Quaker woman. She worked in charities. She visited prisons. She read nothing not approved by the orthodox meeting. She involved herself in no political or "worldly" causes, including abolition, and she spent long, futile years trying to be recognized as a minister.

Those were the years of ferocious battle between the orthodox Quakers and the liberal faction, known as the Hicksites because of their leader, Elias Hicks. One of the most respected woman preachers of the Quaker faith was Lucretia Mott, who also lived in Philadelphia. But because she was a Hicksite, "a despised Hicksite," Sarah did not get to know her until much later.

This is not to say that Sarah's fifteen years in Philadelphia were wasted. They were a critical time of personal growth and intellectual development. She studied and absorbed a vast body of theology and religious interpretation.

Theology was the intellectual currency of the age, and if one couldn't argue in the language of theological interpretation, one couldn't argue at all, whether the subject was abolition or education for women. The Bible was the source for knowledge about human nature. There were very few women who had sufficient learning to even argue the idea that women's supposed inferiority was the result of bad Biblical translation or to make the distinction between the Old Testament, the New Testament, and the King James version of the Bible. A profound understanding of theology and Biblical analysis later went into Sarah's *Letters on the Equality of the Sexes*. The title alone was heresy.

In Philadelphia Sarah had learned the language of theology, but if it hadn't been for Angelina she would never have found the opportunity to use it.

The most significant personal event in this period of Sarah's life was Angelina's conversion to the Quaker faith—Sarah had been sending her literature—and Angelina's emigration to the North in 1829. For years Angelina had spoken out within her church and family against the worst abuses of slavery. When it finally became clear to her that she could do nothing to actually change the lot of slaves, she had a place to escape to.

Her trip to the North had far less emotional capital invested in it than Sarah's had—no call to the ministry for Angelina. She had not gone through a shattering religious conversion, nor had she had to overcome family opposition to going north. She was able to change her residence with the socially acceptable reason of visiting a sister in Philadelphia. This allowed her to be far more detached than Sarah about orthodox Quaker life. "Stultifying" she called it and character-ized orthodox ideas as "soul-quenching . . . which have produced their legitimate fruit of nothingness."

When Angelina arrived in Philadelphia she was twenty-three. After a long involvement with a young Quaker named Edward Bettle, who died of cholera, she grew weary of the restrictions and narrowness of Quaker life. Orthodox Quakers were opposed to any participation in political causes. Angelina wanted to do something about slavery, and in 1834 she joined the Female Anti-Slavery So-ciety of Philadelphia, founded a year earlier by Lucretia Mott. There she heard a brilliant lecture by the British abolitionist George Thompson in which he expressed his belief that the freeing of all human beings from the yoke of slavery was the first obligation of any Christian. The speech made a profound impression on Angelina. The following summer, when she read of Thompson's being at-tacked by an enraged Boston mob and denied a place to speak, she wrote a passionate letter to William Lloyd Garrison, editor of the abolitionist paper the *Liberator*, supporting Garrison's eloquent de-fense of free speech. The letter, which Garrison published, still con-veys the intensity of her feelings about the antislavery cause: "If persecution is the means which God has ordained for the accom-plishment of . . . Emancipation, then . . . Let It Come! for it is my deep, solemn, deliberate conviction that *this is a cause worth dying for.*"

At a time when a woman's name was supposed to appear in print only three times in life—at birth, marriage, and death—a signed letter in support of a controversial cause and a notorious figure like Garrison was a radical act. Angelina admitted that seeing her name in print made her feel "naked." "I cannot describe the anguish of my soul," she wrote. The censure and condemnation from the members of the Quaker Meeting were unanimous; even Sarah was disturbed by such a rash act. But one who had just urged a man "to die if need be" in service to a sacred cause was not about to back down in the face of social pressure.

Soon after the publication of the letter to Garrison, Angelina wrote the antislavery tract *An Appeal to the Christian Women of the South.* (It was burned when it arrived in the post offices of South Carolina, and Charleston authorities issued a warrant for Angelina's

arrest if she ever set foot on South Carolina soil.) Soon the Executive
Committee of the American Anti-Slavery Society in New York realized they had an unusual woman interested in abolition—a South-
erner, a former slaveowner, a literate writer able to convey powerful
emotions. They asked her to become a speaker for the American
Anti-Slavery Society, addressing small groups of women in private
parlors on the evils of slavery. Angelina decided to accept. She
looked on it as her Christian duty.

Sarah was appalled. For one thing, from her efforts to become a
preacher she knew how agonizing it was for a woman to speak in
public. She recalled the rebuffs, the hostility, the venemous resentment toward women who did not stay in their place. Angelina had
never even opened her mouth to attempt a prayer in Quaker Meeting. Sarah also knew that involvement in a worldly political cause
was likely to bring expulsion from the Society of Friends, not a
consideration to be taken lightly. There were few social circles open
to an unmarried woman barred from her homeland.

These considerations were irrelevant to Angelina. She believed
that such a mission was part of her religion and that she was called
to do whatever she was able to on behalf of the slave. Sarah still
disapproved, but she accepted Angelina's decision. She believed that
"their lives were intertwined," and even though it meant risking
expulsion from the only community she had, she offered to accompany Angelina. Sarah believed she could help make arrangements,
assist in the research and preparation of her talks, and play the role
of parent and chaperone.

Their first public assembly took place in New York in November
of 1835 after Sarah and Angelina had attended a convention to train
antislavery speakers. The woman's meeting almost did not take
place because over three hundred women showed up, not exactly
the Anti-Slavery Society's vision of "a small gathering of ladies."
According to Angelina's account of the meeting, it

> was opened with prayer by Henry Ludlow; we were warmly
> welcomed by brother Dunbar, and then these two left us. After
> a moment, I arose and spoke about forty minutes, feeling, I
> think, entirely unembarrassed. Then dear Sister did her part
> better than I did. We then read . . . from papers and letters . . .
> answered a few questions. . . .

The two men left because it was considered indelicate for men to be present when women spoke. Sarah Grimké called this a "ludicrous" practice. "I have blushed for my sex when I have heard of their entreating ministers to attend their association and open them with prayer."

Clearly, even from the beginning, Sarah Grimké was doing more than making arrangements for Angelina. For the three months they remained in the New York area, they conducted small meetings, developed their material, and improved their speaking skills. They were coached by Theodore Weld, the master trainer of the traveling antislavery agents. (Sarah and Angelina were agents of a special category because they paid all their own expenses, but most of their talks were arranged and promoted by the society.) After they had gained exposure and experience, they were invited to New England, the center of radical abolitionist activity and a hive of female antislavery activity.

In the spring of 1837 they arrived in Boston. One of the most prominent local women abolitionists, Maria Weston Chapman, sent out a letter to all the female antislavery societies of New England, asking that they cooperate with the Grimké sisters.

The women of Massachusetts responded enthusiastically. As invitations poured in, Sarah began to realize for the first time that she and Angelina were communicating much more than information about slavery when they stood up in public to speak. They represented the possibility of a new reality, a reality in which women might travel and speak and learn about the larger world. They stimulated imaginations to escape the private existence of home and church and to participate for a few moments in public life, a life that most women only knew about secondhand. Sarah described this period as one where she felt that she had finally emerged into "a world where fresh air circulated," and she could breathe freely and deeply. She was aware that she was not called to speak about slavery in the way Angelina was, and she decided to leave the speaking, "at least on slavery," as she told Theodore Weld, to her sister. What she did not tell Weld was that she was exploring a new subject. It was to become even more controversial than abolition.

By the time they reached Lynn in June of 1837 Sarah knew she had found her calling—advocating equality for a group that did not even know it was "unequal": women. Sarah's vision of human equality was totally outside the moral code of the period. When she offered the idea that woman like man was a "free agent, gifted with intellect and endowed with immortality," a person whose sole duty was to God—not to husband, father, minister, or any other mortal man—she was attacking beliefs that were held as firmly as though they had been cast in concrete in people's minds.

What she said in her talks is not known, for her speeches were never written down and there were no stenographers present. Angelina said that "Sister Sarah" offered her "strange doctrines . . . nobly and fearlessly."

From the articles she published in the Boston *Spectator*, we know something of what she was preaching. *"I ask no favors for my sex. I surrender not our claim to equality. All I ask of our brethren is that they will take their feet from off our necks and permit us to stand upright on that ground which God designed us to occupy."* Compared with the gentle, supplicating prose style women writers generally used, it was like throwing a hand grenade at the reader.

During the three months after their appearance in Lynn, while she and Angelina traveled the northeastern Massachusetts towns of Amesbury, Newburyport, Andover, and Groton, Sarah poured out her blasphemous ideas. "WHATSOEVER IT IS MORALLY RIGHT FOR A MAN TO DO," she wrote in capital letters, "IT IS MORALLY RIGHT FOR A WOMAN TO DO." The clergy looked upon such an idea with the same tolerance they showed toward public nudity. It conjured up a world in chaotic sexual frenzy and a veritable tidal wave of interracial marriage.

When the clergy censured the Grimkés, Sarah responded by telling her "sisters to lay aside their prejudices and examine these subjects for themselves, regardless of the traditions of men."

The clergy could endure ridicule, but they could not tolerate Sarah's plea that no one accept her ideas without first examining the Scriptures. The power of the clergy rested in the pervasive belief that only those who had been chosen and trained were competent to interpret the Scriptures. If people decided that the clergy was wrong in one area, like women's proper role, then it might be shown to be wrong in many others.

It was generally believed, and buttressed by appropriate Biblical quotes, that women had smaller brains and inferior intelligence and that to educate them would destroy their essential nature. Sarah asserted that "intellect is not sexed" and advocated equal education for women. To prove her point she gave examples of women rulers and queens like Queen Elizabeth of England and Cleopatra of Egypt who had been known for their extraordinary intellects. She reviewed the legal system and women's civil death upon marriage. The law held that at marriage, man and woman became one legal person, that person being the man. The woman had no right to own property, keep her own possessions, or maintain custody of her children. Sarah not only proposed equal legal rights for women but also that women be allowed a voice in the writing of the laws, the first step in recognizing women as citizens and ultimately as voters.

When Sarah suggested that women could be preachers—"ministers of the gospel as they unquestionably were in the primitive ages of the Christian church. . . ."—a tornado of protest blew from the pulpit. She was saying, in effect, that women could and should hold power in the Church. This was too much.

Even the most prominent women vigorously attacked her. Catherine Beecher, the pioneer in women's education, was totally opposed to such a vision. "Heaven has appointed to one sex the superior and to the other the subordinate part," she pronounced. "The moment woman begins to feel the promptings of ambition or the thirst for power her aegis of defense is gone." Catherine Beecher was a political conservative who believed that if women wanted to work against slavery they should do so by praying. She was also the daughter of Lyman Beecher, an influential minister who had gained notoriety when his students—Theodore Weld among them—rebelled against the theological justification for slavery.

Only men were supposed to be strong enough to deal with the ultimate issues of life and death. Ministers guarded their spiritual territory with the same ferocity that an admiral did when asked about having a woman as captain of a ship.

Sarah's proposing that women could deal with issues of sin and salvation was roughly parallel to proposing a woman to head the Joint Chiefs of Staff today. What made Sarah so dangerous was the enormous range of Biblical criticism and analysis she had at her command. Using different examples, she argued that God had created man *and* woman in his own image, in perfect equality. "Man" was meant to be a generic term meaning man and woman, and both sexes were equally responsible for evil and the fall from Heaven.

In the storm of opposition that grew up around these new ideas about women's equality, Sarah held her ground. She was not afraid of the power of the clergy. Her years of theological study in Philadelphia were paying off. She knew as much, if not more, theology than many of her opponents; she had a good grasp of church organization; and she had painfully learned a great deal about "ecclesiastical" politics. Two of her major writings were attacks on institutionalized religion. *An Epistle to the Clergy of the Southern States* attacked the Southern clergy's support of slavery. The other, a polemic against the orthodox Quakers for their "separate but supposedly equal policies" for Negroes—black members sat in separate pews at the back of the Meeting House—was never published by the Anti-Slavery Society because it attacked a Northern institution that might be a political ally.

In Boston a huge crowd turned out to hear a debate at the Lyceum on the subject of women's equality, a proposition unheard of until only a few months before. All the debaters were men, because few women were trained to speak in public.

That too was soon to change. Abby Kelly, who had driven the two sisters to one of their meetings, was inspired to follow their example. She became one of the most fiery, dedicated abolitionist speakers and the first woman elected to the Executive Committee of the Anti-Slavery Society. Other women joined the ranks, including Susan B. Anthony and Lucy Stone, who were to become leaders of the woman's rights movement.

Lucy Stone traced her first commitment to the cause of helping women to hearing her minister read the *Pastoral Letter*'s condemnation of the Grimkés. It provoked her interest enough to read Sarah's *Letters on the Equality of the Sexes*, which after appearing in the *Spectator* were published in pamphlet form. Stone immediately wrote to her brother, telling him that if he could read "S. M. Grimké on the Rights of Women . . . I guess you would not think that I was too obstreperous. I tell you they are first-rate and only help to confirm the resolution I had made before, to call no man master."

Among working-class women, the idea of woman's rights took a strong hold, for it was a potent weapon in combating the power of the "boss-fathers," who paid women tiny wages for long, arduous work weeks, sold them a bed and board, judged their morals, and governed their lives. In the Massachusetts textile mills women worked from 5:00 A.M. until 7:30 P.M., six days a week: carding wool and tending looms; pressing, folding, and packing finished cloth. In 1837 a group of women cotton mill workers had gone on strike— "turn-out" was the phrase used at the time—and the *Boston Transcript* reported that the young woman leader of the strike made "a flaming speech on the rights of women . . . which produced a powerful effect on her auditors and they determined to have their own way, if they died for it."

The *Letters on the Equality of the Sexes* did not die out. They posed the basic questions of human equality for most of the century. In 1850 when Lucretia Mott was asked to respond to Richard Henry Dana's attack on women's equality, she took many of her arguments, including exact phrases, from Sarah Grimké's *Letters*. At the end of the nineteenth century, when Elizabeth Cady Stanton decided that a refutation of the Bible's subordination of the female was finally in order, she too returned to Sarah Grimké's biblical analysis before writing her own *Woman's Bible* in 1898.

Even indirectly Sarah Grimké's writings on women and education had an immediate effect. In 1840 Margaret Fuller began her adult education courses in Boston—they were called conversations—on subjects like Goethe and German literature. Before 1837 it would have been difficult for American women to even contemplate taking an interest in such scholarly subject matter, never mind meeting in small groups with men to discuss it.

Yet the woman who acted as a catalyst for all this activity and whose *Letters on the Equality of the Sexes* was described by Lucretia Mott as "the most important work since Mary Wollstonecraft's *Rights of Women* [sic]," is virtually unmentioned in American history texts.

Sarah Grimké is known today mainly as Angelina Grimké's sister and as a manager for her sister's oratorical talents. She did not have a relationship with a man which would have served to define her place in history. She did not die a tragic death (like Margaret Fuller) in the best nineteenth-century tradition. And unfortunately the interrelationship of her personal life with the politics of abolition moved her away from the section of the abolition movement which was most sympathetic to ideas of sexual equality.

Many radical abolitionists, totally dedicated to their vision of a revolutionary era of black and white equality, were appalled at the thought of any change in the social order that might upset their own family and housekeeping arrangements. Most abolitionists believed that the abolition of slavery was a legal and economic problem and that equality for people in slavery could be accomplished without altering attitudes about women.

Only a few abolitionists, William Lloyd Garrison among them, had traced the pattern of sexual violence that ran like a bright ribbon throughout the entire abolitionist struggle.

One of the first antislavery riots, one which had so outraged Angelina Grimké, was in Boston, in 1835, and involved a speech by George Thompson to a female antislavery association. The burning of Pennsylvania Hall in 1838 by a Philadelphia mob took place while a convention of antislavery women was meeting. In both cases black men and white women were attending a public gathering, and black and white women were seen arm in arm in public. According to Garrison's notes: "Attack was against antislavery office; it was directed against a meeting of women; the mayor was neither eager nor able to put it down. [No water was permitted to be thrown on the building.] There is the same spectacle of white women paired with blacks as they leave the hall and make their way through the rioters in the streets."

When a group of Massachusetts women sent petitions to the state legislature urging repeal of all the laws that discriminated against Negroes, including the one which made interracial marriage illegal, the men dismissed the petitions saying, "There isn't a virtuous woman in the bunch." After the burning of Pennsylvania Hall a congressman said that the hall deserved to burn "in order to give an example of the horrors of miscegenation," and a St. Louis newspaper editorialized, "A single shameless instance of a white woman hanging to the arm of a Negro was sufficiently insulting to a people of good taste to justify the demolition of the unholy temple of the abolition lectures."

Garrison was a great supporter of Sarah Grimké's public defense of the rights of women. He printed her articles in the *Liberator* at the same time as they were running in the *Spectator* so that her ideas received a far broader audience. Garrison defended her against the attacks of the clergy. He saw the Church as an enemy, not as a potential ally—"The Church [is] the MAIN OBSTRUCTION to the progress of our cause . . . the foe of freedom, humanity and pure religion." He became such a close friend and supporter that at one time he planned to write Sarah's biography, but old age and ill health overtook him before he could do it. Garrison tried to warn her about those who posed as friends but who might be enemies to her most closely held ideas.

Such a person was Theodore Weld, a man who took second to no one in his commitment to the cause of antislavery, a man who believed in the rights of women—but only after the rights of the slave had been achieved—and the man who was engaged to marry Angelina Grimké. The combination proved a disaster for Sarah.

Weld maintained that he was a committed advocate for the equality of women. He had pioneered in encouraging women to speak out during religious revival meetings during his days as a minister. But he felt that Sarah's timing on this issue of woman's rights was disastrous, and her and Angelina's strategy nonexistent. "What is done for the slave and human rights in this country must be done *now, now, now* . . . woman's rights are not a life and death business, now or never!" Like many religious fundamentalists, Weld's historical perspective was Biblical and there were no qualifications to his views: "Since the world began, Moral Reform has been successfully advanced only in *one* way . . ." and that way was to take one issue at a time, not to confuse woman's rights with slavery.

Theodore Weld was as formidable an opponent as he was a powerful advocate in supporting their original speaking tour. Temperamentally he had the qualities that marked many religious fundamentalists. What he knew was God's truth. There was no room for error or doubt. He confessed to Angelina before their marriage, "I have hardly ever known what it was to experience a counteraction of my will, . . . by any person or persons with whom I was ever associated as long as I can remember." Sarah, unfortunately, had to counteract Theodore Weld's will.

Because she felt so strongly about the moral imperative of the equality of women, she made up her mind to resign from the society rather than agree to be silent on the issue of human rights, both for slaves and women. She had grasped a critical difference in the attitudes of male abolitionists: There were those who accepted women as equals and there were those who allowed women to assume a certain autonomy for a given period of time. Even in a woman's movement proper perceptions of authority demanded that men lead. Sarah told Weld that she was not sure that his allowing women to speak in revivals was proof of his understanding of woman's equality. "I do not think women *being permitted* to pray and tell their experience in revivals is any proof that Christians do not think it wrong for women to preach. This is the touchstone, *to presume to teach.*" She even chided Weld that "if I did not know brother Theodore as well as I think I do, I should conclude his mind was beclouded by the fears which seem to have seized some of the brotherhood lest we should usurp dominion over our lords and masters."

Weld is considered a saint in the abolitionist cause, but his performance toward woman's rights is somewhat shabby. He never saw woman's rights and the rights of people in slavery as part of the same cloth—human equality. He viewed the politics of abolition as a process of gaining allies rather than a process of undermining the accepted authority that made slavery legitimate. He waited for the right moment and then hit Sarah not on the issue of woman's rights, where she was strong, but on her speaking ability, where she was most vulnerable.

A series of six lectures was scheduled by the Boston Female Anti-Slavery Society at the Odeon. Angelina was scheduled to give the first one but because of illness Sarah substituted. Weld wrote to Sarah from New York that he had heard about her speech from some companions he'd chanced to meet on a stagecoach, and that "the anti-abolitionists rejoiced" when she spoke instead of Angelina. He told her he was writing in the spirit of brotherhood and love and knew that she would want to know that her manner of speaking was reported to be "monotonous and heavy" and that rather than "increasing the power of truth" her speaking delivery "weakens it." Honing in on her lack of self-confidence, he made her doubt not only herself but people she trusted, confessing that he was "amazed that the leading abolitionists there in Boston have not frankly told you their feelings on the subject." Some credence might be given Weld's rather brutal opinions had he heard her in person, but he was relaying information he had supposedly heard from nameless stagecoach travelers. People who had heard the speech had quite different views. The women of the Boston Anti-Slavery Society were amazed at Weld's criticisms, and Mary Parker, the president, wrote him a letter praising Sarah's presentation. William Lloyd Garrison told Sarah that the speech had gone well, though she had made him "tremble in apprehension" at her criticism of ideas of armed suppression of the South. Lydia Maria Child raised with her the possibility of starting a woman's rights newspaper should the Executive Committee of the American Anti-Slavery Society in New York succeed in shutting off discussion of the issue. The Female Anti-Slavery Society of Salem made Sarah a lifetime member.

Twenty years later Weld admitted to a fellow reformer, Lucy Stone's husband, Henry Blackwell, that the reason he dropped out of the abolitionist movement and other reform movements was that he found that he himself needed reforming; that "he had been laboring to destroy evil in the same spirit as his antagonists." The ruthlessness he used against Sarah Grimké was certainly in the crusader's spirit of annihilating error. He knew what the effect of such a tactic would be. Sarah had told him of her long futile efforts to speak out in Quaker Meeting, of the rudeness of the elders of the meeting, of the unprecedented action of Elder Jonathan Edwards's asking her to be silent in the middle of her being moved to speak. She had admitted to him in a letter, which was half a report on their speaking tour and half a personal testimony, that until the abolitionist cause her life had been bleak: "My life, what has it been? The panting of a soul after eternity—the feeling that there was nothing *here* to fill the aching void, to provide enjoyment and occupation such as my spirit panted for. The world, what has it been? A waste, howling wilderness."

After receiving Weld's letter, Sarah never spoke again in public.

Sarah Grimké's greatest weakness was a lack of self-confidence. Weld, soon to be her beloved Angelina's husband and therefore to be trusted, had delivered a stunning blow. She wrote to a friend, "After a struggle with my emotions so severe that I was almost tempted to turn back from the anti-slavery cause, I have given up to what seemed the inevitable. . . . I do not know that I shall scribble any more on the objectionable topic of women."

She did, but not for years. After Angelina married Weld, Sarah went to live with them, a common arrangement in a time when large families consisting of husband, wife, parents, and other family members lived under one roof. When Lucretia Mott shocked the

Anglo-Saxon world by attending the World Anti-Slavery Convention in London in 1840, Sarah was not taking part in the defense of women delegates. Instead, domestic duties, helping Angelina with a baby, and running a farm in New Jersey absorbed all her energies. By the time the first woman's rights convention was called in 1848, Sarah was helping to run the school the Welds administered in Eagleswood, New Jersey. Weld had slowly retreated from the abolitionist struggle to a world which was controllable and which behaved according to his ideas.

Considering the power of Sarah's vision of female autonomy, it was remarkable she did not retreat into self-pity so that she would not have to face the reality of having to live out life as someone else's dependent.

It could not have been a happy time living with the Welds and what Angelina became under Weld's influence. Weld later stated that early in their marriage Angelina endured the "shattering of her nervous system," an oblique reference to a breakdown after childbirth. He characterized her as "a light, weak woman, barely able to lift a tea kettle," and said that her "morbid unrest" forced her to avoid "exciting scenes and topics, especially slavery."

Despair was not a stranger to Sarah Grimké, and once she wrote, "I know not what would have become of me but for Angelina's children. . . . My heart has brooded o'er sorrows untold, until my life has seemed an awful blank, humanity a cheat, and myself an outcast."

But something resilient within her would not let her turn her back on life. While at Eagleswood school she taught herself French with such discipline that she was able to translate Lamartine's biography of Joan of Arc, which she published in 1868. She believed it was extremely important to introduce a woman who was personally courageous and a leader of men to the American public. After the Civil War she and Angelina arranged for two freed Negroes to come North to their home in Hyde Park. They were illegitimate sons of her younger brother Henry and a slave woman. Archibald Grimké was the first black to graduate from Harvard Law School. He became the editor of the *Hub* and was one of the most prominent post–Civil War black leaders. Francis James Grimké graduated from Princeton Theological Seminary and became a well-known minister. In order to raise money to send them through college Sarah wrote a novel about the marriage of an octoroon to a white; it was never published because the subject matter was objectionable for the time.

After Weld took a job as a teacher in Boston in 1864, Sarah went back to Massachusetts and seemed to return to her real work. She made herself the agent for John Stuart Mill's classic work *The Subjection of Women*, published in 1869, and walked miles through her neighborhood selling copies and donating the profits to a woman's suffrage journal. She also circulated a petition for woman's suffrage, "traveling all through our town and vicinity on foot." It was "not pleasant work, often subjecting me to rudeness and coldness," she wrote, "but we are so frequently taunted with 'Women don't want the ballot' that we are trying to get one hundred names of women who do want it, to reply to this taunt."

At the age of seventy-eight she walked through a snowstorm in order to vote and thereby test the illegality of denying suffrage to women. She did it at the urging of Lucy Stone.

Sarah Grimké wrote the first statement in America of woman's right to equality. The power of her work stems from its explicitness about the relationship of race and sex in the American social system. Time has borne out her belief that nothing less than a reordering of the accepted ideas about human hierarchy could make racial equality even a possibility. As long as any group of people could be dismissed as inferior in mind, childlike, dependent, unstable, emotional, nervous—another group would be held up as superior in intelligence, mature, independent, stable, capable of leadership: white, adult males.

It is not accidental that it was a Southern woman, born in the heart of the Southern aristocratic ideal, who first traced the pattern of racial and sexual prejudice in America.

Over a hundred years later Gunnar Myrdal, the Swedish sociologist, wrote his classic study of the Negro in American society and he compared the inferior position of women and blacks:

> In drawing a parallel between the position of, and feeling toward, women and Negroes we are uncovering a fundamental basis of our culture. The similarities of the women's and the Negroes' problems are not accidental. They were . . . originally determined in a paternalistic order of society.

This was Sarah Grimké's message, but in 1837 there were only a few people willing to hear it.

One of the most fitting tributes to Sarah Grimké came from Harriet Hunt, a European-trained practicing physician in Boston years before the first woman graduated from an American medical school. In dedicating her memoirs to Sarah Grimké she expressed a thought that must have been true for a number of women who took the first lonely steps against entrenched power and custom in the 1830s. "As a woman, rare and true, you have done much for me, and also for every woman engaged in the reforms of the day. . . . You have elevated, deepened and brightened my public life. . . . I have sometimes thought you a wise magician."

HARRIET TUBMAN

BORN: ABOUT 1820, BUCKTOWN, MARYLAND. DIED: MARCH 10, 1913, AUBURN, NEW YORK. FATHER: BENJAMIN ROSS. MOTHER: HARRIET GREENE. MARRIED: JOHN TUBMAN, 1844. NO CHILDREN. MARRIED: NELSON DAVIS, 1869. NO CHILDREN.

MOST SUCCESSFUL CONDUCTOR ON THE UNDERGROUND RAILROAD. CO-CONSPIRATOR WITH JOHN BROWN. INTELLIGENCE AGENT FOR UNION ARMY DURING THE CIVIL WAR.

*I was always praying for poor old master. 'Pears like I didn't
do nothing but pray for old master. "Oh, Lord, convert old
master; Oh, dear Lord, change that man's heart and make
him a Christian." And all the time he was bringing men
[buyers] to look at me and they stood there saying what they
would give and what they would take, and all I could say
was, "Oh Lord, convert old master."*

*Then I heard that as soon as I was able to move I was to be
sent with my brothers, in the chain-gang to the far South.
Then I changed my prayer, and I said, "Lord, if you ain't never
going to change that man's heart,* KILL *him...."*

HARRIET TUBMAN, AGE FOURTEEN,
QUOTED BY SARAH BRADFORD
IN *Harriet Tubman, the
Moses of Her People,* 1869

In abolitionist literature "the slave" was usually a "he." Almost all the wrenching tales of suffering and cruelty and hairbreadth escapes were generally stories about men in slavery. Little was said about the women who worked in the masters' homes. They were mated like animals for breeding, and in many ways female slaves endured the worst abuse because they had to be available to satisfy the sexual demands of their white masters. The historian John Hope Franklin has called the systematic breeding of slaves "one of the most fantastic manipulations of human development in the history of mankind." In much the same way that experiments were carried out to discover new crops to grow on the exhausted soil, slave women were encouraged to become mothers at the age of thirteen or fourteen, and some had borne five children by the time they were twenty.

Except for the efforts of a few women like Sarah Grimké, the experience of black women in slavery was not depicted in the abolitionist cause. The absence of a historical place for black women has meant that Harriet Tubman has been portrayed as a heroine of folk history rather than a major figure of the radical tradition. Her success on the Underground Railroad as a rescuer of slaves, her support of John Brown's raid on Harper's Ferry, and her work with the Union Army in the South make her a central figure in the events which led to the Emancipation Proclamation in 1863.

Tales of Harriet Tubman's incredible courage and amazing cunning in helping slaves flee the South were told from plantation to plantation, from town to town, along the circuitous rivers and roads that defined the routes known as the Underground Railroad. People described her as the tallest woman who ever walked, a person with eyesight like an eagle, hearing like a deer, and with an ability to silence vicious dogs by her very presence. One current history book describes her as "strong as a man, brave as a lion, cunning as a fox" and recounts that, although she was unable to read or write, she "made nineteen journeys into the Deep South and spirited over 300 slaves to freedom."

No other person, male or female, freed over three hundred slaves and lived to tell about it. Harriet Tubman was the single most successful conductor on the Underground Railroad, a guerrilla operation to help escaping slaves, which many historians consider the major force in intensifying the strife between North and South which brought on the Civil War.

The woman whom John Brown called General Tubman and slaves called Moses was born in slavery to Harriet Greene and Benjamin Ross on a plantation owned by Edward Brodas in Dorchester County, Maryland. She was one of ten or eleven children, and for the first six years of her life she was able to play around the slave quarters and run with the master's children in and out of the "big house." But childhood ended as soon as there was a means of making a slave economically productive and at the age of six Harriet was "hired out" for wages. She was sent to work as a house maid in the home of a woman who lived miles away from the Brodas plantation. Harriet's new mistress, like many slaveowners, believed that whipping made slaves more efficient, and she began every day by whipping her six-year-old servant. Harriet's first lesson was not reading or writing but preparing herself for the system of punishments: each morning she put on every piece of thick, heavy clothing she could find to protect her back.

Her second lesson was in drama. She learned to shriek loud enough so that her mistress was satisfied with the effectiveness of her whipping. Harriet survived the whippings but not the long days of domestic work and even longer nights of rocking the mistress's baby. After six months of daily whippings, insufficient food, and little sleep she was returned to her owner exhausted, ill, and unable to work.

Her mother, Harriet Greene, nursed her sickly child back to health. Greene was a high-strung, nervous woman who was able, even in the fractured social system in which they lived, to give her children a sense of family security and emotional support. The strong ties among the members of the family were unusual, because slavery discouraged marriage bonds and family feelings. The very institution of slavery made a strong and secure family life impossible. Under slave codes people in slavery were property not people and therefore unable to enter into legal contracts. Marriage could not be a legal bond in the same way it was in white society. A husband had few rights or responsibilities. Often he was hired out to another plantation and he saw his family irregularly. Frequently he was like a visitor to his wife and children, and he had to live with the knowledge that one or several of the children were not his. Since any white man could force a slave woman to have sexual relations, there were many mulatto children sprinkled among the black children.

There were seldom courtships or preliminaries to marriage among blacks. Women were often forced to cohabit with men they hardly knew because their masters wanted them to become pregnant. Usually the master had the final decision on which slaves would marry. The children resulting from a slave union belonged—as property—to the white owner. Efforts were made to keep families together, but a couple's children could be taken from them at any time and sold to a plantation hundreds of miles away, as happened to two of Harriet's sisters. When Harriet's biographer wrote that her parents had been able to live together "faithfully" for many years, it meant that there had been no sexual interference from the owner. The two parents built an exceptionally strong and stable relationship between themselves, and throughout Harriet's long life the link with her parents was the one constant emotional tie.

Her father, Benjamin Ross, was a valuable slave, overseeing a lumber operation which sent timbers to the shipyards of Baltimore. As a semiartisan, he earned five dollars a day, a very good sum, which went to his owner. He seemed to have been a shrewd, capable, intelligent man with no illusions about the goodness of "old master."

One of the most agonizing episodes of the family experience occurred when the plantation owner took two of Harriet's sisters and sold them to a plantation in Georgia. Whites have fostered the myth that slaves didn't care about their children, but slave couples fiercely resisted the division of their children by sale. Thirty years after the event, when Harriet brought her parents to Philadelphia, William Still of the Underground office talked with them and recorded in his narratives of escaped slaves that the selling of the two children was still "a source of great anguish and continuing resentment by both parents."

Harriet was just a child when her sisters disappeared, but that experience and the consequent fear of being "sold South" remained with her all her life. She described to Sarah Bradford, who later wrote her biography, the agonized expressions on the faces of her two sisters; the terror of their children, who were wrenched away from their parents; the hopeless grief of her mother; the anguish and despair of her father. The fear of being sold was shared by everyone in slavery, and it was a real one.

As a plantation owner's fortunes declined, especially in border states like Maryland, where the economy was in transition between slavery and paid labor, the owner was often pressed for cash. Slaves were sold off to chain gangs—processions of blacks held together by chains—which transported slaves to the big plantations in the South. The demand for slaves was great in the big cotton plantations of Louisiana, Georgia, Mississippi, and Arkansas, and the fear of being sold South was a primary motivation for slaves to escape.

The first attempt to sell Harriet took place when she was thirteen, after an accident which altered her physical health and mental outlook for the rest of her life. Having been hired out as a field hand because she hated the work of a house servant, Harriet was present when a slave left his work without permission and entered the local supply store. The white overseer found him there and ordered Harriet and others in the store to help tie him up for a whipping because he was disobedient. Harriet refused. In the confusion caused by her refusal the slave ran away. The overseer picked up a two-pound lead weight used on the store's scales and heaved it after him. The weight missed the man and hit Harriet on the head.

No one thought she would live. She was delirious for two months. Her skull was crushed, her eyes were glazed. She recognized no one. Unable to move, she lay on a straw pallet in a corner of her parents' cabin. The incident occurred sometime in late fall and she was not conscious until Christmas. Then she talked to herself, babbled in delirium, and had strange fits of silence, falling asleep for fifteen or twenty minutes. In her later years she had to have an operation at Massachusetts General Hospital in Boston to relieve the pressure on her brain which caused these sleeping seizures.

The only medical care she got was from her mother and other slaves who knew some herbal medicine. Rather than call a doctor, her owner tried to cure the injury by getting rid of the victim. Tubman remembered that, as she lay in the slave cabin in her private agony, her master kept bringing in buyers. "They stood there," she recalled, "saying what they would give and what they would take." But she was so debilitated there were no takers, even at the lowest price, and this when almost anyone would buy a slave at a bargain.

Her first conscious memory was of Christmas. From then until March she remembered only praying for "poor old master." The only person who could help change her situation was her master. The only means she had to change her life was through prayer, so she prayed for the Lord to change her master's heart. "I was always praying for poor old master. . . . Oh, Lord, convert old master. . . ." Then she underwent a remarkable change in perception about her choices in life. When she heard that as soon as she was strong enough to be moved, she was going to be sent in a chain gang to the far South, she changed her prayer: "Lord," she prayed, "if you ain't never going to change that man's heart, *kill* him. . . ." In that instant, when she recognized that her master was never going to change, she began to reject slavery as a normal existence.

Harriet slowly recovered, but there were odd after effects. She would fall asleep for fifteen or twenty minutes no matter where she was, and nothing could wake her up; when she awoke she was drowsy and in a stupor. She had a deep indentation in her head, and sometimes her eyes were glazed and her mouth slack. Unlike most girls her age, her owner did not find her a husband because he did not want to take a chance on being responsible for "half-wit" children. That she was retarded was a notion Harriet encouraged and, like many slaves who developed fake illnesses and hearing problems to harass their masters, Harriet found it useful to fake one of her seizures when someone came around with an unpleasant job for her.

Since she was not much good at domestic work, Edward Brodas let her work first with her father, then decided to hire her out to do man's work—physical labor in the fields, plowing, splitting timber, driving oxen. It was exhausting, but the constant physical activity had beneficial effects on her health. It developed her stamina and endurance, and she did indeed become as "strong as a man," as she was later described. The vigorous labor helped to keep her mind alert even though she was always subject to the sleeping seizures. The physical conditioning and stamina she gained as a girl benefited her throughout her life. Two years after Harriet's accident, Edward Brodas died. His son was too young to assume responsibility, and the plantation was managed by a guardian.

For the next fifteen years she lived a relatively uneventful life—hiring her time, working occasionally for Dr. Anthony Thompson, a physician, real estate speculator, and Methodist clergyman whose father was the legal guardian of Harriet's master, and other white farmers in the area. She bought her own team of oxen, a sign she was able to earn more money than what was owed to her master. In about 1844 when she was twenty-four, she was able to marry a free Negro named John Tubman. Because he was free and because of her advanced age there was no objection to the marriage. John Tubman was an easy-going, pleasant man who didn't do much work. As a free Negro he could not share Harriet's deepest fear—being sold without warning to a plantation in the South.

It was a fear that never left her, and it grew with each failure of the young master's fortunes. As the main house became more run-down, Harriet Tubman knew that the sale of more slaves was imminent. Soon she began having a dream, which repeated itself night after night. She saw horsemen galloping into the slave quarters of the plantation at night. She heard the sobs of agony as mothers and fathers were torn from their children. The sound of horses' hooves receded. Then there was silence.

As rumors of slaves being sold to the chain gang became more frequent, the fear of being sold South obsessed her more and more. Her husband told her she was a fool because she could think of nothing else.

Quite suddenly she began having a different dream, a dream of flight. She dreamed she was actually flying great distances over fields and towns, looking down over rivers and mountains "like a bird." Just as she began to tire she would reach "a great fence" or a huge river, and would exert all her energy. "Just as I was sinking down there would be ladies all dressed in white . . . and they would put out their arms and pull me across."

The second dream was of escape through territory she had never seen, aided by people she did not know. It was a vision of an alternative life, and after she made her escape, she claimed that the territory she crossed and the people who helped her were the same as she had seen in her dream.

The fortunes of the Brodas plantation continued to go steadily downhill. In 1849 the young master died and rumor had it that all the slaves would be sold. Frequently the least docile slaves were sold first. When the slave quarters' grapevine produced the rumor that Harriet Tubman and two of her brothers were next to be sold to the chain gang, Tubman knew she must act. She had the name of a Quaker woman in the area who was reputed to have helped slaves. She and her two brothers decided to flee.

"The true romance of America is not in the New England character, nor in the Virginia planters, but in the story of the fugitive slaves," wrote the Boston journalist Franklin Sanborn after learning Harriet Tubman's story.

The journey of the fugitive slave was an odyssey into the unknown. Black men and women set out by foot to travel at night to a land they had never seen, in order to attain a liberty they had never known. Many turned back when a successful escape seemed impossible. But many, like Tubman, went on, determined that freedom was worth dying for. "There was one of two things I had a *right* to, liberty or death. If I could not have one, I would have the other; for no man should take me alive." She had no idea how many miles it was to Pennsylvania, nor could she have read a map if she had one. She had only two means of determining her way: following the North Star when the weather was clear; feeling the moss which grew on the north side of tree trunks when it was cloudy. After one night in the woods Tubman's two brothers turned back. But Tubman determined to go on—alone.

Traveling only at night, sleeping in the woods by day, fearing even the white strangers who helped the Underground Railroad, remembering the terrible stories of slaves caught by bloodhounds, Tubman made her way over hundreds of miles to Pennsylvania. When she arrived in Philadelphia in 1849, she was about thirty years old. No one had recorded the exact date of her birth. She could not read or write. Every person she knew in the world was back in Dorchester County, Maryland. "Oh, dear Lord," she prayed, "I ain't got no friend but you. Come to my help Lord, for I'm in trouble."

Her exhilaration at being free from slavery—"I looked at my hands to see if I was the same person"—did not last long. She was alone in a city which was like a foreign land compared with the lush Maryland countryside where she had lived her entire life. She felt like a prisoner who had been released from twenty-five years in prison only to come home to an empty place. "The house had been torn down, his family were gone, their very name was forgotten, there was no one to take him by the hand to welcome him back to life. So it was with me. I was free; but my home, after all, was down in the old cabin quarter, with the old folks, and my brothers and sisters."

She found work—first as a domestic servant in Philadelphia, then in the resort hotels in Cape May, New Jersey—and she developed a plan. She would go back for her family. "To this solemn resolution I came: I was free and they should be free also."

Tubman's resolve to go back for her family grew out of the intensity of her belief that she could never be free as long as others were in chains. Her own freedom depended on the freedom of others. In 1850 Harriet Tubman became a conductor on the Underground Railroad, the organized network that helped thousands of slaves flee the South. The Underground Railroad was, in the words of the historian John Hope Franklin, "the most eloquent defiance of slaveholders that abolitionists could make."

Tubman made contact with William Still of the Underground office in Philadelphia and learned about the organization: the names of contacts; people who would supply a boat to cross rivers; other agents, called stationmasters, who provided shelter, food, and information along the various routes; and conductors, the people who guided slaves on their journey. Tubman decided to become a conductor for her family. On her first trip as a conductor she went to Baltimore for her sister and her sister's two children and brought them out. Then in 1851 she returned to Maryland for her brother and two other men. On her third trip, two years after her own escape, she returned to Dorchester County to get John Tubman. In returning to the scene of her own escape, she took an extraordinary risk. She was likely to be recognized and captured by the patrols, a local militia that enforced the slave codes by patrolling an area and picking up any suspicious-looking blacks.

Tubman knew she couldn't go in person, but she sent John Tubman word where she was. His response was devastating: he sent back a message saying that he didn't want to escape. As a free Negro, John Tubman was living with another woman whom he called his wife. According to an account Tubman later gave to the *Freedman's Record* her grief and anger so overpowered her on learning this news that she almost went to his house. "I did not care what master did to me, I thought I would go right in and make all the trouble I could. I was determined to see my old man once more." Finally Tubman decided "how foolish it was just for temper to make mischief," and that "If he can do without me, I can do without him." Instead of John Tubman, she brought out a party of eleven, including another brother and his family.

From that time on she gave up her personal life to become the single most effective agent of the Underground Railroad. William Still wrote that "in point of courage, shrewdness and disinterested exertions to rescue her fellowmen, by making personal visits into Maryland among the slaves, she was without her equal." It was a profession in which one was either successful or died. Only the shrewdest and most skillful conductors succeeded for any length of time. Many were captured; many ended their lives in jail or at the end of a rope. Leading slaves out of the South was essentially a military operation, a form of guerrilla warfare.

Financed in the North with tentacles reaching deep into the South, the Underground Railroad made accommodation between the free and slave states impossible. The flight of slaves made a lie of the Southerners' contention that their slaves were happy and content under slavery.

Politically, the Underground made the live-and-let-live attitude so many Northerners advocated impossible. Economically, the drain of escaping slaves was estimated to be in the tens of millions of dollars. It was also a constant, grim reminder to Southern slaveholders that their slaves, and therefore their way of life, could disappear.

In response plantation owners organized vigilante groups, supported a system of slave catchers, cultivated slave informers, and developed a highly systematic method of posting escape notices. Patrols visited slave quarters to search for weapons that might be used in an uprising and visited assemblies of blacks to search for suspicious slaves.

During the ten years between 1850 and 1860 Harriet Tubman made nineteen trips into the South bringing out over three hundred slaves worth a quarter of a million dollars. She was never captured nor did she ever lose a "passenger." No other person, including John Brown, was so successful in actually liberating slaves. By the end of the 1850s the slaveowners of Maryland had posted rewards totaling $40,000 for the arrest of the woman known to the slaves as Moses. The size of that reward, worth about $200,000 today, is a measure of the fear, anger, and anxiety she provoked among white slaveowners. It is probably the highest price placed on a woman's head in history.

Harriet Tubman was successful because she believed passionately in freedom for black people, and she channeled all her intelligence, her spirit, and her energy toward that end. She had intense dreams and visions and told Thomas Garrett, a Quaker stationmaster for the Delaware Underground, that she "ventured only where God sent her." She understood the minds of the slaves she guided and the mentality of the whites who hunted her. She also had, according to those who worked with her, the qualities of a great leader: coolness in the face of danger, an excellent sense of strategy, and an ability to plan down to the most minute detail. One of her fellow workers described her as having "courage, foresight . . . self-control, subtle perception, command over other's minds."

She never allowed more slaves to join her than she was able to properly care for. She once made a woman leave her two children behind because she did not have sufficient resources to take care of them. She developed contacts along various routes, people who would give her intelligence about the terrain and the whereabouts of "wanted" posters. She was able to arrive in a strange town and find the right person to give her food, money, information, new shoes, medicine, a horse and carriage, or whatever it was that she needed.

She developed a sophisticated system of communication, using songs and Biblical references in order to let her "passengers" know where to find her and the date and time of departure. She usually started out on a Saturday night, the time slaves were allowed to visit friends. Since Negroes were not due back until Monday morning it gave Tubman two nights of traveling time before the alarm was given and the wanted notices posted.

Wanted notices such as this one were often posted, offering a big reward for a particularly valuable slave.

Ran away from the subscriber, on Saturday night, November 15, 1856, Josiah and William Baily. . . . Joe is about 5 feet 10 inches in height, of a chestnut color, bald head, with a remarkable scar on one of his cheeks, not positive on which it is, but think it is on the left, under the eye, has intelligent countenance, active and well-made. He is about 28 years old. . . . A reward of fifteen hundred dollars will be given to any person

who will apprehend the said Joe Bailey and lodge him safely in
the jail at Easton, Md.

If Tubman's party included three females and two men, and
wanted notices had been posted describing each person in the group,
she might have one of the men dress as a woman so that they
appeared as four women and one man. On one occasion a light-
skinned slave "passed" as the white master transporting slaves to
another town.

A $1,500 reward greatly increased the hazards for the entire group,
and on such occasions Tubman would have to take extreme measures. In one town she hired a man to follow the sheriff. As soon as
the sheriff put up a poster and moved on, her man would tear it
down.

In each town there was a new danger. Once when she was about to
put the party aboard a train, a slave-catching patrol entered the
railroad depot. She took the entire group to the other side of the
station and put them on a train going south, assuming that her pur-
suers would not dream of fugitives traveling in any direction except
north. Often if there were no way to cross a river except by a guarded
bridge, she would resort to crawling across a railroad bridge at night.

But the Delaware Bridge which she reached with Josiah Bailey was
the principal crossing from South to North. As the major link between Delaware and New Jersey—slave state and free state—the
bridge was heavily guarded and patrolled by bounty hunters looking
for escaped slaves with a price on their heads. Tubman worked out a
scheme with Thomas Garrett. In the morning Garrett arranged for
two wagonloads of singing and shouting bricklayers to cross the
bridge from the New Jersey side. In the evening the bricklayers
returned across the bridge, still singing and carrying on. Under their
feet lay Josiah Bailey, Harriet Tubman, and three other escaped
slaves. Notices offering $12,000 reward for "Moses" and $1,500 for
Josiah Bailey were posted near the bridge but no one thought to stop
the wagon full of happy bricklayers.

Tubman was always fearful of an infiltrator or informer, a slave
working for a white, who might join one of her groups to betray her.
The story has often been told of her holding a gun to the head of a
man who refused to go on, saying, "Dead niggers don't tell no tales.
Move on or die."

When asked by a reporter if she would really shoot a man, she answered, "Yes. If he was weak enough to give out, he'd be weak enough to betray us all, and all who had helped us; and do you think I'd let so many die just for one coward man?"

Harriet Tubman was a radical because she acted on the belief that slaves had only two choices—freedom or death. She did not believe there was any gradual, easy way to change their lives within slavery, and she infused in others the will to risk everything for freedom. The hundreds of people she guided out of the South were the visible expression of the sentiments of a people allowed no public voice. Southerners contended that the Negroes were happy and content, that slavery was a benevolent institution taking care of irresponsible, happy-go-lucky "darkies." The stream of slaves Tubman and others guided to the North were the most eloquent rebuttal to that argument.

The thousands of slaves who escaped to the North were valued in millions of dollars. During the great debate in 1850 on the Fugitive Slave Law one senator from North Carolina estimated that there were over fifty thousand escaped slaves in the North, worth over fifteen million dollars. The constant stream of escaping slaves had the same effect on slaveowners that the fear of being "sold South" did on the slaves. It was a constant assault on the slaveowners' sense of security and well-being. And it was one of the reasons they offered such enormous rewards for "Moses."

Out of that insecurity came more repressive laws. State legislatures passed laws giving ten- to twenty-year prison sentences to any person circulating printed material which "might incite colored people to insurrection." Maryland courts sentenced a free black to ten years in prison for having in his possession abolitionist literature. In 1851 Congress passed the Fugitive Slave Law, which in effect denied political asylum to slaves in the Northern states by making it a federal offense to help a runaway slave. There were many American citizens who committed civil disobedience between 1851 and 1860 by giving aid and comfort to fugitive slaves. Gerrit Smith, a U.S. congressman, and William Seward, Lincoln's secretary of state, hid Harriet Tubman in their homes and gave food and shelter to the fugitive slaves with her.

After 1851 Harriet Tubman was no longer able to stop in Pennsylvania with her hardy bands of fugitives but had to travel all the way to Canada and safety "under the Lion's paw"—the British flag. It was a journey of over fifteen hundred miles. The distance, the harshness of the climate, the strangeness of the surroundings made it very discouraging. Tubman spent much of her time organizing self-help societies, collecting clothing and food, and organizing the newly freed slaves so that they might survive. A rescue which illustrates both Tubman's genius and the hardship of the Canadian climate was the escape of her parents, both in their seventies and unable to travel by foot. Few aged people escaped from slavery because of the hardships of travel. Tubman brought her parents by carriage and by railroad, traveling in broad daylight, first to Philadelphia and then to St. Catherine's, Canada, where she had made her home since 1851.

When her parents were unable to withstand the severity of the Canadian winter she moved them to Auburn, New York, and with the help of William Seward bought a small farm there.

Effective as the Underground Railroad was in making whites aware of the realities of slavery, it was a pitifully slow and inadequate means for helping those who actually lived in slavery. There were far too many cases like that of Margaret Garner, a young woman from Kentucky who tried to escape without adequate help. When captured in Ohio, she killed one of her children and later tried to jump off a riverboat with her two other children rather than return to the life of a slave and have her children grow up in slavery.

Even as Tubman risked her life in her journeys into the South she grew to believe that far greater penalties must be brought to bear before slaveowners would relinquish the system of slavery. Slavery, she maintained, would be outlawed only when the costs of maintaining it were greater than those of abolishing it. Tubman saw her task in the Underground Railroad to be one of imposing some of those costs. This strategy was one of the reasons she was interested in the scheme of a white man who came to see her in Canada with a plan for a slave insurrection in Virginia.

His name was John Brown, and he had been sent to her by Frederick Douglass, the black abolitionist leader who had joined other militant abolitionists in supporting Brown's plan for a slave rebellion. Brown's idea was to lead a small army of freed slaves and white supporters into the mountains of Virginia to liberate an area from slavery. Then, using the techniques of the Underground Railroad, Tubman and others could lead escaped slaves to the liberated area instead of all the way to Canada. The scheme was based on other successful slave uprisings such as the rebellion against the British in Jamaica and the slave insurrection in Brazil.

Brown held a convention in Chatham, Ontario, in May 1858. He outlined his strategy and drew up plans for a provisional government and constitution for the liberated area. Tubman attended the convention along with thirty-four blacks, many of whom she had recruited. She agreed to help find recruits for the liberation army. John Brown was very impressed with the participation of Harriet Tubman. When he wrote to his son telling of her support, he was able to convey his respect only by referring to her as he. "I am succeeding to all appearance, beyond my expectation. Harriet Tubman hooked on his whole team at once. He is the most of a man, naturally, that I ever met with."

When abolitionist leader Wendell Phillips saw Brown for the last time before the raid on Harper's Ferry, Brown was with Harriet Tubman in Boston. He recalled Brown saying, "Mr. Phillips, I bring you one of the best and bravest persons on this continent—General Tubman as we call her."

"General" Tubman became an active recruiter for John Brown even while continuing to act as a conductor on the Underground Railroad. She became involved with other prominent figures in the conspiracy, such as the journalist Franklin Sanborn and the Unitarian minister Thomas Wentworth Higginson. When Brown finally struck at Harper's Ferry, Virginia (now West Virginia), in October 1859, Harriet Tubman was not with him. Many letters had gone out to notify "the woman," but she had not been found. She was ill in Fall River, Massachusetts. It was the kind of illness that struck her periodically throughout her life, a combination of utter fatigue and complicating side effects from her old head wound. When she was finally on her way, in New York on October 17, 1859, she told the woman she was staying with that she had a premonition something was wrong. She believed that "Captain Brown was in trouble" and that they should soon hear bad news from him. The next day's newspapers brought news of the raid on the federal arsenal at Harper's Ferry and the arrest of Brown and most of his men. Only five persons escaped out of twenty-one participants.

Harriet Tubman, like John Brown, was something of a mystic. She believed in her dreams and premonitions and had learned to trust them. After her very first meeting with Brown in Canada she had a dream she could not understand. "I was standing in a wilderness sort of place all full of rocks and bushes and I saw a serpent raise its head among the rocks . . . it became the head of an old man with a long white beard, gazing at me wishful-like, just as if he were going to speak to me . . . then two other heads rose." As she stood looking at them and wondering what they could want with her, a "great crowd of men rushed in and struck down the younger heads, and then the head of the old man, still looking at me so wishful-like. . . ."

One of Brown's sons was killed during the battle. The other was hanged. John Brown himself was hanged on December 2, 1859. Tubman finally understood the meaning of the dream and she completely understood John Brown's words of explanation at his trial:

> Had I so intervened in behalf of the rich, the powerful, the intelligent, the so-called great . . . and suffered and sacrificed what I have in this [act], it would have been all right. . . . I believe that to have interfered as I have . . . in behalf of His despised poor, I did no wrong but right.

She believed that Brown had deliberately sacrificed his life on behalf of the slaves. "When I think how he gave up his life for our people, and how he never flinched, but was so brave to the end . . ." She also believed that his hanging was the first step leading to war between North and South.

Despite the failure of the Harper's Ferry raid from the standpoint of freeing or liberating territory, the action achieved its ultimate political goal, that of polarizing the country on the issue of slavery. It is possible that Harriet Tubman was one of the few people who truly comprehended the nature of John Brown's vision and the symbolism of his strange assault on Harper's Ferry. The relationship between the two has been curiously interpreted, one writer even suggesting that Brown recruited Tubman to be the "protecting mother" of the newly liberated state. More likely, they each understood the other's unusual gifts. Like Tubman, Brown was deeply religious: he carried with him a heavy sense of destiny; and like Tubman, he was utterly committed to freeing black people from slavery.

On the way to be hanged John Brown scribbled his last prophetic message on a piece of paper.

> I, John Brown, am now certain that the crimes of this guilty land will never be purged away but with blood. I had, as I now think, vainly flattered myself that without *very much* bloodshed it might be done.

The vast company of soldiers that escorted him to the gallows included Robert E. Lee, Stonewall Jackson, and John Wilkes Booth—all to be central figures of the Civil War era.

One historical judgment has made John Brown an ineffectual leader who sacrificed his men irresponsibly, an unstable fanatic who had a family history of insanity and who arrived at Harper's Ferry with no sound plan and little grasp of military objectives. His martyrdom has been attributed less to his understanding of his action than to the haste in which the governor of Virginia hanged him.

Yet even the governor of Virginia did not call him a crazed fanatic: "They are themselves mistaken who take him to be a madman. . . . He is a man of clear head, of courage, of fortitude and simple ingenuousness." While he was in prison, Brown refused all plans for rescue or escape. His words at his trial were measured and powerful. In talking with reporters he never lost track of his central purpose or the true subject of his trial. The *New York Herald* quoted him:

> I am here . . . not to gratify any personal animosity, revenge or vindictive spirit. It is my sympathy with the oppressed and wrong, that are as good as you and as precious in the sight of God. . . . You may dispose of me easily, but this question is still to be settled—the Negro question—the end of that is not yet.

On the day Brown was hanged Harriet Tubman was very agitated, and she went to see Franklin Sanborn, who had also been involved in the Harper's Ferry conspiracy. She told him, "It was not John Brown that died on that gallow . . . it wasn't mortal man, it was God in him." Tubman's religion was personal and profound. It had nothing to do with organized churches. Thomas Garrett said he had never met anyone "of any color, who had more confidence in the voice of God, as spoken direct to her soul. She has frequently told me that she talked with God, and he talked with her every day of her life."

When others said there would have to be peace between the North and South—war between Americans was unthinkable—Tubman said, "They may say 'peace' as much as they like; I know there's going to be war." Within four months of the hanging of John Brown, the South Carolina militia fired on Fort Sumter, a federal fort in Charlestown harbor, and the war for Southern independence began.

With the outbreak of the Civil War in 1861, Tubman guided a last party of escaping slaves to Canada through upstate New York and then returned to Boston. Her former coconspirators in the John Brown affair—Franklin Sanborn and Thomas Wentworth Higginson among others—introduced her to Boston's political and literary elite. She went to the homes of Bronson Alcott, Ralph Waldo Emerson, Mrs. Horace Mann, Lydia Maria Child and mesmerized them with her accounts of slave escapes and the desperate measures needed simply to stay alive. According to Sanborn, "They all admired and respected her. Nobody doubted the reality of her adventures. She was too *real* a person. . . ."

Tubman began speaking at antislavery meetings—often under an alias because she was still a hunted woman—and working with freedman's societies in the Boston area. During this period she gained a great reputation as a speaker. She was hardly a conventional speaker on the abolitionist circuit. Often she had a sleeping seizure while sitting on the platform. Then this black woman, who looked much older than she was, would rouse herself and, to the amazement of the audience, give a spellbinding account of slavery and how slaves escaped to the North. After a meeting in Worcester, Massachusetts, a reporter wrote that the black woman abolitionist spoke

> in a style of quaint simplicity which excited the most profound interest in her hearers. The mere words could do no justice to the speaker and therefore we do not undertake to give them . . . but we advise all our readers to take the earliest opportunity to see and hear her.

She spoke with poetic rhythms in language of striking imagery. Years later, describing an early battle of the Civil War in Charleston, South Carolina, she told her audience: "We saw the lightning and that was the guns; and then we heard the thunder and that was the big guns; and then we heard the rain falling and that was the drops of blood falling; and when we came to get in the crops, it was dead men that we reaped."

A clergyman compared her stories to gospel narratives, compelling in their simplicity of truth. A reporter who interviewed her in her old age said it was worth the day's journey up to Auburn, New York, just to hear her describe one of her exploits. Tubman had great dramatic power. She described a scene as vividly as if she were showing a photograph, and her voice and language changed with the different actors. But always there seemed to be no way to describe her except to compare her to a man. "For sound sense and real native eloquence, her address would do honor to any man," said one newspaper. Even Franklin Sanborn's highest compliment was to compare her to a man: "She has done what can scarcely be credited on the best authority, and she has accomplished her purposes with a coolness, foresight, patience and wisdom, which in a *white man* would have raised him to the highest pitch of reputation."

Through the connections she made in Boston, Tubman's talents were recruited in the service of the Union Army. Unlike other influential blacks such as the extraordinary woman orator Sojourner Truth, Harriet Tubman refused to recruit blacks to fight in the Union Army. She did not believe in a war that did not make the freeing of slaves an explicit goal. Until 1863 and the issuing of the Emancipation Proclamation, the Civil War was fought to prevent the South from seceding from the Union. In 1861 when Tubman met Lydia Maria Child at an antislavery convention in Boston, she told her:

> God is ahead of Master Lincoln. God won't let Master Lincoln beat the South till he does the right thing. Master Lincoln, he is a great man, and I'm a poor Negro; but this Negro can tell Master Lincoln how to save the money and the young men. He can do it by setting the Negroes free.

After their meeting Mrs. Child wrote the poet John Greenleaf Whittier, "Her uncouth utterance is wiser than the plans of politicians."

Tubman may not have had any respect for the way Northern politicians vacillated during the first years of the war, but she did know that there were black people in the South who were victims of a war not of their making. In 1862 the Union forces captured a series of islands off the coast of South Carolina, an area they designated as Department of the South. In the North abolitionists wanted to begin Reconstruction immediately. They raised money to send teachers and volunteers to the Department of the South to begin the process of "educating and enlightening the slave."

The governor of Massachusetts, John A. Andrew, was an ardent abolitionist and a close friend of the Department of the South's commander, General David Hunter. Under Governor Andrew's auspices Harriet Tubman agreed to go to the Department of the South in the service of the Union Army. She carried a military pass which read:

> Pass the bearer, Harriet Tubman, to Beaufort and back to this place, and wherever she wishes to go; and give her free passage at all time on all Government transports. Harriet was sent to me from Boston by Governor Andrew of Massachusetts and is a valuable woman. She has permission as a servant of the Government to purchase such provisions from the Commissary as she may need.

By the beginning of 1862 Harriet Tubman was in South Carolina, on the coast near Beaufort, in the vicinity of the Grimké family plantation, working as an agent for the Union Army and serving as a liaison between the white officers and the slaves—"poor black wretches" as the commander's staff referred to them.

It is popularly believed that the Southern blacks greeted the Northern soldiers as their saviors. In reality they were as terrified of the white Northern soldiers as they were of their own masters, probably more so. The Southern black spoke in a different dialect, one which even Tubman had trouble understanding. "Why their language down there in the far South," Tubman told Sarah Bradford, "is just as different from ours in Maryland as you can think. They laughed when they heard me talk and I could not understand them, no how."

Thousands of slaves were living within the coastal area controlled by Union troops in South Carolina. They were not treated as freed people but rather as "contraband," property taken during war. Cut off from their old way of life, unable to work or cultivate crops, living in a chaotic military encampment, many grew ill, suffering a range of diseases from malnutrition to cholera. Many, especially children, were cut off from their families and were completely disoriented. It was with these people that Tubman worked. She played the role of doctor, dispensing bourbon or whatever else she could get from the military commissary. From her mother she had learned much about the healing properties of herbs, and she gained a great reputation as a healer. A tea that she used for treating yellow fever became famous. She baked pies and sold them to soldiers, teaching other black women how to make goods that could be exchanged for money or supplies.

For the first few months Tubman received a soldier's pay of fifteen dollars a month. Then when the first black troops arrived in Hilton Head, South Carolina, she stopped taking this salary in protest against the half-wage the Negro soldiers were paid. One Negro regiment was from Massachusetts under the command of a Bostonian, Colonel Robert Shaw. The other was under the command of Colonel James Montgomery, a former guerrilla fighter with John Brown in Kansas. Although the black troops were highly motivated, well trained, and had been recruited from free Negroes in the North, someone in the army bureaucracy had decided black troops need receive only half pay—seven dollars a month instead of fifteen. The black troops rebelled, for they knew they would risk their lives the same way whites would.

Tubman was given command of a team of nine scouts and river pilots and had begun leading reconnaissance missions into the interior. They explored rivers, penetrated the defense systems along the river banks, and eventually conducted raids. Disguised as an old, hobbling black woman—a pose she often assumed—Tubman could travel the inland roads of the South without ever being suspected of being a Union spy. She gathered information about troop movements, population, sources of supplies, positions of artillery. Eventually she formulated the strategy for guerrilla raids into enemy territory to draw slaves over to Union control. There were many daring and successful forays into the South Carolina interior, but none was more famous than the one up the Combahee River in which Tubman and her troops surprised two Confederate encampments and freed eight hundred slaves.

A newspaper account of the raid mentions only Colonel Montgomery but acknowledges that the 300 black troops,

> under the guidance of a black woman, dashed into the enemy's country and struck a bold and effective blow, destroying mil-

lions of dollars' worth of commissary stores, cotton and lordly dwellings and striking terror into the heart of rebeldom, brought off near 800 slaves and thousands of dollars worth of property without losing a man or receiving a scratch.

Years later Tubman told a reporter from the *American Review* that after they had gone up the river, surprised the Confederate troops, and broken through their defenses, the slaves refused to come on board the Union boats. Instead, they stood at the river's edge refusing to go back to their quarters even when whipped by the plantation overseers, but equally afraid of boarding the boats.

Tubman described a chaotic crowd of humanity—"men, women children, babies, 'pears like I never seen so many twins in my life"—churning explosively at the water's edge, resisting all entreaties to get aboard "Lincoln's gunboats." Colonel Montgomery said, "Moses, you'll have to give 'em a song," which Tubman did, improvising both words and music:

> Come along! Come along! Don't be alarm.
> Uncle Sam's rich enough to give us all a farm!
>
> Come along! Come along! Don't be a fool!
> Uncle Sam's rich enough to send us all to school!

The musical message reached them. They came aboard. "I never seen such a sight," Tubman said later. "One woman brought two pigs, a white one and a black one; we took 'em all on board, named the white pig Beauregard and the black pig Jeff Davis. . . . Bags on their shoulders, baskets on their heads, and young ones taggin' behind all loaded. Pigs squealing, chickens screaming, young ones squallin'."

The boats took off and brought the eight hundred slaves to the Union encampment. Such raids were devastating to the morale of white Southerners, emphasizing their vulnerability to Union forces even in the deep South.

Colonel Montgomery received all the credit for these raids. Even though he did acknowledge Tubman's part—writing to the commanding general on July 6, 1863, "I wish to commend to your attention Mrs. Harriet Tubman, a most remarkable woman and invaluable as a scout"—there is some question as to the rapport he had with the black troops under his command. One of Montgomery's black soldiers, a former slave named William Henry Singleton, recalled Montgomery's outraged response when his troops refused half-pay following the Combahee raid. Montgomery ranted, "Anyone can see how grotesquely ignorant you are. . . . I used nigger troops in Kansas, niggers and mules . . . a nigger and a mule go very well together."

Despite Montgomery's wrath, his troops continued to refuse to take their pay. Hurriet Tubman was one of them. She received little credit and no compensation. Except for her first few months, she was never paid for the long years of exhausting effort and the risks she took. As a woman she found it virtually impossible to be recognized or compensated as a soldier. All she ever received were a few letters of commendation from her commanding officers. (The obstacle was sex more than race. Anna Ella Carroll, a white woman who had given Lincoln military advice on the Tennessee River campaign, never received recognition or a pension despite years of petitions before Congress and files of testimonial letters.)

In 1864 Tubman requested a leave of absence from the Union Army and returned to Auburn, New York. She was struck with a debilitating illness, and after several months she recovered, but more slowly than in the past. As she grew older her seizures grew more frequent and more severe.

She was still the sole support of her parents. The mortgage on her little house was due. Her financial situation was so poor that Franklin Sanborn put a notice in a Boston newspaper asking for contributions of money and clothing. After putting her financial affairs somewhat in order and recovering her health, she was on her way back to Charleston when she was derouted by several members of the Sanitary Commission who felt she could be effective in protesting the chaotic and unsanitary conditions in the freedman's hospital in Fortress Monroe, Virginia. When the war ended in 1865 she was working as a nurse or "matron" in the hospital, having made numerous trips into Washington to fight for additional funds and supplies as well as to see Secretary of State Seward about her own lack of compensation and the discriminatory pay being given to black soldiers.

At the war's end she was on her way back to New York when she received a nasty sample of what "freedom" was to really mean. The white conductor refused to recognize her military pass, told her she couldn't sit in the passenger car, and when she resisted, physically pulled her from her seat and threw her in the baggage car. Her arm was wrenched so badly that she was in severe pain for months afterward.

She was around forty-five years old, and she was to live for another fifty years. Even though her story was legendary, she could not turn her fame into financial security. Queen Victoria sent her a medal and invited her to visit England. But the U.S. Congress would not take up Tubman's petition for back salary and a pension. She saw the failures of Reconstruction and the terrible social and economic dislocation of the 1870s.

She found herself supporting a never ending stream of visitors and "guests." Whatever money she raised she gave to others. Her most closely held idea was to begin a home, named for John Brown, for the aged. It grew out of her realization that the most disoriented and uprooted people were the old blacks who had no children to help them and no place to go. They were misfits in the post–Civil War era. Although she was never able to raise enough money to start the home, she did organize what became known as the Harriet Tubman Home for Indigent Aged Negroes. Throughout her remaining years money was a constant, continuous source of worry. Her parents lived to be almost a hundred and she was their sole source of support.

In 1865 the Freedman's Association of Boston paid her a salary of ten dollars a month to help freedmen and freedwomen. In 1869, Sarah Bradford, a white woman from her home town, published a biography of Tubman, the proceeds of which were to help pay off the debts on her property. The same year she married again.

Her first husband, John Tubman, had died; he was shot in Maryland in 1868, a casualty of black "freedom." He had refused to stop when a white man asked him to; the white man was tried and acquitted. Harriet Tubman married Nelson Davis, a black soldier she had met in the South. Little is known about the marriage except that a distinguished group of people, including Secretary of State Seward, turned out for the celebration. The marriage did make it possible for her to finally receive a pension after Davis's death. When the U.S. Congress finally succumbed to the pressures of public opinion in 1902—she was about eighty-two years old—and gave her a small pension, they awarded it to Mrs. Nelson Davis, *widow* of a former soldier. They never recognized Harriet Tubman.

With her powers of prophecy it is hard to believe that she was surprised by the chaos that followed the Civil War. She never accepted the false choice between civil rights for blacks and civil rights for women. Susan B. Anthony, an advocate for civil rights for both women and blacks, had often helped Tubman outfit slaves for Canada from her home in Rochester, New York. Tubman belonged to the suffrage organization which Susan B. Anthony—an ardent abolitionist—headed with Elizabeth Cady Stanton. Tubman was visible proof that half the people in slavery were women, and the catchphrase "It's the Negro's hour" really meant "It's the male Negro's hour."

Harriet Tubman's entire life was consistent with the insight she had reached as a girl of thirteen. Freedom must be taken—it cannot be granted. The message of her life lies in the total integrity she brought to applying that truth to the choices confronting her.

In the Boston Common at the corner in front of the State House there is a monument to Colonel Robert Shaw, the white man who gave his life leading the first regiment of black troops into the battle of Fort Wagner in Charleston, South Carolina. He is shown on horseback, sword raised. The black troops surround him, on foot.

To learn about Harriet Tubman is to learn that the Battle of Fort Wagner would probably not have taken place had those troops been white; that Colonel Shaw, like Colonel Montgomery, was not a leader of black people; that were it truly a monument to valor and heroism it would be to the hundreds of unmentioned black soldiers sacrificed in that battle.

The Robert Shaw monument is a monument to the illusion that white people granted blacks their freedom. Harriet Tubman's life is a monument to the reality of black resistance. She, like many others, took her own freedom. She participated in the organized system of resistance known as the Underground Railroad and helped hundreds of other slaves to take their own freedom. She participated in plans for armed rebellion. She was active in the abolitionist movement. She volunteered and fought in the Civil War.

Harriet Tubman's life spans an entire range of black experience and is a radical statement of that experience. She resisted all attempts to soften it in the myths that grew up after the Civil War. Once, when someone asked her if she were sorry that she refused an invitation to visit Abraham Lincoln, she is reputed to have answered that she was—but then Abraham Lincoln hadn't freed her.

After a life of such extraordinary effort, enduring a range of human experience that few people can even imagine, it is hard to comprehend what kept her going. Even Sarah Bradford's book, which was the one public effort of recognition in her life, contained the demeaning disclaimer that Tubman and her family were "different" from the "idle, miserable darkies who have swarmed about Washington and other cities since the War." Since she had devoted her entire life to her people it was fortunate she couldn't read Sarah Bradford's commentary.

Frederick Douglass concluded a famous tribute to her by admitting the measure of her sacrifice: "Excepting John Brown—of sacred memory—I know of no one who has willingly encountered more perils and hardships to serve our enslaved people than you have."

Perhaps a hint of her inner life was provided in an interview with Frank Drake of the *New York Herald* when she was in her eighties. She pointed toward a nearby orchard and asked him if he liked apples. When he answered yes, she inquired if he had ever grown any apple trees. He responded that he had not.

"But somebody else planted them," she said seriously. "I liked apples when I was young, and I said, 'Some day I'll plant apples myself for other young folks to eat' and I guess I did it."

ELIZABETH
CADY
STANTON

———◆•◗◖•◗◖•———

BORN: NOVEMBER 12, 1815, JOHNSTOWN, NEW YORK. DIED: OC-
TOBER 26, 1902, NEW YORK, NEW YORK. FATHER: DANIEL CADY.
MOTHER: MARGARET LIVINGSTON. MARRIED: HENRY BREWSTER
STANTON, 1840. CHILDREN: DANIEL (1842), HENRY (1844), GER-
RIT SMITH (1845), THEODORE (1851), MARGARET (1852), HARRIET
(1856), ROBERT (1859).

ORGANIZER, FIRST WOMAN'S RIGHTS CONVENTION, SENECA
FALLS, 1848. CANDIDATE FOR U.S. CONGRESS, 1866. EDITOR OF
THE *Revolution*, 1868–70. FOUNDER (WITH SUSAN B. ANTHONY)
AND FIRST PRESIDENT OF NATIONAL WOMAN SUFFRAGE ASSOCIA-
TION, 1869–90.

We have a higher duty than the demand for suffrage. . . . We see that the right of suffrage avails nothing for the masses in competition with the wealthy classes, and, worse still, with each other. Women all over the country are working earnestly in many fragmentary reforms, each believing that her own, if achieved, would usher in a new day of peace and plenty. . . . Agitation of the broader question of philosophical socialism is now in order.

ELIZABETH CADY STANTON
IN *New York Journal*, 1898

"She is described by an eyewitness as resembling a man in her dress, having on boots like a man, pants like a man, dickey like a man, vest like a man. . . ." a New York newspaper reported in 1851. Had the newspaper bothered to send a reporter to see Elizabeth Cady Stanton in person, he might have described her quite differently. "A handsome woman in her middle thirties, a mother and a wife, she wore a black taffeta dress with white lace at the collar and cuffs. . . . The dress stopped just below her knees, her legs covered by a pair of trousers made of the same material as her dress," was the description of the same appearance that ran in a local temperance newspaper. Forty years later another reporter compared Stanton to Queen Victoria—"They resemble each other in stature and looks, and are also about the same age." But in 1851 any woman wearing pants or the bloomer, as the new dress was called because it was advocated in a newspaper run by Amelia Bloomer, was an insult to public morality. In an era when sexual anxiety was so high that table legs were covered with cloths to the floor because of their resemblance to human legs, any woman who called attention to her own legs was a ready target for a torrent of bitter, obscene abuse.

The effort to change woman's style of dress was a real health need, unfortunately, and not the amusing diversion some historians have made it out to be. Women's clothes in the middle of the nineteenth century were designed to make them tiny-waisted, large-bosomed, legless creatures. Pinched-in whalebone corsets put a terrific pressure on the liver and kidneys. Long skirts and multiple petticoats were a severe strain on the base of the spine and made the simplest physical exercise an ordeal. Some have suggested that it was at this time the phrase "A dog is a man's best friend" came into vogue, because women were so restricted by their clothes they couldn't go anywhere. Shortness of breath, abdominal pains, fainting, and needless complications from pregnancy and childbirth were all the result of clothes that prevented freedom of movement and any physical exercise.

Harriet Tubman provides as good testimony as any of the need for the bloomer dress. In 1862 she wrote to Franklin Sanborn, telling him that she wanted "a bloomer dress made of some coarse, strong material to wear on expeditions." On the Combahee raids she was carrying two pigs for a woman when the command was given to run: "I started to run, stepped on my dress . . . and fell and tore it almost off. I made up my mind then I would never wear a long dress on another expedition of the kind, but would have a 'bloomer' as soon as I could get it."

Unfortunately, by that time Elizabeth Cady Stanton had long given up on the idea that American women would adopt a sane manner of dressing. Women who wore pants in the middle of the nineteenth century might as well have worn a scarlet A. Elizabeth Cady Stanton is best known for proposing woman's suffrage in 1848, but after what she endured trying to free women from the prison of their clothes, she would not have been at all surprised to learn that women got the vote fifty years before pants on women gained total acceptance in American life.

"I have never wondered since," she wrote of the dress reform struggle of the early 1850s, "that the Chinese women allow their daughters' feet to be encased in iron shoes, nor that the Hindu widows walk calmly to the funeral pyre." The two-year campaign to change women's fashions revealed a great deal about the personal qualities of Elizabeth Cady Stanton—originality, creativity, humor, intelligence, tenacity, a sense of strategy, and an ability to give up when necessary.

In 1852 she decided that too much of her own energy was being consumed in defending the "short dress" and that many of the legal and economic reforms she wanted were being sacrificed to the public fury over "unsexed" women who displayed their limbs in public; she decided it was time to quit. With the same force of personality she had used in urging women to take up fashion reform, she convinced them to give it up. "We put the dress on for greater freedom," she wrote to her friend and coworker Lucy Stone, "but what is physical freedom compared to mental bondage?"

She had perceived that the weight of custom and prejudice was far more powerful than the force of logic or rational argument. It was a lesson she never forgot. She never overestimated the power of logic or reasoned appeal to change people's minds. She understood as few women, either before or after her, that concepts of women's capabilities were rooted in centuries of irrationality and that tactics of a movement to improve the lot of women must shift with the time and the nature of the opposition.

Elizabeth Cady Stanton came to be know as the statesman of the woman's rights movement. Some people called her a "gadfly," flitting from one issue to another—divorce, prostitution, economic independence, suffrage. Others accused her of never having been able to fit her ideas into a coherent system. Yet more than any other woman of her generation she confronted the reality of the role women were relegated to play in American society, and she acted to change it. Change, she believed, came only with a combination of independent thought and political power. Everything she did—beginning with her resolution that women must vote—was aimed at making it possible for women to free themselves from encumbering traditions—economic, political, intellectual, and social. Her advocacy of woman's right to divorce earned her outraged condemnation from the press, from male reformers, and from other women. The women reformers accused her of undercutting their effectiveness with an unnecessary assault on public morality. Women, they believed, could have their rights without gaining the right to divorce. Stanton kept on advocating liberalized divorce laws in the belief that indissoluble marriages made men tyrants and women slaves; marriage was a building block of the larger society and it had to be changed.

"The trouble was," she once admitted, "not in what I said, but that I said it too soon, and before the people were ready to hear it. It may be, however, that I helped them to get ready. Who knows?" Her genius was in focusing on the irrationality of customs dictating woman's place. She believed that they were capricious inventions of men's minds.

Such fresh and creative thinking was not a natural product of her family, which was hardly a hotbed of free thought or radical ideas. Her father, Judge Daniel Cady, disinherited her rather than admit that there was value in her advocacy of woman's rights. He was probably typical of many conservative, landowning lawyers from small towns in agricultural areas. Johnstown, New York, where Stanton grew up, is not far from Albany. Judge Cady was a judge of the State Supreme Court and a member of the U.S. Court of Appeals. He was also, as his son-in-law Henry Stanton noted, "a leader of the New York bar." As a lawyer Judge Cady's skill was legendary, and one attorney who had argued over two hundred cases against him said that on the rare occasions that he won the verdict, he never relaxed for fear that his "secretive, wary adversary" might spring a trap at the last moment. Like Judge Grimké, Stanton's father developed his daughter's interest in the law. Unlike Judge Grimké, Daniel Cady also passed on his skill in legal argument and relish for oral debate.

Many superb talkers considered Stanton "the most brilliant conversationalist" they had ever met. She gained a great reputation as a debater during the eleven years she traveled as a lecturer. She was earnest and logical, never facetious or belittling, and when challenged could respond with wit. During a stop in Lincoln, Nebraska, a man asked her, "Don't you think that the best thing a woman can do is to perform well her part in the role of wife and mother?" He added, "My wife has presented me with eight beautiful children. Is not that a better lifework than that of exercising the right of suffrage?" Stanton surveyed him from head to foot and answered coolly, "I have met few men worth repeating eight times." The story spread over the entire state.

At the Woman Suffrage Convention in Washington in 1869 a reporter from the *Philadelphia Press* noted many of her father's legal and political influences:

> Of all the speakers Mrs. Stanton seemed to me to have the most weight. Her speeches are models of composition—clear, compact, elegant, and logical. She makes her points with peculiar sharpness and certainty. . . . It seems to me that while Lucretia Mott may be said to be the soul of this movement . . . Mrs. Stanton [is] the mind, the "swift, keen, intelligence." [She] has the best arts of the politician and the training of the jurist . . . added to the fiery, unresting spirit of the reformer.

Stanton did have the "unresting spirit" of the reformer. In describing herself before audiences and to newspaper reporters, she tended to overemphasize her father and the qualities of the jurist. She rarely mentioned her mother, Margaret Livingston Cady, who was a splendid politician in her own right.

Margaret Cady's family, the Livingstons, were among the most prominent early families of New York State. Her grandfather had been a colonel at West Point and had fought in the Revolution. Many of the family were important figures in state politics. Elizabeth's daughter, Harriet Stanton Blatch, liked to tell the story about how her grandmother outwitted all the men of her church. When Margaret Livingston Cady wanted a particular minister for the local Presbyterian Church, she knew how to lobby and to count her votes ahead of time. But just before the votes were taken, she heard that the women's votes were to be taken last because all the women of the church supported Margaret Cady's candidate. The church elders planned to take the voting basket outside to count the ballots and to skim a few votes off the top. "Even as my grandmother related the story," Harriet Stanton Blatch recalled, "I could feel her intense interest. . . . It called for secrecy, manipulation, leadership." Margaret Cady arranged for the ballots to be placed in a big jar and for her to be the last person to vote. Instead of dropping her ballot on top, she plunged her hand to the bottom, swishing her arm around as she did so, mixing up all the votes. Margaret Cady's candidate for minister was elected.

Unlike Sarah Grimké, Elizabeth Cady Stanton had a model of a female politician throughout her early years. Margaret Cady may have been fatigued from bearing ten babies, and she may not have spent much time with her daughters, but she was—in the words of her granddaughter—"a born politician." When she wanted something, she was an expert "at winding in and out as she advanced on a position she was determined to take."

Stanton's determination and rebellion stemmed from more than a reaction to her father's authority: she had learned from her mother how to take what she wanted. Stanton told one interviewer, "Whatever success I have achieved I attribute to the self-assertiveness and determination of my character." Then she told the reporter, "Put it down in capital letters, SELF-DEVELOPMENT IS A HIGHER DUTY THAN SELF-SACRIFICE. The thing which most retards and militates against woman's self-development is self-sacrifice."

Judge Cady and Margaret Livingston had six children who survived infancy, all daughters except for one boy, who died at the age of eighteen. Family life was hierarchical, disciplined, and strict. The children were constantly reminded to show respect to parents, teachers, servants. Stanton felt that her parents "were as kind, indulgent, and considerate as the Puritan ideas of those days permitted, but fear, rather than love . . . predominated." They were raised as strict Scotch Presbyterians, a depressing religion which taught man's natural depravity and emphasized the constant presence of the Devil.

To escape the strong discipline and strict religious atmosphere, Stanton often went to the neighboring estate of her reformer cousin Gerrit Smith. His daughter Libby was the same age as Stanton and the two remained close friends for life. Stanton remembered being shown a secret room, where Harriet, a young black girl not much older than herself, was being hidden while en route to Canada. Stanton remembered cousin Gerrit's explaining to her about the Underground Railroad and telling her that his house, a beautiful estate at Peterboro, was one of the "stops." It was at Gerrit Smith's house where she first heard ideas of reform and radical notions of abolition and temperance and free religious thought. Her father thought Smith a dangerous radical, frittering away his fortune on irresponsible causes.

Her other reminiscences of girlhood evoke vivid pictures of elm-lined streets, fresh bread baking in the oven, sunlit summer weddings, country visiting, and the warm, affluent close-knit family life that is the romantic image of nineteenth-century America. Very early in life Elizabeth Cady learned that this picture of domestic tranquility had another, less happy, image on the other side.

When Elizabeth was eleven, she used to spend a lot of time in her father's law office, listening to the legal advice he gave to townspeople and learning about the resolution of conflicts concerning property and inheritances. Flora Campbell was a neighbor who owned a farm, which supplied the Cady family with fresh eggs, butter, milk, vegetables, and chickens. One day Flora Campbell came to the office beside herself with fear and anxiety. Her husband had mortgaged her farm to pay his gambling debts. The bank was going to foreclose. Elizabeth Cady's unbelieving ears heard her father say that Flora Campbell's husband had acted on accepted legal principle. Women, like slaves, had no right to hold legal title to property, and all of a wife's possessions belonged to her husband.

To make matters worse, Judge Cady assured Flora Campbell that once she lost her farm, he would not let her or her children starve. It was an electric moment. Even eleven-year-old Elizabeth Cady realized what a great affront to human dignity it was to offer charity rather than justice. She threatened to cut the offensive laws out of her father's law books with her scissors. He told her that laws were made by men and that the way to change them was not by cutting them out of books but by influencing the men who made them. According to Elizabeth, he told her that when she was older she "must go to Albany and tell the legislators how those laws wrong women." His actions, however, belied his words.

It is almost impossible to believe that conservative, austere, conventional, bourgeois Daniel Cady had the remotest intention of encouraging his daughter to do anything to reform the state of laws regarding women. Judge Cady was a believer in the American faith of amassing wealth and passing it on. He was not interested in poverty or injustice, and years later when Elizabeth Cady Stanton went to the New York legislature to testify on behalf of revised laws relating to women, he believed that her testimony reflected badly on his ability as a parent. "How," he asked, "can a young woman, tenderly brought up, who has had no bitter personal experience, feel so keenly the wrongs of her sex?"

As adults their relationship became a series of battles. Elizabeth was an embarrassment to him. He used one threat after another to prevent her from espousing radical reforms. One evening she read a speech to him that she planned to give to a local woman's organization. She told him proudly that they were going to pay her ten dollars. He answered that if she gave that speech, "it would be the most expensive speech" she ever gave. She said no matter what, she intended to speak on the subject of justice and freedom for women. They each grabbed their candles and marched out of the study by separate doors. Judge Cady made good on his threat. Elizabeth received her ten dollars for a very good speech, and her father wrote her out of his will. (Just before he died in 1859 he relented and put her back in.)

It was not only her father who opposed her public work for women. Her husband was far from sympathetic. Henry Stanton was an "eloquent and impassioned" orator in the New York wing of the abolitionist movement and a close friend of Theodore Weld's. She had met him at her cousin Gerrit Smith's house and found him "a fine-looking, affable young man, with remarkable conversational talent." The last quality she found particularly impressive. He was staying there for a series of abolitionist meetings that were taking place in the area, and as Elizabeth Cady "had a passion for oratory," his talents as an orator stood out to very good advantage. He was also ten years older than she was, "with the advantage that that number of years necessarily gives."

Their marriage did not take place easily. Elizabeth's father objected. And at twenty-four she was not as free from romantic entanglements as she appeared. For a number of years she had been involved in a rather tortuous romance with Edward Bayard, her oldest sister's husband.

She had known Bayard since he had come to read law with her father when she was eleven. Her only brother had died the same year, and Bayard in many ways filled the void in the family. He married the oldest daughter, Tryphenia, and reinstituted birthday parties, picnics, and childhood outings, which had been forgotten during the long period of mourning. Impressed with Elizabeth's intelligence and curiosity, he introduced her to law, history, politics, philosophy, economics, and many other subjects girls did not study. He was also a sympathetic supporter in her futile effort to replace her brother in her father's eyes. She learned to ride horseback, play chess, take first place in Greek. It was an unheard-of achievement for a girl, but her father's only response was, "You should have been a boy."

Almost everyone who had any intimate knowledge of the family admitted that Bayard and Tryphenia were unsuited to one another. Aunt Bayard, as Tryphenia was called, was rather cold, precise, and enjoyed financial matters. Bayard, on the other hand, according to Elizabeth, was "of a metaphysical turn of mind and in the pursuit of truth was in no way trammeled by popular superstitions." He was always asking questions, "like Socrates," and loved to teach girls "how to think clearly and reason logically." From the time she left Emma Willard's school for girls to the time she married Henry Stanton, Edward Bayard was a critical part of Elizabeth Cady's life. She called those years "the most pleasant years of my girlhood." Unfortunately it was an affair with no hope of happiness.

There was no divorce in 1840; an unhappy marriage remained an unhappy marriage. Elizabeth Cady used to meet Bayard in New York at another sister's house. Once he proposed that they run off to Europe together. It was a hopeless situation and perhaps offers a clue to Elizabeth's later willingness to publicly broach the subject of divorce.

All the Cady girls except Elizabeth chose their husbands from the young men who came to clerk for Judge Cady. Henry Stanton was, in Judge Cady's eyes, a thirty-four-year-old ne'er-do-well, a professional agitator in a dubious cause. No daughter of Cady's was going to marry an aimless abolitionist orator. Edward Bayard, for quite different reasons, joined Judge Cady in opposing the marriage. After a long, unhappy struggle Elizabeth broke the engagement.

But she changed her mind when she learned that Henry was going to leave for England for the World Anti-Slavery Convention. She decided to go ahead with the marriage. It was an important step of independence and set a pattern for decisions she would have to take later in life. Without the trousseau or elaborate festivities befitting a Cady daughter she was married in Johnstown, New York, in 1840. She had been able to persuade the minister to omit the word "obey" from her marriage ceremony—although to this day it still remains in most church ceremonies. She believed that the vow of obedience was degrading, and she refused to take it. "I object to the teachings of the church on marriage by which [a woman] is given away as an article of merchandise and made to vow obedience as a slave to a master. . . . When our pulpits declare that the husband is the head of the wife as Christ is head of the church, they simply reflect the opinions of a dark and barbarous age. . . ." At the age of twenty-four she set out with her new husband for London. Henry Stanton represented the branch of the antislavery organization that refused to have women members. Elizabeth Stanton admitted she knew nothing of abolitionist political infighting, and she was hardly aware that the abolitionist organization had split into two groups on the issue of women members. The group that allowed women as full members was the American Anti-Slavery Society. The other group was officially known as the American and Foreign Anti-Slavery Society.

Elizabeth Stanton was not a delegate, and she too tended to oppose the idea of women delegates. Before boarding the ship for London, Henry had taken her to meet his best friend, Theodore Weld. She had heard Angelina Grimké Weld and Sarah Grimké, two women whom she greatly admired, speak against the idea of women delegates, particularly the controversial Lucretia Mott; they were afraid that the woman's issue would harm the cause of antislavery. During the long voyage to England she had listened to tirades about Lucretia Mott from James Birney, her husband's influential sponsor. Birney described Mott as "a very dangerous person . . . a heretic, a disturber of the peace . . . and the woman who demoralized the anti-slavery ranks. . . ." Mott was allied with William Lloyd Garrison and the faction of the movement that called for human rights for women as well as for the slaves. She was in her late forties and an official delegate of the American Anti-Slavery Society.

Elizabeth Stanton found herself seated at the dining table of a London boardinghouse with the notorious Mrs. Mott and four women delegates. Mealtimes became debating matches between the five women and the male delegates of the other antislavery organization. James Birney was so disgusted with the presence of women that he moved to other lodgings.

Despite Mott's reputation among her husband's colleagues, Stanton was charmed by her. For the first time she saw a woman who knew how to defend herself in public debates. "Calmly and skillfully Mrs. Mott parried all their attacks, now by her quiet humor turning the laugh on them and then by her earnestness and dignity silencing their ridicule and sneers." For Elizabeth Stanton, who had "often longed to meet some woman who had sufficient confidence in herself to frame and hold an opinion in the face of opposition," Lucretia Mott was "an entirely new revelation of womanhood." Despite Henry's kicks from under the table, Stanton began taking the woman's part. Lucretia Mott was "the first woman I had ever met who believed in the equality of the sexes and who did not believe in the popular orthodox religion. [Mott], who was a broad, liberal thinker on politics, religion, and all questions of reform, opened to me a new world of thought."

She took every opportunity to talk with Mott, went to hear her preach in a Quaker church, asked her questions about religion and theology. In less than a month she wrote back to Sarah Grimké and Angelina Weld, telling them she found Mott a "peerless woman" and relaying Mott's thinking that the sisters should both resume public speaking in the cause of woman; "Sarah in particular she thinks should appear in public again. . . . She says a great struggle is at hand and that all the friends of freedom for woman must rally round the *Garrison standard*."

In a matter of weeks Elizabeth Stanton had gone beyond the limited thinking of the conservative middle of the abolitionist movement. Mott would continue to have a profound influence on Stanton's development for the next ten years.

Stanton was at a period in which she had strong opinions and ideas but no theoretical framework to hold them together. She was exceptionally curious, but her questions were leading her around in circles instead of into new areas of enlightenment and intellectual growth. Moreover, her newly found independence from her father and family was causing her to question some of her most profound religious beliefs.

Stanton's questions, like those of Sarah Grimké before her, placed her in opposition to the unquestioned authority of the Church. Mott was able to reach Stanton not only because of her political abilities but because in the course of becoming a Quaker preacher Mott had been through a similar spiritual crisis—a total questioning of accepted authority. For twenty-four-year-old Elizabeth Cady Stanton, getting to know Lucretia Mott was

> like meeting a being from some larger planet . . . a woman who dared to question the opinions of Popes, Kings, Synods, Parliaments, with the same freedom that she would criticize an editorial in the *London Times*, recognizing no higher authority than the judgment of a pure-minded, educated woman. When I first heard from the lips of Lucretia Mott that I had the same right to think for myself that Luther, Calvin and John Knox had . . . I felt at once a new-born sense of dignity and freedom; it was like suddenly coming into the rays of the noon-day sun after wandering with a rush-light in the caves of the earth.

What Lucretia Mott gave to Stanton was a sense that each person could interpret her or his own experience with God, that no one had a stranglehold on truth, and that theology, as interpreted by the institutionalized churches, often prevented people from experiencing real religion by making them depend on men trained as priests or ministers.

Religion, Mott explained to her, "is a natural human experience common to well-organized minds." Theology, which is used to define sin and salvation:

> is a system of speculation about the unseen, and unknowable, which the human mind has no power to grasp, or explain; and these speculations vary with every sect, age and type of civilization. No one knows more of what lies beyond our sphere of action, than thou and I, and we know nothing.

Such an existential point of view was like lifting a blanket from Stanton's mind. As a girl she had been overcome with the thought of eternal damnation. The worst emotional crisis in her life occurred when she was sixteen and was caught up in a series of religious meetings by the great revivalist preacher of the age, Charles Finney. She referred to that period of self-immersion in sin and damnation as one of the worst of her life and even at the age of seventy still maintained that "all the cares and anxieties, the trials and disappointments of my whole life are light, when balanced with my sufferings in childhood and youth from the theological dogmas which I sincerely believed."

Finney had also had a great effect on her husband, who had decided to become a minister after participating in one of Finney's revivals. Henry Stanton went to Lane Seminary in Cincinnati where he met another one of Finney's converts, Theodore Weld. Finney's fire-and-brimstone techniques formed the basic methods of the abolitionist orators. However, Weld was twenty-four when he became a Finney disciple and Henry Stanton was twenty-six, a less impressionable age than sixteen.

Lucretia Mott opened up an entirely new way of looking at people and events. She gave Stanton insight into process, the way in which people reach conclusions about the workings of the world. She told her about the Quaker religion and the doctrine of "inner light." She gave her a copy of Mary Wollstonecraft's book, *The Vindication of the Rights of Woman*, written in 1793, proposing equality between men and women. Lucretia Mott recognized in Elizabeth Stanton a curiosity and intellectual energy that was similar to her own and shared her deepest spiritual experiences with her. Meeting Lucretia Mott was a turning point in Elizabeth Stanton's life. She never again had to accept the opinion of a father, a husband, or any man whose supposed superiority was quite unprovable and whose authority was so questionable.

When the time came to vote on the seating of the female delegates at the London convention, Henry Stanton was alone among the members of the new American and Foreign Anti-Slavery Organization, or "New Org" as it was derisively called, to vote *for* the seating of women. It confirmed Angelina Grimké Weld's initial impression of Elizabeth Stanton which she had shared with Gerrit Smith: "We were very much pleased with Elizabeth Stanton who spent several days with us [but] I could not help wishing that Henry was better suited to mold such a mind."

In many ways the battle between domesticity and public life which had taken place between Angelina Grimké and Theodore Weld was to be played out in a different way between Henry and Elizabeth Stanton.

Like his friend Weld, Henry had a reformer's zeal but was a conventional man when it came to domestic relations. Social change was not an organic process to him. It was a series of causes which one ranked in order of importance. The ability to view society as a system in which attitudes of authority and hierarchy affected everyone was simply not part of his intellectual makeup. The marriage between Henry and Elizabeth was not a smooth one. Very early in their marriage Henry wrote from Boston, "I do love you Lizzie! Will you forgive all my coldness and unkindness?" Like Weld, Henry was gone much of the time, leaving the babies and domestic responsibilities to his wife. When their fourth son, named for Theodore Weld, was born in 1851 with a misplaced collarbone, Henry was in the legislature in Albany. He wrote that he was "very distressed," gave her the name of a doctor to call, said he would come home "if my presence is needed," and proceeded to write four pages on the legislative impasse between the Whigs and the Democrats which necessitated his presence in Albany.

His work in the legislature, political campaigns, lobbying in Washington all kept him away from his family. In a letter of the late 1850s he berates Elizabeth for not writing to him—"Why don't you write me? This is the 4th or 5th letter I have written home, and not a word from there! Pray write and tell me how you all are." And then he questions her about the domestic cares that have prevented her from writing—"Have you plenty of wood? Do the potatoes freeze? Is the gutter up? How are the babies? Does Margaret Livingston Stanton go to dancing school?"

The difference in perspective, attitudes, and intelligence between Elizabeth and Henry Stanton is best revealed in their letters to their children. Henry passed on a bourgeois, conventional sense of societal order to his sons Daniel and Henry. He wrote to them on February 22, 1852, while they were students at the Welds' school in New Jersey:

One hundred and twenty years ago today, George Washington was born. Mrs. Weld will tell you who he is. He studied hard, and was very industrious, and very good, when he was a boy; and when he grew up to be a man, he became one of the noblest and best of men in this country. If you are good boys and study well, perhaps you may be as great a man as George Washington.

Contrast this view of proper behavior with Elizabeth Stanton's later letter to her daughter Margaret:

Now improve every hour and every opportunity and fit yourself for a good teacher or professor, so that you can have money of your own and not be obliged to depend on any man for every breath you draw. The helpless dependence of women generally makes them the narrow, discontented beings so many are.

The idea that women *must be* educated to be self-supporting in the same way men are is still not the prevailing viewpoint. One can only imagine how it was viewed one hundred years ago when Stanton offered it as a resolution in public meetings. It was a principle she practiced, earning three to four thousand dollars a year as a lecturer and sending three of her children through college—two of the boys to Cornell and Margaret to Vassar.

The contrast between conventional morality and the creativity of Stanton's mind is most evident in her ideas about children and child rearing, as unorthodox as everything else. She refused to spend weeks and months in bed before and after childbirth, as was the custom, but walked around and moved freely even during the first stages of labor. She developed her own theories of personality development and was far more informal with her children than was acceptable at the time. She held heretical ideas on the parent-child relationship, having no patience with the idea that children owed a debt of eternal gratitude to their parents. She felt that the obligation was on the part of the parents, who "can never do too much for their children to repay them for the injustice of having brought them into the world, unless they have insured them high moral and intellectual gifts, fine physical health, and enough money and education to render life somthing more than one ceaseless struggle for necessities."

Henry had no more understanding of such a viewpoint than he did of many of his wife's other ideas. He accepted some of her activities—writing articles in the local temperance paper, for example, even though it was indelicate for a woman to sign her name. He also supported hiring a housekeeper, Amelia Willard, who freed Stanton from some of the household burdens so she had some time to read and write. But his view of a progressive marriage seemed to have been based on the dominant-subordinate relationship of Theodore Weld and Angelina Grimké.

The Welds and the Stantons were close friends. A Stanton son, Theodore, was named for Weld. The Stanton children went to the Welds' school. But Elizabeth Stanton resisted with all her strength the kind of intellectual thrall that Theodore Weld exercised over his wife.

It was not easy, for the full weight of tradition, custom, and friends rested with Henry. Fortunately, Elizabeth Stanton was helped by an outside source of support and encouragement that Angelina did not have—Lucretia Mott.

After London Mott had kept track of her young friend. When they returned to the United States, Mott corresponded with her, inquiring about her reading, suggesting books, and giving her an outsider's viewpoint on the "right" way to live, reminding her that acts, not thoughts, "are the true test of the Christian faith." Mott provided a beacon of judgment and guidance. When Henry decided to study law with Judge Cady, Mott commented, "I wonder if such a thing is possible as an honest and *Christian* lawyer."

When Henry moved to Boston to take his place as an up and coming lawyer, Mott recalled first meeting him as "an unsophisticated Lane Seminary boy." When Stanton was caught up in taking care of her babies, running a large home, and becoming a renowned hostess, Mott visited her in Boston and reminded her of their idea to have a convention to discuss the subject of woman's rights. When the pressures from Henry Stanton against her public work became great, and Elizabeth desperately tried to recruit the Grimkés into the movement, Mott told her that she should not expect help from that source. "As to the Grimkés," Mott wrote, "I have little hope of them, after such a flash and such an effectual extinguishment—We must not depend on them. Nor upon any who have been apostles before us." Most important, Lucretia Mott was able to give Stanton a sense of history and an understanding of past events.

When the number of woman's rights conventions and meetings had multiplied to almost monthly affairs, Stanton decided to write a book setting out the history of the woman's rights movement. She decided to trace the origins of the first woman's rights convention of 1848 back to the London Anti-Slavery Convention of 1840. Mott approved her plan, but told her she must begin earlier:

> This is the right work for thee, dear Elizabeth, and success will no doubt attend thy undertaking. All the help I can render shall be most gladly given.
>
> Let me suggest then, that the opening chapter go further back than the Anti-Slavery split in 1840—Sarah and Angelina Grimké's labors in Mass. in 1835 and 36 aroused the clergy; and the *Clerical Appeal* and the *Pastoral Letter* were issued. . . . Some prominent abolitionists who had before given countenance to the Grimkés, now, either secretly or more openly acted against women's cooperative action with men. The Tappans—Birney—E. Wright—J. Leavitt and others in New York in '39 and '40 uniting with the New England opposition. . . . During that year Sarah Grimké's *Letters* were written on the *Equality of the Sexes*—the best work after Mary Wollstonecraft's *Rights of Women*. . . .
>
> —In thy coming work, thou must do thyself justice. Remember, the first Convention originated with thee.

Stanton was thirty-three when the first woman's rights convention took place in 1848 in Seneca Falls, New York. It had taken years before the right combination of timing, circumstances, people, and personal discontent came together in such a way as to produce action instead of talk.

Seneca Falls was a small town in a malarial region not far from Rochester, where Henry had gone to practice law when the Boston winters became too harmful to his health. Seneca Falls was also the home of Edward and Tryphenia Bayard. With three active boys—one of whom fancied himself an inventor and had once floated the baby off in a tub to see where the wind would carry him—little household help, a husband often absent for long periods, Elizabeth Cady Stan-

ton began to understand as she never had before "the practical difficulties most women had to contend with in the isolated household." She articulated the housewife's malaise of mental fatigue and
depression from being enclosed in a house all day with small children:

> I suffered with mental hunger, which, like an empty stomach
> is very depressing. . . .
> The general discontent I felt with woman's portion as wife,
> mother, housekeeper, physician and spiritual guide, the cha-
> otic conditions into which everything fell without her constant
> supervision, and the wearied, anxious look of the majority of
> women impressed me with a strong feeling that some active
> measures should be taken to remedy the wrongs of society in
> general and of women in particular. I could not see what to do
> or where to begin—my only thought was a public meeting for
> protest and discussion.

The people to spark such a meeting were her old friend Lucretia
Mott, who came to the area for a yearly Quaker Meeting; Mott's
sister, Martha Wright, who lived nearby in Waterloo; and several
other Quaker women who had seriously thought about women's
social and legal disabilities. Stanton poured out her unhappiness
"with such vehemence and indignation that I stirred myself, as well
as the rest of the party to do and dare anything." The five women
put a notice in the *Seneca County Courier* on July 14, 1848, announcing

> a Convention to discuss the social, civil and religious rights of
> women. . . . The first day will be exclusively for women, who
> are earnestly invited to attend. The public generally are invited
> to be present on the second day, when Lucretia Mott . . . will
> address the convention.

None of them, including Elizabeth Cady Stanton, had any idea
whether anyone would attend.

The timing, however, was perfect. Only a few months before, the
New York state legislature had passed the first law allowing women
limited rights to ownership of property. The bill had been vigorously
debated and passed only because the Dutch landowning aristocrats

of New York were tired of the loss of their property by profligate sons-in-law. They wanted their daughters to be able to inherit their property if they had no male heir. The very act of recognizing the problem of woman's inability to hold property focused attention on the crippling disabilities of women before the law and legitimatized the need to discuss them.

Lucretia Mott was a well-known preacher, highly respected in abolitionist circles, and was a drawing card. Elizabeth Cady Stanton knew many of the active reformers in the area through her husband and Gerrit Smith. Over two hundred people showed up for the meeting. From the very first, Stanton showed herself to be a brilliant politician.

She understood the need to communicate new ideas through traditional forms, and she modeled a statement of principles for the meeting on the Declaration of Independence. The Declaration of Sentiments was a splendid way to point up the gap between political rhetoric and social reality for one half of the population of "democratic" America.

> We hold these truths to be self-evident: that all men and women are created equal; that they are endowed by their Creator with certain inalienable rights; that among these are life, liberty and the pursuit of happiness. . . .

In its description of man's historical tyranny over woman it had much in common with Sarah Grimké's *Letters*.

> He has compelled her to submit to laws, in the formation of which she had no voice. . . .
> He has made her, if married, in the eye of the law, civilly dead. . . .
> He has monopolized nearly all the profitable employments. . . . As a teacher of theology, medicine or law, she is not known.
> He allows her in Church, as well as State, but a subordinate position, claiming Apostolic authority for her exclusion from the ministry, and, with some exceptions, from any public participation in the affairs of the Church.
> He has giv[en] to the world a different code of morals for men and women, by which moral delinquencies which exclude

women from society, are not only tolerated, but deemed of little account in man.

Of the twelve resolutions the most important were those on the need for women to overthrow the male monopoly of the pulpit and to secure equal participation with men in the various trades and commerce and professions. But Stanton succeeded, over the objections of her coorganizers, in including a resolution proposing that women gain the right to vote. Everyone thought she would make the group appear ridiculous, and Henry left town rather than remain around for what he felt could only be a disaster. As usual he underestimated his wife.

She realized that although a resolution calling for political rights for women might be ridiculed if she offered it, it might be given a respectful hearing if offered by someone else. With a sure instinct for choosing allies, she asked Frederick Douglass, the black abolitionist leader, to speak for the vote for women. Douglass offered the resolution, basing his arguments on the need for the oppressed to be able to choose rulers and write laws. The resolution passed.

The reaction of the press and pulpit to the meeting was so venomous that Stanton later confessed, "If I had had the slightest premonition of all that was to follow the convention, I fear I should not have had the courage to risk it." Most of the women who attended the convention and who had signed the Declaration of Sentiments asked that their names be removed. Friends snubbed her. She began to believe that the meeting had been a disgrace.

The meeting, chaired by Lucretia's husband, James Mott, had been a relatively quiet and dignified affair with excellent debates and speaking. In the newspapers it became an orgy of Amazons.

The *Telegraph* in Worcester, Massachusetts, ran an editorial headlined, "Insurrection Among the Women." The newspaper explained that

the Amazons [intend] in spite of all misrepresentations and ridicule, to employ agents, circulate tracts, petition the State and National legislatures, and endeavor to enlist the pulpit and the press in their behalf. This is *bolting* with a vengeance.

The *Rochester Daily Advertiser* told readers that "the women in various parts of the state have taken the field in favor of a petticoat empire. . . ." The *New York Herald* recalled that 1848 was a year of revolutions, mused on the role women had played in the bloody uprising in Paris, and declared the Declaration of Sentiments to be "a most amusing document. . . . The amusing part is the preamble where they asserted their equality. . . ." In many ways translating the Declaration of Independence as a manifesto for woman's equality had been a stroke of genius.

In Philadelphia, the site of the signing of the Declaration of Independence, one of the local newspapers went a bit overboard in its reaction to the idea of women as citizens:

> A woman is nobody. A wife is everything. A pretty girl is equal to ten thousand men, and a mother is next to God, all powerful. . . . The ladies of Philadelphia therefore, under the influence of the most serious "sober second thoughts" are resolved to maintain their rights as Wives, Belles, Virgins, and Mothers, and not as Women.

The comment in the press and pulpit was out of all proportion to the scope and size of the Convention on Women's Rights in Seneca Falls. It became impossible to even pick up a paper without reading some form of ridicule.

Before the Seneca Falls convention ended, the participants had agreed to hold another meeting in Syracuse, New York, the following month. It was with "fear and trembling" that Elizabeth Stanton set out for the second woman's rights convention. She was on the speaker's platform, but she was so taken aback when a woman presumed to chair the meeting that she left the stage. Only as the meeting progressed did Stanton see with great clarity that this was precisely what a woman's movement must be—women must act in their own right, take control of their own meetings and their own lives.

These early conventions were organized spontaneously by local women and without any organizational base. The credit for building a national women's organization must go to Susan B. Anthony, Stanton's coworker for almost fifty years. Anthony was not only an administrative genius, she was responsible for freeing Stanton from the domestic entrapment of six children. Just as Lucretia Mott had been crucial to Stanton's intellectual independence, Susan B. Anthony was crucial to her gaining practical independence. In many ways, Elizabeth Stanton was able to test her talents only in partnership with Susan B. Anthony.

Anthony was five years younger, a Hicksite Quaker from Rochester, New York, who had first met Stanton in 1851 when she went to ask her advice on the problem of the state temperance society's refusal to allow women to speak in meetings. Anthony had not been at Seneca Falls or at any of the woman's rights conventions immediately following it. Stanton advised Anthony not to confront the men in open debate but to organize a convention of all the women's temperance groups in the state. She believed a separate convention would show off the abilities of the women. The first female temperance convention was a great success. Stanton was elected president, and Anthony secretary—a relationship they would continue throughout life. It was at that first women's temperance convention in 1851 that Stanton gave her speech in the "short dress" with trousers, and gained the press commentary that she "resembl[ed] a man."

One of Elizabeth Stanton's unique abilities—but a key one for any public figure—was to know how to use the enemy's reaction to good advantage. She had conquered her fears of appearing ridiculous and of being snubbed by old friends. She was willing to offer herself as a target to keep the woman's rights controversy boiling so that other women would become aware of the cause and become bold enough to act.

She wrote a letter of protest to the editors of the New York paper who had described her so inaccurately, and she made sure that a correct description of her dress appeared in the *Lily*, the temperance newspaper published by her neighbor Amelia Bloomer, whose name eventually became attached to the new dress. Soon Stanton was too notorious for the temperance society, and they voted her out of the presidency because she was devoting too much time to woman's rights and too little to temperance. Susan B. Anthony was so disturbed at the treatment of Stanton that she resigned in protest. It was a sacrifice because at that time Susan B. Anthony's commitment was to temperance not woman's rights. The two causes were a response to the same disease—the abject helplessness and misery of many women and children with a husband and father who was a drunk—but the diagnosis and treatment of one was very different from the other. The temperance people believed that the root cause was liquor; that if liquor were banned a man would not drink away his wages, leave his children starving, or beat his wife in a drunken rage. Woman's rights advocates believed liquor was a symptom not a cause; that men became tyrants because of the helplessness of their wives. Stanton's view was that only when women could keep their own wages, own property, and be legal guardians of their own children would they be able to protect the dignity and integrity of the family. Depriving men of liquor would have little effect. "Waste no more powder on the Woman's State Temperance Society," Stanton told Anthony prophetically, "we have other and bigger fish to fry."

She was right. The woman's movement gained great momentum in the 1850s. Almost every year a National Woman's Rights Convention was held with representatives from many states. They reported on their efforts to employ speakers, distribute literature, and gather petitions to change legislation to allow women to keep their own wages, to maintain property after marriage, and to have the right to guardianship of their own children. Anthony was the organizer of these conventions, and many women who had been prominent in the abolitionist and temperance causes became active in the cause for women. It was a far more unpopular movement than abolition, and the women in it were subjected to ridicule, humiliation, threats of violence, and hostility from men and women alike.

Elizabeth Stanton was determined to stay with the movement she helped to create, but the demands of her home and family were in constant conflict with her public life. Often she had to call Anthony to take over the house and children so that she could gain enough hours of uninterrupted concentration to write a speech or respond to a newspaper attack or get a day or two away from home to attend a local convention of women. Anthony often became impatient with the speeches that never got written and the obligations that weren't met. In 1852 the National Woman's Rights Convention went on without Stanton because she was giving birth to her fifth child and first daughter, Margaret. She never appeared for an extremely important speaking engagement in Boston because she was too ill from her sixth pregnancy. After the sixth child, her daughter Harriet, she wrote to Susan:

> Your servant is not dead but liveth. Imagine me, day in and day out, watching, bathing, dressing, nursing and promenading the

precious contents of a little crib in the corner of my room. I pace up and down these two chambers of mine like a caged lioness, longing to bring to a close all housekeeping cares. . . .

Now that I have two daughters, I feel fresh strength to work. It is not in vain that in myself I have experienced all the wearisome cares to which woman in her best estate is subject.

Sarah Grimké, who knew from her own experience and that of her sister exactly what domestic burdens did to aspirations for outside work, wrote to Stanton in 1854 thanking her "in the name of humanity for thy able address in Albany" and congratulating her for her success in addressing the New York legislature. She added a personal appreciation of Stanton's struggle. "Oh, Liz, if you were not tied hand and foot by domestic duties, what a glorious work you would do for woman. As it is you do much, very much."

The address Stanton gave to the New York legislature in 1854 was on the disabilities of women before the law. She was the first woman ever invited to address a committee of the legislature, and with Anthony's help the event was magnified fifty times over. Anthony made sure the speech was written ahead of time, arranged for Stanton to deliver it to the New York Woman's Rights Convention, and circulated 50,000 copies to the press, women's groups, temperance groups, and reform organizations all over the country. It was the beginning of Stanton's reputation as the legal brain of the woman's movement. It was also the beginning of much greater public visibility. Speaking invitations poured in from all over the state, and Horace Greeley asked to publish her columns in the *New York Tribune.*

The public career she was developing brought her into an exhausting struggle with her family. Her father, her husband, and her friends were all opposed to any activity which took her out of her "true sphere," the home. It is a conflict that women then and now solve by volunteer work, charities, or outside pursuits that do not require the discipline of sustained commitment. That was the pattern Stanton had been following—retreating from the woman's movement when family obligations interfered. But a terrible fight with her father forced her to make a "fierce decision." She wrote to Susan B. Anthony, who was campaigning in New York State with petitions to change the laws affecting women:

I wish I were as free as you and I would stump the State in a twinkling. But I am not, and what is more, I passed through a terrible scourging when last at my father's. I cannot tell you how deep the iron entered my soul. I never felt more keenly the degradation of my sex. To think that all in me of which my father would have felt a proper pride had I been a man, is deeply mortifying to him because I am a woman.

That thought has stung me to a fierce decision—to speak as soon as I can do myself credit.

It was not only her father. It was also her husband. "Henry sides with my friends, who oppose me in all that is dearest to my heart. They are not willing that I should write even on the woman question. But I will both write and speak," she concluded.

Despite the burdens on her time and the distractions of her family, Stanton deeply enjoyed her children. Her daughter Harriet said she had a marvelous way with children, both her own and her grandchildren.

She was a famous story teller and whenever there were children in the house they gathered about her knee at bedtime to hear one of her heart-thrilling fairy tales. . . . Her imagination and the ability she had to put herself back into any period of her life, made little children feel that she was one of them.

Four years after her last child was born she moved to New York City, where Henry was appointed a customs inspector. By the time the Civil War ended, she was forty-nine years old, her children were growing up, and she was just about to embark on a second career. Once she had confessed to Susan B. Anthony in a letter she asked her to keep strictly confidential, "Sometimes, Susan, I struggle in deep waters. . . . However, a good time is coming and my future is always bright and beautiful." It took a number of years, but she was right.

The Civil War had brought a halt to the momentum of the woman's movement. Susan B. Anthony was a devoted abolitionist, spending an entire year speaking in the abolitionist cause and working with fugitive slaves. Anthony recorded in her diary in 1861 that she "outfitted a slave for Canada with the help of Harriet Tubman."

But she had wanted to continue building an organization throughout the war. She was outvoted by those, Stanton included, who felt that woman's first duty was to support the Union. When the war ended, Elizabeth Stanton was one of the first to admit that Susan B. Anthony had been right. The proposed Fourteenth Amendment to the Constitution would have given political rights to the newly emancipated slaves, but it used the word "male." "Put the word male in the constitution and it will take fifty years to get it out," Stanton argued. But there was no organized movement to hear her. It was five years since women had met to debate woman's disabilities. During the war years women had spent their efforts in organizing the Sanitary Commission and the Woman's Loyal League.

As though to dramatize the need for a new infusion of energy into the woman's movement, Elizabeth Cady Stanton announced in 1866 that she would run for Congress. She did so to demonstrate that even though women could not vote, they could hold office if elected. She ran as an independent in the Eighth District of New York City on a platform of free speech, free press, free men, free trade, and universal suffrage. The campaign stirred up a great deal of debate and publicity, although far less than her campaign fifteen years earlier to change women's style of dress. The first woman to run for Congress, she received twenty-four votes.

But more was needed to infuse new life in a woman's movement than a campaign for Congress. A referendum was held in Kansas on the vote for women and the vote for blacks. Both Stanton and Anthony went to Kansas to speak on behalf of the referendum. If woman's suffrage could be won in Kansas, it would be an important test of public sentiment. Woman's suffrage lost—as did votes for blacks—but during the trip Stanton met a man who offered to back a newspaper devoted to the cause of woman's rights. A flamboyant character named George Train became the chief financial backer of a newspaper called the *Revolution*. Susan B. Anthony was publisher, Elizabeth Cady Stanton and a writer, Parker Pillsbury, made up the editorial staff.

Stanton called the two years she spent writing for the *Revolution* the happiest of her life—and the most valuable. She was able to express her ideas on women's oppression with the confidence that she was writing for an audience who wanted to hear what she had to say. She covered an extraordinary range of subjects, many of them taboo—prostitution, prison reform, infant killings (as a form of birth control), and the seduction of servant girls. One historian of the woman's movement, Eleanor Flexner, has said of the *Revolution:*

> [It] made a contribution to the women's cause out of all proportion to either its size, brief lifespan, or modest circulation. . . . Here was news not to be found elsewhere—of the organization of women typesetters, tailoresses, and laundry workers, of the first women's clubs, of pioneers in the professions, of women abroad. But the *Revolution* did more than just carry news, or set a new standard of professionalism for papers edited by and for women. It gave their movement a forum, a focus, and direction. It pointed, it led, and it fought, with vigor and vehemence.

Elizabeth Stanton wrote about women's low wages and about every new occupation that opened to women. Her point of view was for equality for women in every aspect of American society. She believed in the woman's movement in the broadest sense. External circumstances forced her attention to focus on the single issue of suffrage.

Former abolitionists who had organized with women in the Equal Rights Association took the position that the urgency of the vote for the Negro far overshadowed the need for the vote for women. Ignored was the fact that half the black race was made up of women. Harriet Tubman believed in her political rights and was a member of the Stanton-Anthony group even when it split from the Equal Rights Association. After the Fourteenth Amendment passed and the men insisted that women work for the Fifteenth Amendment, which would give the vote to blacks, the women answered that they would work for an amendment that gave political rights to both blacks and women. Women were being asked to betray their own constituency.

The issue was more than a false choice between the women's political rights and the Negro's political rights. It was a question of denying a social reality. Although blacks and whites had been rigidly separated by law, there was, in fact, an elaborate and complex set of social relationships between them. Except for a few people like Sarah Grimké, there was little analysis in the North as to what would happen in the public imagination when black men, former slaves, became white women's political superiors. The editorial in the *Revolution* which was considered a "deadly insult" to the Negro was in actuality quite hard-nosed.

> Just as the Democratic cry of "white man's government" created the antagonism between the Irishman and the Negro, which culminated in the New York riots of 1863, so the Republican cry of "manhood suffrage" creates an antagonism between black men and all women, which will culminate in fearful outrages on womanhood especially in the Southern States. . . . The Negro will be the victim for generations to come of the prejudice engendered by making this a white man's government. . . .

Unfortunately, it was Stanton's old ally, Frederick Douglass, who made the most compelling case against linking women's suffrage with the vote for black Americans: "When women because they are women are dragged from their homes and hung from lampposts; when their children are torn from their arms . . . then they will have an urgency to obtain the ballot equal to the black man."

Stanton and Anthony were accused of irresponsibility, self-ishness, and treason to the cause of human rights when they refused to support the Fifteenth Amendment. Clearly women were not equals in the Equal Rights Association. The men who led the association followed custom and expected that "their" women would accept their leadership. Much of the outrage that surrounded the walk-out of women from the Equal Rights Association was the result of the totally unexpected independence of action by the women. Even the most radical of men could not understand the thorough-going idea of woman's autonomy that Elizabeth Stanton envisioned.

On May 14, 1869, a handful of unhappy women met in the offices of the *Revolution* to decide what to do about an organization dedicated to equal rights which was not upholding its own purpose. Only the most radical women were there: Lucretia Mott; the brilliant woman from Poland Ernestine Rose, whom Wendell Phillips had identified as a "threat" to the cause; the famous orator Anna Dickinson; and a number of others. No men were present. Never one to lose an organizing opportunity, Susan Anthony called for a meeting. The result was the formation of the National Woman Suffrage Association. Its purpose was to advocate an alternative amendment, the sixteenth constitutional amendment, which Stanton drafted and which stated simply that the rights of citizens of the United States should not be denied on the basis of race, color, sex, or previous condition of servitude. They also resolved to work against passage of the Fifteenth Amendment: "We oppose the measure, because men have no right to pass it without our consent," Stanton wrote in the *Revolution*. If women were ever to act on the basis of equal rights, they had to begin.

A tidal wave of bitterness swept over them. As a countermeasure, the moderate women of the Equal Rights Association organized the American Woman Suffrage Association, with prominent male reformers as officers—Henry Ward Beecher, Wendell Phillips. Their goal was largely identical to that of the parent organization, that of "step[ping] aside so that the Negro may have the ballot," in Julia Ward Howe's famous phrase.

But the woman's movement was not large enough to support two suffrage organizations with two newspapers. The Stanton-Anthony group had fewer resources, made many enemies, assaulted public sensibilities, and soon was in deep financial trouble. Several moderate women offered to help them financially, but only on condition they change the name of their newspaper to something less inflammatory. Stanton said no!

A journal called the *Rosebud* might answer for those who come with kid gloves and perfumes to lay immortal wreaths on the monuments which in sweat and tears others have hewn and built; but for us . . . there is no name like the *Revolution!*

In 1870 the *Revolution* was absorbed by another newspaper.

Twenty years later the two separate woman's suffrage organizations merged, each unable to meet the demands of political action, organization, education, and money that the woman's suffrage campaign entailed. Before women gained the right to vote it took millions of dollars. Fifty-six different campaigns for state referenda, four hundred eighty campaigns to urge legislatures to put woman's suffrage on the ballot, forty-seven campaigns for state constitutional conventions, thirty campaigns to urge presidential party platforms to include woman's suffrage as a plank, and nineteen lobbying efforts with nineteen successive Congresses before the Nineteenth Amendment was proposed in Congress in 1919 and ratified August 26, 1920, giving women a right that immigrant men had the minute they took out naturalization papers. The main opponents of woman's suffrage were the liquor interests. They believed woman's suffrage was synonymous with Prohibition, and they fought "votes for women" in every state it was put on the ballot.

Elizabeth Stanton never confused the woman's rights movement with the campaign for suffrage. She was the first president of the united suffrage organization—Susan B. Anthony succeeded her three years later—but she outraged many of the new recruits to the woman's movement, many of whom brought the religious piety of the temperance organizations from which they had come. Her *Woman's Bible,* published in 1898, was repudiated by the very organization she had helped to found. In her efforts to challenge religious teachings, which relentlessly preached women's inferiority, she stirred up the clergy, caused libraries to refuse to circulate the book, and fostered a storm of criticism in various newspapers. The Woman's Suffrage Association announced that it had "no official connection with the so-called Woman's Bible." She was eighty years old and still considered a dangerous radical.

Her sympathies were changing in the labor turmoil that grew in the decades following the Civil War. The woman's movement was operating in a different economic system from when she had first struck out in 1848.

> The strikes and mobs . . . of the masses warn us that, although we forget and neglect their interests and our duties, we do it at the peril of all. . . . The impending danger cannot be averted by any surface measures; there must be a radical change in the relations of capital and labor.

In her eighties she began to study socialism. In 1894 she wrote about the railroad strikes in Chicago.

> A Mr. Debs seems to have inaugurated the movement. The strikers make many blunders. But . . . it is natural for the masses to occasionally ask why we have these extremes of riches and poverty. There must be something rotten in Denmark. My sympathies are with [the strikers].

Elizabeth Cady Stanton was basically a politician, but a politician for a small heretical movement which, like the abolitionists, had limited means to power. She did not like organizational infighting or the demands of administration. Her greatest gifts were in articulating issues, gaining the public's attention, orchestrating demands for reform. She was not afraid to make herself a target, to draw lightning while other people decided if they were brave enough to step out. She had a politician's love for getting the ideas of people, stepping into a crowd and "pressing the flesh," enjoying the energy that flows from an audience. The most joyful moments of her autobiography are those in which she describes her tours in the tiny towns of the West, traveling alone, telling how she talked to people on trains. She instructed mothers on how to take care of their babies, gave one baby a bath while its exhausted parents slept, opened the windows in waiting rooms because she felt that fresh air was good for everyone, slept in a Kansas farmhouse while mice ran across her pillow, convinced train conductors to let her off at unscheduled stops.

She also had several other qualities of a great politician—energy to burn, a great sense of humor, and the ability to inspire great loyalty. People were often exasperated with her, angry at her constant shifts of attention, annoyed with her devotion to what were considered irrelevant subjects, yet few people end their lives with so many old friends around them.

Even Frederick Douglass, her arch opponent in the 1868 debate about "the Negro's hour," remained a lifelong friend. When Douglass married a white woman he learned exactly how limited were the ideas of equality held by his old abolitionist friends. In the storm of public condemnation, from blacks and whites alike, Stanton wrote Douglass a warm letter of congratulation. Douglass responded:

Much as I respect the good opinion of my fellow men I do not wish it at the expense of my own self-respect. . . . You, dear Mrs. Stanton, could have found a straight smooth and pleasant road through the world had you allowed the world to decide for you your sphere in life. That is, had you allowed it to sink your moral and intellectual individuality into nonentity. But you have nobly asserted your own and the rights of your sex and the world will know hereafter that you have lived and worked beneficially in the world.

You have made both Mrs. Douglass and myself very glad and happy by your letter and we both give you our warmest thanks for it.

At the age of eighty a tribute was held for her in New York in the Metropolitan Opera House, with over three thousand people in attendance. The New York *Sun* reported on November 12, 1895, "This is Stanton day in New York. The brave and estimable woman will be honored today as no other American woman ever was honored in her lifetime." It was an extraordinary testimonial to a woman who had spent most of her life abused and criticized. When she died seven years later in 1902, the most appropriate tribute was in a note written by Susan B. Anthony. "Well," she said, "it is an awful hush."

MOTHER JONES
(MARY HARRIS JONES)

———————◆—◆◆—◆———————

BORN: MAY 1, 1830, CORK, IRELAND. DIED: NOVEMBER 30, 1930, SILVER SPRING, MARYLAND. FATHER: RICHARD HARRIS (NATURAL-IZED AMERICAN CITIZEN). MOTHER: NAME UNCERTAIN (BELIEVED TO BE MARGARET OR ELLEN). MARRIED: GEORGE JONES, 1861. FOUR CHILDREN, NAMES UNKNOWN (ALL DIED 1867).

JOINED KNIGHTS OF LABOR, 1879. COFOUNDER, INDUSTRIAL WORKERS OF THE WORLD, 1905. ORGANIZER, UNITED MINE WORKERS, 1900–20.

I went up to the miners' camp in Holly Grove where all through the winter, through snow and ice and blizzard, men and women and little children had shuddered in canvas tents that America might be a better country to live in. I listened to their stories. I talked to Mrs. Sevilla whose unborn child had been kicked dead by gunmen while her husband was out looking for work. I talked with widows, whose husbands had been shot by the gunmen; with children whose frightened faces talked more effectively than their baby tongues. I learned how the scabs had been recruited in the cities, locked in boxcars, and delivered to the mines like so much pork.

"I think the strike is lost, Mother," said an old miner whose son had been killed.

"Lost! Not until your souls are lost!" said I.

MARY HARRIS JONES IN 1914
FROM *The Autobiography of
Mother Jones*, 1925

Mother Jones's name weaves in and out of the major events of labor history: from the time the first union admitted women in 1879, to the formation of the Industrial Workers of the World in 1905, to the Great Steel Strike of 1919. She captured the imagination of American workers in a way that no one else has before or since. To know of her life is to know that for millions of immigrant laborers, life in America was hell. Her will to resist the tyranny of industrial owners was legendary among workers. Her courage was infectious, and it was this the owners feared most.

Consistent with the legend of Mother Jones, any account of her life begins in controversy. She claimed to have been born on May 1, 1830, in Cork, Ireland. The place is probably right and the month and day may be right, but the year seems to be wrong. According to school and work records she would have had to have been born in 1838 or 1839. Toronto Normal School records show that in 1858 a student named Maria Harris was eighteen. The signature of Maria Harris corresponds to that of Mother Jones. If one accepts Mother Jones's 1830 birthdate, there is a span of nine years in her youth that is completely unaccounted for. It may have been that as she grew older her flair for the dramatic prompted her to capitalize on a "grandmother image" and magnify her years. Under oath in court she tended to be more truthful about her age. At her trial in West Virginia in 1902, a newspaper reported that "She confessed to sixty years."

The image of a pink-cheeked old woman who dared to go to the center of brutal strikes was potent and effective. Like Harriet Tubman's poor-old-bent-over-black-woman disguise, Mother Jones's grandmother role was inspired camouflage. Her sense of drama enabled her to capture public attention for the plight of people who were politically powerless.

She was drawn to the miners, although it was child labor that aroused her most spectacular activities. Although she had ample opportunities in countless newspaper interviews, public hearings, and other forums to tell about her childhood and youth, she never did. The only personal details she provided were those that she shared in common with the anonymous immigrants who made up much of the American labor force. It was as though she wanted people to know that the only parts of her life that mattered were her personal suffering, struggle, and resistance. In the opening statement of her autobiography she summed up the themes of her life.

> I was born in the city of Cork, Ireland, in 1830. My people were poor. For generations they had fought for Ireland's freedom. Many of my folks have died in that struggle. My father, Richard Harris, came to America in 1835, and as soon as he had become an American citizen he sent for his family. His work as a laborer with railway construction crews took him to Toronto, Canada. Here I was brought up but always as a child of an American citizen. Of that citizenship I have ever been proud.

Her father, Richard Harris, had settled in Burlington, Vermont, and he became a naturalized American citizen in 1850. The knowledge Mary Harris gained from her father about the working of railroads gave her a mobility not available to many other union organizers. She once evaded a two-hundred-man militia in Colorado by avoiding the train stations and going at night to the section house, where the cars stood ready to be coupled to the train. An old section hand found her walking the ties. Mother Jones introduced herself, said she had a ticket on the "sleeper going south," and asked to be put aboard. She was sound asleep by the time the train eased into the station to let its first passengers on under the watchful eyes of the soldiers.

In Toronto Mary Harris went to public school and then to Toronto Normal School, a teachers college, from which she was graduated in 1859. Her first job was in Monroe, Michigan, as a teacher in a convent school. According to the convent records, "Miss M. Harris entered the house as a secular teacher on August 31, 1859. . . . She remained until March 8, 1860 at which time she was paid in full . . . $36.43."

Although she claimed she never liked teaching, she was a natural teacher. Every speech she gave was a history lesson in the labor movement. Between strikes she used to talk at union meetings about the development of the labor movement in England, and at the end of the meeting she sold a book called *Merrie England*, which described socialism in the simple personal terms of the workers' struggles in England. She always encouraged "her boys," as she called them, to learn more English, improve their minds, and read rather than spend time in the saloon. Some of them listened to her, and she was their first impetus for self-education.

What she didn't like about teaching was "bossing little children," and after almost seven months in the convent school she left to try to be a dressmaker in Chicago. By the following fall she had given up on dressmaking and was in Memphis, Tennessee, for another teaching job.

For her time Mary Harris was a well-educated woman. Although she could always pull out an Irish brogue when she needed it, she spoke well and wrote extremely well. Her letters have few misspellings, excellent punctuation, and good grammar. Had she wanted, it would have been very easy for her to marry into the middle class. Instead, she married George Jones, an itinerant blacksmith and organizer for the Iron Moulders' Union in Memphis, Tennessee. They were married in 1861, and she did some traveling with him—"missionary work" she called it—trying to convince iron workers to overcome the threats of blacklisting, firings, and cries of "traitor" to join the union. The Iron Moulders' Union had been founded only in 1859, and it was the first successful union to organize members across state lines.

The Joneses lived in a poor section of Memphis, not too far from the foundry where George Jones worked. They had four children—three boys and a girl—within four years. The Civil War did not seem to greatly touch their lives except to increase work for iron workers.

In 1867, an epidemic of yellow fever broke out in Memphis. The rich left town; the poor had no place to go. There were few doctors or nurses to help the poor. Once a house was known to have a fever victim, the house was quarantined to visitors. The air was filled with the stench of burning sulfur, for it was believed that sulfur fumes warded off the fever. City officials banned all public assemblies. Churches were closed. People did not leave their homes if they didn't have to. Wagons driven by masked and hooded men creaked through the streets to pick up the dead. It was not so very different from the death wagon drivers who called "Bring out your dead" in the plague-infested towns of the Middle Ages.

Across the street from Mary Jones, ten persons lay dead from the plague. "The dead surrounded us. . . . All about my house I could hear weeping and the cries of delirium."

One by one Mary Jones's children caught the fever and slowly died. "I washed their little bodies," she said simply, "and got them ready for burial." Then her husband caught the fever and died. "I sat alone through nights of grief. No one came to me. No one could. Other homes were as stricken as mine. All day long—all night long, I heard the grating of the wheels of the death cart."

Some inner resource saved her from the abyss of personal despair. Over fifty years later, when the women of Colorado saw their husbands shot down and their children burned to death in a fourteen-month struggle culminating in the Ludlow Massacre, she knew from her own experience what they suffered. "Get out and fight," she told them. "Fight like hell till you go to heaven!" She explained, "That was the only way I knew to comfort them." It was either fight or not survive.

After the Iron Moulders' Union buried her husband, she got a permit to help nurse the remaining victims. When the epidemic was over she packed up her few belongings and went back to Chicago.

For the next four years she worked as a dressmaker. Apparently she was very good and opened her own shop on Washington Street near the lake. Dress was always significant in her life and she was concerned about her appearance, which was impeccably ladylike. Her demure costume was a wonderful foil for her fiery speeches and rough language. As one news reporter wrote:

> A casual glance at the blue-eyed, pink-skinned, white-haired woman, in her mid-Victorian dress of black, with its fussy touches, and her bonnet of black lace, with its violets and lavender ribbon . . . does not suggest that here is the greatest fighting spirit that American womanhood has developed in our time.

A West Virginia miner's daughter remembers that when Mother Jones used to come around she showed the miners' wives how to make bonnets and encouraged them to give up the kerchiefs they always wore on their heads. Perhaps it was her way of trying to break down the dress distinctions that separated the miners' wives from the mine owners' wives. Another West Virginia woman, Mrs. Utt, remembers that her mother would not let her go to Mother Jones's meetings because her language was so rough. Mother Jones used a lot of "damns" and "hells" in her speech and was not afraid to use strong words, especially in relation to the "pig-eyed" mine owners or other enemies of the workers. It was a way of deflating authority, of thumbing her nose at those who were in power, and letting her audience know that they could do it too. During a particularly brutal strike in West Virginia one mine owner remembers her referring to the governor of the state, a man named Glasscock, as "Crystal peter" and "Crystal cock."

It always gave a wonderful lift to the miners' spirits to see this tiny—she was about five feet tall—sedately dressed woman, swearing like a trouper.

The course of her dressmaking business changed in 1871 when Mrs. O'Leary's cow tipped over the lantern and caused the Great Chicago Fire. Three hundred people died. The fire destroyed eighteen thousand houses, and ninety thousand people were left homeless. Mary Jones was burned out, her business and home completely destroyed. All she had left after the fire were the clothes on her back. For the second time everything in her life had been obliterated—and after that it was as though she had nothing left to fear.

Never again did she try to accumulate any possessions or make a home for herself. "I reside wherever there is a good fight against wrong," she used to say and it was true. Home was never again a fixed place.

"After the Chicago fire," Jones said, "I became more and more engrossed in the labor struggle and I decided to take an active part in the efforts of the working people to better the conditions under which they worked and lived."

Like many women in the labor movement, Mary Jones got involved because of the work of her husband. She got to know many of the Iron Moulders in Chicago who were affiliated with a two-year-old organization known as the Knights of Labor. According to its founding charter, the Knights of Labor was "an organization of working people of every craft . . . skilled and unskilled . . . with members of every creed and color. . . ." After the fire Mary Jones began to go to meetings that the Knights of Labor held in an old fire-scorched building near St. Mary's Church, where she had been living along with hundreds of other homeless refugees. To her the Knights, which had to hold meetings secretly because people who attended were persecuted and blacklisted by employers, seemed "a worthy, even sacred cause." She became a supporter—women were not officially admitted as members until 1879—listing her trade as "dressmaker" on the application. The cause of labor and the vision of the Knights of Labor opened a new world to her. She began to spend her "evenings at their meetings, listening to splendid speakers. . . ."

Three important developments occurred during these Knights of Labor meetings. First, she was exposed to the ideas of socialism and the historical facts behind the organization of workers in England and other European countries. (She went to Europe in 1873 and again in 1881 to learn more about the conditions of workers in England, Ireland, France, Austria, and Germany.) Second, she began to discover her own skills as a speaker and debater. She began by asking questions of the speakers and found that she had a commanding presence and an ability to make people listen to what she said. Although the Knights of Labor did not yet admit women workers as full members, Mary Jones unofficially joined the Knights as a supporter and agitator and began recruiting for them.

She was sent out by the Chicago office to speak to workers and try to persuade them to join the Knights of Labor. She was persuasive, dynamic, personal, and she developed into a fiery speaker, able to inject energy and determination into a crowd. One reporter covering a labor rally described her as "an energetic, white-haired, bright-eyed little woman [whose] earnestness would carry conviction to a steel magnet itself." Tom Tippett, who worked with her in the United Mine Workers, said,

> In the union office she was out of place quarreling with officials, offering no constructive policy of her own and constantly violating union policy. It was in the field that she made her real contribution. With one speech she often threw a whole community on strike, and she could keep the strikers loyal month after month on empty stomachs and behind prison bars.

In her later days she could draw immense audiences from all segments of society—society women, factory girls, laborers, town fathers, business representatives, black and white, and all nationalities. She spoke out of total conviction, and she never said what she didn't believe. At a banquet of the National Woman's Suffrage Association in New York a woman asked her how women could help laborers when women didn't have the vote. She answered, "I have never had a vote and I have raised hell all over this country. You don't need a vote to raise hell! You need convictions and a voice!"

She did not exactly charm the five hundred members of her audience, all of whom were dedicated to the woman's vote, but very few walked out on her. No one ever accused her of currying favor with an audience. Her job was to shake an audience out of its apathy, energize people, and get them acting instead of talking.

Elizabeth Gurley Flynn, known as the Rebel Girl of the IWW and one of its outstanding organizers, considered Mother Jones "the greatest woman agitator of her time." As a professional agitator herself she knew that the greatest enemy was public indifference and was a keen judge of what moved an apathetic audience to action. The first time Flynn saw Mother Jones was at a Bronx, New York, open-air meeting. "She was giving the 'city folks' hell. Why weren't we helping the miners of West Virginia? Why weren't we backing up the Mexican people against Diaz? We were 'white-livered rabbits who never put our feet on Mother earth,' she said."

The third important result of the Knights of Labor was Mother Jones's meeting with Terrence Powderly, the leader of the Knights and a man who would remain one of her close friends and confidants throughout her lifetime. They maintained a correspondence for years, and when Mother Jones was unable to travel any more she went to Powderly's home near Washington, D.C., and then spent her last years nearby at Mrs. Walter Burgess's in Silver Spring.

Powderly was a gentle, philosophical man who was thirty years old when he took over the Knights in 1878. He was greatly criticized later for the policies the Knights pursued and for his failure to use strikes as a prime tactic. Powderly was a laborer himself, who had worked his way up through the railroads, had quit to study law, had managed a grocery store, and had even served a term as mayor of Scranton, Pennsylvania. He had been greatly influenced by William Sylvis, the founder of the Iron Moulders' Union and a hero of Mother Jones's husband. He detested strikes because he felt they cost the workers far more than they gained and that they rarely brought lasting benefits. At a time when labor agitators were branded as socialist traitors, and a major preoccupation of the Catholic Church was fighting socialism—the majority of the laboring classes, Irish, Polish, Italian, German, Slavic, were all Catholic—

Powderly deserved credit for making a union a "moral, godly" organization in the eyes of its Catholic membership. The local Catholic Church was the one stable element that immigrant workers had in their lives, and they would not support an organization that had a hint of what the parish priest called "the evils of socialism." Some priests even refused to bury the early organizers in Catholic cemeteries.

Realistically, socialism offered the only theoretical basis for labor unions. When Powderly was under severe attack for his failure to incorporate militant tactics and socialist ideas into unionism, Mother Jones wrote to him, "Though all the world may abuse you there will still be one who will defend you. . . . You were rocking the cradle of the movement. You made it possible for others to march on."

Some of Powderly's ideas were visionary. He refused to accept the idea that women or blacks should be barred from labor unions even though they worked for lower wages. A year after Powderly assumed leadership, the Knights admitted women as equal members, the first labor organization to do so. (It did not, however, admit blacks.) Powderly often shared a speaker's platform with Elizabeth Cady Stanton or Susan B. Anthony, and he spoke for the woman's vote while they spoke for the rights of women in the mills and factories. He made Susan B. Anthony a member of the Knights of Labor. He advocated joining the Communist International Workingmen's Association, an organization that Karl Marx had started in London in 1865. But in many ways he was not in touch with the tactics needed to deal with the raw struggles that were to take place between capitalist owners and the people who worked for them.

The profound friendship he developed with Mother Jones, which lasted over fifty-five years, reveals a great deal about both of them. Both were excellent judges of human nature. Both had had profound spiritual experiences connected with the miners. And in both of them there was an intermingling of religious sensibility with the impulse for radical action. In Powderly, however, the religious sensibility predominated, which may have been why he was so successful in negotiating with the Catholic Church. In Mother Jones the taste for battle dominated. Mother Jones's religion took a different form from Powderly's—a militant, defiant, unaccepting view of the application of Christian values.

Mother Jones, like Powderly, often referred to the "greatest agitator of all time"—Jesus Christ. She portrayed Christ as an organizer and worker for the industrious poor. She explained that Christ could have been honored by the rich of his day. Instead, he chose to die rather than betray the poor. Unlike Powderly's, her language was that of the people not the Church. "Christ walked among the poor and the despised and the lowly and he agitated against the powers of Rome. . . ."

She had a strong sense of religion but very little faith in the Catholic Church. Often in a mining town all public buildings were owned by the mine owners—even the churches. In one mining town she found the men meeting in the Catholic church, the candles lit, the priest collecting the union dues. She told the men, "This is a praying institution. You should not commercialize it." She told everyone to get up and go outside. When they were out in the open air she told the men: "Your organization is not a praying institution. It's a fighting institution. . . . Pray for the dead, but fight like hell for the living."

Unlike Dorothy Day who thirty years later would join radical action with Catholicism, Mother Jones did not believe that the Catholic Church was of much help to laborers. Nonetheless, she was aware of the limitations of labor experiments that did not contain religion. When she was asked to join a socialist colony in Ruskin, Tennessee—one of the worker communities that had become fashionable—she refused, saying, "Only religion can make a colony successful and labor doesn't have religion."

At heart she believed that there was no way for the lot of working people in America to improve until they faced the hard task of organizing. Her life was devoted to making that possible. She was out of place in the union office or around the negotiating table. Her real contribution was in the field.

From 1871 to 1900 it is hard to put together a clear chronological record of Mother Jones's activities. In many of her speeches she implied involvement with the Pittsburgh railroad strike in 1877, the Haymarket Riots of 1886, the founding of the United Mine Workers in 1890 (when it merged with another group of miners in the Knights of Labor), the Populist Army of 1892, the Pullman strikes organized by Eugene Debs in 1894, Coxey's poverty march of the

same year. She never said what she had done, but she spoke about
them in such a way that her audience saw themselves as part of a
great tradition of struggle, resistance, and the will to overcome.

Often her itinerary was not fixed by the union office but by a call
for help from individual workers. Her personal correspondence contains more than one urgent call for help from an anonymous miner.
Her reputation as a savior of hopeless situations brought her telegrams such as this one from Shamokin, Pennsylvania:

> MOTHER THERE IS A STRIKE AT THE SILK MILLS HERE   WILL YOU
> COME AT ONCE   I KNOW YOU CAN DO LOTS OF GOOD
> COME IF POSSIBLE
>
> FROM A MINER

Often immigrants were recruited to work in the mines by the
promise of free land to farm. When they arrived, there was no land,
and there was no way to express grievances. They lived in a company house, bought their food from a company store, saw a company
doctor if they were sick, and sent their children to a company
school. Often they were paid in company scrip instead of real
money, so they couldn't leave town. If a worker expressed too much
discontent, credit was cut off at the store, and he found an eviction
notice at his house.

In 1897 Mother Jones began working with coal miners in West
Virginia and Pennsylvania. It brought her to the attention of John
Mitchell and other leaders of the struggling mine workers union,
and she was hired as a field organizer. In 1900 they paid her $494.91
for work done, and by 1904 she was listed as one of sixty walking
delegates receiving $4 a day. It was just about the same salary that
the miners received. She stayed with workers, shared their food, and
any money she raised she turned over to others.

Textile strikes, streetcar strikes, silk mill strikes, ironworker
strikes, railroad strikes—nothing absorbed Mother Jones in quite
the same way as the desperate struggles of the mine workers. When
Clarence Darrow wrote the introduction to her autobiography he
said it was

> the mountainous country, the deep mines, the black pit, the
> cheap homes, the danger, the everlasting conflict for wages and
> for life [that] appealed to her imagination and chivalry. . . . In
> all her career, Mother Jones never quailed or ran away. Her

deep convictions and fearless soul always drew her to seek the spot where the fight was hottest and the danger greatest.

If there is a key to Mother Jones's life, it is to be found in her identification with the miners. There she saw in stark forms the human costs of America's progress. And it was there that she first became known as Mother. She tells of a terrible incident when she stayed up all night with a dying man whose head had been bashed in by one of the mine detectives. "We took him to the hotel and sent for a doctor who sewed up the great open cuts in his head. I sat up all night and nursed the poor fellow. He was out of his head and thought I was his mother." She was in a sense a mother for many people—children whose fathers had been lost in the mines, women who married young and had had too many babies and had little hope left in their lives. The struggle of the men and women who lived in isolated towns tucked away in mountains was in many ways the grimmest battle of the American labor movement. Mother Jones succeeded in bringing that story down from the hill towns into public notice. Many of the names are lost to American history— Bruceville, Arnot, Fairmont, Trinidad. She depicted the life of the miners and their families, and she did nothing to soften the reality. But as in Harriet Tubman's descriptions of the lives of slaves, there was a sense of the poetry of human experience in Jones's images of the men who

crawl through dark, choking crevices with only a bit of lamp on their caps to light the silent way; whose backs are bent with toil, whose very bones ache, whose happiness is sleep, and whose peace is death.

She told of families that

lived in company-owned shacks that were not fit for pigs. Children died by the hundreds due to the ignorance and the poverty of their parents. Often I have helped lay out for burial the babies of the miners, and the mothers could scarce conceal their relief at the little ones' deaths.

She understood the isolation of spirit of the miner's life:

Mining at its best is wretched work, and the life and surroundings of the miner are hard and ugly. His work is down in the black depths of the earth. He works alone in a drift. There can be little friendly companionship as there is in the factory, as there is among men who build bridges and houses, working together in groups. The work is dirty. Coal dust grinds itself into the skin, never to be removed. The miner must stoop as he works in the drift. He becomes bent like a gnome. His work is utterly fatiguing. Muscles and bones ache. His lungs breathe coal dust and the strange damp air of places that are never filled with sunlight. . . . Around his house is mud and slush. Great mounds of culm, black and sullen, surround him. His children are perpetually grimy from play on the culm mounds. The wife struggles with dirt, with inadequate water supply, with small wages, with overcrowded shacks.

She described sitting with a miner on a culm pile, while he ate lunch with grimy hands, or talking with his wife over the washtub, while she washed coal dust out of her white curtains.

"We came like missionaries," she wrote of her first experiences organizing among miners. "We held revival meetings at which we called on our congregations to seek salvation, not in the 'blood of the lamb' but in the United Mine Workers." About the success of these efforts she said:

> Our task was not safe or easy. . . . Men who joined the union were blacklisted. Their families were thrown out on the high-ways. Men were shot. They were beaten. Many disappeared without a trace. Storekeepers were ordered not to sell to union men or their families. . . .

It was painful, bitter, lonely work. Often it seemed hopeless. Joining a union became a death warrant in many mining towns. But in others it was a source of strength. One strike at the Dripmouth mine in Arnot, Pennsylvania, in 1900 revealed a lot about Mother Jones's persistence, her ingenuity, her judgment of people, and her infectious spirit.

A strike of the miners had been going on for five months without making headway. The mine owners had sent the doctors, the school-teachers, the preachers to the homes of the miners to get them to sign a document saying they would return to work. Then they brought in substitute workers, called scabs, to keep the mines working. In those days there was no money with which to pay strike benefits and many strikes were broken simply by the owner's ability to outwait the strikers.

Mother Jones told the demoralized men, "Stay home with the children for a change and let the women attend to the scabs." She organized the miners' wives into "an army" and armed them with tin washtubs, mops, brooms, and pails of water. She knew she would be arrested if she were seen at the head of the troops, and since nothing more effectively stopped rebellions than the arrest of a leader, she chose another woman to lead the army.

> I selected as leader an Irish woman who had a most picturesque appearance. . . . She wore a black stocking and a white one. She had tied a little red fringed shawl over her wild red hair. Her face was red and her eyes were mad. I looked at her and felt that she could raise a rumpus.

She told the woman to lead the woman's army up to the entrance of the mine and "hammer and howl and be ready to chase the scabs with your mops and brooms." Her final instructions were, "Don't be afraid of anyone."

The women weren't. They knocked down the first guard who tried to stop them. They ran after the workers who tried to enter the mines. The mules that pulled the coal cars out of the mines started bucking and kicking. What began as an ordinary workday became utter chaos. As miners started to leave their houses to go to work the women chased them back inside. One man was thrown over the fence to land at the feet of his mother. Thinking he was dead she ran for a bottle of holy water yelling, "For God's sake come back to life . . . and join the union." According to Mother Jones, "When he opened his eyes and saw all the women standing around him he said, 'Sure and I'll go to hell before I'll scab again.' "

The march of the miners' wives turned the strike around. The men resolved not to go back to work and to stay out until they gained some of their demands. For days and nights the women guarded the mines so the company would not bring in scabs. "They were heroic women," said Mother Jones. "In the long years to come the nation will pay them high tribute for they were fighting for the advancement of a great country."

That strike in Arnot was won. But there were many that weren't, many that were gruesome in their violence and brutality. At Stanaford Mountain Mother Jones said she went into a corner "and wept like I hadn't wept since the death of my husband and four children in 1867." She had seen a miner's shack soaked red with blood. The miner had had his head blown off and his wife and four children were riddled with bullets.

She accepted the decision of the community at Stanaford Mountain not to continue the strike. "No strike has ever been won that didn't have the support of the women," she used to say and she was right. It is a truism that has been strangely neglected by labor historians. Men did not stay out on strike when their wives were pushing them back to work. Her ability to work with the miners' wives was one of the reasons for her extraordinary success. She understood the totality of the miners' lives. She had good rapport with the women, and she understood their children.

There was nothing delicate about miners' wives. Most of them had spent their own childhoods working in the silk mills. They married young, had too many children too quickly, and aged before their time. As Mother Jones told it:

> Many a time I have been in a home where the poor wife was sick in bed, the children crawling over her, quarreling and playing in the room, often the only warm room in the house. I would tidy up the best I could, hush the little ones, get them ready for school in the morning, those that didn't go to the breakers or to the mills, pack the lunch in the dinner bucket, bathe the poor wife and brush her hair. I saw the daily heroism of those wives.

The breakers were chutes in which coal was separated from slate in the mines. Boys as young as six and seven were hired to do this work. The silk mills were small mills which grew up around mining towns where women and children were sent to work. Women and children were less trouble than men. They worked long hours for a pittance, and they didn't organize or strike for higher wages.

When Mother Jones went to Kensington, Pennsylvania, in 1903 to assist in a textile strike she learned that ten thousand of the seventy-five thousand strikers were children, many of them under ten years old. "Every day little children came into Union Headquarters, some with their hands off, some with the thumb missing, some with their fingers off at the knuckle. They were stooped little things, round shouldered and skinny." When she asked the reporters why they didn't publish the facts about child labor in Pennsylvania, they answered they couldn't because the mill owners had stock in the newspapers. "Well," she said, "I've got stock in these little children. I'll arrange a little publicity."

She asked the parents if they would let her take their children for a week or ten days. They consented and Mother Jones began what became known as The March of the Mill Children, a procession from Kensington, Pennsylvania, to Oyster Bay, New York, where President Theodore Roosevelt was vacationing. She thought it would be beneficial if "President Roosevelt might see these mill children and compare them with his own little ones who were spending the summer on the seashore."

As they marched reporters began to cover their progress and the meetings that Mother Jones arranged in each town and city she went through. She was a member of the Socialist party, and Socialists in each of the towns helped with arrangements and organizing crowds. At a mass meeting in Philadelphia she introduced some of the children to the crowds. "Here's a textbook on economics," she said as she introduced James Ashworth, a little boy who was stooped over like an old man from carrying bundles of yarn that weighed seventy-five pounds. "He gets three dollars a week and his sister who is fourteen gets six dollars. They work in a carpet factory ten hours a day. . . ." To an immense crowd in New York City she showed little Eddie Dunphy, "a little fellow of twelve whose job it was to sit all day on a high stool handing the right thread to another worker . . . eleven hours a day . . . for three dollars a week." Then she introduced Gussie Rangnew, "a little girl from whom all the childhood had gone. Her face was like an old woman's. Gussie packed stockings in a factory."

The *New York Times* covered every day of the march. Farmers brought out fresh food to the children. The marchers cooked in washtubs along the road. Trainmen gave them free rides. In Princeton, New Jersey, Grover Cleveland lent them his barn to sleep in. Senator Thomas Platt, one of the political bosses of New York, arranged to meet them in a fancy hotel in New York, but he went out the back door after he saw the "little army." When the manager of the hotel served them a sumptuous breakfast, Mother Jones insisted it be charged to the good senator. She talked about how she wanted a federal law prohibiting the exploitation of children and enforcement of child labor laws already on the books. The newspapers gave enormous amounts of publicity to the issue of child labor, and within a year Pennsylvania had passed a law to keep children out of factories until they were fourteen. President Roosevelt, however, refused to see Mother Jones, and child labor legislation and enforcement was left to the state legislatures, many of which were under the control of the industrialists. Enforcing even the mildest child labor laws was difficult. Mothers lied about the ages of their children so that the children could work. It was a question of starvation or perjury, explained one group of mothers in Kensington. The fathers had been killed or maimed at the mines, and the children's wages were needed to pay for food.

Also, according to the ground rules of capitalism, human laborers, regardless of age or sex, were considered part of the machinery. "When my machines get old and useless," explained a New England mill owner, "I reject them. . . . These people are part of my machinery." If an owner paid more than the lowest wages, he was considered to be working against his stockholders. Children were the ideal laborers. They worked for pennies a day and were docile. Child labor legislation was defeated for years on the mindless charge that it was a Communist plot for the government to take over private enterprise. As far as capitalist owners were concerned, human rights did not matter.

There are a number of brutal strikes that have been immortalized in labor history, but nothing quite points out the greed at the heart of the American energy to industrialize than the mindless destruction of the lives of thousands of children. In 1904 Mother Jones went to the mills in the South, which were operated principally by women and children. She took a job as a laborer just to see what it was really like. The mill owner hired her only after she said she had six children that she would bring from the North.

What she saw in the mills made her feel that the mining towns were a haven of hope. Few descriptions surpass Mother Jones's account of the cotton mill where she worked in Cottondale, Alabama:

> Little girls and boys, barefooted, walked up and down between
> the endless rows of spindles, reaching thin little hands into the

machinery to repair snapped threads. They crawled under machinery to oil it. They replaced spindles all day long, all day long, all night through. Tiny babies of six years old with faces of sixty did an eight-hour shift for ten cents a day. . . . The machines, built in the north, were built low for the hands of little children. At five-thirty in the morning, long lines of little gray children came out of the early dawn into the factory, into the maddening noise, into the lint filled rooms. Outside the birds sang and the blue sky shone. . . . At the lunch half hour, the children would fall to sleep over their lunch of cornbread and fat pork. They would lie on the bare floor and sleep. Sleep was their recreation, their release, as play is to the free child.

She saw children's fingers snapped off by machines. She saw the body of her landlady's eleven-year-old daughter carried back from the mill one evening, her scalp torn off when her hair had been caught in a machine.

Wages were so low no one could save enough money to escape. One woman had three children working in the mill. Her husband had died of tuberculosis, and the family had run up a debt of thirty dollars for the funeral, which they tried to pay back penny by penny to the mill owner. Mother Jones was determined to rescue them. Once again her knowledge of the inner workings of the railroad provided her the means of escape. Like the passengers of the Underground Railroad, they fled in the night.

I arranged with the station agent of the through train to have his train stop for a second on a certain night. . . . In the darkness of night the little family and I drove to the station. We felt like escaping Negro slaves and expected any moment that bloodhounds would be on our trail.

The train made its unscheduled stop and, "away we sped, away from everlasting debt, away to a new town where they could start anew without the millstone about their necks."

But escape was possible only for very few. There seemed to be little real way to help the children except by working for a decent wage for their parents. When Mother Jones returned to New York she held several meetings and tried to publicize the conditions in the southern mills, most of which were owned by northerners. She became depressed and engulfed in hopelessness. "I could scarcely eat," she said. "My food ... at times seemd bought with the price of the toil of children."

As she had done before in her life she refused to give in to despair. She turned suffering into a source of strength and decided that she would concentrate on the miners and the mountain camps "where the labor fight is at least fought by grown men."

In 1905 the Western Federation of Miners sent her to Chicago to participate in the founding of a radical labor union. It was to be a union which would offset the conservative bread-and-butter approach of the American Federation of Labor. Eugene Debs and Daniel De Leon, both leading Socialists, were on the platform, along with Father Thomas J. Hagerty, a "labor" priest; William D. "Big Bill" Haywood, also of the Western Federation of Miners; and Mother Jones. The Industrial Workers of the World came out of the meeting as forceful and radical a labor group as America has ever seen. Whites, blacks, foreign-born, native, skilled and unskilled workers were all welcome in a union that was dedicated not only to revolutionary labor relations but to changing American society. Mother Jones was to have disagreements with the Wobblies, as they were popularly known, but she always respected the courage and integrity of the leaders and the idealism on which the organization was founded.

To break the unions, business leaders, in collusion with public officials, framed labor leaders for crimes they didn't commit. A highly publicized trial grew out of the outrageous framing of IWW leaders Bill Haywood, George Pettibone, and Charles Moyer for the murder of an Idaho governor in 1906. The three were kidnapped and brought across state lines so that they could be arrested and brought to trial in Idaho. Mother Jones became one of their chief fund raisers.

The three were arrested in February 1906, but their trial did not begin until May 1907. During those fifteen months, Mother Jones traveled the length and breadth of the country, speaking at meetings, rallies, dinners—wherever there was an audience. She wrote a stirring article on the frame-up for a Socialist paper, claiming, rightly, that the arrests and the trial were attempts to break the hold of the Western Federation of Miners in the western mining towns by depriving the miners' union of its best leaders. She brought national publicity to Haywood and the IWW. There is no record of how much money she raised, but there is proof that she was able to raise five to six thousand dollars at one dinner. She was one of the biggest drawing cards of the Haywood-Pettibone-Moyer Defense Committee, and when it had enough money, it hired Clarence Darrow, the best defense attorney in the country. The ultimate acquittal of all three defendants was an important milestone in establishing the legitimacy of the union. Mother Jones never missed a session of the trial, and it was the beginning of Clarence Darrow's friendship with her. He wrote:

> Some of the fiercest combats in America have been fought by the miners. These fights brought thousands of men and their families close to starvation. They brought contests with police, militia, courts and soldiers. They involved prison sentences, massacres and hardships without end. Wherever the fight was the fiercest, Mother Jones was present to aid and cheer. In both the day and the night, in the poor villages and at the lonely cabin on the mountain side, Mother Jones always appeared in time of need.

The most ferocious conflict in the history of American labor and industry was fought by the miners in the coalfields of Colorado in 1913 and 1914. George McGovern and Leonard Guttridge have written in *The Great Coalfield War:* "The story's essentials are uncomplicated: intolerable work conditions fomenting labor insurgence, capitalist resistance followed by strike culminating in strife.... The United States had experienced no domestic bitterness of comparable intensity since the Civil War." Mother Jones was there.

Every battle skill she had was called upon—her ability to give solace and relief from suffering, her adroit defiance of police and military, her use of trains for slipping through guarded strike zones, her knack for making a remote struggle in the mountains real to city people, her talent as a fund raiser, and her name as a drawing card. The mine owners had purposely put together the most hostile ethnic groups in order to maximize internal hostilities among the workers. But conditions were so bad in the Trinidad coalfield that common interests prevailed over national hatreds.

The miners had gone on strike to obtain the following: an eight-hour day (a law already passed by the Colorado legislature but not enforced), the right to choose their own doctors, wage increases, mine safety inspection, and recognition of collective bargaining through the miners' union. The Colorado mining interests, dominated by the Rockefeller-owned Colorado Fuel and Iron Company, refused to see the strike leaders or union officials to discuss the demands—because to do so implied recognition of the union. They hired scabs at twenty dollars a head in Mexico—company agents promised the Mexicans land—and hauled the men over the border in cattle cars. They brought in thugs, armed gunmen who traveled in a specially designed armored car known as the Death Special, and the Boss and Felts Detective Company to harass and force the miners back to work. But these techniques had been used too many times before. By 1913 the majority of the miners were former scabs, strikebreakers from previous strikes, and they knew the routine all too well. Many of them had high thresholds of intimidation.

The intransigence of the Colorado mine owners was rooted in the absentee ownership of John D. Rockefeller, Jr., and a stubbornly held belief in the authority of ownership which violated common sense and humanity. The Colorado Fuel and Iron Company dominated all other mining companies, and was responsible for almost 40 percent of the mining in Colorado, a state which was the chief production area for coking coal west of the Mississippi.

Rockefeller, who lived in New York and had been to Colorado only twice, saw the struggle in Colorado as no simple, isolated strike; he saw it as one which could affect the entire course of industrial development in America. The cherished principle of the open shop—an owner had the right to hire and fire as he chose—was the bedrock of American capitalism, and Rockefeller later expanded on this theme when called before a congressional committee investigating the Colorado coal wars:

We believe the issue is not a local one in Colorado. It is a national issue whether workers shall be allowed to work under conditions as they may choose. As part owners of the property, our interest in the laboring men in this country is so immense, so deep, so profound that we stand ready to lose every cent we put in that company rather than see the men we have employed thrown out of work and have imposed upon them conditions which are not of their seeking and which neither they nor we can see is in our interest.

Unfortunately, the principle Rockefeller felt he was upholding precluded a careful examination of the miners' grievances. Congressman Martin Foster asked Rockefeller, "You are willing to let these killings take place rather than to go there and do something to settle conditions?" Rockefeller answered:

There is just one thing that can be done to settle this strike and that is to unionize the camps, and our interest in labor is so profound, and we believe so sincerely that that interest demands that the camps shall be open camps, that we expect to stand by the officers at any cost.

"And you would do that, if that costs all your property and kills all your employees?" Congressman Foster continued.

Rockefeller responded, "It is a great principle."

Yet it was a principle which shielded the owners from any understanding of the lives of the people who produced their great fortunes. Under further questioning Rockefeller admitted he knew nothing of the Colorado coal miners' wage scales; was unable to name the counties where Colorado Fuel and Iron Mines were located; knew nothing of miners' housing facilities and could not say if miners worked twelve hours a day or seven days a week.

The myth of outside agitators stirring up the satisfied natives is a ploy that has successfully been used in busting unions, discrediting political demonstrations, and interfering in foreign countries. In Colorado, this charge diverted attention from the real issues of the strike and the misery of the miners' working and living conditions.

Before the long Colorado coalfield war was over, sixty-five persons were killed, forty-three of them women and children. Mother Jones had been in the strike zone in January 1914.

My eyes ached with the misery I witnessed. My brain sickened with the knowledge of man's inhumanity to man . . . I sat through the long nights with bereaved widows watching candles burn down to their empty sockets . . . I nursed men driven nearly mad with despair. I solicited clothes for children . . . I helped bury the dead. . . .

Detectives followed her every move. State militia guarded every railway station so that the strikers would be cut off from outside help. But her knowledge of the railroads helped her sneak through. Other union organizers also got in. Some were arrested. Some were beaten up. Some were killed in ambush. Finally, Mother Jones was arrested. After refusing to leave the state, she was held for a month in a dank cellar underground. "I slept in my clothes by day and fought off rats with a broken beer bottle at night." The imprisonment of an old woman, supposedly in her eighties, caused a great public outcry, but the mine owners preferred the bad press to having Mother Jones loose in the field.

The strike dragged on for fourteen months. After the company evicted them from their homes, the miners moved into tents near Ludlow, where they lived through the mountain winter. Rockefeller claimed he had no idea of the violence perpetrated by the mine owners in Colorado, but subpoenaed correspondence later showed that he was in daily contact with his Colorado agents. In April 1914 the Colorado National Guard moved three machine guns into the hills surrounding the tent colony. The National Guard, paid by the mine owners, had deteriorated to the level of a band of mercenaries. A squad of soldiers went into the camp to ask a strike leader, a Greek man named Louis Tikas, to turn over two Italian workers for infraction of some newly invented military rules. Tikas asked for a warrant; the soldiers had none. Tikas refused to surrender the men. The soldiers retreated to the hills around the tent colony. Mother Jones described what followed:

> Immediately the machine guns began spraying the flimsy tent colony, the only home the wretched families of the miners had, spraying it with bullets. Like iron rain, bullets fell upon men, women and children. The women and children fled to the hills. . . . The men defended their homes with their guns. All day long the firing continued. . . . The little Snyder boy was shot through the head, trying to save his kitten. A child carrying water to his dying mother was killed. . . . Louis Tikas was riddled with shots while he tried to lead women and children to safety. They perished with him. Night came. A raw wind blew down the canyons where men, women and children shivered and wept. Then a blaze lighted the sky. The soldiers, drunk with blood and with the liquor they had looted from the saloon, set fire to the tents of Ludlow. The tents, all the poor furnishings, the clothes and bedding of the miners' families burned. . . . In a dugout under a burned tent, the charred bodies

of eleven little children and two women were found—unrecognizable. Everything lay in ruins. The wires of bed springs writhed on the ground as if they too, had tried to flee the horror. . . .

For the first time public sentiment turned against the Rockefellers. Four men, three women and eleven children had been killed in this one tragic event, the worst of a long series of deaths throughout the strike. Mother Jones knew that with this violence the Ludlow strike would finally reach public attention. She had seen too much not to be cynical about the press: "Little children being roasted alive makes a front-page story. . . . Dying by inches of starvation and exposure does not."

At the time of the massacre Mother Jones was in Mexico—trying to convince the Mexican scabs that the company agents' promises of free land would not materialize if they went to work for the Colorado Fuel and Iron Company. She immediately left Mexico and began a public tour describing what had happened in Ludlow. She knew that public opinion had to be enlisted in the aid of the strikers, and money had to be raised for the eight thousand homeless mountain refugees. Again she traveled the country—Kansas City, Chicago, Columbus, Cleveland, Washington, D.C.—describing the massacre.

President Wilson sent in the U.S. Cavalry to restore order and offered a truce that gave the miners some of their demands. Rockefeller hired a team of publicity men to explain the strike from a supposedly "neutral" point of view. A series of pamphlets on each major issue of the strike was sent to a carefully selected list of writers, editors, magazine publishers, public interest groups, political organizations.

One pamphlet was devoted to Mother Jones and portrayed her as a violent Anarchist with a criminal record, known for murder and violence. The bulletin quoted General Chase, who was in command of the Military District of Colorado during the strike:

She is an eccentric and peculiar figure. I make no mention of her personal history, with which we are not concerned.

She seems, however, to have in an exceptional degree the faculty of stirring up and inciting the more ignorant and criminally disposed to deeds of violence and crime.

Prior to the advent of the state's troops she made a series of speeches in the strike zone, of which I have authentic and verbatim reports.

These speeches are couched in coarse, vulgar and profane language, and address themselves to the lowest passions of mankind.

I CONFIDENTLY BELIEVE THAT MOST OF THE MURDERS AND OTHER ACTS OF VIOLENT CRIME COMMITTED IN THE STRIKE REGION HAVE BEEN INSPIRED BY THIS WOMAN'S INCENDIARY UTTERANCES.

The allusion to her "personal history" referred the reader to the *Congressional Record* of June 13, 1914, where Congressman George Kindel of Colorado had inserted a number of newspaper reports about her. One alleged that she had once run a whorehouse in Denver "with the highest stake poker games and the best looking girls in town."

The attempt to blame the violence of the Ludlow Massacre on Mother Jones was not only a cheap tactic; it didn't work. At his first appearance before the Industrial Relations Commission, Rockefeller introduced himself to Mother Jones and invited her to meet with him to discuss the problems of the miners. She accepted. After the meeting he publicly intimated that Mother Jones would accompany him on a tour of the Colorado Mines. To the press he gave a long statement on how amiable and agreeable his meeting with Mother Jones had been.

If nothing else, Rockefeller's wooing of Mother Jones illustrated that she was a power to be reckoned with; her integrity and honesty were unquestioned by workers and she stood for the legitimate demands of the working class. The public relations people hired by Rockefeller failed to ruin her reputation; in a cynical turnabout they then tried to present her as being on their side.

For her part Mother Jones said Rockefeller was "a nice young man." But she went away from their meeting feeling "that he could not possibly understand the aspirations of the working class. He was as alien as is one species from another; as alien as is stone from wheat."

Mother Jones could not be bought off by luxurious dinners, introductions to private clubs, or a trip on a yacht. She never yearned to be a "respectable" labor leader. Her strongest impulse was to give voice to the mute workers who had no other means of expression. She was able to travel from a miner's shack to the offices of John D. Rockefeller, Jr., without ever forgetting where she came from. A letter from Katherine Schmidt of the Office Employees Union reveals the essential integrity she represented for the rank and file. After lamenting the fact that other labor leaders had been corrupted by "big dinners, joy rides, sporting women," she told Mother Jones that "Smidie [her brother] says, and so do I, that we'd bet our last cent on Mother Jones . . . you cannot be touched with money, and you don't want a political job so they cannot reach you no how."

Having witnessed so much violence she did not believe that men and women should be defenseless. When the Industrial Relations Commission asked her if she had advocated that the West Virginia miners buy guns she had answered, "I not only advised the miners to buy rifles, but I personally raised the money which paid for them." She was conscious of the effect of public statements, and she said that no one should be helpless in the face of brute force.

But she also believed that nothing was ever won from violence and that personal resistance was the strongest weapon. In a letter to Tom Mooney, a labor leader who was framed for a bomb explosion in San Francisco and who wrote asking for help, she said

> I am opposed to violence because violence produces violence and what is won today by violence will be lost tomorrow. We must ever and always appeal to reason, because society after all has made all the progress it has ever made by analyzing the situation carefully and bringing the matter before the public.... The taking of human life has never settled any question.

Mother Jones was a giant in the labor movement. She has been neglected largely because the history of the labor movement has neglected women, both as workers and as wives of workers. There is no framework in which to understand Mother Jones unless there is a perception of the total society of men and women who struggled for workers' rights to life and a living wage.

When twenty-four-year-old Mary Petrucci went to Washington to tell her story to President Wilson about the burning of her three children at Ludlow, Colorado, she went with the strength and consciousness of a woman who knew what her life was about and why she had suffered as much as she had. She was very much like Mary

Jones back in 1867. Mary Petrucci was able to explain to newspaper reporters:

> You're not to think that we could do any differently another time. We are working people—my husband and I—and we're stronger for the union than we were before the strike. . . . There's sadness in our hearts and there always will be, but there isn't . . . despair.

It was from such people that Mother Jones took and gave strength and it was in the conviction of the goodness and rightness of the working class, "her class," that she made her choices and cleared a path.

Mother Jones has been criticized for taking many contradictory positions in her life—opposing suffrage and temperance for example. She opposed suffrage because she was separated from the middle-class traditions that believed in the legitimate workings of law and political rights. "If the women of the country would only realize what they have in their hands there is no limit to what they could accomplish. The trouble is they let the capitalists make them believe they wouldn't be ladylike." She lived where the Constitution was meaningless and the ballot had no power to change economics. The women of Colorado had had the vote for two generations before the Ludlow massacre, and it was like a feather before the wind of company-owned judges, juries, congressmen. Temperance she saw as an effort to create a more sober, efficient working class—an effort of the capitalists to deprive men of their one escape in life. She called Prohibition "the worst affliction the country has." She was a Socialist yet she didn't campaign for her old friend Eugene Debs when he ran as the Socialist candidate for the Senate in Indiana. Senator Kern, the Democrat incumbent, had gotten her out of a West Virginia prison when she had been sentenced to twenty years. She never forgot a friend or a personal favor.

She aged, but she never mellowed. Tom Tippett covered the United Mine Workers annual convention in 1923 at which there was a terrible credentials fight over the Kansas delegation.

As the delegates reached fever heat Mother Jones walked quietly to the front of the stage and held up her hand. "I never go to Washington without paying my respect to a monument erected along the way in memory of another man from Kansas who fought the chattel slavery of this country. That man, John Brown, is a national hero today . . . and the name of the judge who sentenced him has long been forgotten."

She then compared the leader of the unseated delegation to John Brown and read a speech from the women of Kansas, who appealed for justice for the ousted delegation. According to Tippett, "The crowd seemed to go mad as they cheered this wonderful old soldier of theirs that has been in the front lines of every battle in the miners' union." When she "was a hundred years old" a big birthday celebration was held for her in Silver Spring, Maryland, outside Washington, D.C. It was a "who's who" of the labor movement, and even John D. Rockefeller, Jr., sent a warm telegram.

But the most appropriate tribute was an army of poor, bedraggled workers, who marched out from their camp in Washington, where they were staying to illustrate the plight of the poor. The Great Depression had begun. With a black man, "King" Jeff Davis, leading the march, the demonstrators walked the eight miles out to Silver Spring to pay tribute to one of the original poverty marchers.

As Mother Jones said, "The militant, not the meek, shall inherit the earth."

CHARLOTTE PERKINS GILMAN

BORN: JULY 3, 1860, HARTFORD, CONNECTICUT. DIED: AUGUST 17, 1935. FATHER: FREDERICK BEECHER PERKINS. MOTHER: MARY A. FITCH WESCOTT. MARRIED: CHARLES WALTER STETSON, 1884. CHILDREN: KATHERINE (1885). DIVORCED, 1894. MARRIED: GEORGE HOUGHTON GILMAN, 1900.

POET, LECTURER, AUTHOR OF *Women and Economics*, 1898; *The Home: Its Work and Influences*, 1903. EDITOR AND PUBLISHER OF THE *Forerunner*, 1909–16.

From the day laborer to the millionaire, the wife's worn dress or flashing jewels, her low roof or her lordly one . . . these speak of the economic ability of the husband. . . . All that [a woman] gets—food, clothing, ornaments, amusements, luxuries—these bear no relation to her power to produce wealth, to her services in the house, or to her motherhood. These things bear relation only to the man she married, the man she depends on—to how much he has and how much he is willing to give her. The women whose splendid extravagance dazzles the world, whose economic goods are the greatest, are often neither houseworkers nor mothers, but simply the women who hold most power over the men who have the most money.

CHARLOTTE PERKINS GILMAN
IN *Women and Economics*, 1898

The Beecher family name runs through many of the most dramatic events of nineteenth-century American history. Lyman Beecher was the towering minister who presided over the great theological debate about slavery at Lane Seminary in Ohio, a debate which grew so violent—Beecher and the seminary trustees supported slavery—that two of the seminary's most promising young ministers—Theodore Weld and Henry Stanton—withdrew from the ministry to become abolitionist orators. Catherine Beecher, one of Lyman's daughters, was a pioneer in women's higher education. She was also an ardent antifeminist, a highly visible and respected critic of Sarah and Angelina Grimké. Another daughter, Harriet Beecher Stowe, wrote *Uncle Tom's Cabin*, the book reputed to have changed the hearts and minds of America on slavery. A son, Henry Ward Beecher, was said to be "the greatest preacher the world has seen since St. Paul preached on Mars Hill." He also was a principal in the greatest scandal of the century, the Beecher-Tilton trial over an illicit love affair. The genius of the Beechers was in finding the true center of public opinion and articulating it with great style in the language of progress and liberal reform. They were never ahead of public thinking and more often they were behind it.

The only Beecher who was an original thinker was a granddaughter, who has generally not been treated as a Beecher at all. Charlotte Perkins Gilman was the greatest theoretician the woman's movement ever produced. One historian described her as "the Marx and Veblen of the woman's movement." Even today many people regard Charlotte Perkins Gilman as one of the most important thinkers and social critics of the early twentieth century. Her significance lies in the integrity of her life, in her acts as much as in her beliefs. Her autobiography, *The Living of Charlotte Perkins Gilman*, is the story of her insistence on her right to be treated as a human being, to choose work which defined her, to be a producer rather than a consumer. With a consistency that borders on the obsessional, she rejected in her own life every social, economic, political, and ethical principle society held up as defining the true nature of woman. The themes she explored in her books—women in industrial society, economic survival, unpaid domestic drudgery, work as a means to identity, service to humankind rather than individual accumulation of goods—were rooted in the experiences of her life.

Her grandmother on her father's side was described by a family historian as "an anomaly; she [Mary Foote Beecher] was the only purely private Beecher. She never wrote a book, article, made a speech, gave a lecture. . . . This lack was more than compensated for by her granddaughter." Mary Beecher quietly married a man named Thomas Perkins and had four children. Frederick, the oldest, was Charlotte Gilman's father. He was a librarian, a magazine editor, and a man of some prominence.

When Charlotte was seven, her father left the family. She remembered him as "an occasional visitor, a writer of infrequent, but always amusing letters with deliciously funny drawings, a sender of books. . . ." Her impressions of his rare visits included "some black Hamburg grapes he brought to Mother, a game of chess, one punishment [he spanked her for spitting down the stairwell onto the bald spot of the landlady's head], and a gun" he brought for her brother.

He apparently had little interest in the development of his children and was not conscientious about sending money or making sure that they were well taken care of. Gilman often saw her mother, Mary Fitch Wescott Perkins, completely without funds or hope of support in the near future. When their debts piled up and their credit ran out, they took the inevitable step for renewed economic liquidity: they moved. They moved eighteen times in fourteen years, most of the moves from one city to another. It was a life of hand-me-down clothes, boardinghouses, rented rooms, indefinite stays with relatives, "railroad journeys, mostly on the Hartford, Providence and Springfield . . . occasional steamboats . . . the smell of hacks [horse-drawn taxis] and the funny noise the wheels made when little fingers were stuck in little ears and withdrawn alternately."

They were not poor in the same way that the women who worked fourteen hours a day in the textile mills in Providence were poor. They would never have been allowed to starve or wear rags on their feet in winter or to die of disease because they could not afford a doctor. But Charlotte's mother was unable to provide security for her children; they had no fixed place of residence, little continuity in schooling or friends, no resources with which to ward off the unknown disasters of the future. Charlotte Perkins Gilman was not just poor, she was a "poor relation"—a situation that is as much social as it is economic.

The dreary deprivations of her life were alleviated only by occasional visits to Beecher relatives. Charlotte vividly recalled "a soul-expanding" experience at the grand house in Connecticut that Aunt Harriet had built from the proceeds of *Uncle Tom's Cabin.* It had gables and turrets, towers and chimneys and a beautiful conservatory with fountains. Charlotte remembered the feeling of sunlight and space in the conservatory and "Aunt Harriet at a small table . . . looking out at the flowers and ferns and little fountain while she painted in water-colors." It was during these childhood visits with Harriet Beecher Stowe that Charlotte got her desire to paint. In her late teens, when she had the opportunity to go to the Rhode Island School of Design, she specialized in still lifes of flowers.

Another group of Beechers lived in Boston, and there she had her first exposure to how exhilarating a real social life could be. During one visit to Cambridge she was a great hit among the young cousins who went to Harvard. She marveled in her diary, "I never was so courted and entertained in all my little life . . . to find Lewis Greeley actually loitering about to see me! I cannot understand it."

Being a poor relation of a successful family was a central tension in her development. She often referred to her poverty as a child, the hard labor, the waking up at four in the morning to do the chores. But in later life she exhibited an unconcern about money that is characteristically upper class. She refused to worry whether she would be paid for a lecture; often she set out on a journey without enough money to make her destination; and she always had difficulties with agents and publishers in making sure she was properly reimbursed for her writings. She described her lack of concern about money as an attitude similar to that of a Buddhist monk's.

Charlotte Perkins Gilman may have often been strapped for cash, but she was from a special upper middle-class kind of poverty. The family may have been wealthy, but a woman without a husband had no resources. Charlotte saw what happened to a woman who had no man to support her, and she saw beyond the class mythology of woman's role to the economic reality. Later that gave her the perspective to analyze all women as a service class.

Her mother's only source of income was from one of the few

respectable professions allowed women—an extension of mothering—teaching young children. Mrs. Perkins was an excellent teacher and gave her own children a fine appreciation of good reading. But teaching was never remunerative enough for a living, and Mrs. Perkins was hounded by debt. Consequently she could never make a life for herself. At first she took her children to live with her parents, then with her husband's parents, then with aunts, relatives, and "in various houses here and there where he [Frederick Perkins] so installed her, fleeing again on account of debt." Charlotte described her mother's life as "one of the most painfully thwarted I have ever known. . . . After her flood of lovers, she became a deserted wife." Apparently a popular belle in her youth, Mrs. Perkins never accepted that her husband had rejected her and tried to prevent her children from knowing similar pain.

In what can only be termed a misguided sense of parental protection, Mrs. Perkins tried to prevent her children from craving affection and tenderness by denying them any. She never permitted any signs of physical affection or tenderness between herself and her children, and the only brother-and-sister relationship they knew was a teasing or roughhousing one. After Charlotte realized that her mother sometimes cuddled her brother, Thomas, and herself at night after they had gone to sleep, she tried to keep herself awake by sticking pins in her arms.

Since her mother was the only emotional support in her life, Charlotte was an exceptionally obedient and dutiful child, rarely questioning or disobeying her mother's commands. But at the same time she built an elaborate fantasy world in which "a Prince and Princess of magic powers . . . went about the world collecting unhappy children and [took] them to a guarded Paradise in the South Seas." She wrote in her autobiography, "I had a boundless sympathy for children, feeling them to be suppressed, misunderstood."

As Charlotte entered her teens, her mother forbade her from reading novels, having close friends, going to parties, or attending the theater. Charlotte reacted by refusing to admit that she wanted any of these pleasures of life. But her greatest love was the theater, and she was unable to deny that to herself. When a cousin once invited her to attend a performance of Hamlet and her mother refused to let her go, Charlotte admitted that "something broke" within her.

In her teens she and her brother and mother went to live in a house in the country, where they remained for two years. She was completely isolated, having no friends and no schooling. It was during this important period that she developed her inner resources. Almost as a game she trained her capacity for concentration and played with her own powers of self-discipline. She decided to develop one new personality characteristic each year. She was particularly gratified when she heard an aunt who had once complained about her self-centeredness expressing pleased surprise about "how thoughtful" Charlotte had become.

Another example of her appreciation of self-discipline was physical fitness, an interest she took up as a teenager after hearing a woman doctor speak in Providence. At a time when fainting was considered the badge of femininity Gilman ran a mile twice a week, learned gymnastics, and wore clothing as light and as loose as possible. The physical conditioning stayed with her. At the age of forty-two she played basketball with her daughter at Barnard, and at the age of sixty-five she followed up a lecture at the University of Oklahoma by swinging two lengths of the parallel rings. She had no vanity about her looks, but she did admit that she was vain about her physical condition.

Her formal schooling consisted of four years spread out among seven different institutions. Her intelligence was obvious, but there were enormous holes in her background because of the erratic path her education had taken. She excelled in reciting poetry and in elocution, gifts she later attributed to the "Beecher skill" for preaching. For her, school was simply another life game, an environment to be tested and experimented with. Once, in the midst of a silent study period, she shouted out "it" into the quiet. When the teacher called her to the head of the class to explain what she had done, Gilman answered that she simply wanted to see what would happen.

The neglect of Gilman's formal education was due to her sex, not to the family's poverty. When her brother Thomas was sixteen the Beecher family sent him to Massachusetts Institute of Technology in Boston.

Instead of formal schooling Charlotte Gilman received a reading list from her father. He also sent some issues of *Popular Science* magazine and some books. At that time Frederick Perkins was the librarian of the Boston Public Library, and the course of reading he sent her was a critical influence in disciplining her mind and organizing her ideas. At the age of sixteen she began, for the first time, to read books in sequence, relating the random information she had been collecting to an overall system. It was, she later remarked, the beginning of her real education and seemed to compensate for the formal schooling she had been denied. It did not compensate for the lack of friends or the lack of support that comes from the resources of a large institution.

The relationship with the Beecher family was always problematical. After thirteen years of desertion Mrs. Perkins finally divorced her husband. The Beecher family was bitter. Regardless of the expansive sentiments and humanitarian ideas that the Beechers put forth on printed page and from the pulpit, they were no different from the rest of bourgeois America in their respect for money and their mania for surface conventionality. "Good families" simply did not have divorces during the nineteenth century. And so Gilman learned the hard lesson that only the woman as victim can claim respectability; the woman who asserts herself loses social legitimacy. "So long as 'Mary Fred' [her mother] was a blameless victim, they [the Beechers] pitied her and did what they could to help, but a divorce was a disgrace."

She, however, strongly identified with being a Beecher and throughout her autobiography are self-descriptive references to "being a Beecher" or "having the Beecher gift" or the "Beecher skill." She never mentions being a Wescott, her mother's maiden name which traced back to the days of Roger Williams. Only once does she mention inheriting the traits of her mother's family, that of "a deep sympathy for children."

One relationship with a branch of the Beecher family was of particular importance, that with her father's sister's family, the Gilmans. During the period of bad feeling about the divorce, Charlotte and her mother visited the Gilmans at their home in Connecticut. The Gilmans had also been through a recent family crisis, and each family was a source of support to the other. When Charlotte and her mother returned to Providence she began a remarkably frequent correspondence with her cousin, George Houghton Gilman. He was twelve, she was nineteen. The two, despite the differences in ages, developed a warm, affectionate, trusting relationship. Their letters, filled with humorous drawings and diagrams, were sensitive and literate and contained an undercurrent of a real need to communicate. The correspondence lasted three months.

While attending the Rhode Island School of Design in Providence, Rhode Island, Charlotte met a young artist named Charles Walter Stetson. (A family friend had paid the tuition.) While her own assessment of her own talent was that she was a craftsman rather than an artist, she became extremely skilled in miniatures and still lifes. Until the age of twenty-four she lived with her mother, supporting herself by teaching art, drawing designs for monuments, painting advertising cards for a soap company, and selling some of her own paintings.

She knew that she was an impressively disciplined young woman intellectually but quite stunted emotionally. It may have had something to do with her feeling that marriage was not necessarily the right conclusion for her relationship with Stetson, but in 1884 there wasn't much room for social experimentation. She married and became a "wife." Within a year their first and only child was born and she was also a "mother." It was a disaster. She was utterly unprepared for both roles. Instead of the joy and fulfillment society told her she should feel, she felt hostility, resentment, and rage at the new little being that was utterly dominating her life. It was like expecting Albert Einstein to give up all his mathematical equations once he'd become a father. She had a severe postchildbirth breakdown.

She lost all her energy. She was depressed, cried a lot, and didn't know why. She couldn't concentrate. "Here was a charming home, a loving and devoted husband, an exquisite baby . . . and I lay all day on the lounge and cried." After five months' recuperation, she took a trip to California to visit friends. "From the moment the wheels began to turn . . . I felt better." Her lethargy disappeared, she was able to concentrate, she enjoyed her surroundings. As soon as she returned to husband and baby the same depression descended on her.

In the nineteenth century and for a good part of the twentieth there was only one theory on postpartum depression: it was the triggering of a deep-seated mental illness by the ordeal of labor and childbirth. As Gilman's condition became worse, she finally went to see Dr. Mitchell Weir, the "greatest nerve specialist in the country." This giant of the medical profession informed her that he had already had the misfortune to treat two "Beecher women," indicating that he believed there was a family strain of nervous disorder if not insanity. His prescription was for Gilman to give up all intellectual work, to "never touch pen, brush or pencil" as long as she lived, and to devote herself entirely to husband and baby. Years later she said that if her writings and work had done anything to change the treatment of mental illness, "I will not have lived in vain."

Weir's advice was guaranteed to turn what is now viewed as a period of common emotional disturbance into a chronic mental illness. A recent British study showed that 64 percent of one hundred and thirty-seven mothers revealed emotional and psychological symptoms similar to Gilman's following childbirth.

They relived the traumas of their own childhood. They experienced acute anxiety, depression, or had fantasies of suicide or of abandoning the baby. They had decreased ability to concentrate and a greatly shortened attention span as well as severely disturbed dream patterns and mental imagery.

Identical patterns of depression and anxiety have been observed in new fathers and in adoptive mothers, leading to the rejection of the theory that it is a hormonal condition. Today there is some acceptance that social pressures and discontinuity with the past are major causes of postchildbirth depression and that societal pressures on women to drop all outside interests and activities for motherhood is a major factor in severe emotional breakdowns following childbirth.

In Gilman's day men could be both fathers and philosophers, but a mother was "safeguarding civilization." The mystique of motherhood, the mythology of woman's fulfillment through child care, made any accurate diagnosis of her disorder impossible. There were countless women of Gilman's era who went into mental asylums and never came out because of "insanity caused by childbirth."

It was like telling an athlete who had spent his entire life training for the Olympics that he should never exercise again and must banish all thoughts of athletics from his mind. Forbidden from work—her one source of continuity with her past—she sank further and further into the recesses of her mind. "The mental agony grew so unbearable," she wrote, "that I would sit blankly moving my head from side to side—to get out from under the pain. . . . I made a rag baby, hung it on a doorknob and played with it. I would crawl into remote closets and under beds—to hide from the grinding pressure." Given the degree to which her mental and emotional control declined, it is a measure of her inner toughness, of her sheer refusal to turn her back on life that she was finally able to take measures to help herself survive. She later used this experience as the basis for her renowned short story "The Yellow Wallpaper." The heroine of the story is a young mother who has been sent to a house in the country to rest. She finds herself alone, lethargic, dispirited. Her overprotective physician husband blames her active imagination and urges her to rest and stay away from all stimulating ideas. But her imagination urges her on, and for a brief moment she wonders if the true source of her illness might not be her husband and the constrictions he places on her. Alone in her bedroom, she begins to fantasize about the hidden forms she sees in the wallpaper's pattern. She sees a woman caught behind bars. Trying to free her, she rips off the wallpaper and tells her husband, "I'm free at last." The nameless heroine of the story wants to "write a little [to] relieve the press of ideas." . . . She is sure that "congenial work, with excitement and change, would do me good." Instead, blocked from any self-expression and outside stimulus, she goes mad.

In a moment of lucidity Charlotte Gilman and her husband agreed to temporarily separate. In 1888 she went back to where she had first experienced a relief from the pressures of her breakdown—California. She took the baby, Katherine, and a nurse and went to Pasadena, where old friends from Providence were living. Although life was difficult, she soon began to write and work well again. In one year alone, 1890, she wrote thirty-three articles and twenty-three poems. Her husband had followed her in 1889 and had stayed in California for a year. They agreed that there was no hope for a life together and worked out the arrangements for a final separation and divorce.

Then began Charlotte's own experience of what life was like for a woman who did not have a man to support her. She tried running a boardinghouse. She wrote articles for newspapers and magazines. She worked in plays for the Pasadena Playhouse. Despite the hand-to-mouth existence, she was asserting herself and discovering what she was capable of doing. It was a restorative period. Considering the state of helplessness she had reached, it was a wonder she was able to do any productive work at all. After *New England Magazine* published her short story "The Yellow Wallpaper," in 1892 a doctor wrote to her, asking if she could possibly have been writing out of her own experience of "incipient insanity." She answered, "I went as far as one could go and still get back." Slowly she recovered, but she was left with severe headaches, a greatly decreased attention span, and a low threshold of endurance of emotional conflict.

Gilman reveals very little sense of humor in her personal relations, but she does reveal another side of her personality in her poems—witty, fluid, light, brimming with humor at the absurdities of life. A volume of poems, *In This Our World*, published in 1893, touched a responsive chord in the public. She was a student of Darwin's theories on evolution, and her poems pointed out the follies of human social ideas if viewed through evolutionary time. One, "The Survival of the Fittest," brought her fame:

> *In northern zones the ranging bear*
> *Protects himself with fat and hair.*
> *Where snow is deep, and ice is stark,*
> *And half the year is cold and dark,*
> *He still survives a clime like that*
> *By growing fur, by growing fat.*
> *These traits, O Bear, which thou transmittest,*
> *Prove the survival of the fittest!*
>
> *In modern times the millionaire*
> *Protects himself as did the bear.*
> *Where Poverty and Hunger are,*
> *He counts his bullion by the car.*
> *Where thousands suffer, still he thrives,*
> *And after death his will survives.*
> *The wealth, O Croesus, thou transmittest*
> *Proves the survival of the fittest!*

She began to come into demand as a speaker and lecturer before women's clubs and political clubs. In 1891 she moved to Oakland and became active in the Pacific Coast Women's Press Association in San Francisco. She had found an audience because of her satirical poems. They were in harmony with the groups called Nationalist clubs, which had grown up around Edward Bellamy's utopian novel *Looking Backward,* a vision for a tranquil America in the year 2000. Without actually using the word socialism, Bellamy presented a world in which socialist ideas were put into practice—public ownership of railroads and utilities, civil service reform, government aid to education. Rather than Darwinian survival, cooperation and community were the key ideas. Bellamy published her poems in his newspaper the *New Nation* and told her that the reading of her poem "The Survival of the Fittest" "has formed a feature of club exercises."

Her Socialist speeches to Bellamy's Nationalist clubs were so well received that a Los Angeles newspaper said that "Mrs. Charlotte Perkins Stetson's [address] . . . was in every way so masterly that it is much to be regretted that its length precludes us from publishing it entire."

Charlotte Gilman discovered that she had talent as a speaker: "I had plenty to say and the Beecher faculty for saying it." She was a slight, handsome woman, with a soft, easy voice that reached the back rows. She was forthright in her delivery, strongly opinionated, and incapable of saying anything in which she did not believe. One listener likened her to a "militant madonna." Another described "the beautifully shaped head with its soft hair gathered at the nape . . . the keen features, the firm mouth, the brilliant eyes."

The problematical relationship with her mother continued. Mrs. Perkins moved to California to take care of Katherine, but she soon became so ill that she herself required constant nursing. Gilman refused to put her mother in a nursing home—even though she risked another mental breakdown herself—telling her doctor, "I do not wish to have it said that I have failed in every relation in life." Her mother died in March 1893. A year later Gilman's divorce from Stetson became final. (Walter Stetson had unsuccessfully sued for divorce in Rhode Island in 1892. Two years later a California court granted Gilman a divorce.) He immediately remarried. His new wife was the author Grace Ellery Channing, the friend with whom Gilman had originally stayed in Pasadena.

Since Gilman did not believe that her daughter should be deprived of a father the same way she had been, she arranged for Katherine to live in New York for an indeterminate amount of time with the Stetsons. "Since her father longed for his child and had a right to some of her society; and since the child had a right to know and love her father—I did not mean her to suffer the losses of my youth—this seemed the right thing to do." The divorce combined with the separation from her daughter brought her notoriety in Boston and California newspapers. At the time it was said she was a woman "who had given up her child," an act of moral degeneracy that had no equal in the nineteenth century. Even sympathetic historians see her through nineteenth-century glasses. William O'Neill disposed of her personal crisis by explaining that "she solved her dilemma by divorcing an entirely satisfactory husband and giving up an agreeable child. Having thus cleared her decks, she went on to enjoy a successful career as a writer and feminist theoretician." The reality was somewhat different. Sending her child off was not easy.

I took her to the uptown station in Oakland, where the Overland trains stopped for passengers; her grandfather appeared; she climbed gaily aboard. She hurried to the window and looked out, waving to me. She had long shining golden hair. We smiled and waved and threw kisses to each other. The train went out, farther and farther till I couldn't see her any more. . . .

That was thirty years ago. I have to stop typing and cry as I tell about it. There were years, years, when I could never see a mother and child together without crying. . . .

With the death of her mother, her divorce from her husband, and the departure of her daughter she closed out the first part of her life. It was 1895 and she was thirty-five years old. She wrote in her diary her assessment of herself: "A failure, a repeated cumulative failure. Debt . . . no means of paying, no strength to hold a job if I got one."

From 1895 until 1900 she lived in no fixed place, traveling across the country lecturing in different cities. She left California without really knowing where she was going. Her first stop was Chicago, where she stayed with Jane Addams—"her mind had more 'floor space' in it than any other I have known"—at Hull House. Then she went to Washington, D.C., where she attended the annual suffrage convention and where she met Lester Ward, a man who was the single greatest influence on her intellectual and professional development.

Ward was the founder of sociology as a discipline in America. He was the leader of a group of intellectuals who challenged Herbert

Spencer and Charles Sumner's social application of Darwin's theories of evolution and survival of the fittest. Ward believed that Social Darwinism, as it came to be known, was a simple apology for the brutality of capitalist competition and that if Darwin's ideas were accurately interpreted they would show that cooperation, not competition, was the means of survival for the higher species. Within this framework he saw the role of women and the selection of such characteristics as weaknesses and prettiness as an evolutionary aberration. Ward assumed that male and female were equal in nature and that society had distorted their functions. Gilman called his "gynacocentric theory," which had been first set out in a well-known article called "Our Better Halves," "the greatest single contribution to the world's thought since evolution." It was one of the first modern writings to discuss matriarchy as the original form of social organization.

The seeds of Lester Ward's ideas germinated while Gilman was in England in 1896 on her first trip outside the United States to attend the International Socialist and Labor Congress. Traveling abroad led to new growth in her self-confidence and her belief in her own talent.

Although not a member of the Socialist Party, she was one of the few prominent women lecturers on Socialist thinking, and she was placed on the speakers' platform with George Bernard Shaw during a great peace demonstration in Hyde Park. Beatrice and Sidney Webb, the leaders of the Fabian Socialists in England, invited her to their home, where she met some of the noted thinkers of English intellectual life. Ramsay MacDonald, a future prime minister, interviewed her for a Socialist journal. She also met a woman who was to become a good friend and an important feminist, Harriet Stanton Blatch, Elizabeth Cady Stanton's daughter. Harriet Stanton Blatch had married an Englishman and later brought to America the militant tactics English feminists used in their struggle to get the vote.

When Gilman returned from England in 1897 she took two important steps: she looked up her old friend and cousin George Houghton Gilman, since become a New York lawyer; and she began writing a book on the need for women's financial independence. The book made her famous. She eventually married her cousin. The two events were not unrelated. Marriage had not been an easy decision, Gilman having concluded she was unsuited to marriage. The torrent of correspondence between them from 1897 to 1900 shows the terrible emotional ordeal that all personal relationships had become for her. At the same time she desperately needed someone to communicate with. Her cousin was able to break through her unwillingness to commit herself emotionally because he represented more than an isolated love affair. He was a Beecher, and he was a link to a family and a past that she had been deprived of. In letters that run twenty-five and thirty pages she confided to him her entire past history, the reasons for her mental illness, her anguish in trying to feel and express emotion. Finally, she admitted, "Not till I am again surrounded by numbers of pleasing and desirable relatives shall I know whether I 'love you for yourself alone' or as an epitome of the family!"

The marriage to a Beecher in 1900 gave her a sense of place and roots that she had never known before. Twenty years later when they moved from New York to one of the old Beecher homes in Norwich, Connecticut, she wrote, "This is my native state, and while the town is not my ancestral home, it is my husband's. . . . It has more of the home feeling than such a nomad as I ever hoped for."

The marriage was successful, but it took place only after she had achieved a public identity by publishing her first and most famous book, *Women and Economics*, in 1898. Lester Ward's ideas had given her a different perspective from most feminist theoreticians, and rather than focusing on the disabilities of women in American society, Gilman concentrated on male and female relationships in equilibrium. Her concern was with the health of society as a whole. She did not blame men for the lowly position of women. Rather she believed that men, too, were victims of archaic social forms developed in the agricultural past, utterly unsuited to technological living. Nor did she believe that suffrage was the answer for changing the role of women in an industrial society.

> The political equality demanded by the suffragists [is] not enough to give real freedom. Women whose industrial position is that of a house-servant, or who do no work at all, who are fed, clothed, and given pocket-money by men, do not reach freedom and equality by the use of the ballot.

Women and Economics is not a tract on economics but a thoroughgoing analysis of the economic basis of freedom for women. It is a comprehensive study of all the service functions in society that are performed by women for free. Borrowing from Lester Ward she advanced the radical idea that in the human species, unlike other species, the female had become totally dependent on the male for food and shelter (or the money to buy them); consequently, those aspects of her personality involved in her relationship with the male—the sexual and maternal—had overdeveloped, while her ability to participate and contribute to the larger community had atrophied. *Women and Economics* contained most of the major themes that she later developed in other books: the narrowness of the home, the damage done to children being brought up by one parent, the need for cooperation and new forms of social organization, the effects of religion. Her purpose was not simply to argue for the economic liberation of women but to show the harm done by continuing the economic slavery of women in industrial society and the value to be gained by freeing them.

> It is not that women are really smaller-minded, weaker-minded, more timid and vacillating; but that whosoever, man or woman, lives always in a small dark place, is always guarded, protected, directed and restrained, will become inevitably narrowed and weakened by it. The woman is narrowed by the home and the man is narrowed by the woman.

She wrote *Women and Economics* in less than six months. When it was released in 1898 she achieved instant fame. The founder of the National Consumer League, Florence Kelley, a Socialist, reported to her that "Miss Addams called it a 'Masterpiece.'" And Jane Addams wrote that "Mrs. Kelley says that it is the only real contribution to economics ever made by a woman...."

Gilman went on to attack the single-family home as economically wasteful, isolated from the community, and necessarily restricting in its view of the world. In 1903 she proposed in *The Home: Its Work and Influence*, the professionalization of housecleaning, the use of services—laundry, diaper, food preparation—instead of buying more machines which kept a woman chained to the home.

She believed that the biological accident of giving birth did not define a human being's contribution to society. She viewed work in modern society as a means of identity, a clarification of function.

The idea that all women were allowed motherhood as their only "work" deprived society of valuable talent and did irreparable damage to women who were no more suited for devoting their lives to being mothers than all men were to being fathers. "Each woman born," she wrote in *Human Work*, published in 1904, "has had to live over again in her own person the same process of restriction, repression, denial; the smothering 'no' which crushed down all her human desires to create, to discover, to learn, to express, to advance." Work in modern society, she believed, was "an end in itself, a condition of [a person's] existence and their highest joy and duty."

She was not afraid to attack basic institutions—law, government, education, fashion, games, sports, the courts—which enforced the idea of man as the superior sex and women as passive, "helpless" servants to their husbands. Her style was light enough and her scientific perspective distant enough so that she was able to get away with such attacks on taboo subjects. But soon she found that even as her fame grew she had more and more trouble getting published.

She remembered Theodore Dreiser, the editor of a magazine called the *Delineator*, telling her, "You should consider more what the editors want." She answered, "If the editors and publishers will not bring out my work, I will!" She began her own magazine, the *Forerunner*, and many of her most adventuresome ideas were worked out first there.

In other books, such as *The Man-Made World or Our Androcentric Culture* (1911), she analyzed the destructive effects of arranging life so that men are allowed fatherhood and productive work, while women are forced to "choose" between motherhood or work in the world. She suggested that such a choice meant that society was deprived of women's qualities of cooperation, peacefulness, life-orientation. Man's domination of the world meant a continuation of a social order organized around competition, destruction, and war.

In *His Religion and Hers* (1923) Gilman suggested that religions in the West have been morbidly preoccupied with death, principally because they have been almost totally developed by men. She proposed that women, who are more in touch with the processes of birth and life, would have a more life-oriented approach to religious beliefs if they were allowed to participate in the churches as ministers.

All these themes—the need for economic independence, the organization of home and family life in industrial society, the influence of religion on enforcing behavior patterns—were themes which had been developed in a different form by Sarah Grimké and Elizabeth Cady Stanton. In 1897, during the early years of Gilman's preeminence, she had an opportunity to meet Stanton. She remarked, "Of the many people I met during these years I was particularly impressed by Elizabeth Cady Stanton." Gilman was a successor to Stanton in that she had many of the same insights, but Gilman was able to frame her ideas in language which is meaningful today—the language of economics, anthropology, sociology. Her writing shows the clear influence of the dominant intellectual currents of the late nineteenth century—theories of evolution, Darwin's ideas on the development of the species, a belief in America's uniqueness. A good illustration of the difference between the era of Charlotte Perkins Gilman and Elizabeth Cady Stanton is the way they dealt with a similar problem—that of young immigrant servant girls made pregnant by male employers and sent into the streets by the "lady of the house."

In 1869 Stanton poured out her outrage into the pages of the *Revolution* over the case of Hester Vaughn, a Welsh girl seduced by her employer, then evicted from the home destitute and pregnant. The girl had nowhere to go and finally gave birth in an unheated attic room to a child who died. Vaughn was brought to trial by the state of Pennsylvania on charges of murder. Unable to speak in her own defense because she was a woman, she was tried and convicted for murder and sentenced to *hanging* for the "inhuman murder of a helpless baby." Stanton learned more details about the case, found that the girl was desperately ill from malnutrition and exhaustion, that the baby was undoubtedly dead at birth or died soon after, and that Hester Vaughn was unable to even give her side of the story at her trial. After a long series of articles about the case, Stanton and Susan B. Anthony organized a large demonstration of women in New York. Then she and other feminist leaders went to see the governor of Pennsylvania. Eventually the sentence was commuted, and Hester Vaughn was sent back to Wales.

Forty-seven years later Gilman took an identical situation and wrote it up as a short story in her magazine the *Forerunner*. Instead of a wife who threw the girl out, she created a "new woman," a wife who took the girl off to live with her in another house in another town. In a brilliant analysis of a man's sense of violation of property rights, Gilman describes the husband's hiring of a private detective to find his wife, his mystification at her protection of the servant girl, the final conclusion in which the wife tells her astounded husband that she is happier living without him.

Like the *Revolution*, the *Forerunner* rejected advertising it didn't like, had a small circulation, and was constantly in debt. The real revenue was in the form of personal letters of deep personal appreciation from women who had no other link with ideas from a radically changed world. It is hard to know how such ideas could have been kept alive if Gilman had not taken on the responsibility and the staggering workload of writing and publishing the magazine for seven years (1909–1916), the equivalent of writing over a book a year. The years she was writing the *Forerunner* were the doldrums of the suffrage movement. It took a broader perspective than short-term politics to keep a feminist vision alive.

There is no way of knowing how influential her ideas were, but they have endured in different people's writings. Walter Lippmann borrowed many of her ideas for his analysis of the woman's movement in his book *Drift and Mastery*. "Housekeeping and baby-rearing," wrote Lippmann, "are the two most primitive arts in the world. . . . Almost in vain do women like Mrs. Gilman insist that the institution of the family is not dependent on keeping woman a drudge amidst housekeeping arrangements inherited from the early Egyptians."

William Dean Howells, the influential editor of the *Atlantic Monthly*, proclaimed that Charlotte Perkins Gilman had "enriched the literary center of New York. . . ." A year before Thorstein Veblen had coined the phrase "conspicuous consumption," Gilman had written about "the consuming female . . . the priestess of the temple of consumption [who] creates a market for sensuous decoration and personal ornament, for all that is luxurious and enervating. . . ."

The *Nation* praised *Women and Economics* as "the most significant utterance on the subject since [John Stuart] Mill's 'Subjection of Women'."

Gilman's analysis of American society was lucid, her intelligence extraordinary, her perceptions devastating. She recognized that in olden times, as the messenger of bad tidings, she would have been killed. But modern societies have developed more subtle ways of eliminating their messengers. Fame, then plagiarism and dilution of her ideas, then obscurity was the fate of Charlotte Perkins Gilman.

Her death was utterly consistent with her life. At the age of seventy-five, after the pain of terminal cancer made it impossible for her to continue to work, she took her own life by chloroform, leaving a note which read in part:

Human life consists in mutual service. No grief, pain, misfortune or "broken heart" is excuse for cutting off one's life while any power of service remains. But when all usefulness is over, when one is assured of unavoidable and imminent death, it is the simplest of human rights to choose a quick and easy death in place of a slow and horrible one.

Public opinion is changing on this subject. The time is approaching when we shall consider it abhorrent to our civilization to allow a human being to die in prolonged agony which we should mercifully end in any other creature.

ANNA LOUISE STRONG

———◆◆◆———

BORN: NOVEMBER 14, 1885, FRIEND, NEBRASKA. DIED: MARCH 29, 1970, IN PEKING, CHINA. FATHER: SYDNEY STRONG. MOTHER: RUTH TRACY. MARRIED: JOEL SHUBIN, 1932, IN THE SOVIET UNION. NO CHILDREN.

JOURNALIST, AUTHOR AND EDITOR OF *Letters from China*, A NEWSLETTER FROM PEKING, 1959–69. AUTHOR OF *I Change Worlds: The Remaking of an American*, 1935; *China's Millions*, 1928; *China Conquers China*, 1949; AS WELL AS OVER TWENTY BOOKS ON THE SOVIET UNION, SPAIN, MEXICO, AND INDOCHINA.

I know that the first essential to survival is to believe that you can survive. And next, to identify the enemy and know your own mistakes and strength. And I take heart from the fact that the Pentagon which boasts that it can "overkill" the planet has not yet been able to take Korea or Cuba or Vietnam or Laos because of the complex pressures that get in the way. So the Chinese may be right in thinking that, as men grow steadily more conscious, they will master the forces of nature and the mechanisms of men's hands. . . . In China . . . there is still the faith that ordinary men are greater than the powers of nature. . . . They still hold that victory depends not on the power of weapons but on awakening the consciousness of man . . . that was why I came to China at the age of 72.

ANNA LOUISE STRONG
IN *Letters from China,* (1959)

The labor movement produced many radical figures. Some, like Mother Jones, came from immigrant backgrounds. Others, like Anna Louise Strong, came from upper class families where the American Puritan tradition prevailed with all its certainty that Americans were more virtuous than other peoples of the world. Anna Louise Strong spent the first thirty years of her life accepting this unquestioningly. The Everett Massacre and World War I made her decide that was a myth she could no longer afford.

Everett, Washington, a city twenty-eight miles north of Seattle on Puget Sound, was the site of a labor battle in 1916 that became known as the Everett Massacre. Two hundred and fifty laborers were caught in a boat on the Snonomish River, ambushed by two hundred vigilantes hidden in warehouses along the shore and in tugboats in the water. The resulting five dead, thirty-one wounded, and countless drowning fatalities made national headlines. Nobody knew who actually fired the first shot, but the responsibility for the deaths of two deputized vigilantes was laid to the workers. Seventy-four men—none of whom were shown to have been carrying a firearm—were arrested on charges of murder and brought to trial in Everett. The event became one of the great causes of the labor movement, and some of the best coverage was a series of articles in the *New York Evening Post* by a young free-lance reporter from Seattle named Anna Louise Strong.

She was an unlikely labor reporter. She was thirty-one years old, a member of the Seattle school board, a member of the Federation of Women's Clubs, and the daughter of a a well-known Seattle minister, Sydney Strong. The Seattle labor movement was not exactly where one would expect to find a minister's daughter with a Ph.D. in philosophy. The workers of the area were principally loggers and shipyard workers, nomad laborers with no vote and no political voice. The loggers were men without families, who drifted into the city when snow closed the logging camps. The only labor organization that would embrace such a motley constituency was the Industrial Workers of the World, the Wobblies.

The Wobblies wanted a single union for an entire industry rather than unions divided according to crafts. In the Everett strike, which preceded the massacre, their demands were for the right to organize, minimum wages, and an eight-hour day. The IWW had changed greatly since 1905, when Mother Jones had sat on the platform of the organizing convention. But the opposition of industry owners to labor organizers had not changed. When the IWW tried to organize a meeting in Everett, the police broke it up with clubs and shotguns. Any worker suspected of being a Wobbly was run out of town. The roads and railroads were patrolled by the police and vigilantes hired by the lumber companies so that no "outsiders" could come in. The public officials of Everett, in collusion with the industry owners, systematically denied the workers the right of free speech and the right to assemble.

The Wobblies were famous for their imaginative tactics and called a meeting to take place in a prominent Everett square. To make sure that the city's swollen police force would not arrest them on the roads into the city they arranged to travel from Seattle by boat at night. The *Verona* left Seattle at midnight with two hundred fifty workers on board, most of whom were unarmed. The police, acting on the information of an informer, deputized two hundred men, who waited at the docks hidden in warehouses and tugboats. As the boat pulled in the guards at the docks began firing. And the vigilantes in the tugboats caught the *Verona* in a crossfire as the boat tried to pull away. It was generally believed that two deputized vigilantes were shot in the confusion by their own men. The workers had clearly not expected an armed battle at the docks.

Anna Louise Strong insisted in the best tradition of journalism that "I was not taking sides in any struggle; I merely sent the news." But the news as she saw it was that the government of the city of Everett had denied the workers their constitutional right to land at a public dock and to speak on behalf of the working men. In addition it had acted in collusion with the lumber companies, hired thugs, and deputized vigilantes in order to deny those rights through violence. A noted historian of the IWW, Melvin Dubovsky, wrote of the Everett Massacre, "Perhaps the lesson Anna Louise Strong drew from the trial was the most important: The fruit of war is war and yet more war." The labor struggles continued, culminating in the Seattle General Strike of 1919, the only general strike that America has ever known. By that time Anna Louise Strong was on the inside, as a member of the Strike Committee.

Unlike generations of women preceding her, Anna Louise Strong had received one of the best possible formal educations available for women. Her mother, Ruth Tracy Strong, was one of the few women college graduates. She had attended Oberlin College and had focused much of that education on making her children as brilliant and as independent as one woman could. At the dinner table she read the classics while her children ate their dinners, or she led word games so that they learned vocabulary, pronunciation, and spelling. By the age of six Anna Louise, who was the oldest, was able to write in verse. Her first two books were of poems she had published while she was still in college.

Mrs. Strong encouraged her daughter's independence and fearlessness by permitting Anna Louise to travel by herself. At the age of eight she was encouraged to go on an overnight railway trip alone to Cincinnati to visit her grandmother. She handled her own ticket, gave a tip to the porter, and took a cab from the train station to her grandmother's house. She called it, "My big day of independence."

Mrs. Strong also understood childhood terrors. When the children huddled inside, afraid of thunderstorms, she sent them out on the porch to watch the lightning and hear the thunder. She made it a "treat" for good behavior. It must have worked because Strong said, "I think it is due to this training that in later life when death has actively threatened . . . I have not known fear; I have known increased capacity for cool action and even a thrill of joy. . . ."

Although Strong described her mother as a "modern, progressive mother, unlike the clinging mothers of the past," she recognized that her mother had been unable to give her children the freedom to see any evil in the world or to experience any of the violence of real life. After the family had moved from Nebraska to Ohio, Strong was put in local public schools. When a teacher shook her by the ear for filling her inkwell without permission, Mrs. Strong promptly took Anna Louise out of public school and put her in Cincinnati's best private school. Anna Louise questioned the overwhelming poverty she saw on Chicago's West Side, and her mother told her it was the result of the "ignorance" of the people who lived there. Hers was a very sheltered childhood which did not question the rightness of her family's way of life or the superiority of its progressive ideas. "I grew up expecting justice and kindness as natural rights of man," she wrote. "If anyone treated me with unkindness, I assumed it must be . . . my fault." It was only after World War I, when she was in her mid-thirties, that she began to realize that justice must be fought for, that there were people in the world who meant their acts to be destructive, that poverty and misery were not the result of individual ignorance but the product of systematic exploitation.

Her own drive and intelligence, combined with the amount of private tutoring she received, meant that she skipped several grades in school. This too contributed to her social isolation. She was always at least three to five years younger than anyone else in her class, and she finished high school at fourteen.

Oberlin would not accept her as a student until she was sixteen, so her parents sent her to Europe to learn languages for a year and then to Bryn Mawr for another year. She was bright but did not have many friends. "I shone in . . . marks. I did not shine in the good times." With embarrassment she remembered being chosen to read aloud *The Rape of Lucretia* because the teacher thought she was too young to know what rape meant.

After graduating from Oberlin at the age of nineteen, Strong went on to the University of Chicago to get a doctorate in philosophy. She wrote a dissertation on the psychology of prayer, defended it before the combined theological and philological faculties, and at twenty-three was the youngest student ever to receive the Ph.D. from the University of Chicago.

Unfortunately, contrary to what Sarah Grimké and other early feminists had hoped, an education in itself did not lead anywhere. The major occupations open to women were still teaching, housework, and prostitution. As many women were to find out, education was a fine attainment as long as they didn't try to do anything with it.

Looking back, Strong said that the most valuable activities were the odd jobs she took to support herself through school. She made felt pennants, tutored other students, typed papers. These taught her to support herself, to discipline her time, and helped her to understand people. She learned that she could always be economically independent if she did not become a slave to luxury and comfort. "I resolved to keep myself independent by never becoming habituated to a soft standard." She decided never to accumulate more goods than the ability to earn at odd jobs would allow her to sustain. She also decided that work and education should never be separated, which she acted on throughout her life.

In many ways she was very much like Charlotte Perkins Gilman as a young woman—dedicated, serious, constantly analyzing herself and her activities. She was also quite lonely and had few friends. Unlike Charlotte Gilman, she was only occasionally able to analyze her problems as cultural rather than individual. Also unlike Gilman, she seemed to have absolutely no sense of humor, nor as a friend later remarked, "did she see any need for one."

She believed she could do anything. She wanted to be a North Pole explorer, a pilot, a great writer. She chose writing because it seemed an appropriate occupation to combine with marriage.

Like many women before and after her, she failed to find an ideal husband and she failed to find rewarding work. Her first job after graduation from Oberlin was as a reporter for a religious newspaper in Chicago, the *Advance*. She was hired to write verse, report on news for the women's pages, and fill in as a general assignment reporter. She threw herself into the work and was both a success and a failure. The publisher praised her work but fired her after six months. Only an understanding editor who saw the effect of this blow was willing to tell her that it was the publisher's standard procedure to hire talented young people right out of college, use their energies, and fire them after their efforts had succeeded in obtaining subscribers. It was after this rude experience in the outside world that she decided to continue her education. She got a scholarship and enrolled in the philosophy department at the University of Chicago. "After the first six months of the dry philosophy of the University of Chicago, I knew that I hated it," she admitted years later.

Her mother had died while she was at Oberlin, and Strong made her home with her father on the West Side of Chicago, where he did settlement work. Her father, Sydney Strong, was one of the major influences in her life. He was a descendant of John Strong the Elder, the seventeenth-century pioneer who seemed to have single-handedly populated the Connecticut valley from Hartford to Northampton with preachers, educators, farmers, writers, and military men. There were many clergymen in the family and Sydney Strong was one of them, but he was not a traditional one. A Congregational minister, he was also an activist and a liberal thinker. He believed in Darwin's theories of evolution at a time when such theories were still heretical. He was a pacifist and a supporter of organized labor. Strong attributed her convictions and sense of rightness to her father. "By word and life he taught me that neither money, nor fame, nor human opinion are to be counted against being 'right' in one's soul."

While in graduate school at Chicago she wrote a book with him entitled *Patriarchs and Pioneers, Biographical Portraits from the Bible*. Anna Louise Strong could not be a patriarch but she could be a pioneer, and it is the word that she used most often to describe herself.

The only critical comment she ever wrote about her father revolved around a sermon he gave when she was in her teens. The subject was sexual attitudes and "cheap girls." "I don't think this talk about cheap girls goes well with Christian ethics," she told him. "Jesus tells us to love everybody and to give all we have to the world without questioning the return. . . . It would really be more Christian to be 'easy.' " Despite her father's progressive social views he had traditional attitudes about sex and marriage.

Nonetheless, her father was a source of support throughout her life. When she later made her home in Russia he visited her there, and his views on international understanding greatly influenced her own. After completing her doctoral degree she went to Seattle, where he had taken a post as a minister, and he helped her to create a job for herself, one which fully utilized her skills and energies. She set up "Know Your City Institutes," lectures and discussions about civic affairs combined with tours of the cities. They became popular in the West, where people felt a lack of roots and were eager to develop a sense of historical pride. The success of those seminars earned her a job in New York as an organizer of the New York Child Welfare Exhibit. She gained a reputation as an expert in public exhibits, which in fact she had become, and ended in Washington, D.C., as a coordinator of exhibits for the newly formed Children's Bureau. She said of this experience, "One's first responsible job is the great revealer far more than school."

During her years in Washington she was to learn three skills that in the future would serve her extremely well: one was the presentation of complicated information to an uninformed public in a way that would create excitement and enthusiasm; second was learning how to deal with people in authority; and third was an understanding of the inertia of bureacracy and how it works. The last she never mastered. Her mind was best at grasping individual tasks not whole systems. One of the people who most influenced her during this period was Leonard Ayres of the Russell Sage Foundation. He introduced her to the idea that good works can have harmful effects and that unless she made an effort to understand the total system in which she was operating, many of her best efforts could do more harm than good.

It was not easy, understanding that one's best work can do damage, but in 1915, after organizing a series of exhibits on the West Coast, she "refused to return to the deadening life of Washington, D.C.," and went back to Seattle to visit her father. The grandeur of the mountain setting, "added to a belated sense of duty" to her father, made her decide at the age of thirty to settle down and put out some roots. She ran for the school board and won. She joined many organizations. She wrote for local newspapers. She had been there for a little over a year when the Everett Massacre took place. She covered the trial and sold her articles to the *New York Evening Post.*

But the time in Seattle was a period of personal crisis for her. She had no work that was of great value to her. The hours spent at school board meetings, she said, were "the most completely boring of my life." She had no personal life to speak of. A man whom she loved and wanted to marry was already married, and the conflict resulted in an emotional breakdown. Rewi Allee, the editor of *Eastern Horizon* and a neighbor of hers in Peking, said that when Strong was in her eighties she began reciting poems she had written in her twenties for a man she had wanted to marry. "She would laugh at these old memories," Allee recalled, "but she had memorized the poems and remembered them clearly."

She reenergized herself through physical activities. Mountain climbing became a "new form of opium," as she called it. Like everything else she did, her energies were prodigious and her commitment obsessive. She organized the first winter climb of Mount Hood—which was almost her last climb because of an unexpected blizzard. When other mountaineers berated her for being foolhardy, she found it hard to explain why she had gone. The "mysticism of the adventurer," she called it, "conquering the unconquerable forces of desolate nature." In the expanse of glaciers and wilderness, ice and sky, she found a source of the mystical feeling that runs throughout her life. Mountains never ceased to fascinate her. In her seventies she climbed over ten thousand feet of mountain roads to Lhasa in Tibet, the first American to do so.

Her personal crisis in 1916 coincided with an historical crisis, the United States involvement in World War I. Strong threw herself into every antiwar organization active on the West Coast—the Anti-Preparedness League, the American Union Against Militarism, the Emergency Peace Federation. She organized meetings, arranged for speakers, distributed pamphlets. She conducted a plebiscite in Seattle on voter attitudes toward entering the war, and she sent the results to Congress.

She used all the skills she had learned in Washington to articulate public dissent. When the United States declared war in April 1917, she said, "Nothing in my whole life, not even my mother's death so shook the foundations of my soul. . . . I could not delude myself that this was a 'war to make the world safe for democracy'; I had seen democracy slain in the very declaration of war. . . . There had been a deep mistake in the whole basis of my life. Where and how to begin again I had no notion." World War I marked the end of her career as a liberal reformer and the beginning of her life as a radical activist. Mr. Wilson's war, as some called it, was also described as "the war to end all wars." It ushered in a new era of repression of intellectuals, radicals, pacifists, and dissenters in general.

Congress immediately fortified the war effort by creating a Committee on Public Information to censor press criticism of the war. Within eight weeks of the declaration of war it passed the Espionage Act, a law which imposed up to $10,000 in fines or twenty years in prison or both for anyone who interfered with the draft or attempted "to cause disloyalty." Less than a year later, Americans were forbidden under the terms of the Sedition Act to "willfully utter, print, write, or publish any disloyal, profane, scurrilous or abusive language about the form of government of the United States" or to "urge, incite or advocate any curtailment of production in this country or anything or things, product or products, necessary or essential to the prosecution of the war."

In the Justice Department's zeal to rid the country of what it considered subversive and traitorous persons and groups, men and women were imprisoned not only for acts but also for saying such things as the war should be financed by higher taxes instead of bond sales or for criticizing the Red Cross or YMCA. One woman was sentenced to ten years in jail for stating, "I am for the people and the government is for the profiteers."

Strong's first anti-war act was to testify on behalf of four men arrested under the Espionage Act for distributing an anti-conscription pamphlet which she had authorized while an officer of the American Union Against Militarism. Her testimony resulted in a hung jury:

> What's unlawful about that dodger [pamphlet]? Printed before the conscription law was passed, wasn't it, when nine-tenths of this country thought conscription un-American? Even if it hadn't been, who prevents free-born Americans from attacking an oppressive law?

Her strategy of outraged respectability was effective, but as she sadly observed, "After [the trial] I was the best-known woman in Seattle; I was no longer among the most respectable."

The influential members of the city establishment and the women of the middle-class woman's organizations were no longer eager to be associated with someone whose politics were so disruptive. They drafted a petition to recall her from the school board and circulated it throughout the city. The need to be effective, the need to be legitimized by the so-called responsible elements of the community became progressively less important to her. Her revulsion against the war and the domestic repression that went with it had created a profound moment of conscience.

Anna Louise Strong protested the war by publicly associating with a woman Anarchist arrested for sending seditious literature to soldiers. Strong's description of Louise Olivereau can describe herself as well:

> She was one of those poetic souls to whom war never became a statistical movement of forces, but always vividly remained torn flesh, scattered brains and blood. She heard in her soul the shrieks of each murdered victim and hated war with emotion.

Louise Olivereau was a typist in the IWW office who spent her tiny salary mimeographing statements against war by Tolstoy, Abraham Lincoln, Thoreau, and the Bible and sending them to lists of drafted soldiers. She was tried for violating the Espionage Act.

Louise Olivereau knew Anna Louise Strong from her visits to the IWW offices during the labor battles, and she asked Strong to sit beside her in court so that she might have a few encouraging words. Strong knew how futile a gesture it would be. Olivereau refused an attorney, tried to defend herself, and declared herself an Anarchist before a staid Seattle jury. Eight-column headlines announced to the Seattle public that Anna Louise Strong sat beside the Anarchist in court. Louise Olivereau was convicted, and Anna Louise Strong was recalled from her position on the school board.

It was then that she began her new vocation, that of journalist, reporting on the problems of working people. She began working for a Communist paper, the *Daily Call*, and when its presses were wrecked for publishing items critical of the war effort, she went to work for a Socialist paper, the *Union Record*. Under the pen name Anise she wrote verses with themes about the exploitation of labor and published them in workers' newspapers throughout the country. She knew practically nothing about Marxism or socialism but she read everything she could find about the Russian Revolution of October 1917. Her editor told her that the shipyard workers liked the "Russian stuff," and so she kept writing about workers' management in factories, revolutionary tribunals, rationing of children's food, women's equality.

She understood her own naiveté and admitted that she was like many American leftists who were "cheerfully unaware of the theoretical basis of Russia's revolution and ready to cheer any workers who had taken power." Her articles made the *Union Record* the only newspaper in the United States to give positive coverage to the events in the Soviet Union from 1917 to 1919.

In some ways the Russian Revolution was felt more immediately by the workers of the Northwest. One reason was geography. When laborers in New York thought about Russia they turned toward the Atlantic and imagined a long trip across the history, traditions, politics of all the European countries in between them and the Russian border. The activists of the Northwest turned toward the Pacific and saw Russia as a huge land mass of Asia. There were not the same intermediary political or economic structures to cross. This lack of barriers has much to do with the fact that it was the papers of the Northwest which carried more news of the Revolution than the Socialist papers of the East.

It was also a time when the entire American journalism profession was making its reputation on European battlefronts or at Versailles. Strong stayed in Seattle reading pamphlets, translations of Lenin's speeches, learning about the Revolution from every journalist or traveler who came through Seattle. She recalled going to hear Louise Bryant, a well-known foreign correspondent whom she described as coming through Seattle "to dazzle the smoke laden air of the close packed longshoremen's hall with her gorgeous amber beads and the glamour of the forbidden border." She spent hours, sometimes days, with these messengers of revolution and wrote whole series of articles from what they told her. She interviewed the wife of Krasnoschekoff, president of the Far Eastern Republic who had fled eastern Russia when the Japanese invaded. From her she gained some knowledge of Soviet schools and new ideas on child care in the Soviet state.

Like Charlotte Perkins Gilman's, Strong's first ideas about socialism had come from Edward Bellamy's book *Looking Backward,* a utopian novel about socialism. The political and economic theories of Marx or the humanitarian socialism of Europe that Gilman came to know in England was not part of Strong's experience. Strong was puzzled when Louise Bryant told her that the Russian Communists were violent. "You mustn't think they are pacifists over there because they withdrew from the war," Bryant said. "They believe in armed uprising. . . ."

It was difficult for Strong to fit that information into the situation in Seattle. She believed in workers' control, but she couldn't visualize an armed uprising against Mr. Skinner, the owner of the Seattle shipyards. She had prepared a pamphlet on Lenin's speech about workers taking power in a Russian city. With characteristic confidence she disregarded the scholarly introduction that had been written by the translator of the speech, put tight headings on each paragraph, and wrote simple summaries of Lenin's thoughts. The pamphlet was seen all over Seattle, on streetcars and ferries, where dockworkers carried Lenin's thoughts to and from work.

In January 1919 the accumulated discontent of workers which had been building throughout the war erupted in Seattle in what snowballed into the first general strike in America. American firms made huge profits during the war, and for many the war years were the most prosperous of their existence. Yet workers' real wages had remained the same from 1916 to 1919 while prices had risen up to 50 percent. The strike in Seattle was the first of a wave of strikes that spread across the country. It was only with the Seattle strike that Anna Louise Strong came face to face with the staggering gap between workers' consciousness and the realities of power. Responding to a call from Seattle's Central Labor Committee, sixty thousand workers in all industries left their jobs. For five hectic days the industry of the city was almost paralyzed. As a member of the Strike Committee, Strong was torn by the conflicts of theory and reality. Who would drive ambulances when all the drivers were on strike? How could the telephones operate when all the operators went on strike? How could children get milk when the milk wagon drivers were on strike? Should they keep the street lights on in order to prevent looting? These were only a few of the questions the Strike Committee had to try to answer.

She saw that none of the leaders had clearly worked out all the consequences of the strike. Nor did they have a taste for the demands of battle. "The strike could produce no leaders willing to keep it going. All of us were red in the ranks and yellow as leaders," Strong wrote. Mother Jones, who was traveling through the country in 1919, wrote of the fragmented labor movement, "If a revolution started tomorrow, I don't know where they would get a leader." After five days the labor leaders called the strike off. The mayor blamed it on a Bolshevik plot, and a strong wave of antilabor opinion rolled over the city. The Seattle strike marked the beginning of a national Red Scare. It was easier to blame the thousands of strikes throughout the country on a Communist conspiracy than to examine the real sources of worker discontent.

Strong was arrested although not imprisoned for her role as historian of the Strike Committee. She called some of her writings of that period "beautiful mists of hope. . . . We passed quite unconsciously over the whole problem of the conquest of power." Unlike Mother Jones, who took an active role in the Great Steel Strike which began a few months later, Anna Louise Strong and the union leaders of Seattle lacked any real taste for battle. They had no sense of what they would do against the National Guard or a deputized militia. "We lacked all intention of real battle," she wrote. "We expected to drift into power."

The postwar economic depression hit Seattle before the rest of the country. The shipyard workers drifted to other cities and the best went first. The composition of the labor movement changed, and workers spent most of their time fighting each other for scarce jobs. The outward forms of comradeship remained, but old friends called each other traitors. Like other dissenters who found the repression intolerable, Strong longed to flee from the ashes of the "Seattle revolution," from the insoluble problems around her. But where was she to go?

Lincoln Steffens, one of the most creative journalists of the era, was in Seattle. He was on his way back from accompanying President Wilson's special emissary, William Bullitt, to the Soviet Union. When Strong expressed her eager wish to see the realities of socialism in practice, Steffens asked mildly, "Why don't you go?"

"It was one of those moments in life," she later reflected, "when we veer in a sharp direction that seems unrelated to the old, yet which is already determined by a hundred unnoticed influences which have heaped themselves within us." Steffens gave voice to a desire that she had not dared to acknowledge. When he finally said it, she knew that was what she was going to do.

At the time Lincoln Steffens was encouraging Anna Louise Strong to go to the Soviet Union, it was not easy for an American to travel through Russia. The Russians, understandably, were suspicious of Americans. The United States had joined the French and English governments in trying to unseat the Bolshevik regime immediately after the Revolution. A campaign was launched by Japan and the United States in the far eastern Russian provinces, and the Allied forces took the ports of Murmansk and Archangel in the North. There were American troops in Archangel until the end of 1919. All aid from the Allies went to the right-wing forces. The only Americans allowed into the country were relief workers assigned to the American Friends Service Committee, an international Quaker organization. Anna Louise Strong applied to the committee, was unable to get an assignment in Russia, and accepted work in Poland. She was thirty-five years old when she left Seattle for Warsaw in 1921.

In Poland she promptly got dysentery and lice and worked herself to exhaustion. The head of the mission, Florence Barrow, told her it was merely her "Russian training." At the first opportunity Strong asked Barrow for permission to go to Moscow. Her tenacity of will,

combined with the power of her personality, made her the first of all
the eager American Friends Service volunteers in Poland to get to
Moscow in late 1921. A friend of hers, Ida Pruitt, who knew her in
China said, "When she wanted something, she was like a
dreadnought. She cut through everything. Nothing stood in her
way."

From Moscow she traveled aboard the first railway train to carry
food and medical supplies to the victims of the famine along the
Volga River. The country had been so devastated by the civil war
that the train had no fuel and had to stop along the way for wood to
be cut. A thirty-hour trip took fourteen days. At first she could
hardly comprehend what she was seeing. Women gave their babies
away or left them on the platforms of the railway cars because they
had no food. She saw thousands of children, "standing weakly on
their legs," lining the tracks.

> I heard the cry of hundreds of gaunt, dirty children: "Bread for
> the love of God, a crumblet, a little crust of bread." Their thin
> legs hardly supported them; they raised thin hands and wailed
> in thin voices. Huddled for warmth against the night in tiny
> stations I saw throngs of peasants, men, women, children, all
> armed with government transportation permits in lieu of
> tickets, all waiting for trains to take them to regions of bread,
> and dying as they waited.

Typhus raged. In the hospital in Samara she watched a doctor
become hysterical on being told that after her family had had to sell
all its jewels to buy food, the food had been stolen. Strong had
thought she would find a brave new world beyond the Polish border.
She found instead a country in chaos, a people whose experience had
been so grim that death had become a minor event. After four weeks
she herself succumbed to typhus.

"I was relieved when the doctor said I had typhus. Typhus excuses
everything." She was in delirium for a week. Her head ached so
badly she went for six days without sleeping. When she began to
recover, she was so weak she was unable to bear the stories about
the hunger and death of the people around her in the hospital. A
letter was delivered to her from America containing the menu from
a trans-Atlantic steamer. As she read it aloud she became hysterical.
"Olives and pickles and two or three kinds of soup . . . three entrees,

meats and fowl and salad . . . desserts and five kinds of cheese. . . .
We read it aloud in the hospital and laughed and wept." In Samara
there was no bread, and the one lemon they had obtained for her had
been smuggled past a blockade in Turkestan.

The Volga famine in which tens of thousands died of starvation
marked another dividing line in her life. After seeing the limits of
human survival it was impossible for her to ever again go back to
reporting on the problems of property and corruption. The immediacy of death made her conscious of the need to find meaning in her
own life. After the Volga famine she was a survivor. Her mentality
changed to that of someone who had participated in a great catastrophe and lived to tell about it. She had to find the significance of
her own survival. It was as much a religious experience as it was a
political one.

During the four months she spent in bed recovering from typhus,
she met no important officials and saw only nurses, doctors, and
peasants. She had seen none of the efficiency or achievement that
the Revolution was supposed to bring; instead, she had to cope with
unlit streets, fuelless trains, ruined factories, and starving villages.
In her own words, her most vivid impression was of "a filthy sprawl-
ing city by the Volga where the world lay dying." Unlike many
idealistic American leftists, her desire to remain in the Soviet Union
was not a romantic one.

> In place of the united country of convinced socialists defying
> the world which I had expected to find as soon as I crossed the
> border, I found grumbling, ill-fed folk, many of them barefoot,
> many cheating the government, most of them discontented.
> But there were people here and there . . . who quietly, doggedly
> and even cheerfully disregarded their own lack and gave their
> thought to keeping the country alive. . . . Even they had no
> energy left for enthusiasm; they needed their energy for
> struggle.

In 1921–22 many more Americans went to the Soviet Union, to
work in factories, to provide technical skills, to experience some of
the energy of the "workers' state." Some were recruited by the American Communist party, others went out of their own curiosity, and
still others were business promoters seeking concessions. On her
own initiative Strong proposed a Russian-American club, which

could serve as a central meeting point for Americans and furnish services like translators, office space, and housing referrals. It was a good idea, badly needed, and it received the enthusiastic support of both Americans and Russians. She set about the business of getting a charter, finding a house, going through the formalities of organization.

Unfortunately, setting up such a club in a foreign country called for many more skills than she possessed at that time. Her strengths were in blithely barging into offices, intimidating people into giving her the information she wanted, overwhelming them by the sheer force of her presence and determination. In America it always worked. In the Soviet Union it didn't. She was a pushy American outsider.

She needed intricate political skills, a sense of the niceties of the bureaucracy, a diplomatic feel for the interrelationships of one governmental office with another. She was operating on the basis of old IWW slogans and half-thought-out ideas of workers "bringing order out of chaos." After three months of futile organizing she described her feelings of frustration and futility as so great that she "would rather go through typhus again than through that summer."

When the Russian Foreign Office told her to drop the scheme, she went into one of the rages for which she was famous. She called the Russians "damned Asiatics! Polite and shifty liars who never tell you frankly what they do." She called herself a failure. "This was failure, utter and crushing, which left marks . . . on my soul that will never entirely pass."

She was a woman of enormous energy living in a foreign culture which really did not have any use for her. It was a terrible blow to her confidence and self-esteem.

She became the correspondent for *Hearst's International Magazine* in 1922 and three years later became the Russian correspondent for the North American Newspaper Alliance. She always wrote for an American audience, trying to translate the Russian Revolution in a way that would make it understandable to Americans. Rewi Allee said that she tried always to appeal to "the revolutionary spirit of the American people which she believed to be very much alive."

In addition to her articles she gave English lessons to Trotsky; provided Krupskaya, Lenin's widow, with the latest books on education from the United States; started an English-language newspaper, the *Moscow News* (not the same as a later paper *Moscow Daily News*); and raised money for food and equipment for the communes instituted for the packs of children left homeless during the Revolution.

Every year she returned to the United States and lectured to political organizations, labor unions, and colleges such as Wellesley, Smith, Vassar, Columbia, and Stanford. Nym Wales, Edgar Snow's first wife, said that "on the platform she was impressive, forthright and open. . . . She was quick, bright, fast spoken with no time or energy to waste. Her face was finely modeled with a good sharp New England profile. In her youth she must have been unusually handsome with fair skin and expressive features."

She began to gain a reputation in the United States as an expert on the Soviet Union and was invited to talk to businessmen about trade. Henry Ford sent for her when the Soviet Union began to order tractors. She said that "for a whole hour . . . he talked in the platitudes of a high school orator," bemoaning the tragic death of the Russian tsar. The public relations director of Standard Oil invited her to an elegant dinner of businessmen and their wives as living proof that "an American woman could emerge in health and confidence after four years in Soviet Russia." Standard Oil was interested in the oil reserves of the Baku region. The former president of the First National City Bank of New York, Frank Vanderlip, invited her to dinner at his home to discuss the unpaid tsarist loans. She reported his comment: "I personally know that the claims are grossly exaggerated." The refusal of the United States to reopen diplomatic relations with the Soviet Union was largely based on the insistence of the First National City Bank, the House of Morgan, and other financial institutions that the repayment of outstanding loans be made a conditions of diplomatic recognition. The Russian regime claimed they were the tsar's debts and refused to pay.

She met with Gerard Swope, president of General Electric, to discuss business concessions and credit in the Soviet Union in exchange for company property that the Russians had confiscated. A year after her meeting with Swope, General Electric was the first major American company to resume dealings with the Soviet Union.

In a certain sense Anna Louise Strong was an ambassador without portfolio. There was no diplomatic recognition between the Soviet Union and the United States until 1933. She had an extremely ambiguous political identity—the Russians considered her a capitalist and the Americans considered her a Communist. There were, however, very few people who had access both to the industrialists of the United States and the top officials of the Soviet government. By the mid-1930s she had gained a great reputation as a Soviet expert. She had published the first interview with Stalin. When she was in the United States, Eleanor Roosevelt invited her to the White House to brief the president, and the two women corresponded frequently after that.

In some ways she was like the disillusioned young intellectuals of her generation who became expatriates and made a life for themselves in France or Italy. Unlike them she was an expatriate operating in a vastly different culture. In the Soviet Union she was seeing her first cultural revolution, a country moving from the Middle Ages to the twentieth century. The task was far greater than politics or economics. It was one of changing centuries of thought, of moving from an agricultural to an industrial society. The realization of the cultural basis of revolution gave new insight to her reporting and a better understanding to her personal friendships.

Even the Russians she became closest to were outsiders. One of her best friends was a Russian professor named Valentina, with whom she shared an apartment for two years.

> We had discussed at length and repeatedly our souls, our views of men and our attitude to the party. We had no use for any men who were not "responsible party members" . . . we ourselves were intending to join the party someday, but always at the last minute we found some flaw in our souls or in the party to cause another delay.

As they evaluated life around them—a worker who was evicted, some person unjustly jailed, starvation among the peasants—they concluded, "This country is worse than capitalism. It evicts workers, starves peasants, and jails innocent citizens."

In 1932 she married a Russian agronomist named Joel Shubin. He was a Communist, and she told Rewi Allee that "perhaps we married because we were both so doggone lonely. But we were very happy."

He traveled with her in the United States when she came back to visit. They had no children. He was killed during World War II.

Even after twenty years in Russia and marriage to a Communist, Strong never joined the Communist party. She never took sides in the deep rifts in the Communist party. Her bedrock experience was American, and she always referred back to it. When a coworker accused her of being a Trotskyite, she answered, "I've got too much experience in the labor movement of Seattle to go against a workers' movement because it throws out a candidate I like." It took a while before she realized what she really was, a journalist and an outsider, a writer for the capitalist press. But there were very few American journalists who actually made their homes in Moscow.

Strong believed in efficiency. She loathed waste. She had no understanding of the uses of corruption. She had absolutely no sense of how to create an enterprise from the bottom up. Her skills were in organizing from the top down, imposing order on disparate groups below. She had a Western sense of hierarchy, and she had no patience for consensus decision-making. Periodically she flew into "passionate rages," as she called them, at a system that wasted her energies and would not use her efficiently. She had no skill at deciphering how different values put a completely different light on the same event.

When she was working on the *Moscow News,* she would rush back to the paper with her scoop on the speech of some minister at an official meeting. The editor of the paper would not use it, telling her that it was impossible to write an article on the minister's speech until the official version had been released by Tass, the official government news agency, and printed in *Pravda.* Scoops did not exist, nor did condensing or summarizing official remarks. The thought that a newspaper played a very different function in Russia from what she had been taught in America did not occur to her. She became frustrated, outraged, and ended in a fury of resentment. "It seemed to me that everyone had cynically exploited all my aspirations to betray me . . . to chain me to failure and to keep me chained."

At a critical point in her conflict with the Russian system she almost gave up. But it seemed to her that she would be giving up in the same way she had once before in Seattle—rejecting the school board, the reform organizations, the peace groups, everything that reminded her of her own failure. She toyed with using a very potent weapon, telling her story to the Western press. There were many "my-disillusionment-in-Russia" stories circulating in the United States, and her story was eagerly sought after. It was a difficult time for her, and she admitted that she "played with that thought [of going to the Western press] as a desperate man plays with suicide, when all of his deep instincts cry for life."

Her weaknesses were the opposite side of her strengths. The same determination and single-mindedness that made her so difficult to work with prevented her from taking the most sensible way out of an intolerable situation. Instead of writing an exposé for the *New York Times* she wrote a letter to Stalin describing her situation on the *Moscow News*. She had resigned from the newspaper, but the editor refused to accept her resignation, telling her it was "an anti-Soviet act," and continued to use her name on the paper. The letter led to personal interviews with Stalin, Voroshilov, Kaganovich, and other Russian leaders. It was yet another turning point in her life, for she began to get an instinct for the system she was in . She began to get a feeling for process, for the means by which life in the Soviet state was carried on. It was a beginning of her sense that life is organized at many levels, and documents like speeches, constitutions, and statements of intent are only the crust at the top.

For the first time she began to contemplate the idea that her failures in the Soviet Union were not entirely due to others but were rooted in herself, in her own lack of self-knowledge and unrealistic expectations.

> For Russia I had no background of discrimination; I saw Russia and its communists mystically. . . . I accepted them as almost superhuman beings. With that sentimental American inclusiveness which asks moving picture stars their views on politics and accepts from illiterate politicians advice on science or women, I was ready to take a Russian communist as an oracle, not only on revolutions, but on personal plans and details of personal life.

The feel for cultural traditions, the sense of subterranean political process, the realization that leaders come in many guises—these are evident in her excellent writing about China. In 1925 she was forty years old and on her way back to the United States to lecture and to

arrange for publication of some of her materials when she visited
China for the first time. It was a labor strike that drew her, and Russian connections took her into the city of Canton.

Strong was able to get into the center of China's infant revolution
through Fanny Borodin, the wife of Mikhail Borodin, the secret advisor to the revolutionary Chinese nationalists and later her editor on
the *Moscow News*.

Within the Soviet Union the exact nature of the Chinese political
upheaval had been a source of controversy among political theorists.
Some said it was a genuine uprising of the proletariat. Others said it
could not lead to genuine Communist revolution because it was an
agricultural country with no worker class to sustain revolution.
Consequently, Stalin's government recognized the official Chinese
government but surreptitiously gave arms and aid to the revolutionary forces led by Dr. Sun Yat-sen. China was ruled by competing
warlords. In the south a new revolutionary government had been set
up in Canton by Dr. Sun Yat-sen.

In Canton a hundred thousand workers had organized a strike
against the British port of Hong Kong. The Strike Committee allowed no foreigners to enter the city, but Fanny Borodin said, "I'll
ask the strike committee to break the rule and let me meet you. It is
really important that you see Canton." Using her own and her husband's connections she obtained a permit and personally arranged
for Strong's transfer from a British steamboat to a small Canton
motor boat. "It was the first time for months a Canton boat had met
that British steamer," she said. "I swiftly stepped into the boat and
departed amid the astonished stares of sailors."

Until Strong visited Canton she had not understood what China
was really about. The exotic courts, the gossip of the foreigners
about the warlords, the confused theories of the Peking students
about communism, socialism, democracy, the strange customs of
politeness—these combined to make her feel that the Chinese were
indeed an "inscrutable people." When she arrived in Canton she
recognized what she was seeing and could understand it. "The
Canton strike was hard, ruthless, definite. It was organized labor
on strike in Seattle. . . . I felt it the moment I entered strike headquarters. This was no alien, exotic country; this was home. Here
were peasant workers grown industrialized and feeling their power."

Fanny Borodin arranged for her to address a mass meeting of Chinese women.

> I talked to them of the conditions out of which Russia made her revolution, the old patriarchal household, the ignorant village, the enslaved women, the factories with their barracks life. . . . Those women understood the details of the Russian revolution as no American audience of mine ever had. It was their own life I told, as it had been and might be.

That speech reflected the framework for her understanding of China. It was her Russian experience she drew on. "I saw peasant populations essentially similar over the greatest land area of earth," she wrote. "I began to see the Russian revolution . . . as the first stage in the awakening and industrialization of Asia." In 1925 the meeting of women represented a new consciousness, since footbinding, child marriages, marriage by purchase were still prevailing customs. The meeting organizer was a widow whose husband, a strike leader, had been assassinated. Her presence was an insult to the traditional Chinese family because a woman was supposed to retire to her home for years after the death of her husband.

Although Rewi Allee calls many of Strong's reactions from those days "to be those of ordinary middle-class western people of her time," her eye for the details of organizing new political structures on old social forms was excellent, and she captured aspects of the struggle in China that went completely unnoticed by other Western reporters. For example, in 1927 when she went to Wuhan in central China—a city where all foreign concessions had been revoked—she wrote about the early labor unions and their support for women's rights. She saw the practices that the workers were rebelling against—punishing children by shutting them overnight in wooden cages so small that the children could not lie down, bribing foremen in order to hold jobs, beating women workers for the slightest fault, reduction of wages for any infraction of rules or mistakes in work. With great sensitivity she wrote of the courage of the "bobbed-haired girls" who, although illiterate and half-starved, cut their hair as a symbol of defiance against the traditions of centuries. Among the Westerners there were rumors that the women of Wuhan had celebrated their new freedom by parading naked through the streets, but Anna Louise Strong knew and publicly said that this was simply a horror story designed to create passionate opposition. When an area went from the control of the revolutionaries back to the old rulers, as happened with great frequency, the "bobbed-haired girls" were the first to be executed.

One description of her in Hankow came from an American civil engineer who had been working on the Yangtze River conservation project: "There was a big strong American woman reporting from there—she seemed to be everywhere. Then there was another one, also an American, a red-headed one." The big one was Anna Louise Strong (as she became older she gained weight and came to weigh close to two hundred pounds). The red-headed one was Rayna Prohme, a former University of Illinois roommate of Dorothy Day's, a Communist, and an agent of Mikhail Borodin's.

As relations between the Russian and Chinese governments became strained Mikhail Borodin was "asked" to leave China. Fanny Borodin was jailed but eventually escaped. All Russians in Shanghai were arrested on the grounds of aiding the revolutionary forces. Rayna Prohme was given the task of smuggling Sun Yat-sen's widow out of the country (which she did successfully), and Anna Louise Strong was allowed to join Borodin's expedition back to Russia across the Mongolian desert.

The book that she wrote on this period, *China's Millions*, is a classic. (On Strong's eightieth birthday Chou En-lai presented her with a new edition printed by the Peking Press.) It includes an account of Borodin's voyage and reads like a trip back into the Middle Ages, except that they traveled in cars. It was a trip of almost two thousand miles through country under the control of competing warlords, a region where the roads often stopped at rivers without bridges.

Strong's account of the journey gives a good indication of her ability to endure hardships, her willingness to take risks, and her capacity to overcome fear of the unknown. It also gives an extraordinary glimpse of life in the northern provinces of China at a time when few Westerners ever ventured beyond the major cities. Except for a few scholars and missionaries, few Westerners had occasion to travel through this vast region.

Borodin's caravan of automobiles, which carried its own gasoline, had to reach towns by sundown because the gates of the walled cities were locked shut. Bandits infested the hills and lived by robbing and looting. When they passed from Honan into Shensi Province there were customs officials at the gates of departure and entrance. Food distribution between provinces was almost like that between foreign countries. One province was rich with fresh fruits and vegetables, while the next was dry and poor with shortages even of rice. Throughout the trip Strong kept a running account of the warlords and generals and petty officials they met and dined with. She also recorded Borodin's cynical but prophetic prediction, "Only the workers and peasants can unify China." He concluded, "Miss Strong is unlucky in her revolutions. She was too late for the Russian revolution and she is much too early for the Chinese."

When the caravan reached the Soviet Union and the Trans-Siberian railway, Strong had the feeling they were emerging from a trip back in time. She became acutely aware of how time and distance are recorded and measured in the modern age. Road posts marked off kilometers; trains ran on fixed schedules; letter boxes indicated mail service. And for the first time in weeks she saw land enclosed by fences.

Not long after this China trip Strong went to Samarkand in the Soviet Union. It was a territory that was Moslem and where the women were in purdah, wearing a form of the veil which made them look like mummies encased from head to foot in coarse material with only slits so they could see. The Soviet government had granted Moslem women political rights, had outlawed polygamy and purdah, and had stipulated that women be allowed to learn to read. But in the Moslem provinces Moslem custom prevailed. It was considered a man's right to murder his wife, and many women were found murdered for having discarded their veils or for having joined the "emancipated" women who came from Moscow. Strong traveled on horseback and several times was almost killed for being a dangerous example of "the emancipated woman." Her book on this trip, *Red Star in Samarkand*, is an original and unusual piece of reporting. In many ways it was the work of an explorer for nothing had prepared her to analyze the politicizing of Moslem women. She often harked back to the Seattle General Strike in her reporting of the strikes and revolutionary demonstrations in other countries, but she had no reference point with which to decipher these remote Asiatic provinces.

When she wrote her autobiography in 1933 it was an autobiography written thirty years too soon. Lincoln Steffens read a draft of the book and wrote to her, "The transition the Revolution is making in you is not yet finished." He told her she had not completed the process she was describing, that of transcending national identity. "They have an entirely different culture, more different than the Christian was from the old Greek. . . . You really do not get the Russian culture. You will. Don't worry. And when you do, I think you'll want to write another book."

He was right. Strong never really did "get" Russian culture, but what she learned in Russia allowed her to make a unique connection with the emerging modern Chinese state. Her writing from 1927 to 1949 covers revolution and political upheaval in many countries. But her political growth and international understanding is most evident in her writing about China. Through the years of her travels back and forth between the Soviet Union and China she got to know many of the leaders of the Communist Revolution of China, and in 1946, she was able to fly into the area held by the revolutionary army of Mao Tse-tung. Her description of the period in Yenan approached that of a religious experience.

In Yenan there was time and space. There was expansion of thinking. . . . Not for years, and perhaps never, had I so felt my concepts of the world sharpening, developing as in those Yenan talks. . . . I thought I had a grasp of two great systems. . . . Then there in China was something different from either. A new birth of the world's most ancient people. . . . It was like Columbus sighting America. It was like being young again.

Others who were there had the same reaction. Ida Pruitt, an American who was born in China of missionary parents, said that

everyone was dedicated to the revolution. . . . Everyone who saw Yenan came out with an exalted feeling. Perhaps the special quality was that we saw people working for revolution for the people, not just making revolution for the leaders.

Yenan had once been a walled city, situated at the intersection of three valleys, and a center of travel. During World War II the Japanese had bombed the city. With all the buildings destroyed, the inhabitants dug themselves into the caves in the hills around the city. It was there that Mao Tse-tung, Chou En-lai, General Chu Teh and other legendary figures of the Chinese Revolution had their headquarters. During a truce in 1946 Strong flew into Yenan on an American plane that was patrolling the area.

She lived the daily life of Yenan. Her home was in a cave. She met with people, got to know the women soldiers, went up to Radio Hill, where a powerful receiver monitored news from all over the world, debated theory with some of the intellectuals, and participated in Yenan social life. In light of the imposing mythology that later grew up about these men, it is somehow reassuring to know that during Yenan dances Chu Teh danced as though he were marching, a steady one-step all the time; Chou En-lai was an excellent waltzer; and Mao sat out most of the dances.

Mao did, however, enjoy talking, and the interview he granted Strong became, justifiably, one of the most famous and the most important of her career. She asked him about the strength of his enemies and the threat of American imperialism.

American imperialism . . . it becomes lonely. So many of its friends are dead.

Before the February Revolution in Russia the Czar looked strong and terrible. But a February rain washed him away. Hitler was also washed down by the storms of history. So were the Japanese.

They were paper tigers all.

What became known in the entire Western world as "the paper tiger" interview actually could have been the "scarecrow" interview. The translator first translated Mao's words as scarecrow and Mao asked what it meant. Then he said no:

A paper tiger is not something dead stuck in a field. It scares not crows but children. It is made to look like a dangerous beast. But it is really only pressed paper which softens when damp.

The interview produced some of the most quoted ideas of Mao, such as his thoughts on the atom bomb: "The birth of the atom bomb was the beginning of the death of the American imperialists. For they began to count on the bomb and not on the people." He talked about the strength of peoples' consciousness and the nature of American imperialism. Strong reached into the full range of her past experience for that one interview.

When Mao and his troops had to evacuate Yenan because of the advance of Chiang Kai-shek's nationalist troops, he told her to take the story of the "liberated areas" out of China. She wanted to go with them, but she was over sixty years old then and she knew she couldn't keep up with the march. Back in America she tried to sell articles on the civil war in China and to explain that the United States was backing the wrong side, but no one was interested.

In 1949 she was unceremoniously expelled from the Soviet Union. She had written a book on the Chinese Revolution, *The Chinese Conquer China*, and distributed drafts of it to a number of publishers in Europe and the Far East. Even though China was not of great interest to Americans until it seemed they had "lost" it, it was of concern to the Japanese, the Indians, the Southeast Asians. In the book she praised Mao and used the term "Maoism," claiming he had given an Asian form to Marxism. She also gave information on how little help the Russians had given the Chinese Communists, a point that touched nerves in the Soviet Union. Immediately after publication of this book on China she was expelled from the Soviet Union.

She was denounced by the Russians as "an American spy" and "a tool of Wall Street" and left the Soviet Union the way she had come in, through Poland, this time via Lubianka prison instead of the American Friends Service Committee mission. It was a terrible blow. She was never told why she was being deported, and in the Communist world her denunciation meant that no American Communists or leftists would talk with her.

When Mao finally marched triumphantly into Peking in 1949, Anna Louise Strong was in Connecticut, an outsider in her own country. "She was angrier," Ida Pruitt said, "at missing the revolution in China than she was at the outrageous behaviour of the Soviets. I met her in New York when she first arrived and we went to see Arthur Miller's play, *Death of a Salesman*." It is a tribute to her fund of knowledge of the world that she refused offer after offer from the American press "to tell her story." Instead she told the reporters who hounded her for anti-Russian statements:

> Do not use me to inflame international friction. News today is like an atom bomb. It can explode and destroy worlds. More than your lives or mine . . . more than justice or injustice to any individual is the question of war or peace.

She gave no opinions about the Soviet government, nor did she express many opinions about life in the United States. It is hard to imagine how she lived through the era of Senator Joseph McCarthy and the fear of Communist infiltration that pervaded America. What could she have thought when the *New York Times* reported that the secretary of defense had distributed a pamphlet entitled *How to Spot a Communist* with a list of "danger signals indicating communist beliefs"? Could she have understood the mentality of the secretary of health, education, and welfare, Oveta Culp Hobby, who called a plan for free polio vaccine for children "a back door approach to socialized medicine"?

In 1956 the State Department returned Strong's passport—their right to withhold it on grounds of political beliefs had been declared unconstitutional—and she decided to return to Peking. "In China . . . there is still the faith that ordinary men are greater than the powers of nature. . . . They still hold that victory depends not on the power of weapons but on awakening the consciousness of man. . . ." She was seventy-one years old.

In the internecine struggles of the Communist parties of the world, it is remarkable that Strong was always able to preserve her sources. Somehow, over forty years she maintained the integrity of her position as an American outsider, an observer looking in. If she had been considered an insider she would never have been welcome, as she manifestly was, in Peking or Moscow or Hanoi. No member of a clique in any government survives the ups and downs of rival power factions unless he or she maintains a safe island of neutrality.

Her remarkable career was possible because she was an American, and she never represented herself as anything but an American. The vantage point from which she viewed the Soviet Union, China, and later Vietnam was as an American explorer for whom the unmapped areas of the world were not territorial but political. She was also the fortunate beneficiary of the revolutionary maxim that peoples are distinct from governments; and while the Communists might use all manner of adjectives to describe American imperialism, they went out of their way to make it clear that they never confused the U.S. government with the American people. Even the South Vietnamese delegates at the 1965 Hanoi International Conference ("For Solidarity with the Vietnamese People Against U.S. Imperialist Aggression and for Defense of Peace") assured her that they discriminated between the American people and the U.S. government.

She was now seventy-nine years old but she stayed throughout the conference, interviewed Ho Chi Minh, and wrote with clarity and fervor about the bombings of North Vietnamese villages. Her sources and her skills held out so long that years before there was any mention of American involvement in Laos, she had written a long account describing the strategic relationships of Cambodia and Laos to control of South Vietnam. From the beginnnings of American involvement in Southeast Asia she referred to the "Indochina War." She analyzed American strategy with the help of those who remembered the Japanese domination of Indochina in World War II. The names changed but the strategic points remained the same. She drew on the reporting experience of years and described the napalmed children, the organization of the women guerrilla fighters, the strength of the indigenous forces in South Vietnam. Patiently she wrote of the strength of the Vietnamese and recounted the eloquent words of a Western reporter observing the French withdrawal from Hanoi after their defeat in 1954: "The victor came in sandals, bearing machine-guns on tote-poles; the vanquished left in tanks."

Eventually her aging body overcame her will. She still wrote her newsletters, *Letters from China,* and gave first-hand accounts of the Cultural Revolution and the Red Guards in China. In 1967, at a time when almost all her old friends were vilified by the Red Guards, she was given a red armband and entertained publicly by Mao to make it known that she was not to be molested. She continued to write, but it became more and more difficult. By her last year she could no longer concentrate long enough to put her thoughts on paper. Her friends said that "she could still laugh at a good joke, and got a good deal of pleasure out of a pot of spring blossoms brought to her. She still reacted indignantly to new reports of U.S. duplicity in Laos and U. S. lies on Vietnam, but she was not well enough to write again."

Because of the lack of diplomatic relations between the United States and the People's Republic of China, it was impossible for her to return to her country. But she was planning for the future and in her eighty-fifth year she announced, "When it becomes possible to visit the U.S.A. freely, I intend to do so, and to lecture there about what I have seen in China."

She died before that became possible. It is hard not to have the feeling that we are the losers for not having been able to hear what she had to say. There are few Westerners who have lived the history of modern China, who knew men and women who have become legends, who understood the realities underlying the slogans and clichés.

When she died in 1970 the *New York Times* carried a front-page article on her life, calling her "one of the most prominent Americans living in Asia." They recounted the birthday party Mao had given her when she was eighty, a huge celebration in Peking with many prominent members of the Chinese government in attendance.

The French newspaper *Le Monde* called her one of the most significant journalists of the twentieth century. By her own description "a specialist in social revolution," she was the author of more than thirty books on the development of Socialist revolution throughout the world. She was also a tireless traveler who never wrote a story from a government handout if she could travel to the spot in person.

Ida Pruitt said, "She was first and foremost a newspaperwoman. She thought of herself as a journalist all her life. She never dwelt on the past. She saw the present and the future. She was a doer." She was known in China as Shih Teh-long, "the especially brilliant one," and part of her brilliance was her capacity to keep learning, to never rest with old answers.

Her death in Peking was the end of a long journey from Friend, Nebraska, where she had been born eighty-four years before. During her childhood Benjamin Harrison was president. His wife, Lizzie Lord, was Strong's great-aunt. When Strong died, Richard Nixon was president. The man who had done so much to perpetuate the irrational fear of communism in America considered his greatest accomplishment his reception by China's leaders in Peking in 1972, when the United States rediscovered China. "Victory depends," Anna Louise Strong wrote in 1956 when she went to live in Peking, "not on the power of weapons but on awakening the consciousness of man. . . ."

DOROTHY DAY

BORN: NOVEMBER 8, 1897, BROOKLYN, NEW YORK. FATHER: JOHN
DAY. MOTHER: GRACE SATTERLEE. COMMON-LAW MARRIAGE TO
FORSTER BATTERHAM, 1925. CHILDREN: TAMAR TERESA (1927).

CONVERTED TO CATHOLICISM, 1928. FOUNDER (WITH PETER
MAURIN) OF THE CATHOLIC WORKER MOVEMENT, 1933. EDITOR
OF THE *Catholic Worker*, 1933–   . AUTHOR OF *The Long
Loneliness*, 1952; *On Pilgrimage: The Sixties*, 1972; *Loaves
and Fishes*, 1963.

I have come here to express my sympathy for this act of non-violent revolution, for this act of peaceful sabotage which is not only a revolution against the State but against the alliance of Church and State which has gone on much too long. . . . Only actions such as these will force the Church to speak out when the State has become a murderer. . . . I've been in jail for civil disobedience more often than any of you and I know more clearly than any of you the courage it entails . . . and I know we must hang on to our pacifism in the face of all violence. . . . It's the most difficult thing in the world, and the one that requires most faith.

DOROTHY DAY AT A RALLY FOR
NINE CATHOLICS ON TRIAL IN
CATONSVILLE, MARYLAND, FOR
BURNING SELECTIVE SERVICE
FILES, 1968

In 1972 Dorothy Day wrote in the *Catholic Worker*, "The greatest tribute I can pay to my friend Anna Louise Strong . . . is to say that I will study further the rise of the People's Communes which she wrote of in the letters she sent out these last ten years. It always made me happy to see the postmark *Peking* on the newsletters. . . . The mail service did indeed transcend all national boundaries."

The *Catholic Worker* is a newspaper Dorothy Day began in 1933 with Peter Maurin, and it too has transcended national boundaries. Colman McCarthy, an editor with the *Washington Post*, has called the *Catholic Worker* "an exceptional achievement. Easily it is the only paper in the country to have kept so long to one editorial line, to one typographical tradition and to one price." It is still the same price that it was in 1933, a penny a copy. And it still is the center of a movement dedicated to a Christian Communism—voluntary poverty, feeding the hungry, sheltering the homeless, absolute pacifism, and communal living. Over the years it has attracted many people— intellectuals, political activists, artists, writers, reformed alcoholics, many seeking a life in which spiritual values could be combined with political activism.

James Forest, one of fourteen young men who poured napalm on draft files in Milwaukee in September of 1968, explained that napalm was immorally and illegally destroying lives in Vietnam. The Catholic Church had been silent. He and the others were speaking out in the name of Catholicism and Christianity. "After all," he asked, "what are we taught in the Worker Movement? To let human need control property. To work for a radical change in the social order. To create our own lifestyles. To extend works of mercy into works of peace."

Dorothy Day is a Catholic. But her religion is different from the Catholicism that many of us learned in Sunday school. It is a political Catholicism, a belief that loving God must be transformed into love for people. It is a Catholicism that means helping the poor, protesting the State's infringement on individual liberty, continually seeking personal understanding of who we are, where we've been and where we are going. It is in the tradition of Lucretia Mott's admonition to Elizabeth Stanton that acts, not thoughts, "are the true test of the Christian faith."

A Catholic bishop said, "We think of church history as being made by Popes, but Dorothy Day has transformed the Catholic Church in America more than anyone."

It was not expected to be that way. She was not born Catholic and did not join the Catholic Church until she was in her thirties. The first part of her life was in radical politics.

She divides her life into two parts: the first was a time of experimenting with different political and social causes; the second was devoted to building the Catholic Worker movement. In her autobiography, *The Long Loneliness*, a classic in the tradition of St. Augustine's *Confessions* or Thomas Merton's *Seven Story Mountain*, she writes: "The first twenty-five years were floundering, years of joy and sorrow, it is true, but certainly with a sense of insecurity one hears so much about these days. I did not know in what I believed, though I tried to serve a cause."

Dorothy Day was born in 1897 in Bath Beach, Brooklyn. When she was six years old, her family moved to Berkeley, California, where her father took a job on a newspaper; he was a sportswriter. Her one vivid memory of California was the San Francisco earthquake, "an event which threw us out of our complacent happiness into a world of catastrophe." Rather than fear or terror at the havoc the earthquake had wrought she recalled "the joy of doing good, of sharing whatever we had with others."

Her father sold all their furniture and belongings and moved the family to Chicago. For a while they were in tight economic circumstances. It was the first time they didn't have a servant, and her father had trouble finding another job.

> I was much ashamed of the house in which we lived, and used to walk down the street with my little school friends who lived on Ellis Avenue and duck into the apartment house on 37th Street, pretending to live in that more respectable building instead of in a flat over a saloon. . . .

Her father was originally from Tennessee. Although he was a sportswriter for most of his life—he was a founder of the Hialeah racetrack in Florida and later worked for a racing newspaper in New York—he occasionally tried to write short stories or a novel. He was extremely proud to have made the *Saturday Evening Post* before he died. The techniques and traditions of journalism were a strong influence in the family, and Day traces her own journalistic skills back to Chicago. "We [her brothers and sister] started writing newspapers when I was ten years old. . . ." There were no picture books, detective stories, or "trash" allowed in the house. Dorothy and her three brothers and sister were not allowed to have friends in because it would interfere with their father's privacy. There were few distractions or diversions. She remembers "sad summer afternoons when there was nothing to do and suddenly everything palled and life was dull and uninteresting. . . . There were times when my sister and I turned to housework out of sheer boredom." It was not until she and her sister had grown up and left home that they had their first serious conversations with their father. "We children did not know him very well, so we stood in awe of him, only learning to talk to him after we had left home and he began to treat us as friends— casual friends it is true, since he was always impatient with our ideas and hated the radical movement which both my sister and I were involved in later."

Her mother, Grace Satterlee, was one of the first women trained as a stenographer, and Dorothy says, "I have a picture of her in a high-collar blouse, and long skirt, sitting on a stool." When Dorothy later became interested in workers and working-class movements, her mother told her about her work in a shirt factory in Poughkeepsie as a girl. She did not have the same romantic view of "the workers" as her daughter did.

In Chicago Dorothy went to public schools and read voluminously on her own. She was deeply moved by Dostoyevsky's *The Brothers Karamazov*, and she was fascinated with *Memoirs of a Revolutionist* by the Russian anarchist Prince Peter Kropotkin. He, like Lester Ward and other social critics opposed to Social Darwinism, believed that higher forms of animal life developed on the basis of cooperation rather than on the principle of "the survival of the fittest." She was also influenced by the writings of another revolutionary anarchist, Vera Figner, a woman who spent twenty years in solitary confinement in a Russian prison for her part in terrorist activities.

But the book that made the most significant impression was Upton Sinclair's *The Jungle*, a book exposing the meat-packing industry of Chicago and the slum poverty of Chicago's West Side. That novel moved her to walk rather than think, and she explored the streets of the slaughterhouse section of the city while she took her baby brother John on his daily walk. Instead of repelling her, slum poverty gave her an insight into her future vocation.

> Though my only experience of the destitute was in books, the very fact that *The Jungle* was about Chicago where I lived, whose streets I walked, made me feel that . . . my life was to be linked to theirs; . . . I had received a call, a vocation, a direction to my life.

At the age of sixteen she received a Hearst scholarship to go to the University of Illinois in Urbana. She subjected herself to such austerity—going without meals, working at several jobs at once, keeping long, exhausting hours—that she experienced an overwhelming period of homesickness and depression. During her first year at the university she joined the Socialist party, which turned out to be quite dull, and made few friends. During her second year she wrote an article for the college newspaper on the experience of going hungry, which brought her to the attention of Rayna Prohme, a brilliant, wealthy fellow student who was at the center of a group of aspiring writers. "The only benefits those two years at college brought me," she wrote her brother, "was my friendship with Rayna and my own sense of complete independence." Rayna invited Dorothy to share a room with her, paid the rent, and helped her in many ways. Dorothy was profoundly grateful for Rayna's generosity, and her sophomore year became more of a youthful college experience—attending lectures by prominent Socialists and activists, listening to readings by poets such as Edgar Lee Masters, John Masefield, Carl Sandburg, and Vachel Lindsay.

Dorothy continued to write, and Rayna enthusiastically encouraged her. Endowed with exceptional intellectual abilities, both were propelled toward what George Bernard Shaw has called "a clear comprehension of life in the light of an intelligible theory."

Rayna found her theory in communism. She later became an agent for Mikhail Borodin in China, smuggled Sun Yat-sen's widow out of China to Moscow in 1926, and was nursed through the last stages of encephalitis by Anna Louise Strong. At the time Rayna Prohme died, she was just about to enter the Lenin Institute, an act described by Vincent Sheehan as comparable to taking religious vows.

After her sophomore year Dorothy left the university and moved to New York. It was 1916, a year before the United States entered World War I.

Her first months in New York were extremely difficult even though her family was there; her father had a job on the *Morning Telegraph*, a horse-racing newspaper. She was no longer able to fit into the family, yet she had no other life that was hers. Day described that period as a time of "great suffering. . . . I found no friends; I had no work; I was separated from my fellows. . . . My own silence, the feeling that I had no one to talk to overwhelmed me so that my very throat was constricted. . . . I wanted to weep my loneliness away."

Eventually she got a job on the *Call*, a Socialist newspaper, which hired her for five dollars a week. She began to learn that helping the poor can be complicated. While covering strikes, pickets, bread riots, marches to City Hall, community demands for housing, schools, health, she learned that each political group had its own program for the poor. There were constant squabbles among the Socialists, Anarchists, the American Federation of Labor (AFL), and the Industrial Workers of the World (IWW), each with their separate constituencies and leaders. In the political turmoil of Greenwich Village life she saw or heard many of the leading radicals of the day, like Elizabeth Gurley Flynn, the celebrated "Rebel Girl" of the IWW. "I heard Gurley Flynn, as she was called, speak at meetings for the Mesabi Iron Range Strikers and I was thrilled by her fire and vision." She heard Alexander Berkman and Emma Goldman, the famous Anarchists; Bill Haywood and Arturo Giovanitti of the IWW. She interviewed Trotsky before he went back to Russia in one of his innumerable disguises.

Within a year she had moved to another paper, the *Masses*, acclaimed as one of the liveliest radical monthlies in the country and the center for a group of writers, artists, intellectuals, reporters, and various other Greenwich Village bohemians. The literary crowd that centered around the *Masses* included such figures as Malcolm Cowley, John Dos Passos, Eugene O'Neill, actors from the Provincetown playhouse, and a number of artists. An often told but apocryphal story is that Dorothy Day was the model for Marcel Duchamps's painting, *Nude Descending a Staircase*. She did, however, model for art classes.

She may have been part of an avant-garde crowd, but she quickly learned that ideas were separate from actions. Claude McKay, the black poet, frequently went to the same Village restaurant as many of the *Masses* editors and frequently heard them refer to "niggers." Once, he remembered, a young woman got up and told a particular editor that if he used the term again, she'd slap his face. The young woman was Dorothy Day.

She considered herself a radical and she was part of a politically conscious crowd, but looking back she admits to a certain lack of honesty with herself. The real motivation for her political involvement, she believed, came from "much ambition and much self-seeking. . . . I was not a good radical."

Her friends were Communists, Socialists, and Anarchists. She was impatient with the theoretical squabbles among the Socialists, the doctrinal controversies among the Communists. She liked anarchism philosophically but felt it was a philosophy for an elite not for the masses. She joined the union Mother Jones had helped to found, the IWW—a loose movement of blacks, immigrants, and migrant laborers who tried to revolutionize industrial capitalism and American society. A month before her twentieth birthday she was in Madison Square Garden, singing the worker's hymn celebrating the Russian Revolution, convinced along with many others that salvation for the wretched of the world would come only through a workers' revolution.

It was a naive hope. On April 6, 1917, the United States entered World War I against Germany and the Central Powers.

Since it was the Anarchist and Socialist publications that were most skeptical of the war effort and cynical about a "war to end all wars," they were harassed and eventually suppressed. Day's editor at the *Masses,* Max Eastman, was twice brought to trial for impeding the war effort. She was called to testify. Pacifists, antiwar Socialists, war resisters, alleged German sympathizers were persecuted or beaten, and some were murdered. One of Dorothy's friends at the *Masses* was the artist Hugo Gellert. His younger brother was put in an army prison for refusing to put on a uniform, and he never came out. The army claimed he committed suicide, but prison deaths of war resisters were common and the causes suspicious.

Meetings of liberal political groups were raided. In Montana a crippled IWW organizer was dragged from his bed by masked men and hanged. The Justice Department had ransacked the halls and headquarters of IWW offices throughout the country.

In Washington, D.C., women from all over America exercised their right to petition for redress of grievances. They picketed President Wilson at the White House on behalf of woman's right to vote. They carried banners which called the president "Kaiser Wilson," and superpatriots, some in military uniform, physically attacked the women while the police stood by. On June 22, 1917, the police began arresting not the assailants but their female victims. They were violating no law and the only charge ever filed against them was that of obstructing sidewalk traffic. Yet sixty of them, including Alice Paul and other leaders of the National Woman's party, a militant feminist organization, were put in Occoquan, a prison facility known for its cruel and inhumane treatment of prisoners, and held for thirty days without being arraigned. The rights of free speech and petition were not upheld, and the feminists were the first victims of the war. Dissent would not be tolerated in wartime.

Dorothy Day was among the demonstrators and was one of those arrested. She was kicked to the floor by guards and beaten before being flung into a cell with one of the leaders, who was handcuffed to the bars. The prisoners were threatened with the whipping post, bloodhounds, and other punishments. They were not allowed to see their lawyers, and when, to keep their protest before the public, the women began a hunger strike they were brutally force fed. One historian described the treatment of the women prisoners at Occoquan as "a miniature reign of terror."

Many older radicals, schooled in a European tradition which separated political crimes from felonies, lived in the continual expectation of going to prison. If they had not done time themselves, they had friends who had and were therefore emotionally and intellectually prepared for prison life—the tension, the ultimate sense of coercion, the inability to experience any sense of free choice, the regimentation, the absence of interpersonal relationships—everything that strips a person of his or her humanity. Since Day was neither an experienced radical nor a professional criminal, she was completely overwhelmed by prison.

I lost all consciousness of any cause. I had no sense of being a radical, making a protest against a government. . . . I lost all feeling of my own identity. I reflected on the desolation of poverty, of destitution, of sickness and sin. That I would be free again after thirty days meant nothing to me. I would never be free again.

When she and the other demonstrators were finally released after weeks in jail, Day returned to New York to find that she was unable to pick up where she had left off. Refusing to work for anything that would assist in the war effort and overwhelmed by what she called "the tragic aspect of life," she became a nurse in King's County Hospital in Brooklyn and worked there until the end of the war.

When the war ended in 1918 Day, like many American writers and disillusioned intellectuals, fled to Europe. However, she did not stay to become one of the "lost generation" of expatriates. She returned to America in time for the Red Scare and the Palmer Raids, which were the peacetime sequel to wartime repression.

Americans in general seemed to find little incongruity in fighting a war for liberty by suppressing individual rights; they had grown accustomed to repression. In 1919, when many employers refused to raise wages to match price increases, workers from coast to coast participated in a series of strikes—3,630 of them to be exact. The Seattle General Strike in which Anna Louise Strong had participated was only the beginning. The strikes, which involved over four million workers, together with a number of Anarchist bombings, were taken as proof of a Red attempt to take over.

The attorney general, A. Mitchell Palmer, who had been appointed by Woodrow Wilson, took the initiative in a crusade by the Justice Department against the labor movement, radical political groups, left-wing publications, blacks, strikers, foreigners, Socialists—any group that called for change. Palmer had been a former head of the Pinkerton Detective Agency and had compiled extensive files on dissenters, Socialists, especially on labor organizers. In a nationwide series of raids of offices, homes, and boarding houses, Palmer's agents rounded up twenty five hundred "aliens" and "members of the Communist party" for deportation. Dorothy Day had her second experience in jail as a result of a Palmer "Red raid."

She was in an IWW boarding house in Chicago when the Palmer agents invaded. Assuming that any women in the house were prosti-

tutes (the woman Day was visiting had once been in the profession),
the agents arrested Day and booked her as a prostitute. She was
stripped, searched for drugs, dressed in prison clothes, and thrown
into a cell with prostitutes. It was a different prison experience from
her first.

There were no schoolteachers from Connecticut calling out commands for courage and resistance. A drug addict went through withdrawal in the next cell, screaming in agony and hitting her head
against the bars for the entire night. Even more important was that
there was no reason for Day's being there; it was only her own
innocence that had landed her in jail.

> It was as ugly an experience as I ever wish to pass through, and
> a useful one. I do not think that ever again, no matter of what I
> am accused, can I suffer more than I did then of shame and
> regret, and self-contempt. Not only because I had been caught,
> found out, branded, publicly humiliated, but because of my
> own consciousness that I deserved it.
>
> When Eugene Debs wrote, as he did in his innocence, that as
> long as there were men in prison he was one with them, they
> were noble words and went down in history. But I have always
> felt that he could never have suffered, noble and gentle man
> that he was, the same shame and self-contempt that I felt and
> that I felt in common with the prisoners with whom I was
> confined.

Some of her cellmates told her that the prison matron ran a house
of prostitution and used some of the women prisoners on busy Saturday nights. "Why," Day began to wonder, "were prostitutes prosecuted in some cases and in others respected and fawned on? . . . Why
were some termed criminals and others good businessmen? What
was right and wrong? What was good and evil?" What, she wondered, really constituted criminal behavior? Why were prostitutes
arrested, but not their customers?

Such questions were not easily answered by political or economic
theory. After she finally got out of jail she began to realize how
much of her time had been spent in talking and theorizing about
helping the poor, and how little in actually doing it. She said of
herself and her friends that "we helped others . . . but we did not
deprive ourselves in order to help others. We had no philosophy of

poverty. We were outraged by injustices and . . . revolted at the idea of a doled out charity. . . . The true meaning of the word we did not know."

The national hysteria against Reds and aliens and dissenters continued. Day went to Chicago and held a series of jobs, working as a secretary, a clerk in Montgomery Ward's, a librarian, a cashier, and as an assistant to the editor of a Communist monthly called the *Liberator*. The climate toward leftist publications was so hostile that the editor of the magazine, Robert Minor, told Day to end all his letters with the information, "At the moment of this writing there is a man standing in the doorway across the street who has been shadowing me for the past week."

She left Chicago for a newspaper job in New Orleans. Her first assignment was to work as a taxi dancer in a cheap dance hall on Canal Street and write a story on the lives of the women who worked there. In New Orleans she learned that A. & C. Boni would publish her first novel, *The Eleventh Virgin*, and that the movie rights to it had been sold for $5,000, a small fortune in those days. Day quit her job, moved back to New York, and bought a cottage on Staten Island, then a quite rural artists' and writers' colony. It was 1924 and she was twenty-six years old.

On Staten Island she moved into another bohemian literary circle. One of her closest friends, Peggy Baird, had married Malcolm Cowley, and a stream of talented writers came to their house on the island as weekend guests.

Day had been seriously involved over the years with a number of men—a newspaperman in Chicago; Mike Gold, a leader in the American Communist party; a writer with whom she had traveled in Europe—but none of these liaisons resulted in an enduring relationship. While living on Staten Island, she did meet a man who took a permanent place in her life. "The man I loved, with whom I entered into a common-law marriage, was an anarchist, an Englishman by descent, and a biologist."

Forster Batterham made gauges during the week in New York City, but his consuming passion was ecology, the interrelatedness of human beings and the environment. An Anarchist, he had no use for any of the established institutions of society—Church, State, or marriage—and in the bohemian environment in which they lived, there was no need to formalize a marriage. Batterham moved into Day's cottage, and they lived together for four years. It was an extremely happy period for her. She loved the sea and the life they lived on the island. During the winter they shared an apartment with her sister in Manhattan.

In March 1927, when she was twenty-nine, she had her first and only child, Tamar Teresa. The birth of the child was a dividing line in her life. She found it to be a wonderfully joyous event, but, as for Charlotte Gilman, it marked a life crisis, an urgent need to reevaluate her past. It was a moment of self-recognition that she had glimpsed years before when she had heard Eugene O'Neill recite "The Hound of Heaven" in a Greenwich Village cafe—an undeniable need "to pause in the mad rush of living and remember my first beginning and my last end." The entry of a new life into the world made her acutely aware of the finite limits of her own.

She began to feel that it was too frightening to take responsibility for a child in a godless world. She began reading books about philosophical and spiritual questions, such as William James's *The Varieties of Religious Experience*, which surveyed the infinite ways in which people in all societies and civilizations have coped with mystical faith. She reread *The Brothers Karamazov*, and she read *The Imitation of Christ* by Thomas à Kempis. She told Dwight Macdonald that "it was St. Augustine's *Confessions*, Dostoevsky and William James that turned me on religiously." She said in her autobiography: "One afternoon as I sat on the beach, I read a book of James's essays and came on these lines:

Poverty is indeed the strenuous life—without brass bands or uniforms or hysteric popular applause or lies or circumlocutions; and when one sees the way in which wealth-getting enters as an ideal into the very bone and marrow of our generation, one wonders whether the revival of the belief that poverty is a worthy religious vocation may not be the transformation of military courage, and the spiritual reform which our time stands most in need of. Among us English-speaking peoples especially do the praises of poverty need once more to [be] boldly sung. We have grown literally afraid to be poor. We despise anyone who elects to be poor in order to simplify and save his inner life. If he does not join the general scramble, we deem him spiritless and lacking in ambition. We have lost the power even of imagining what the ancient realization of poverty could have meant; the liberation from material attachments, the unbought soul, the paying our way by what we are and not by what we have. . . ."

It was a direction that could only take her farther away from her atheist husband. The conflict brought about a crisis. At one point the tension was so great that she constantly felt a great weight on her chest and would wake up in the middle of the night unable to breathe. She finally went to the hospital to have tests. The doctors told her it was nerves.

The schism between her spiritual life and her daily existence became so great that she finally converted to Catholicism and had the baby baptized in the Catholic Church. That act set in motion events that were beyond her control. A practicing Catholic was out of place in a bohemian community. She realized she had to leave not only her husband but her past.

At the age of thirty, Dorothy Day moved into Manhattan to begin the second part of her life. Never did a new spiritual life begin with less clarity. On August 15, 1929, less than three months before the Wall Street crash, she received a job offer as a screenwriter for Pathé studios in Hollywood. She left for California with her daughter in hope "of living a stimulating creative life with time to read and study and write." She found that she couldn't save a penny, she had no productive work, and she was "lonely, deadly lonely."

I was to find out then, as I found out so many times, over and over again, that women especially are social beings, who are not content with just husband and family, but must have a community, a group, an exchange with others. A child is not enough. A husband and children, no matter how busy one may be kept by them, are not enough. Young and old, even in the busiest years of our lives, we women especially are victims of the long loneliness.

When her contract ran out she went to Mexico where she might have stayed if Tamar had not become sick. In May 1930 she was back in New York. She found a job as a library researcher, and she shared an apartment with her brother John and his new wife. She sent Tamar to live with her sister, Della, and her family in the country, spending only the weekends with her daughter. In her spare time Day tried to write another novel, and she wrote free-lance articles for a number of magazines, including the *Catholic Reporter* and *Commonweal*, both Catholic magazines.

Her Catholicism was not a public affair. She never thought in terms of Catholics acting together for social and political causes. Her religious faith was not rooted in the bloated bureaucracy of the Catholic Church but in the ideas of men and women who had described deep spiritual experiences. Her faith—despite the inward-looking nature of the Church—was always outward-turning. When one priest told her that it was too late to do anything in the world except prepare for death, she changed priests.

What little formal religion there had been in her family was Episcopalian and that only because the local Episcopalian minister needed her brothers to sing in the choir. But in her autobiography Day recognized that many of her religious impulses came from childhood. She had once barged into a friend's house looking for her. The friend's mother, who was on her knees, turned to tell Dorothy that "Kathryn and the children had all gone to the store," and then went on with her praying. "I felt a burst of love toward Mrs. Barrett that I have never forgotten. . . ." Another came from an Irish girl, Mary Harrington, who first told Day about the life of a saint, a spiritual adventure that she had never even dreamed existed.

Her perceptions of Christianity—charity, helping the poor, sharing with others, pacifism—were at odds with the realities of a Church which owned enormous amounts of property, had huge financial investments in the capitalist system, and more often than not associated itself with economic privilege and power. Despite the bourgeois Catholicism she saw around her, she believed that it was the Church of the poor, of the masses. Like Mother Jones, she retained those parts of Catholic history which carried the story of helping the poor and the weak—giving strength to the beggars, the crippled, the rejects and unused of society. The problem was how to find a bridge between the faith she professed and the life she saw around her.

In 1932 there were over twelve million unemployed people in the United States. There was no such thing as unemployment insurance or Social Security pensions, no welfare for families who were unable to pay rent or buy food. The Great Depression was going into its fourth year when the Communist party and one of its affiliates organized out-of-work men and women to march on Washington to petition for relief. The Hunger March was to illustrate that President Herbert Hoover's bromides about good old American self-reliance and character were not going to fill the stomachs of hungry children.

The politicians and the capitalist press played up the march as the first stage in a Communist takeover. The straggling, hungry marchers who arrived in Washington on a cold December day were billed in feverish editorials as "shock troops in the class struggle."

Day had lost touch with most of her old radical friends, but Mike Gold often dropped in to see her. He was working on the preparations for the march. She decided to report on the Hunger March for the Jesuit periodical *America* and for *Commonweal*.

When she arrived in Washington she saw a ragged, harassed group of men and women camped out in the streets of the city, surrounded by an army of police and troops armed with machine guns, sawed-off shotguns, tear-gas bombs, nightsticks, and rubber hoses. The marchers had been denied a permit to proceed down Pennsylvania Avenue to the Capitol and were forced to remain in the streets—without heat, sanitary facilities, food, or water—for two days while the question of allowing American citizens to petition their government to take measures so that they and their children might not starve to death was debated.

Day traveled with Mary Heaton Vorse, a veteran labor reporter. Vorse had reported on Mother Jones's activities during the Great Steel Strike of 1919, and she was one of the few reporters that Mother Jones respected. Day and Vorse found that the only organized groups to support the demands of the marchers—demands that we now consider the basic rights of citizens—were women's organizations, pacifist groups, Quakers, and a few other religious groups. There were no Catholics supporting the Hunger Marchers. As Day watched the army of the poor straggle down Pennsylvania Avenue she thought:

Far dearer in the sight of God, perhaps, are these hungry ragged ones, than all those smug well-fed Christians who sit in their homes, cowering in fear of the Communist menace. . . . How little, how puny my work had been since becoming a Catholic. How self-centered, how ingrown, how lacking in a sense of community.

That was soon to change. Five months later she published the first issue of the *Catholic Worker*, a newspaper that would continue without interruption up to the present. The idea for the paper came from Peter Maurin, who was waiting to see her when she returned from Washington, about whom she said, "Peter, the French peasant, whose spirit and ideas will dominate . . . the rest of my life."

Peter Maurin was a drifting reformer who talked to anyone who would listen in a thick French accent. He was at least twenty years older than Dorothy Day, and he had worked his way across the United States and Canada doing everything from stringing telephone lines to digging sewers. He was eager to meet Day because he had read some of her articles in *Commonweal* and felt that she was the person to promulgate his ideas on radical action in accordance with Christian values.

During his itinerant life he had never stopped reading and studying, and according to people who knew him, he was a total intellectual: only ideas mattered. When Dorothy's brother John found Maurin at the door of his apartment, he thought Maurin was an unbalanced Anarchist; Maurin looked like a Bowery bum. But the relationship that grew out of the meeting with Dorothy was that of teacher and pupil. "I revered him and listened to him as one would to an old *starets* or guru," Dorothy explained.

Maurin explained his program to her. It was utopian, Christian communism. He offered a synthesis of radical action and Christian faith, a joining of ideas that was precisely what Day had speculated on during the Hunger March. Why must one be an atheist to be a political radical?

Maurin's most compelling idea was for a newspaper. He believed that journalists should influence the time in which they write, that there was no such thing as objective reporting. Journalists had to be propagandists and agitators. He wanted Day to start a newspaper called the *Catholic Radical*, which would carry his Christian political theory. He reduced his ideas to a rhythmic form he called Easy

Essays, which were actually more complicated than they looked. Communism for example he explained in this way:

> The name Communism
> does not come from Karl Marx
> it comes from Proudhon
> Proudhon was a Frenchman
> and France is a country with a
> Catholic tradition
> And Catholic tradition
> gave to Proudhon
> the word Communism
> The name commune exists
> in French history
> Since the 11th century. . . .

Day liked the idea but wanted to call the paper the *Catholic Worker*. Within four months the first issue was distributed on May 1, 1933, in Union Square. It was called the *Catholic Worker*, and in a sense the newspaper became the novel of social significance that Day had always wanted to write. From the very first issue it had great personal style, gave much attention to the details of people's lives, and had the warm appealing quality of a good novel. It was a personal paper, and the ideas that formed the basis of its philosophy were explained through the acts of real people. For over forty years those ideas have remained intact—voluntary poverty, feeding the hungry, sheltering the homeless, absolute resistance to war, and communal living.

Throughout the years of Day's collaboration with Maurin, he gave her a philosophical basis and confidence in her ability to act. He was, however, hopeless in dealing with practical realities. When she asked him how they would raise money for the paper, he told her to read the lives of the saints. "In the history of the saints," he told her, "capital was raised by prayer. God sends you what you need when you need it." Maurin was the spirit of the Catholic Worker movement, and Dorothy, with her skills as a journalist, politician, and administrator was the glue that held it all together. Ammon Hennacy, a Catholic Anarchist and an editor of the *Catholic Worker*, wrote, "Without her [Day's] patience and knowledge, the *Catholic Worker* could not have lasted six months. She knew what an issue was and she knew how to write it up so as to be understood by the reader."

The first editorial announcing its purpose is still dramatic reading:

> It's time there was a Catholic paper printed for the unemployed.
>
> The fundamental aim of most radical sheets is the conversion of its readers to radicalism and atheism.
>
> Is it not possible to protest, to expose, to complain, to point out abuses and demand reforms without desiring the overthrow of religion?
>
> In an attempt to popularize and make known the encyclicals of the Popes in regard to social justice and the program put forth by the Church for the "reconstruction of the social order" this news sheet, the *Catholic Worker* is started.

From the beginning its growth was phenomenal. It was a penny a copy; it is still a penny a copy. Many issues were given away. People handed it out on street corners, and college students distributed it to strikers. Circulation grew by word of mouth. People recognized that here was something that could make a difference in the way they approached political and economic problems. It broke down their sense of isolation and made them part of a family.

By 1939 the circulation was one hundred thousand, reaching practically every politically or socially conscious Catholic in the country. Abigail McCarthy, the former wife of Senator Eugene McCarthy, was a student in St. Catherine's college in Minnesota when the newspaper first started to appear in the Midwest. It made her completely rethink religious principles. "The Catholic Worker movement was a whole new way of looking at things," she said. "[I think] it was the single biggest influence on Catholic intellectuals in the 1930s. . . ."

Much to the dismay of the dean of St. Catherine's, Abigail and some of her friends handed out copies of the *Catholic Worker* to the strikers at the Ford Motor assembly plant, quite a radical act for "St. Catherine's girls." When World War II began Abigail worked at a Catholic Worker house in St. Paul, one of some thirty-five Catholic Worker houses that had grown up across the country.

Catholic Worker houses became a focus for action by Catholics on behalf of the workers. People who had never before involved themselves in a public demonstration found themselves collecting clothes, joining picket lines, feeding strikers, organizing workers. Day traveled all over the country as a reporter and as an activist. In 1936 she went to Detroit to report on the sit-down strike out of which came the United Auto Workers Union. She fed pickets at a textile workers strike in Lowell, Massachusetts. When the CIO (Congress of Industrial Organizations) was trying to get support for organizing the steel workers, Day went to Pittsburgh and visited every liberal or labor priest in the city to get his support. In 1937 the Catholic Trades Unionists, the first Catholic labor group, was organized at the Catholic Worker offices in New York.

It has been said that the Catholic Worker movement changed the direction of Catholicism in America, but the story of its influence in the labor movement is still to be written. The effect of the Catholic Worker movement cannot be evaluated until we know more about the role of the Catholic Church in inhibiting the growth of a politically conscious labor movement. The reason Mother Jones was buried in Mount Olive Cemetery in Illinois is that it was a nonsectarian cemetery, founded for two strikers killed in a labor struggle. The Catholic Church would not allow them to be buried in consecrated ground. For the millions of immigrants who came to work in America's mines and industries, the Catholic Church was the only stable cultural element in their lives. The Church opposed the "godless" Socialist or Communist union organizers. The union had to take second place to the Church. The Catholic Worker movement made an incalculable contribution by joining Communism and Catholicism.

The vitality of the Catholic Worker movement sprang from its authentic sense of community and its ability to provide real help when all other institutions in the society failed. There are hundreds of stories like that of Herbert Joyce, who hitchhiked to New York from West Virginia with his two-and-a-half-year-old son. He arrived on a winter night in the midst of the Depression, when every bed in the Catholic Worker house was filled. His wife had run off. He had no job, no money, no place to go. Not wanting to send him away in the cold with the little boy, Day said she would go with him until he found a place.

They went to the police, the hospitals, an orphanage, a social agency. No person and no institution was equipped to help a penniless, unemployed man with a baby. After hours of futile pleas for help, she took him back to the Catholic Worker house, gave him her bed, wrapped the baby in blankets, and moved in with someone else.

The Catholic Worker houses developed organically as more and more people became involved in putting out the paper and distributing food and clothing to the unemployed. The first house was on Mott Street in the heart of Chinatown in New York.

As usual Maurin had a theory for what to everyone else was a natural development. For him it was a house of hospitality, modeled on the religious hospices of the Middle Ages, where anyone could find food and shelter in time of need. Similar houses of hospitality sprang up in other cities, and it became a model for others to follow. No matter what seemed to evolve, Peter Maurin had a theory for it. Evening lectures with speakers became round-table discussions. When the Workers bought their first farm, in Easton, Pennsylvania, and began a communal farming venture, Maurin called it an "agronomic university." This ideological base of the movement should not be underestimated, for it was what allowed the ideas to spread and to take form in different places.

When Paul Moore, who is now the Episcopal Bishop of New York, graduated from the Episcopal Seminary, he and his wife, Jenny, decided to take an assignment in a poor black section of Jersey City. According to Jenny Moore, "Dorothy was very influential in our decision to move there and on the way we saw our lives. Our house in Jersey City was very Catholic Workerish." They had met Day when she came to speak to a group of seminary students. "She was like a wind from another land," Jenny Moore recalled, "very exciting and a little frightening."

When World War II was declared the political climate changed dramatically. Workers were called upon to put patriotism first. The position of the *Catholic Worker* did not change. Dorothy wrote a moving editorial in 1939, calling on the workers to resist war:

> No matter how the legislative tide turns, no matter what laws are passed abridging the neutrality of the United States, you hold it in your power to keep our country aloof from a European war. This is our appeal, that you use your power as workers to refuse to manufacture or transport articles of war that are intended for foreign nations, warring or neutral. That you serve notice on your employers, in organized fashion, that

you will have no part of such blood money, and that you will strike if necessary to maintain your position.

She helped to organize the Association of Catholic Conscientious Objectors, the only group in the country that provided the opportunity for Catholic pacifists to carry out alternative service.

The ideas of the Catholic Worker movement have had an odd staying power, resting dormant and then germinating in unexpected ways. The size of the movement expanded or contracted according to the times. Stanley Vichnewski, who has been with Dorothy Day since the very beginning, recalled when a young man named John Kennedy came down to the Worker house in the late 1940s on Mott Street. "I remember distinctly how bewildered he was at the sight of the poverty and the misery of the place."

Fifteen years later another young man, Michael Harrington, came to the *Catholic Worker* as the editor of the paper. His work there formed the basis of a book called *The Other America*, one of the first nationally recognized books to outline the depth and extent of poverty in affluent America. In the early sixties the book came to the attention of President John Kennedy, and this chronicle of the plight of the poor in America marked the beginning of a "war on poverty," a war which unfortunately gave way to a real war on the people of Vietnam.

The Vietnam conflict produced a core of Catholic radicalism that had never been seen in this country. Priests in white collars demonstrated in front of the Pentagon, poured napalm on draft files, encouraged men to burn draft cards. Nuns spoke out against American imperialism in South America. The dissenters were supported and held up by the tradition of the Catholic Worker movement. The spirit of that tradition was stated very well by Father David Kirk of Emmaus House who described himself as "a spiritual stepchild of Dorothy Day," and Emmaus House as "a stepchild of the Catholic Worker Movement, which was the cradle of Catholic radicalism in this country." He continued, explaining how important it was that people understand that Christianity is political, "Since the thirties *The Catholic Worker* has used the word revolution in its non-violent sense. The Catholic Worker Movement brought about social change by forming little groups . . . small communities that challenged the values of the existing order."

In November 1972 Dorothy Day was seventy-five years old. During a television documentary on her life and her work she refused to allow any glamour to be attached to her life and her cause.

> The great city of New York just a short month ago came into our door on First Street with a poor little woman who was covered with lice from head to foot from sleeping out in filth in broken-down buildings, with some loathsome sores and, to be very indelicate, a prolapsed rectum, covered with filth, excrement, urine and head-lice and body-lice and they sent her to us—the police, the Brooklyn police. This is how extreme we can get, this happens over and over again in the history of the *Catholic Worker*. Why not take her into the Woman's Municipal Lodging House? . . . There is no room. Why not take her to Bellevue Hospital with her physical condition? . . . St. Vincent's hospital?
>
> I don't know how over the years you can accumulate such a tremendous saga of rescue; but in the City of New York, the greatest, richest city in the world we have to bring in this woman from the streets.

In less than a minute she had forcefully conveyed a message that is central to the Catholic Worker movement: the failure of government, the failure of the State to provide for individual needs. The solution to society's problems must begin with the individual. "We begin with ourselves and give what we have, and the movement spreads."

Many people have called the Catholic Worker movement a scandal, after seeing the reality of the poverty, the dirt, the smells, the utter destitution. In the last quarter of the twentieth century there is nothing romantic in the poverty of the Bowery, nothing remotely political can be visualized emanating from the human wreckage of New York—the alcoholics, the mentally disturbed, the mumbling men and women with their shopping bags, the refugees from the single-room-occupancy hotels. Yet in the starkest terms it is possible for an outsider to see the most elemental needs of society—food, shelter, community—and how monumentally American society has failed to provide them for so many of its members.

In the best sense of the word, this is a scandal, and that may be why it has such an effect on people. Dorothy Day has been criticized for romanticizing poverty, for refusing to criticize the Catholic

Church bureaucracy, and for stressing an impractical back-to-the-land movement. Many of the Catholic radicals she helped to create disagree with her refusal to challenge Church tradition in areas such as abortion, birth control, liturgy, or unquestioning obedience to Church hierarchy.

Her survival has depended on appealing to the radicalism of Christian values rather than threatening the political institution of the Church. Publicly she has said, "If the Chancery ordered me to stop publishing the *Catholic Worker* tomorrow I would." But in private she said that she would pack everything up, go across the river out of the Cardinal's jurisdiction, and start publishing again.

Dorothy Day has been described as a woman who has had more influence on the Catholic Church than anyone in this century. She is known throughout the world. The Catholic Worker house in New York and the farm in Tivoli, New York, receive a stream of visitors from all over the country and all over the world. Many of the people who have written about her refer to her as a saint. And she may be but perhaps in the terms that William James used to describe Saint Teresa of Avila: "She had a powerful intellect of the practical order. She wrote admirable descriptive psychology, possessed a will equal to any emergency, great talent for politics and business, a buoyant disposition and a first-rate literary style."

When a television reporter asked Day whether she had sympathy with what women were trying to do today in the woman's movement and in politics, she answered, "If I stayed long enough in one place . . . I would be very interested in local politics . . . I think that's very necessary. I think that when it comes down to it . . . the state should be a community of communities. . . ." Then very deftly she switched the conversation and read this quotation from William James:

> I am done with great things and big things, great institutions and big success, and I am for those tiny invisible molecular moral forces that work from individual to individual, creeping through the crannies of the world like so many rootlets, or like the capillary oozing of water, yet which, if you give them time, will rend the hardest monuments of man's pride.

FANNIE
LOU
HAMER

———————◆◆◆◆◆———————

BORN: OCTOBER 6, 1917, MONTGOMERY COUNTY, MISSISSIPPI.
DIED: MARCH 14, 1977, RULEVILLE, MISSISSIPPI. FATHER: JIM
TOWNSEND. MOTHER: LOU ELLA BRAMLETT. MARRIED: PERRY,
"PAP" HAMER, 1944. ADOPTED CHILDREN: DOROTHY JEAN (D.
1967), VIRGIE LEE. VICE-CHAIRMAN, MISSISSIPPI FREEDOM DEMO-
CRATIC PARTY CANDIDATE FOR CONGRESS, 1964; CIVIL RIGHTS
LEADER; FOUNDER OF FREEDOM FARM AND OTHER AGRICULTURAL
COOPERATIVES IN SUNFLOWER COUNTY, MISSISSIPPI.

The Old South! History and romance faithfully preserved. Enchanting antebellum homes, historic parks and battlefields and a storied past reminiscent of hoop skirts, steamboats on the Ol'Man River and cotton plantation. This is Mississippi!

Mississippi News and Views,
JUNE 1964

They beat me until my body was hard, 'til I couldn't bend my fingers or get up. . . . That's how I got this blood clot in my left eye—the sight's nearly gone now. And my kidney was injured from the blows they gave me in the back. . . . I was in jail when Medgar Evers was murdered.

FANNIE LOU HAMER,
ABOUT WINONA, MISSISSIPPI, 1963

Fannie Lou Hamer walked into history in August 1964 when she stepped before the national television cameras at the Democratic National Convention. An African American women with a deep southern accent and imposing physical presence, she appeared before the credentials committee to challenge the legitimacy of the all-white Mississippi delegation.

A poor sharecropper, one of twenty children, a woman who did not set foot outside Mississippi until she was forty-five, Mrs. Hamer, as everyone called her, also held credentials as vice-chairman of the newly created Mississippi Freedom Democratic party. She gave the members of the Credentials Committee—and the nation—an electric account of what it meant to be black and smart *and* political in the Delta region of Mississippi. Her testimony was so emotionally compelling that by the end of the day, the Democratic party headquarters was swamped with telegrams and phone calls from indignant voters wanting to know what was going on in Mississippi.

America had never before seen or heard anyone quite like Fannie Lou Hamer, someone who spoke authentically for the marginalized poor of Mississippi—the sharecroppers, hairdressers, postal clerks, small store owners, rural tenant farmers. These were people who had been invisible in national politics since the Civil War. Her testimony was so shocking, so mesmerizing, so ineluctably true that it cut through the chaos and confusion of a national political convention. She reminded people what democracy was supposed to be about.

Watching the televised convention from the White House, President Lyndon Johnson jumped to his feet when Hamer began talking. Who was this woman bringing the most vexing problem of the Republic—the racist brutality of the South—right out into the open on national television? Johnson was beside himself with fury. The Democratic convention was supposed to be a conflict-free ceremony illustrating democracy in action. Johnson had become president only nine months earlier, after John F. Kennedy's assassination, and he needed a triumphal nomination. Recently transformed from a parochial Texan into a statesman with a theoretically international perspective, Johnson knew America's political image would be marred by having the closed society of Mississippi revealed in such a powerful way. He also knew his future presidency would be immensely complicated if the highly combustible "race issue" slipped from his grasp. The delegates of the eleven southern states, segregationists all, were predisposed to cause trouble if their states' rights position was not upheld. Between the time that Mrs. Hamer introduced herself—she was allotted only eight minutes—and her tearful conclusion, Johnson had called a press conference, strolled into the White House press room, and terminated her national television coverage by uttering a few unimportant announcements about vice presidential selection. The networks had to cut from the convention to Johnson's remarks.

Johnson's success in pushing Hamer off the airwaves was short-lived. By the evening news, all the networks were running long excerpts from Hamer's testimony. National audiences were riveted. For one thing, in the early 1960s women in America were rarely heard in public, and those who were, like Jackie Kennedy or actress Marilyn Monroe, talked largely about domestic issues. For another, the civil rights spokesmen previously shown on television were black ministers whose oratory was filled with ornate language and call-and-response cadences. Hamer spoke directly and clearly. She came from the grassroots of Mississippi, and she brought the plight of the southern sharecropper to the attention of the nation in such a pitch-perfect appeal she could not be ignored. Bob Moses, a civil rights field-worker in Mississippi who had worked with her since 1962, said "Mrs. Hamer [always] spoke from the heart. When she spoke at Atlantic City in front of the national TV, she spoke the same way." Civil rights historian Taylor Branch said she testified "with the spare cadence of a biblical text," and Martin Luther King, also a witness supporting the Mississippi challenge, told the Credentials Committee that "it is in these saints in ordinary walks of life that the true spirit of democracy finds its most profound and abiding expression."

Hamer concluded her testimony with a description of a savage beating she had received in a Mississippi jail only a year earlier, punishment for attending a voter registration workshop. The effort to control her emotions was so great that her eyes brimmed with tears, and she had to pause before she could go on.

"Is this America?" Hamer finally asked. "Where we have to sleep with our telephones off the hook because our lives be threatened daily because we want to live as decent human beings in America?"

It was a resonant question, and during those eight minutes in 1964, Fannie Lou Hamer became a national figure. All across the country people wanted to know, who is this Fannie Lou Hamer? How did she move from the cotton fields of Mississippi into national politics?

She was born Fannie Lou Townsend on October 6, 1917, in rural Montgomery County in the center of the state. Her grandmother had been a slave; her parents were sharecroppers. She was the last and youngest of Lou Ella and Jim Townsend's twenty children. (Her parents were born in 1875 and 1873, respectively.) When she was two years old, the family moved to Sunflower County in the Delta, a rich agricultural area of twelve counties formed in the triangle of the Mississippi and Yazoo Rivers. There, the Townsend family eked out a living chopping cotton, growing vegetables, and doing odd jobs. The Delta region had been reclaimed from cypress swamps in the 1880s for cotton cultivation, and it was a flat, steamy, unforgiving landscape. People who know the Delta describe it as oppressive, for both whites and blacks. Cotton pickers worked in ninety-eight-degree temperatures covered head to toe in clothing to keep insects away, hanging long burlap sacks around their necks that became heavier as they picked the cotton bolls with hands that became raw and bloody from the sharp-pointed hulls. Unita Blackwell, one of Fannie Lou Hamer's colleagues in the Freedom party, said Delta sharecroppers had a love-hate relationship with the land: "We worked that land and we put our blood into that land." They got little back.

Like most sharecroppers, Hamer's parents had to do other work to get by. Her mother did laundry and domestic work for white families. Her father preached in the local churches and was a bootlegger—an "upstanding bootlegger," according to Hamer's niece. On weekends he ran a juke joint, the black southern equivalent of a speakeasy, from which he sold liquor. These activities were not mutually exclusive in rural Mississippi.

Jim Townsend was a well-known and prominent man in the community, and Hamer grew up knowing what it was to be part of a family that was respected for miles around. Even before the passage of national prohibition in 1920, Mississippi had many dry counties because of the antiliquor ordinances passed by the influential Baptist churches. If people wanted a drink, and many did, the only way to get it was from a bootlegger. The making and distribution of illegal spirits was a well-established business in rural communities, white and black, throughout the South.

While Mississippi tourist brochures boasted of "enchanting ante-bellum homes" and "a storied past of hoop skirts and steamboats," Mississippi was notorious because it had the greatest income dispar-ities between rich and poor of any state in the South, and therefore, in the country. The state was also known for frequent lynchings, murders of blacks, and terrorism carried out by the virulent Ku Klux Klan. "Even in Alabama," wrote Nobel award–winning author V. S. Naipaul, "I found that Mississippi had a reputation for poverty and racial hardness." In 1960 well over half of black families in Missis-sippi lived below the federal poverty level. Many black families had cash incomes that averaged no more than $300 a year. Churches and juke joints were the main institutions of rural social life. Juke (or jook) joints were usually located at a crossroads deep in the country where liquor, blues, dancing, gambling, and the occasional knife fight came together. "Musically speaking, the jook is the most im-portant place in America," wrote folklorist and novelist Zora Neal Hurston. Carried out of the cotton country by musicians like B. B. King and John Lee Hooker, the famous Delta blues were complex laments that went back to slavery and West Africa. John Lee Hooker once said that his songs were so sad that sometimes he made him-self cry. The *Concise Oxford Dictionary of Music* defines the blues as a "slow jazz song of lamentation, generally for an unhappy love affair. Usually in groups of 12 bars, instead of 8 or 16 . . . tonality predominantly major, but with the flatted 3rd and 7th of the key (the 'blue notes')." Historians consider juke joints as important as any institution in black America, except the church. As Anthony Walton wrote in *Mississippi: An American Journey*, in the black church a woman might sing:

Amazing grace, how sweet the sound
That saved a wretch like me
I once was lost, but now am found
Was blind but now I see.

While a man in a juke joint might sing:
When a woman get the blues
She hang her head and cry

When a man get the blues
He catch a freight and ride.

Fannie Lou Hamer grew up knowing both the church and the juke.

Hamer's childhood essentially ended when she was twelve years old. Her father had made an enormous effort to help his family escape the sharecroppers' fate of desperate poverty and unrelenting physical labor. By 1929 he had saved enough money from his preaching and bootlegging to lease land and move his family to a new farm. He purchased his own farm equipment and animals, including a plow and two mules. He even bought an automobile and began to make repairs on the house that came with the property. It looked as though the Townsend family might actually break out of the sharecropper's cycle of poverty, landlessness, and constant debt.

Sharecropping was a postbellum system designed to replace slavery as the cheapest source of labor. Some said it was as bad as slavery. Sharecroppers worked an assigned section, or share, of land while the landlord provided housing (usually a shack with no sanitation or good water), seed, fertilizer, and farm equipment from his own store, at usurious rates. The plantation owner kept the books. When the harvest was done, sharecroppers usually found they had nothing left, no profit and no crops, because the owner deducted hundreds of dollars for supplies. No sharecropper could challenge the owner's accounting system or audit the books because education for most Mississippi blacks ended at the sixth grade. It was almost impossible to work one's way out of the sharecropping system. Blacks had no means of entry into the political system. Mississippi dealt with discontent by providing young black men one-way bus tickets to northern cities like Chicago or Detroit, where they found work in the steel or automobile plants.

Hamer was in the sixth grade when disaster struck. While the family was away, one of their white neighbors, wanting to illustrate the futility of black ambition and to set an example for other black families, put an arsenic-based fertilizer in Townsend's animal feed. Called Paris Green, the fertilizer poisoned the animals, and they all died. Without the mules the Townsends could not plow the land they had leased; without plowed land they couldn't plant seed; without crops they couldn't make payments on the lease. In the end, they lost everything. The family had to go back to sharecropping, now worse off than before. The white planters who controlled land in the Delta viewed Jim Townsend's ambitions to become a landowning farmer with the same savage animosity with which they would view his daughter's ambition to vote thirty-three years later.

Fannie Lou had to quit school and work full-time in the fields. She remembered this period as a time of near starvation—greens and gravy were all they had to eat—and her days transformed into grueling work, from dawn to sunset. Most of all, she regretted having to leave school.

She was in the sixth grade and loved reading. A good speller, known for winning spelling bees, she had an excellent memory and liked to recite poetry, an activity encouraged by her teacher, Thornton Layne. He took an interest in her and helped her years later when she was on the run from the Klan. In order to keep reading, she joined the Strangers Home Baptist Church, where she learned the Bible and went to Sunday school. She also sang in the choir. Even as a child, she had a rich singing voice and an instinct for performing. When she was little, her brothers or sisters used to lift her up on a table and tell her to perform a song for them. Supposedly her signature song, "This Little Light of Mine," went back to her childhood.

Although Vice President Hubert Humphrey called Fannie Lou Hamer illiterate during the 1964 convention negotiations, a sixth-grade education was the norm for blacks in Mississippi. (An eleventh-grade education was typical for whites.) Education, the one tool that could abate poverty, was denied Mississippi sharecroppers because the plantation owners controlled the educational system. Expenditures on black education were scandalous. In North Pike County, for example, the government spent $30.89 per white child and only $.76 per black child; in Holly Bluff the government spent $191.70 per white child and $1.26 per black child. Overall, black education in Mississippi received less than 3 percent of the state's education budget—and blacks made up almost 50 percent of the population. The academic year for black schools was three months shorter than that for white schools so that black children could work in the fields. Not only were books and equipment in black schools out of date and insufficient; many of the reading primers included a Sambo-like main character called Epimandius, a numbingly stupid black child. Most of Mississippi's counties had no bookstores, and over one-third of its eighty-two counties had no public library. Black children could not use the library even if their town had one. Until the 1950s, Mississippi's capital city of Jackson had only one bookstore, and that was a Baptist-run religious bookseller. Mississippi per-pupil expenditures were the lowest in the nation. Education was not easy to come by.

Even if somehow a black student had managed to graduate from high school, Mississippi blacks could not enter all-white public colleges or go to the University of Mississippi. They could not eat at a restaurant or sit at a lunch counter. They could not sit down in an empty seat on a bus, even when the black section was full. All public accommodations were designated "white" or "colored." Medical care was limited, and white plantation owners did not call doctors easily. Even when they did, many white doctors often refused to physically touch black patients. In 1959 the National Association for the Advancement of Colored People (NAACP) counted one black dentist, five black lawyers, and sixty black doctors in the entire state.

The year 1929 marked the beginning of America's Great Depression. For Fannie Lou it meant the beginning of a life of full-time hard work. As a group, Delta sharecroppers lived with terrible deprivation—children's feet wrapped in newspapers for shoes, corn shucks for beds, no running water, constant malnutrition in one of the richest agricultural areas in the country. They worked "from dark to dark" and still had nothing. Lou Ella Townsend, now fifty-seven, took on every job she could find. In addition to picking cotton, she washed the laundry of the white owner's family, cleaned homes for white people, killed hogs (she was given the feet, intestines, and head to take home), and brought up twenty children (she lost only one). She also struggled with poor nutrition and little medical care. Fannie Lou recalled never getting enough to eat during her teenage years and later explained to white audiences that being overweight resulted from a diet made up of too many starches and too little protein. Jim Townsend, who never fully recovered from the blow of losing everything, died ten years later of a stroke.

Fannie Lou's mother did not give up. She had a reputation for being feisty, and, as would later be said of Fannie Lou, she was a woman who was not easily intimidated. Some people said she was just plain crazy because she "didn't have sense enough to be afraid of white folks." Lou Ella Townsend was known as a fighter because she would not let the bossman on the plantation hit her children, even though it was common practice. Fannie Lou said that every day when her mother left for the fields, she carried a bucket in each hand. In one bucket was lunch; in the other, a gun.

Lou Ella passed on stories of her own upbringing. She had twenty-three siblings, many of them light-skinned with blue eyes. Fannie Lou's mother told her that twenty of her aunts and uncles were the products of rape, all by white men. Her mother, Liza Bramlett, had been a slave, and Lou Ella herself was one of only three children, out of the twenty-three, who was the product of a consensual relationship with a black man. Hamer described some of this mixed-race family history to an audience at the NAACP Legal Defense Fund dinner. The subject was black women. "The special plight . . . of black women is not something that just happened three years ago. We've had a special plight for 350 years. . . . I remember my uncles and some of my aunts. . . . I'm very black but [they] was as white as anybody in here, and blue-eyed, and some kind of green-eyed—and my grandfather didn't do it, you know."

One of Fannie Lou's sisters, Laura Townsend, told a Hamer biographer about how their mother described the fate of their grandmother, about "how the white folks would do her" and how "they sho done Grandma bad. . . . The man would keep her as long as he wanted then trade her to another white man for a little calf; then the other man would get to keep her for as long as he wanted—she was steady having babies—and trade her off for a little sow pig." The tales of Liza Bramlett's survival under slavery socialized Fannie Lou and her sisters for black southern womanhood. When she was beaten in the Winona jail, it was as though three generations of black women's rage was tapped. Instead of backing down, she became as determined as death.

In 1940, the year after her father's death, she took over some of his bootlegging business. She met Perry Hamer, nicknamed "Pap," a tractor driver on a nearby plantation. He was five years her senior, had been married before, and had a daughter. Together Fannie Lou and Pap ran her late father's juke joint, from which they also sold bootleg liquor. When they married in 1944, she left her family home and moved to the plantation in Ruleville where he worked. Although she began working there as a common field hand, the plantation owner, W. D. Marlow III, soon realized she was smart, was good with numbers, and could read and write. He gave her the job of time-keeper—keeping track of each field hand's working hours, the number of bales picked, and the amount of money owed. The timekeeper's job was important, located near the scales where the cotton was weighed, and it elevated Fannie Lou a step above the ordinary field hand. The job also gave her a glimpse into how the scales were artificially weighted in the owners' favor. When it came time to "settle up," she saw why no sharecropper got a fair day's wage for a full day's work.

As a teenager she had picked over two hundred pounds of cotton for a dollar a day. As the years went on, she developed a realistic appreciation of why the key agricultural unions in the South—the Sharecroppers Union and the Southern Tenant Farmers Union—had never been able to establish a presence in Mississippi. As soon as anyone was suspected of being a union organizer, he would disappear, the victim of a lynching, a murder, or an unexplained trip. Mississippi led the nation in racial murders and disappearances. The state's virulent racial brutality, enforced by the Ku Klux Klan and, after 1954, the White Citizens Council, kept labor organizations out.

Mississippi essentially remained unchanged since the defeat of Reconstruction in 1875, maintaining a legal system of segregation that kept blacks and whites separated. Called "Jim Crow" after a black minstrel caricature popularized during the 1830s, this system of state laws, known as the Mississippi Code, imposed segregated Jim Crow schools, Jim Crow restaurants, Jim Crow water fountains, Jim Crow transportation, and Jim Crow customs. Although white supremacy and segregation were bedrock values throughout the South, Mississippi was known as the most segregated and inhumane of the southern states. "Change" was not a word that had a positive value in Mississippi. Yet change was coming because tens of thousands of young black men had served in World War II and fought for democracy against the Germans and the Japanese. They had seen a larger world, and when they came back to Mississippi hometowns where they could not vote, go to college, or find a job, they refused to accept the status quo. One of those young veterans was Medgar Evers, who founded the first branch of the NAACP in Mississippi after being unceremoniously turned down for law school at the University of Mississippi.

In 1951 Lou Ella Townsend had a debilitating accident and came to live with Fannie Lou and Pap in Ruleville. She had been clearing land for cultivation (at $1.25 a day), chopping up cypress logs, and had been hit in the eye with a wood chip. Partially blinded, she had not received medical attention in time to save her sight and had to move in with the Hamers. Fannie Lou continued to work as a timekeeper for Marlow, looked after her mother, and regularly attended church. As families went in the Delta, she thought hers was doing pretty well. She and her husband had steady jobs. They had an automobile. Her niece remembers that when she and her parents went to visit, Fannie Lou served the best pecan pie she ever had. "She was a great cook," said her niece. Fannie Lou described the house they lived in as "pretty decent," with running water and a bathtub, but no hot water and no flush toilet. Her awareness of the differences in living standards for whites and blacks came unexpectedly. One day while she was doing domestic work in the Marlow house, she became enraged when the daughter told her not to clean one of the bathrooms because it was where the family dog stayed.

Fannie Lou and Pap had no children of their own. In 1954 they took in a child from the community whose parents were impoverished. Dorothy Jean, nine years old, was the offspring of a single mother unable to adequately care for her. It was the same year the NAACP achieved its historic victory in Brown v. Board of Education, a decision in which the Supreme Court unanimously ruled that segregated schools were both illegal and unconstitutional. Consequently, the South needed to plan for racially integrated education, a future that met with outraged opposition and racial attitudes of stunning viciousness. "What is the real purpose of desegregation?" a white southern politician demanded. "To open the bedroom doors of our white women to Negro men."

Although the Supreme Court decision might seem distant from the experiences of ordinary Mississippi sharecroppers, it would have a significant effect on their lives. In 1954 white Mississippi responded with the formation of the first White Citizens Council. Composed of urban, middle-class, white men, it was a new kind of white hate group that added another layer of brutality to the hysteria of racial relations. The sexual pathology of the South required maintaining the blissful mythology that white men were both benevolent and chaste with their black women workers. In reality, white men had unchecked sexual access to black women, both under slavery and under the sharecropping system. White men projected on to black men their own libidinous desires even though the reality was that many prosperous white families had unacknowledged, but similar-looking, black cousins. (It took the advent of DNA testing to demonstrate that Thomas Jefferson, who freed only a handful of his two hundred slaves, had fathered at least one son with a young slave woman named Sally Hemmings.) Southern white women poured their suspicions about the parentage of many of their servants into their unpublished diaries. Novelist Ralph Ellison wrote about the ambivalence of the sexual South in this poem about the death of the white master:

"I dearly loved my master, son," she said.
"You should have hated him," I said.
"He gave me several sons," she said, "and because I loved my
   sons I learned to love their father though I hated him too."
"I too have become acquainted with ambivalence," I said.
"Then, tell me, who is that laughing upstairs?"
"Them's my sons. They glad."

Some called the White Citizens Councils the "white-collar Klan." Instead of cross burnings and shootings, the White Citizens Councils aimed to control blacks through economic reprisals. One leader summed up their program by saying they wanted to "make it difficult, if not impossible, for any Negro who advocates desegregation to find and hold a job, get credit, or renew a mortgage." The state accelerated its program of giving black people one-way tickets to northern cities. Senator James O. Eastland of Sunflower County, one of the most powerful men in the state, became a voice for the new resistance, repudiating the authority of the federal government and the Supreme Court: "On May 17, 1954, the Constitution of the United States was destroyed because of the Supreme Court's decision. You are not obliged to obey the decisions of any court which are plainly fraudulent [and based on] sociological considerations," he told the citizens of Mississippi.

The following year Fannie Lou and Pap took in another child, Virgie Lee, a five-month-old baby who had been badly burned and whose parents were too poor to provide medical care. They adopted both girls and raised Dorothy and Virgie as their own. That same year there were several brutal murders in Mississippi. Two of the victims were NAACP organizers trying to register black voters. The third was a fourteen-year-old boy. Emmett Till's murder took place only twenty miles away from Ruleville in the rural town of Money; it was a racial murder so brutal that it eventually made the front page of every black newspaper in the state and country.

Emmett Till had traveled to Mississippi by train from Chicago to visit his mother's relatives during summer vacation. He had a stutter and was in the eighth grade, and his Chicago elementary school classmates later described him as a boy who liked pranks. On a hot Wednesday night in August, he and his cousin drove to the nearby country store and stood outside talking to some local boys. On a dare Emmett went into the store and as he was leaving said "Bye, baby" to a white woman standing at the cash register. Four days later his tortured, distended body was pulled out of the Tallahatchie River, his face so badly beaten it was unrecognizable. One eye had been pulled from its socket. His frantic mother insisted the body be returned to Chicago to make sure it was her son, her only son. When *Jet* magazine published a photo of Emmett Till's mutilated corpse, the image was carried by every black newspaper in the country. The fate of the boy moved people, black women particularly, in a way that the Supreme Court ruling on desegregation could not. It meant that male children were not safe from brutal murder. There was no common sense in Mississippi's racial system.

Medgar Evers came to Money from Jackson to investigate the murder for the NAACP. Wearing sharecropper overalls, he went out into the country and talked to witnesses and got enough information to make sure there would be a trial. He even found Mose Wright, Emmett Till's sixty-four-year-old uncle, who had been in hiding ever since the murder but who had seen the men who took the boy away the night of the kidnapping. The trial brought press and observers from around the country, including Congressman Charles Diggs from Michigan. He sat at the segregated black press table and said when Mose Wright stood up, "It was the first time in the history of Mississippi that a Negro had stood in court and pointed his finger at a white man as a killer of a Negro." If not technically the first, it was a rare and courageous act. The Klan had warned Wright he would not live to be sixty-five if he testified. Even though the murderers were acquitted, it was a historic trial.

The Klan was generally made up of poor, rural, white men who met wearing white robes and hoods that covered their faces. The members of the Klan described themselves as true Christians whose religious mission was to root out communists and satanic evildoers. They defined satanic people as Jews, communists, civil rights advocates, and labor organizers. Their principal activity was to set burning crosses in the yards of people they thought were not true Christians. This included anyone identified with organizations like the NAACP, the Congress for Racial Equality (CORE), and the Student Nonviolent Coordinating Committee (SNCC) and any other Negroes who exhibited behavior that showed they "didn't know their place." The burning cross was a warning; after that they resorted to beatings and murder.

After the Emmett Till trial in September, black attitudes in the South began to shift towards resistance, particularly among women. Two months later, in December, a seamstress in Montgomery, Alabama, took a seat in the white section of a segregated bus. When the driver told her to move to the Negro section, she refused. Rosa Parks was arrested and jailed. The day before her trial, a black teacher who also had been unceremoniously thrown off another Montgomery bus for the same reason mobilized the black community by writing and distributing thirty-five thousand mimeographed flyers calling for a bus boycott the day of Parks's trial. "Three fourths of the riders are Negroes," Jo Ann Robinson wrote, "yet we are arrested or have to stand over empty seats. The next time it may be you, or your daughter, or mother." The Women's Political Council of Montgomery circulated the anonymous leaflets through the stores, schools, bars, and churches of the black neighborhoods. Not only were the Montgomery buses empty of black riders the day of Parks's trial; they remained empty for the following year until the city leaders finally negotiated a satisfactory end to segregated seating and the beginning of hiring of black bus drivers. The Montgomery bus boycott, as it was known, also thrust a young minister named Martin Luther King into civil rights leadership and precipitated the organization of the Southern Christian Leadership Conference (SCLC) as an alternative to the traditional black Baptist organizations which were resolutely apolitical.

Fannie Lou now had two girls to look after, and her mother was becoming more sickly and required more care. Although the Montgomery, Alabama, bus boycott might have appeared geographically removed from Ruleville, the newspaper headlines and television coverage of civil rights events kept increasing. In the neighboring state of Arkansas, federal troops had to be sent in to protect nine young black students who integrated Little Rock Central High School in 1957. That same year the first civil rights bill since Reconstruction passed Congress. By 1960 Hamer was hearing the terms "sit-ins" and "freedom riders." Black college students in Greensboro, North Carolina, had begun a spontaneous "sit-in"—sitting down at a segregated white lunch counter—insisting that if national chains like Woolworth's could sell merchandise to blacks, they could also serve them at their lunch counters. These sit-ins spread to cities all over the South, organized at a grassroots level by black college students. They were soon followed by "Freedom Riders," teams of black and white students who took interstate bus trips throughout the South to test the federal ruling that any carrier engaged in interstate commerce could not maintain Jim Crow—white and colored—facilities.

Fannie Lou's mother grew more ill, and Fannie Lou regretted that she could not do more to alleviate her suffering. Although she was pleased she had been able to provide her with a home for the past ten years, she grieved deeply when her mother died in 1961. Within months she herself went into the hospital to have a cyst removed from her uterus. When she came out, she found that while she was in the hospital the doctors had performed a hysterectomy without her knowledge. (Involuntary sterilization was imposed on many poor black women in the South, as well as on Indian women on reservations.)

Hamer was still grieving her mother's death and her own sterilization when, in August 1962, her friend and neighbor Mary Tucker asked if she was going to the meeting at a church in Ruleville to hear the young people. What young people? Hamer asked. Talking about what? Voting, Tucker answered. "Until then, I didn't know that Negroes could vote," Hamer explained later about the meeting she did attend at the Williams Chapel Missionary Baptist Church.

That particular Wednesday night the young men leading the meeting were James Bevel, a staff member of the Southern Christian Leadership Conference (SCLC), and James Forman, Bob Moses, and Reginald Robinson, field-workers for the Student Nonviolent Coordinating Committee (SNCC, pronounced snick). These "young people" were students and former teachers who had volunteered to do voter registration work in the rural towns of Mississippi. It was the most dangerous work in the South. SNCC was an organization of student activists, loosely allied with SCLC, that had formed in 1960 specifically to conduct voter registration in rural areas.

Although the meeting was about voting rights, the organizers opened with a song and a prayer. It was the first time Hamer had heard "freedom songs," church spirituals adapted to the political message of the civil rights movement. The music sanctified the political action by fusing it with biblical songs. Like the coded messages embedded in the songs used by agents of the Underground Railroad in the nineteenth century, the freedom songs created free space. "I felt as though I was called," Hamer said later of that first meeting. Music was the language of the movement, and Fannie Lou Hamer was fluent in that language. From childhood, she had sung in church, read the Bible, and through musical expression had a sense of the power of her own voice. "We Shall Overcome" was an old Baptist hymn, but infused with the message of freedom and political rights, it became the "Marseillaise" of the civil rights movement and endowed people with courage and a sense of unity.

"Ain't Gonna Let Nobody Turn Me Round," "Keep Your Eyes on the Prize," "This Little Light of Mine"—these songs expressed both a political message and a vision. The lyrics infused the idea of going to vote with the traditional slave spirituals of being delivered from bondage and overcoming fear. The songs had their roots in spirituals, gospel, blues, rhythm and blues, calypso, chants, and the African American musical culture that grew up in black churches and juke joints of the South. Music was one way black people could talk back without being directly confrontational. Freedom songs were a vehicle in which they could give voice to their commitment to change and to freedom.

After a meeting in which participants told about some of the merciless atrocities committed against black people, freedom workers sang with a passion that used every cell in their bodies. One SNCC volunteer described the singing as so intense that "nobody could imagine what kept the church on its four corners." Sally Belfrage, a northern civil rights volunteer who had come to Mississippi, described small meetings in rural churches where the power of the message came only through song. "The moral came through the music and the people gave themselves to the message of the meeting."

Spoken words could never rival the effectiveness of song for a population of sharecroppers, many of whom who could not read or write. Fannie Lou had spent a lifetime singing in church, and she was a good song leader—musically, organizationally, and spiritually. Musically, she knew all the songs and hymns, and she had mastered the techniques of black church singing—the vibrato, a range that can go from smooth and clear to a gravel-like tone, the ability to sing several notes on one syllable, to scoop and glide, to "grow" the song with call and response from the congregation. Organizationally, she knew how to project strength, energy, and enthusiasm and to select the right song for the spirit of the moment. Spiritually, she had deep religious conviction, which she conveyed in the quality of her singing. When asked to describe the quality of Fannie Lou Hamer's voice, Harry Belafonte said technically it might be called a contralto, but it was a voice with "a mission." Bob Moses said, "When she sang she was someone who was opening up her soul and really telling you what she felt."

In many ways, freedom songs were sermons set to music. Although the civil rights movement was a political movement with tactics and strategy, many of its participants proceeded largely on religious faith. The absolutism of white supremacy had a rigid grip on the white mind in Mississippi. Everyone agreed that Mississippi was the worst state in the nation for allowing African Americans political voice, "unarguably the most supremacist and segregated state in the country," wrote Juan Williams. Its government recognized neither the authority of the law nor the power of the courts. For blacks the act of registering to vote was more than a rebellious act against a tyrannical system; it represented a symbolic key to entering the modern world. It offered hope to ordinary sharecroppers that they could break the cycle of poverty and powerlessness, a way out of the apathy and fatalism that marked their lives. Fannie Lou Hamer was one of them. So when James Bevel and Bob Moses asked for volunteers to go to the county courthouse in Indianola the next day to register, Hamer was one of the eighteen who raised their hands. Hamer described the following events in her testimony at the Democratic Convention:

It was the 31st of August in 1962 that eighteen of us traveled twenty-six miles to the county courthouse in Indianola to try to register to try to become first-class citizens. We was met in Indianola by Mississippi men, highway patrolmens, and they only allowed two of us in to take the literacy test at the time. After we had taken this test and started back to Ruleville, we was held up by the City Police and the State Highway Patrolmen and carried back to Indianola, where the bus driver was charged that day with driving a bus the wrong color. After we paid the fine among us, we continued on to Ruleville, and Reverend Jeff Sunny carried [drove] me four miles in the rural area where I had worked as a timekeeper and sharecropper for eighteen years.

Although the process for a black resident to register was theoretically the same as that for whites, in practice it worked quite differently. An African American had to go in person to the county courthouse, fill out a questionnaire of twenty-one questions, take and pass a literacy test, and then interpret a clause of the state constitution selected at random. These were requirements that few whites, including most of the county clerks administering them, could pass. This practice allowed county governments wide latitude in voter registration: illiterate whites successfully registered while most blacks, even well-educated blacks, were rejected. In addition, at a time when sharecroppers' cash wages were no more than $1.50 a day, they also had to pay a poll tax of $2.00. (The poll tax was later declared illegal.)

Not only did Mississippi have the lowest rate of black voter registration in the South; it also had unusual "voter anomalies." Some counties in Mississippi had majority black populations and *not a single* black registrant. Other counties had a white registration rate of *96 percent*. Mississippi had less than 6 percent of its black population registered to vote. The next-worst state, Alabama, had registered 23 percent of eligible black voters. Mississippi maintained its segregated politics by means of harsh economic and social penalties. A black person who registered to vote was usually evicted from the plantation where he or she worked and had great difficulty ever finding work again. Fannie Lou Hamer described what happened to her when she returned from trying to register to vote:

I was met by my children when I returned from the courthouse who told me the plantation owner was angry because I had gone down to try to register. After they told me, my husband came and said the plantation owner was raising cain because I had tried to register, and before he quit talking the plantation owner came and said, "Fannie Lou . . . did Pap tell you what I said?"

I said, "Yes, sir."

He said, "I mean that. . . . If you don't go down and withdraw your registration, you will have to leave. . . . then if you go down and withdraw you might have to go because we are not ready for this in Mississippi."

I had to leave that same night.

Hamer left because it was too dangerous for her family if she stayed. Technically, voting might be a constitutional right, but the names of black registrants were printed in the local newspapers. Soon after their names were published, either the Ku Klux Klan or its commando subsidiary, the Christian White Knights, arrived in the middle of the night. The Klan did the shooting; the Knights did the bombing. Their logic seemed to be that any black person who wanted to vote was either satanic or communist. Hamer went first to stay with Mary Tucker, the friend who had told her about the voter registration meeting: "On the 10th of September, 1962, sixteen bullets was fired into the home of Mr. and Mrs. Robert Tucker for me. That same night two girls were shot in Ruleville, Mississippi. Also Mr. Joe McDonald's house was shot in."

Cars filled with armed white men fired bullets into various homes where Hamer was believed to be staying. After the Tucker shootings, two girls were wounded the same night in a drive-by shooting at another home. Joe MacDonald saved himself by jumping into the bathtub for protection. Since law enforcement officers were often members of the Klan, no one was ever indicted, charged, or prosecuted. Soon afterward, the White Knights bombed the Williams Baptist church where the initial voter registration meeting had been held.

Because it was so dangerous for anyone to shelter her, Hamer left the county entirely, taking her two girls and traveling north to Tallahatchie County, where she stayed with relatives and picked cotton to support herself. While she was there, Hamer learned about an extraordinary event of racial integration taking place less than a hundred miles away at Ole Miss in Oxford, Mississippi. It was an event of such historic significance it changed the course of many people's lives, not just in Mississippi but throughout the country. (In California, the award-winning author Ernest Gaines said it motivated him to revise his first novel for the twentieth time and to keep writing about the black quarters of Louisiana where he had been raised.) A black man named James Meredith had entered Ole Miss, as the bastion of the white University of Mississippi was called. The admission of Meredith, the first black man in the history of the state to enter (and graduate) from the university, caused riots that left several people dead. President Kennedy had to federalize the National Guard to control the mobs that swarmed the campus. No black person in the state was unaware that for the first time in anyone's memory, help had come from the outside to prevail over Mississippi state authorities on behalf of blacks. Something was changing. The implications of this event affected many people throughout the nation, including Fannie Lou Hamer. By the end of October she decided to stop hiding out. She and the girls, she announced, would return to Ruleville.

Although Pap Hamer had stayed on the Marlow plantation until the harvest was completed, Marlow fired him anyway. Pap had worked for Marlow for thirty years. When a sharecropper was evicted, he or she lost everything—house, furniture, equipment, animals, crops—because the plantation owner claimed everything belonged to him. Marlow confiscated all the Hamer family's furnishings, took their automobile, and told Pap that he still owed him $300 for overdue bills.

Helped by friends, family, and the SNCC voter education project, the Hamers moved into a house on Lafayette Street in the black section of Ruleville. Because Fannie Lou had to flee before the harvest, she had not been able to can any food. The family was dependent on donations. Pap could not find another job because no one dared hire him. It was a hard winter. As it progressed, Fannie Lou only seemed to become more determined. Bob Moses arranged for her to attend a leadership training conference at Fisk University in Nashville. At the age of forty-five, Hamer finally returned to school. She participated in workshops about voting, nonviolence, communications, and economics. She absorbed everything. When she returned to Ruleville, she continued her voter registration canvassing. Defiantly, she told the registrar at the Indianola courthouse, "I'll be here every thirty days until I become a registered voter." In January 1963 she passed.

Fannie Lou Hamer was exactly the kind of person the SNCC organizers hoped to find in rural communities: someone who was a natural leader, prominent in the community, and fearless. SNCC signed her up as a field-worker in its voter registration project, giving her a small stipend for going out into her community to tell her neighbors that they had a right to register and to vote. Her leadership qualities came from her parents' prominence in the community, her role as a timekeeper on the plantation, and her own considerable indignation about the inequities of Mississippi life. "My parents helped make this town and this county what it is today, because it was out of their sweat, tears, and blood that they [whites] got as much land that they have here and I got a right to stay."

The politics of voter activism were not simple. The key organizers in Mississippi came from the Student Nonviolent Coordinating Committee, a student group originally formed in 1960 under the auspices of the Southern Christian Leadership Conference. Ella Baker, a longtime activist and SCLC employee—who would become a great friend and supporter of Mrs. Hamer's—encouraged the students to keep their own organization independent of the more conservative ministers. At the same time, she persuaded Martin Luther King to support the students even though they were frequently arrested and required lawyers and bail money. The main source of scarce funds was the NAACP, which wanted to be the leading civil rights organization in Mississippi. But because many of its members were middle-class blacks in other states, and because the NAACP was considered communist and an active target of the Klan, membership in the Mississippi NAACP was at a standstill. Fannie Lou Hamer would experience increasing friction with the middle-class civil rights leaders and the black ministers of the large Baptist church organizations, but she would become lifetime friends with the more radical SNCC workers and Ella Baker.

As a field-worker, she began visiting her neighbors and attending church groups, explaining how to register, how to pass the literacy test, and other intricacies of Mississippi voting law. She was not afraid to go door-to-door, and she would talk to anyone. Her motivation was rooted in a deep conviction that it was the historical mo-

ment for black people to act. If not now, when? She continued to en-
large her political education, attending workshops and training ses-
sions about electoral politics. In June 1963 SNCC sent her to South
Carolina for another workshop on voting rights. On the return trip,
the worst experience of her life was waiting for her in Montgomery
County, where she had been born.

> And in June, the 9th, 1963, I had attended a voter-registration
> workshop [in South Carolina] and, was returning back to Mis-
> sissippi. Ten of us was traveling by the Continental Trailways
> bus. When we got to Winona, Mississippi, which is Mont-
> gomery County, four of the people got off to use the wash-
> room. . . . when I looked through the window and saw they had
> rushed out, I got off the bus to see what had happened, and one
> of the ladies said, "It was a state highway patrolman and a
> chief of police ordered us out."

They were all arrested and loaded into waiting police cars. During
the trip across Alabama to the Mississippi border, the bus driver had
phoned ahead to warn the Winona police that he had some Negro
passengers who were challenging the segregation laws. The passengers were arrested and taken to the booking rooms. When it came
time for Hamer to be interrogated, the police wanted to know if she
was the Hamer from Ruleville. By then she was considered a known
troublemaker.

> After I was placed in the cell I began to hear sounds of
> licks and screams. I could hear the sounds of licks and
> horrible screams, and I could hear somebody say, "Can
> you say yes sir nigger? Can you say yes sir?" . . . And it
> wasn't too long before three white men came to my cell.
> One of these men was a State Highway Patrolman and he
> asked me where I was from and I told him Ruleville. He
> said, "We are going to check this." And they left my cell
> and it wasn't too long before they came back. He said . . .
> "We are going to make you wish you was dead."

The officers took Hamer to another cell where they had two Negro prisoners. They gave one of the prisoners a blackjack, loaded
with lead weights, ordered Hamer to lie face down on a bunk, and
ordered the prisoner to beat her.

I was beat by the first Negro until he was exhausted and I was holding my hands behind me at that time on my left side because I suffered from polio when I was six years old. After the first Negro had beat until he was exhausted, the state highway patrolman ordered the second Negro to take the blackjack. The second Negro began to beat and I began to work [move] my feet. . . . The state highway patrolman ordered the other Negro to sit on my feet. My dress pulled up and I tried to smooth it down. One of the policemen walked over and raised my dress as high as he could.

This was the testimony Lyndon Johnson tried to prevent reaching America's living rooms. Hamer's kidney was injured from the blows she received on her back, and she got a blood clot in her left eye that left her with deteriorating eyesight for the rest of her life. She was left in jail without medical care for three days until Andy Young, then an aide to Martin Luther King, came from the SCLC office in Georgia to bail her out. She was rushed to a hospital in Greenwood, but she was so badly beaten and her injuries so extensive that she had to be moved to Atlanta. While she was in the hospital, she learned that the same night as her beating, Evers was shot in the back by a sniper on his own front steps.

As the head of the NAACP branch in Jackson, Evers had put the NAACP behind James Meredith's admission to Ole Miss. The success at the University of Mississippi led him to plan another project to integrate the buses, parks, and lunch counters in Jackson. To raise cash for bail money, he recruited singer Lena Horne to give a benefit performance in Jackson. Five days after the concert, which had turned out a crowd of five thousand and raised a lot of money, he returned to his home late at night. A sniper waiting in the bushes shot him in the back at his front door. His funeral procession, in which the police ordered a crowd of over a thousand to disperse from Jackson's main business street, almost caused a riot. Evers was buried at Arlington National Cemetery. (His killer was acquitted after two trials ended in hung juries.) His brother Charles took over as NAACP field secretary.

Hamer's injuries were so severe that she would not let her husband or children visit her for weeks. Even then her injuries were shocking to look at. Her sister Laura, who did visit, said she was barely able to recognize her "because they had beat her so bad. I woulda' stopped after that beating, but Fannie Lou just kept right on going." Even after the visible physical injuries faded, the psychological trauma never left her. For the rest of her life, she repeatedly told the story of the "most horrifying experience I have ever had in my life." During the summer while Hamer recuperated, political tension in the United States mounted. In August civil rights groups organized a massive march on Washington in which Martin Luther King gave his famous "I Have a Dream" speech. In September the White Citizens Council bombed a church in Birmingham, Alabama, killing four little girls. In November President John F. Kennedy was assassinated in Dallas, Texas.

In public President Lyndon Johnson dismissed Hamer's testimony as ragtag and the challenge of the Mississippi Freedom Democratic party (MFDP) as not amounting to a hill of beans; in private he was beside himself. Indignant Democrats were calling the White House wanting to know what kind of politics were practiced in Mississippi. The Freedom party had done its homework and had developed support from big northern states like Michigan and New York, which had large black voting populations, many with original family members from Mississippi. Johnson spent much of the next twenty-four hours following Hamer's testimony on the phone with southern leaders. "The thing is out of hand now!" exclaimed Senator James O. Eastland in one of five telephone conversations he had with the president.

In a neat dramatic irony, Eastland, one of the most important men in national politics, came from Sunflower County, where he lived on his family's five-thousand-acre cotton plantation. He was Fannie Lou Hamer's neighbor. As chair of the U.S. Senate Judiciary Committee, he held as much influence as any man in the country over black people's political rights. Having defeated all but 1 of the 120 civil rights bills that had come before his committee, Eastland also held power over all Johnson's federal judicial appointments.

Eastland, who was back home in Mississippi directing his people from a distance, would have no part of Johnson's efforts to broker a deal. Johnson had proposed a compromise in which the regular Mississippi delegation would remain seated while the Freedom Democrats would get two at-large nonvoting seats. Admonishing the president that there could be no settlement with the challengers, Eastland added that the Mississippi delegation wanted to endorse Goldwater, Johnson's Republican opponent. Johnson quickly told him they must also want him to cut off the cotton subsidy program, hardly a toothless threat, since millions of federal dollars went into Mississippi's one-crop cotton economy. Eastland himself was a multimillionaire by way of cotton subsidies.

The next morning the governor of Georgia called to warn the president about the possibility of a wholesale walkout by all eleven of the southern delegations. "It looks as though we're turning the Democratic party over to the Nigras," he told the president. Johnson was exasperated and told the governor they had to give the Mississippi challengers something, because the white party regulars in Mississippi were not upholding even minimal standards of political participation. "Pistols kept 'em out," he said heatedly.

> "These people [the Mississippi Freedom Democrats] went in and begged to go into the conventions. They've got half the population and they . . . lock 'em out. . . . You and I just can't survive our modern political life with these goddamn fellas down there [Eastland, Stennis, the Klan, the White Citizens Council] that are eatin' 'em for breakfast every morning. They have got to quit that. And they got to let 'em vote, and let 'em shave, and let 'em eat, and things like that. And they don't do it."

Johnson knew a lot about the sixty-four black and four white delegates of the Mississippi Freedom Democrats because he had ordered thirty FBI agents to monitor their telephones, infiltrate their headquarters, inform on their strategy meetings, and follow the delegation's every move. He sent Hubert Humphrey, his vice presidential candidate, to broker the compromise. The two at-large seats were to go to two specific men on the delegation, no one else. Why not Fannie Lou Hamer? asked Bob Moses. "The President will not allow that illiterate woman to speak from the floor of the convention," Humphrey answered, softening the statement by explaining that the president meant only that she spoke too emotionally to help the party. In fact, Johnson did not want to let her get to the microphone again.

On the second day of the challenge, when Johnson's good friend Governor Connolly of Texas called to warn him of "a wholesale walkout from the South," Johnson's exasperation turned to panic. Connolly was a trusted moderate who had been rallying southern delegates for Johnson. If he could not hold the line, no one could. Now Johnson believed he was caught between tectonic forces he could not control. How could he keep the white southerners behind him while keeping the black voters in northern cities loyal to the Democratic party? The intransigence of both sides precluded a successful negotiation. Johnson became so agitated and depressed that he gave his handwritten notes for a withdrawal statement to his wife and to his shocked press secretary, George Reedy. He would rather withdraw than have the South walk out on him. Johnson then drew the shades and retreated to his bed. Lady Bird Johnson later described that day in her memoir: "I do not remember hours I ever found harder."

Johnson came from Texas; he had grown up poor; he had fought the Klan; he had picked cotton; he knew how black sharecroppers were treated in the South. He understood that the Mississippi challenge represented something far larger than the sixty-eight delegates at the convention. It was the product of four years of hard and dangerous organizing. The challengers had convened their own Freedom Democratic party convention, supported four black candidates for Congress, of whom Fannie Lou Hamer was one, registered over one hundred thousand voters in their own party registration, and recruited and organized eight hundred northern college students, three-fourths of them white, to go to Mississippi to do voter education work. The white students brought the white press with them, and when three volunteers disappeared outside Philadelphia, Mississippi, the press attention was relentless. Unlike the dozens of anonymous black bodies turned up during the search, the press wanted to know exactly what had happened to the three young civil rights workers. When the bodies were found in an earthen dam just eighteen days before the 1964 convention, Dr. David Spain told the press after he performed the autopsy on James Chaney, one of the murdered volunteers, "I could barely believe the destruction to these frail young bones. In my twenty-five years as a pathologist and medical examiner, I have never seen bones so severely shattered, except in tremendously high speed accidents or airplane crashes. It was obvious to any first-year medical student that this boy had been beaten to a pulp."

Many of those same white volunteers were holding vigils outside on the boardwalks of Atlantic City, telling any reporter who would listen about how over ninety-three thousand black Mississippians had cast their votes for the MFDP at tables set up on sidewalks and in barber shops and beauty parlors in Mississippi. Black voters had chosen Mrs. Hamer in the second congressional district over Jamie Whitten, giving her thirty-three thousand votes to Whitten's fifty-nine. But those votes were not counted by the regular Democratic party in Mississippi.

In the end nothing was as it appeared. The southerners did not stage a walkout. The Mississippi Freedom delegates did not accept the compromise. "We didn't come all this way for no two seats," was Hamer's much-quoted response. President Johnson was renominated by acclamation and won the election by the largest margin in history. The delegates from the Freedom Democratic party thought they had accomplished little. They were so disillusioned that Harry Belafonte raised the money to send a group of them, Hamer included, to West Africa to recharge their batteries and gain a larger perspective.

Beneath the surface, however, everything had changed. The credentials committee passed new rules stipulating that state delegations had to be integrated and reflect the composition of their populations. The national Democratic party would never be the same. Lyndon Johnson launched a bitterly unpopular war in Vietnam that so divided the country that four years later he did use his withdrawal statement and did not run for reelection. The Freedom Summer volunteers went back to their colleges as some of the most savvy political organizers in the country and became the future leaders of the free speech, antiwar, and feminist movements. At the 1968 convention Hamer was a fully credentialed delegate who received a standing ovation when she walked to the podium. She was able, as a member of the newly integrated Mississippi Loyalist delegation, to support the successful credential fights by the black Alabama and Georgia delegations. They had modeled their challenges to the all-white delegations on those of the Mississippi Freedom Democratic party four years earlier.

During the trip to Senegal and Guinea in 1964, Hamer had seen for the first time black people running their own governments and their own businesses. It gave her a larger sense of what politics could do. She began to think historically about slavery and its long-term cultural and psychological consequences. She began to understand how Mississippi oppressed poor whites as well as blacks. "Politics is my baby," she told a television interviewer in 1974. "My fight goes beyond the black community. My fight goes towards any oppressed people—white, black, brown, green. You have to always try to be involved in politics."

After returning from Africa in the fall of 1964, Hamer turned her attention to the congressional challenge she and the other candidates, Annie Devine and Victoria Gray, had decided to mount in Congress. The three women set up an apartment in Washington, D.C., so they would be on hand to contest the seating of the white Mississippi congressmen. They were not timid supplicants. When Hamer testified before the closed hearing of the House elections subcommittee, she told the members, "If Negroes were allowed to vote freely, I could be sitting up here with you right now as a congresswoman." Victoria Gray and eleven MFDP supporters were jailed for taking part in a sit-in in the office of the Clerk of the House of Representatives after he refused to publish their challenge documents. Although they lost the challenge, they raised the costs of keeping blacks out of Mississippi politics. Lyndon Johnson invited Mrs. Hamer to some of the inaugural festivities, and Speaker McCormack of Massachusetts arranged, while their case was being heard, for the three women to sit on the floor of the House, possibly the first women, white or black, from Mississippi ever to sit in Congress.

Many national organizations invited Hamer to speak, and she traveled around the country raising money for local projects in Mississippi. She did not see herself staying in Washington. In Mississippi she began working in the new poverty programs initiated by the Johnson administration, such as Head Start for children, food programs for the needy, job training, and housing. Traditionally, the state of Mississippi had refused federal food surplus aid or job training programs because they required participation by both whites and blacks. Under the new antipoverty laws, local groups could apply for money directly to the federal government. Hamer joined with Annie Devine at a conference in Oxford, Mississippi, to teach black women how to write grant proposals. Pap Hamer got a job as a driver for Head Start, the first regular job he had had since being evicted from the Marlow plantation. Hamer's goal was to build institutions that could help her community. "She didn't want to enrich herself," her niece observed, "she wanted to enrich her community."

She spoke on behalf of the Child Development Group of Mississippi and led protests at the county seat to stop efforts by the state to eliminate local poverty programs. She also traveled frequently to tell national organizations about the extent of poverty in Mississippi. When a reporter from *The Nation* asked if she had any desire to leave Mississippi to live somewhere safer, she answered: "We're tired of all this beatin' we're tired of takin' this. It's been a hundred years and we're still being beaten and shot at, crosses are still being burned, because we want to vote. But I'm goin' to stay in Mississippi, and if they shoot me down, I'll be buried here. . . . All my life I've been sick and tired. Now I'm sick and tired of being sick and tired."

In 1964 President Johnson signed the Civil Rights Act and in 1965 the Voting Rights Act, a bill that provided for federal marshals at southern polling places, did away with the white-only primary, and provided for the basic constitutional right for blacks to vote. These were the most significant civil-rights laws to be passed since Reconstruction. Within ten years many segregationists lost seats of power. By 1984 black mayors had been elected in 255 cities. Andrew Young became mayor of Atlanta; Unita Blackwell became mayor of Mayersville, Mississippi. Charles Evers, Medgar Evers' brother, became mayor of Fayette. As author Juan Williams wrote in *Eyes on the Prize*, "Voting, access to public accommodations and an equal education were no longer matters of local largess; they were matters of law."

In 1971 Hamer went to Washington for the founding of the National Women's Political Caucus and became a member of its steering committee. She spoke up for the need for women, both white and black, to enter politics. At the time, women politicians were pioneers. There were only thirteen women in the House and two in the Senate. Shirley Chisholm was the first black congresswoman, elected that year. Hamer decided to run for the Mississippi State Senate, and Liz Carpenter, former press secretary for Lady Bird Johnson, came to help her campaign. (Other celebrities who participated in the campaign were feminist Betty Friedan, folksinger Pete Seeger, and civil rights attorney Joe Rauh.) Hamer's house was firebombed. Although she did not win the election, by 1972 Mississippi had 60 *percent* of eligible blacks registered to vote. Fifteen years later the first black congressman since Reconstruction was elected in the congressional district where Hamer first ran against Jamie Whitten. Hamer turned her attention to economics.

In Africa she might have heard the saying "Give us a fish and you feed us for a day; teach us to fish and you feed us for a lifetime." Hamer believed it was important to address some of the structural problems of food and shelter for Mississippi sharecroppers. She poured her considerable energies into the organization of economic cooperatives in Sunflower County. With the financial support of the National Council of Negro Women and several other northern organizations, she created the Pig Bank, a project that loaned a pregnant female pig to a needy family who later, after the birth of a litter of baby pigs, returned the mother sow to the bank. By the time the Pig Bank ended in 1973, nine hundred families had participated, and thousands of pigs had been born and raised. Hamer had started the pig farm with a 40-acre purchase of land. That land acquisition led to the purchase of 640 acres of land divided into plots where needy families could raise cash crops and vegetables. The financial commitment to the property, called Freedom Farm, was considerable, and she was under continual financial pressure to raise more money. (The total cost for the land was $288,000, with a down payment of $85,000 and annual mortgage of $19,000.) To make the land fully productive, she also had to help raise money to buy irrigation pipes and pumps, cotton trailers, seed, fertilizer, hand tools, ladders, and buildings to store the equipment. The planning for the equipment buildings led to her third and most ambitious project—housing.

"We decided to organize everybody that lived in a shack—which was most of us . . . and teach them how to take advantage of low-cost FHA and farm mortgages. Once we got started, we found that so many people wanted to take part that we didn't have time to give the organization a name. We just sort of call it 'The Co-op.'" With revenues from Freedom Farm crops (primarily cotton and soybeans) and small loans from friendly banks, the Freedom Farm Co-op provided thirty-five families, including the Hamers, with down payments on FHA-financed homes in and around Ruleville. For many it was the first time they had lived in anything but a shack. What pleased Hamer the most was a remark she often heard on winter mornings. "You'll see two men walking out their front doors. One will kind of stop, look around and say, 'Phew I didn't realize how cold it was outside!' Everyplace they ever lived in before, it was always just as cold inside as it was outside.' "

Unfortunately, Hamer took on more financial commitments just as her health began to deteriorate. She had both diabetes and hypertension. Her resources were thin, her health was poor, and she was always controversial. She did not get along with many of the luminaries of the civil rights movement. She fought with the black ministers over funding and recognition and resources. Black male ministers were famously negligent in giving recognition or public authority to women.*

Fannie Lou Hamer did not mince words when it came to expressing her lack of respect for some of the ministers of the black Baptist organizations and their efforts to enrich themselves at the expense of their congregations. She argued with the staff of the national civil rights organizations over leadership decisions, funding, and what she perceived as lack of respect for local poor people. She was contentious and argumentative, and she believed that the middle-class black leadership was out of touch with grassroots Mississippi. Although she was right, by 1972 financial troubles, ill health, and chronic fatigue caught up with her. She was hospitalized for nervous exhaustion. No one else could replace her as a speaker and fundraiser, and the flow of money began to dry up. By 1974 all but forty acres of Freedom Farm were lost to creditors, and Hamer sank into a deep depression. The loss must have tapped memories of her father's failure and the traumatic loss of their land when she was a child. Again she was hospitalized for exhaustion and depression. When she recovered, she and her husband celebrated their thirtieth wedding anniversary at a big party in Greenville. Although Pap had found employment again as a driver for Head Start, he lost the job in the

---

*Author and attorney Pauli Murray expressed the views of many black women when she wrote: "It was bitterly humiliating for Negro women on August 28 [1963] to see themselves accorded little more than token recognition in the historic March on Washington. Not a single woman was invited to make one of the major speeches or to be part of the delegation of leaders who went to the White House . . . It is also pointedly significant that in the great mass of magazine and newsprint expended upon the civil rights crisis, national editors have selected Negro men almost exclusively to articulate the aspirations of the Negro community."

politics over the poverty programs. Consequently, the Hamers had neither medical coverage nor disability income. In 1976 Fannie Lou was diagnosed with breast cancer; after she underwent surgery, Charles Evers, the NAACP field secretary, led the efforts to raise money for her medical bills.

Fannie Lou Hamer died of heart failure in March 1977 at the age of fifty-nine. She would be remembered by children who never knew her. Author Anthony Walton, who was born in 1960, grew up in the Midwest, and went back to Mississippi as an adult to explore the world of his parents, called Hamer a "genius" and wrote: "In the end, what is most intriguing about Dorothy and Claude [his parents], Medgar Evers and Fannie Lou Hamer and thousands of others is not that they suffered but that they stayed intact, human, and did not push their suffering down into another generation. This was true emancipation."

Symbolically, Hamer's funeral service took place at the Williams Chapel Missionary Baptist Church in the town of Ruleville, the same place where fifteen years earlier she had first raised her hand to volunteer to vote. Hers was a simple but radical act, and she never shrank from its consequences. Mississippi politics and national Democratic party politics were never the same again. Few people had made such a difference to so many in their lifetimes. Many of the people who spoke at the funeral had started out with Hamer in the early years of the civil rights movement: Stokely Carmichael (Kwame Toure), Ella Baker, Hodding Carter III, and Dorothy Height. Many had gone on to fame and prominent careers. Andrew Young, who had been a young SCLC organizer and aide to Martin Luther King when he bailed Hamer out of the Winona jail, was ambassador to the United Nations. He arrived in Mississippi in a U.S. government plane. The *Washington Post* marveled that a tiny town like Ruleville could host such an extraordinary funeral.

In Young's eulogy he described Hamer's significance and the moment of history she represented:

Everything I learned about preaching, politics, life and death, I learned in your midst. The many people who are now elected officials would not be where they are had we not stood up then. And there was not a one of those that was not influenced and inspired by the spirit of this one woman, Mrs. Hamer....

Women were the spine of our movement. It was women going
door-to-door, speaking with their neighbors, meeting in voter-
registration classes together, organizing through their churches,
that gave the vital momentum and energy to the movement.
Mrs. Hamer was special but she was also representative. . . . She
shook the foundations of this nation.

Fannie Lou Hamer had a radical vision. She created an experiment
that broke with the established order and allowed people, white and
black, an empowering glimpse of possibility. What people took from
that experiment was a sense of a different way of life, a vision of
community with high moral purpose, and a sense of themselves that
was far more exhilarating than anything they had known before. All
the people who spoke at her funeral said the same thing: knowing
Mississippi and Fannie Lou Hamer had changed their lives.

Her headstone reads, "I'm sick and tired of being sick and tired."

BELLA
SAVITSKY
ABZUG

BORN: JULY 24, 1920, BRONX, NEW YORK. DIED: MARCH 31, 1998,
NEW YORK CITY. FATHER: EMMANUEL SAVITSKY. MOTHER: ESTHER
TANKLEFSKY. MARRIED: MARTIN ABZUG, 1944. CHILDREN: EVE
(1949); LIZ (ISABEL JO; 1952). GRADUATE, COLUMBIA LAW SCHOOL,
LAW REVIEW, ADMITTED NEW YORK BAR, 1945. NATIONAL LEG-
ISLATIVE CHAIR AND EARLY FOUNDER OF WOMEN'S STRIKE FOR
PEACE, 1961. FIRST JEWISH CONGRESSWOMAN AND FIRST WOMAN
ELECTED TO CONGRESS ON PLATFORM OF PEACE AND WOMEN'S
RIGHTS, 1971–76. GLOBAL ACTIVIST FOR ENVIRONMENTAL JUS-
TICE, CONVENOR OF WOMEN'S CONGRESS FOR A HEALTHY PLANET,
1991; COFOUNDER, WOMEN'S ENVIRONMENTAL DEVELOPMENT
ORGANIZATION, 1990.

As we contemplate this, the bloodiest century of human history which dawned at Sarajevo with an incident that launched a world war . . . and is ending in Sarajevo with brutal murders of children, women and men, . . . is it not time to admit that the present dominance, style and conduct of male leadership has been a disaster? . . . Our call is to build communities, not only markets. Our call is to stop nuclear testing. Our call is to scale the great wall around women everywhere.

BELLA ABZUG, PLENARY SESSION,
FOURTH WORLD CONFERENCE ON WOMEN,
BEIJING, 1995

When Bella Abzug died in 1998, few Americans realized she was better known internationally than she was within the United States. As Secretary General Kofi Anan reminded the audience at her memorial service at the United Nations, it was Abzug who assembled the first women's caucus on the environment in Rio de Janeiro in 1992, and "there has been no turning back since then."

In death, as in life, Abzug brought together an unlikely mix of men and women from different continents and social classes. Diplomats, UN officials, colleagues, local and national politicians, representatives of nongovernmental organizations, movie stars, actors, musicians, family and childhood friends—over fourteen hundred people assembled for an unprecedented service held in the General Assembly of the United Nations. They spoke about her extraordinary career and how they came to know her and how she had affected their lives. Peace, feminism, environmentalism, human rights, military policy, and global economics were all part of her philosophical and political framework, and she made friends in every field. "The tribute that really captured who she was," said author and feminist Gloria Steinem, "was the woman from Africa who got up and sang a song she had written for Bella and got everyone else to sing it with her." Not only did Abzug have a wonderful singing voice; everyone agreed that one of Bella Abzug's salient personality characteristics was an ability to get people to do things they never imagined they could, or would, do.

Although it seemed she led and served in causes of great diversity, she always saw them as part of an integrated whole. From the very beginning, when she started out as a lawyer, she had an internationalist's vision of global politics and a sense of America's role in the world. "I am not a centrist," she said proudly. While she gained most notice in the United States for paving the way for other women to enter American politics, she used her political skills and knowledge of governmental agencies to create new networks and international coalitions of women around the world. "Never underestimate the importance of what we are doing here," she told the Fourth World Conference on Women. "Never hesitate to tell the truth. And never, ever, give in or give up. We must elect more women—yes. But we must transform those structures to which we elect women . . .

because present institutions will not do. In my heart I believe that women will change the nature of power rather than power change the nature of women."

The two operative words in Bella Abzug's biography are "voice" and "first." When she decided to become a lawyer, still in high school in the 1930s, it was a time when only one out of a hundred practicing lawyers was a woman. The sign that defined her professional identity still hangs outside the offices of the Women's Environmental Development Organization (WEDO) in New York:

Bella S. Abzug, Esq.
Attorney at Law

Even as a young woman, her mission as a lawyer was to give voice to the oppressed, to use the lawyer's skills to fight the good fight. After she was elected to Congress and became a public figure in the 1970s, the press usually photographed her with her mouth open, jabbing a finger at someone outside of the picture frame. Because she was first, because she was forceful, because she did not speak quietly or deferentially, as women were supposed to, the media called her loud, abrasive, angry, brash, rude, and profane and turned her into a caricature of "Battling Bella." Even in 1995, during the Fourth World Conference on Women in Beijing, China, former president George Bush, also in China at a convention of agricultural executives, said, "I feel sorry for the Chinese having Bella Abzug running around China." When Abzug, who was in a wheelchair at the time, was told of the remark, she said with her typical quickness, "He's at a fertilizer convention, right?" He was.

She knew the stereotypical image overlaid on her was a technique for diluting her influence. "There are those who say I'm impatient, impetuous, uppity, rude, profane, brash, and overbearing," she wrote in the autobiography of her first year in Congress, *Bella!* "Whether I'm any of those things, or all of them, you can decide for yourself. But whatever I am—and this ought to be made very clear at the outset—I am a very serious woman."

WOMEN'S STRIKE FOR PEACE

I still remember the first big demonstration we had outside the United Nations to protest resumption of nuclear testing. We carried balloons and signs and some of us were holding babies

in our arms. We were scared as hell about Strontium 90 from
nuclear fallout poisoning our kids' milk. From out of nowhere
it seemed, thousands of women turned up at the UN that day.
Most of us didn't know each other. We didn't even have a name
for our group yet.

Bella!

In the 1950s many American households bought their milk from a
local milk delivery service. Daily or every other day, a milkman arrived by truck to deliver fresh milk in glass bottles, the kind we now
buy in expensive natural food stores. At some moment in the early
1960s, families across America began finding "Dear Neighbor" notes
slipped in between the newly delivered bottles. "This milk could
contain Strontium 90, which is very dangerous to children," the letter warned. "Strontium 90 causes leukemia in children." The signature belonged to a group identified as the Women's Strike for Peace
(WSP) Radiation Committee.

Doctors had been diagnosing unusual clusters of childhood leukemia in unrelated sections of the country. At first they thought
contaminated water was the source of the illness, but this explanation raised unanswerable questions: How could the same contami-
nant be found in completely different states supplied by distinctly
separate watersheds? Although the government admitted nothing
about the medical effects of atmospheric nuclear tests, scientists familiar with nuclear medicine believed there was legitimate cause
for alarm. Air currents did not respect state lines or national borders. While most of the nuclear tests were conducted at sites in the
Nevada desert (or Pacific islands), winds carried radioactivity thousands of miles from the sites, with reports coming from as far away
as Canada.

Strontium 90 was a chemical by-product of the radioactive fallout
that came from nuclear testing. It entered the atmosphere during the
nuclear test explosion, traveled by wind, mixed with rain and snow,
fell to the ground, percolated into the water table, was absorbed into
vegetation, including grass, and was ingested by cows. Strontium 90
entered the human food chain through milk. Children were particularly vulnerable because they drank large quantities of milk. As small
amounts of Strontium 90 built up in their bones, it caused leukemia
or other childhood cancers in epidemic numbers. The U.S. govern-

ment's Atomic Energy Commission (now in the Department of Energy) denied any connection between children's leukemia and nuclear testing. The commission also denied that nuclear tests were taking place, even though the United States had conducted over two hundred tests in the previous fifteen years, averaging over fourteen per year.

In November 1961 women in sixty cities around the country organized simultaneous demonstrations to protest the dangers of nuclear testing. They came out of the PTA and the League of Women Voters and were mostly middle-class housewives. They were rightly concerned about a nuclear foreign policy that affected their children's health and well-being. They opposed America's resumption of nuclear testing, publicized the effects of nuclear fallout, and criticized the government's lack of accountability. They saw their role as one of moral witness and public education. They did not see themselves as political actors. Although Congress did everything possible to paint their leaders with a Communist brush—within weeks of that first demonstration their leaders were called before the House Un-American Activities Committee—they tapped a largely spontaneous outpouring of anxiety by other women across the country who were appalled at the direction of America's leadership. Unlike their husbands and fathers, they thought the macho values of the Kennedy administration were creating nuclear havoc in the world. Even though it was the height of the cold war, and paranoia about the Soviet Union permeated public life, the leaders of WSP publicly suggested that "better dead than Red" did not constitute a viable foreign policy. (The concept of "victory" under a Mutual Assured Destruction [MAD] postulated a nuclear exchange with Russia that would leave fifty million Russians dead to thirty million Americans.) Similar anxieties over a nuclear future created women's movements in England, France, Italy, Germany, Russia, Australia, and New Zealand. Women's Strike for Peace was part of an international reaction to governments' seeming indifference to the consequences of a nuclear exchange.

At the same time, however, women in postwar America had little public presence or political voice. Except for Eleanor Roosevelt, it was rare to hear women speaking in public. The best known, like Jackie Kennedy or actress Marilyn Monroe, had high pitched, whispery, girlish voices and were unfailingly gracious. The idea of articulate, assertive, political women was lost with the return of soldiers to civilian life and the removal of women from the "men's" jobs they had held so successfully during the war. The push for suburban housing and massive developments (like Levittown) for returning veterans further removed women from centers of civic activity. Commercial and political goals were intertwined in the mass removal to the new suburbs. Women were busy buying new furniture for their new houses, driving new cars, going to the new shopping centers that were being built on former farmland, and, in the absence of public transportation, consuming ever more oil and gas in order to transport their children. Women had neither the time nor the possibility for civic life.

Consequently, the two decades after World War II (1945–65) constituted one of the most romanticized periods of women's domesticity in American history. Women were keeping house, raising children, buying appliances, entering bake-off's, decorating the perfect home. The middle-class American woman was Queen of the Kitchen. One of the most popular shows on television was *Ozzie and Harriet*, and in most episodes Harriet—who in real life had been a feisty jazz singer—appeared in the kitchen wearing an apron while Ozzie and their two sons got in and out of various scrapes. Women supposedly aspired to nothing more than a well-run home, well-brought-up children, and a successful, wage-earning husband. Middle-class women attended college. Many became teachers or nurses. Working-class women were secretaries or factory workers. But the engagement of either class of women in the public world usually lasted only until they married. Politically, they voted like their husbands, and politicians saw them in domestic terms.

It was in this cultural context, in December 1961, that Bella Abzug showed up at a planning meeting of the women who would form the New York branch of Women's Strike for Peace. Although Abzug was a mother and a housewife, she had a résumé that was considerably different from that of other women in the room. She had gone through law school at the top of her class, passed the bar exam, endured discrimination from male lawyers, started her own law firm, solved child care arrangements at a time when mothers didn't work outside the home, and litigated several highly visible labor and civil rights cases, of which the most notorious was the trial of Willie McGee in Mississippi.

Unlike most of the women in the room, she had real knowledge of how the legal system worked. She also understood long-range political strategy and tactics. She told the members of the planning committee that their demand to stop the arms race simply was not enough. A negative demand was not good politics. We need to ask for a specific piece of legislation we want Congress to adopt, she told them, like a treaty banning nuclear testing. She proposed that the next demonstration combine a march in Washington with a lobbying effort in the halls of Congress for a test ban treaty. If they didn't know how to lobby, she would teach them. Public demonstrations, she pointed out, brought publicity, but they needed to be combined with legislative pressure. Amy Swerdlow, who knew Abzug from Hunter College and who attended the same meeting, remembered, "We appointed her the New York legislative chairperson on the spot. It was so obvious that she knew much more than we did." The strategy of combining demonstrations with lobbying became the template for all future WSP actions, and within the year she became legislative director for the national organization of Women's Strike for Peace.

That is not the same thing as saying Abzug's leadership was easily accepted or that women were grateful for her political direction. As Amy Swerdlow documents in her book *Women's Strike for Peace: Traditional Motherhood and Radical Politics in the 1960s*, the majority of women who joined WSP were well educated but identified with being mothers and housewives. (Swerdlow herself, at the time a young mother and housewife, later went back to school, received a Ph.D. in history, and became a professor of women's studies at Sarah Lawrence College.) They were not political and didn't want to be. As Swerdlow points out, "WSP leadership was convinced that the movement's greatest appeal lay in . . . notions of *moral motherhood* and its dissociation from male political culture—both of the Right and the Left" (italics added). The members saw themselves as simple housewives trying to make the world safe for children; they did not see themselves as activists lobbying for new laws. They knew nothing about women's history or the suffrage movement and saw their activism as sui generis. They viewed politics as a dirty business. A WSP memo of the period expressed a commonly held opinion: "We can't beat the devil at his own game, and we really shouldn't be in there trying. Politics is dirty, immoral, corrupt."

Bella Abzug's view was that politics may be a dirty business, but it's our business. It is a measure of her natural political gifts that she was eventually able to transform the consciousness of some of the apolitical women who saw demonstrations as public housekeeping into effective lobbyists and political operatives. While the ethos of the organization was primarily about motherhood and moral witness, Bella's activism was rooted in understanding the deep structures that create policy and law. At a fundamental level she also believed that a movement was not just about the achievement of goals: it created structures; it instructed its participants in analysis; it taught members how to think. She believed that the notion of moral motherhood prevented women from forming a sophisticated understanding of militarism and the ways that domestic structures supported militaristic ends. This sophisticated perception of the relationship between social constructs and an aggressive foreign policy was a consistent theme throughout her life.

In 1961, however, Abzug looked similar to the other middle-class mothers assembling to plan a march on Washington. She was forty-one. She lived in Mount Vernon, a Westchester County suburb, with her stockbroker husband, Martin Abzug, and two young daughters, Liz, age nine, and Eve, age twelve. But unlike the others, she was commuting daily to her law office in New York City. Amy Swerdlow remembered Abzug as being different right from the beginning. "We were housewives. She was out in the world. It showed."

GROWING UP IN THE BRONX

Bella Abzug was born in 1920, the year the women's suffrage amendment passed. As she often described herself, "[I am] a lawyer, social reformer, wife, mother and independent woman who, happily, was born the year that suffrage was approved." She grew up in an Orthodox Jewish, Russian immigrant family in the Bronx. Her father was one of many Russian Jews who emigrated to New York to flee the czar's pogroms and anti-Jewish edicts of the turn of the century. Emmanuel Savitsky left Russia to escape being conscripted into the czar's army during the Russo-Japanese War of 1905. He met Bella's mother, Esther Tanklefsky, on the Lower East Side, where he ran a butcher shop. (During World War I he renamed the shop "The Live and Let Live Meat Market" to express his humanist values and opposition to war.)

When their first child, Helene, was born, the Savitsky family moved to the Bronx, a considerable step up from the Lower East Side of Manhattan. They brought Old World culture with them. Although the Savitsky household was not luxurious, there was always money for music lessons. Bella's parents followed opera, classical music, and ballet. My father, she said, "was always singing folk songs in Yiddish and Russian, and when he wasn't, his favorite Caruso record was on the Victrola." The Savitskys made sure their children had a musical education. Bella's older sister, Helene, studied piano and later became a classical concert pianist. Bella played the violin. "Later I taught myself the mandolin—it's easier." Throughout her life Bella enjoyed opera, attended ballet, and sang in public when the occasion arose. People were always surprised to hear what a fine singing voice she had. The year before she died, she strolled onstage in a top hat and black tails in the middle of a Leslie Gore concert and sang a pitch-perfect rendition of Marlene Dietrich's "Falling in Love Again," bringing down the house. Feminist leader Gloria Steinem recalled her breaking cultural barriers at international conferences by singing folk songs or playing the mandolin. Music was an important part of her life, and her oratory showed a musician's sense of rhythm.

"She first became a feminist," says her sister Helene, "when she was segregated in the temple." Orthodox Judaism was the framework of her childhood. Her grandfather, Wolf Tanklefksy, lived with the family and used to take Bella along when he went to daily services at the synagogue. By the time she was seven, she had learned to recite all the complicated Hebrew prayers "like a wizard," in her own words. Her grandfather was so proud of her, "he always made it a point to show me off to his friends." While she enjoyed the recognition, she also had questions: Why, she wanted to know, are women assigned the last rows in the balcony? Why don't women have a role in the service? Why do men speak during the services and women don't? Her grandfather's answer—"That's the way it is"—was not good enough for her.

When Bella was twelve, her grandfather died. Then, suddenly, a year later, her father died. The Savitskys became a family of women. Who would say the year of mourning prayers for her father? The Orthodox Jewish religion allowed only men to recite prayers for the dead, and the Savitsky family no longer had any immediate male family members. Bella took it upon herself to go to the temple every day to say kaddish, the daily prayers, for her deceased father. When an interviewer asked her how she did it, she answered, "I just stood in the corner and prayed and the rabbi looked away."

Her mother, Esther, had to take over. Emmanuel's death led to a dramatic change in the family's economic circumstances and made a deep impression on Abzug about the vulnerability of a woman with children to support and no male breadwinner. Orthodox Judaism did not prepare women to assume a public or economic role. Despite having had little preparation, Esther rose to the challenge. She took two jobs, working as a department store saleswoman by day and a cashier by night. She used the insurance money to send her older daughter, Helene, to college and later to music school. Five feet tall and driven with energy, Esther wanted nothing but the best for her daughters. In a book Bella wrote about her first year in Congress, she included her mother in the dedication: "To Mama, who cared first."

The Savitsky family was ambitious, intellectual, and talented, and the children were encouraged to develop their gifts. An outstanding student at her Hebrew school, the Talmud Torah, Bella's Hebrew was so good that she got an after-school job teaching the language at a Jewish center in the Bronx. Later she studied Jewish history at the Jewish Theological Seminary in Manhattan. She credits one of her Hebrew school teachers, Levi Soshuk (whom she also describes as very political and very handsome) as the person who first introduced her to Labor Zionism. She was eleven when she first joined the Hashomer Hatzair, the Young Guard, a Zionist Socialist youth group whose aim was to create a Jewish homeland and to educate Jewish youth for kibbutz life in Palestine. It educated its members in socialism, collective action, the history of the Jewish people, and the origins of the historical Jewish homeland in Palestine. The movement also, in its emphasis on collective action, influenced Bella's social life. Abzug studied with the members of her youth group, socialized with them, and after school joined them when they went as a group to try to collect pennies on the subways. It was where she also began her first public speaking:

I used to go to the subway collecting money for what was known as the Jewish National Fund, and when I went into the

subway to collect this money, . . . people did not know what I
was talking about, what Zionism was. . . . I noticed that at the
age of twelve. So in between subway stops I used to make
speeches . . . with my little blue box, telling people they had to
contribute. So I came home late at night.

As an adolescent in the Hashomer Hatzair and growing up in the
middle of the Great Depression, Bella had to have been profoundly
impressed by both the group's vision and its socialist principles.
Among the key beliefs was socialism: "For a Jewish state to come to
be, it must, from the very beginning avoid all the ills of modern
life. . . . Its guidelines must be justice, rational planning and social
solidarity. . . . The Jewish state can come about only if it is socialist." The power of the collective stayed with Abzug all her life. One
of her exhortations to activists was to never do it alone. Find allies.
Build coalitions. Throughout her career, she insisted that the only
time individuals have real power is when they act collectively. Not
only was Labor Zionism her first experience of collective action; it
also gave her an awareness of her talent for public speaking. She noticed that she collected more money when she gave a speech on the
subway.

By the mid-1930s America was approaching the worst of the depression. Abzug's teenage years were filled with labor strikes, pa-
rades, and demonstrations on behalf of economic reform. She grew
up seeing the consequences of poverty and economic exploitation.
Unemployment was pervasive. Families were struggling to make
ends meet. Everyone talked politics—both American politics and,
after 1933, German politics and the events that were affecting Jews
in Germany with the rise of Nazism. At an age when many American girls were pinning up photographs of movie stars on their bedroom walls, Abzug's dream was to go to Palestine. "All I could think
about was working on a *kibbutz* and going to Palestine to build a
Jewish homeland." Her participation in labor Zionism, which combined the spiritual roots of Judaism and the political analysis of socialism, gave her a political and spiritual framework that remained
with her throughout her life.

In an oral history interview with Amy Swerdlow, Bella recalled
that her deep sense of injustice and her interest in the causes of violence emerged from the era in which she grew up: "I was always sort

of interested in peaceful conflict resolution. In many ways, when I look at what I've done over the years on many levels, there's a strong trend of being very much against violence . . . whether it's the violence of racism or sexism or between nations."

Abzug's decision to become a lawyer, made when she was still in her teens, emerged from that same early personal history: she believed that by defending those who were unjustly persecuted, she could make things right. She felt that "the establishment and institutions do great violence to people" and that lawyers were the people who had the tools to fight back. When she told her family she wanted to be a lawyer, everyone except her mother thought it was a passing phase. "Why don't you marry one?" her relatives responded.

She went to an all-girls school, Walton High School, where she was elected president of her class and had a chance to develop her leadership skills free from the male authority patterns that prevailed in coeducational high schools. A former teacher, who was only four years older than the sixteen-year-old Bella, recalled that even in high school she was exceptionally outspoken. "How can you be my teacher?" Abzug demanded of the youthful-looking twenty-year-old teacher. "You look like a student." According to her Walton classmate and lifelong "co-thinker" Mim Kelber, a journalist and writer who would work with Bella throughout her life, Abzug was extremely athletic in high school and until her sophomore year was something of a tomboy. Then, in her junior year, she emerged as a well-dressed young lady wearing suits that her mother made for her. "We all wore suits then," Kelber said. And sometimes hats.

Bella attended Hunter College in Manhattan, then a woman's college, where she was class president for all four years. When Eleanor Roosevelt visited the college during Bella's senior year, Abzug was photographed on the podium with her, both of them wearing hats. She was a brilliant student and in her senior year applied to law school in spite of the considerable barriers she faced. (In addition to Jewish quotas, professional schools either excluded women or admitted only a handful, a policy that prevailed until the 1970s.)

Everyone told me that if I wanted to be accepted as a lawyer, I should go to the best law school, . . . [but] when I applied to Harvard, I received a letter stating that it did not admit women. . . . I was outraged—I've always had a decent sense of outrage—so I turned to my mother. In those days there was no women's movement, so you turned to your mother for help. "Why do you want to go to Harvard, anyway?" she asked. "It's far away and you can't afford the carfare. Go to Columbia University. They'll probably give you a scholarship and it's only five cents to get there on the subway."

Her mother's unqualified support gave her a sustaining confidence and prevented her from being sabotaged by the self-doubt that blunted the aspirations of many talented women of the era. She did go to Columbia Law School; she did get a scholarship; she did take the subway, and, as she said later, "I've been an advocate of public transportation ever since." She was one of nine women out of a class of eighty-five, the unusual proportion of women attributable to the world war and the fact that many men were away in the military. In 1942 college-educated women worked as nurses or teachers, but they were not visible as lawyers, doctors, or professors, as women had been in the first decades of the twentieth century. The medical, academic, and business professions were largely male. (One estimate holds that by the 1940s women made up only 3 percent of those professions, and an even smaller percentage practiced their profession after getting a degree.) At Columbia, Bella worked hard, was at the top of her class, and became editor of the *Columbia Law Review*, a position and class ranking that should have ensured her a job in one of New York's top firms. But she was a woman and Jewish, and the prestigious firms were made up of white Protestant men, so her choices were considerably circumscribed.

In 1944 Bella had married Martin Abzug, an aspiring novelist and future stockbroker whom she met in Miami while they were both on the way to the opera. When Bella graduated from law school the following year, Martin joined her mother in encouraging her to become a practicing attorney. After she passed the New York bar examination, Bella Abzug went to work in a small law firm specializing in labor law. Even though the firm was made up of "liberal" labor lawyers, her male colleagues were unable to think beyond cultural stereotypes and often treated her like a secretary. She quickly learned to tell them she didn't know how to type. (In truth, she didn't.) Although she handled cases for the local unions like the United Auto Workers, the Mine, Mill and Smelting Workers, and local restaurant workers, she got tired of being taken for a secretary wherever she went. "When I was a young lawyer, I would go to people's offices and they would . . . say, 'Sit here. We'll wait for the lawyer.' " No one believed *she* was the lawyer. So she started wearing hats every day. A hat was the visual equivalent of an officer's stripes. Professional women wore hats. Soon a hat was her signature, and by the end of her life she had a collection of designer hats that identified her in any crowd. (When she was a member of Congress, an extended debate took place on the issue of whether or not she would be allowed to wear her hats on the floor of the House.)

She lasted two years with the labor lawyers—"I left those dopey lawyers because they treated me like shit," she told Amy Swerdlow. She decided to build a general practice. Handling wills, divorces, and daily legal problems, she opened her own law office and never again worked for anyone else.

"I handled divorce cases in which my clients were all too often women who had been trained only for marriage and home and suddenly found themselves facing poverty when their husbands left them." The dilemma of women without a bread-winning male made her think more systematically about the economic inequities in women's lives and the inability of women to be trained or to find work that made them financially independent. She also took on civil liberties cases referred by the National Lawyers Guild, a left-wing organization that provided legal services to clients who were too poor to pay for attorneys or who were involved in prominent constitutional cases.

She began to build a reputation as a skilled litigator and good trial strategist. In the Red-hunting hysteria of the Cold War 1950s, she frequently appeared as counsel with people from the entertainment industry who had been called before the House Un-American Activities Committee or Senator Joe McCarthy's committee to answer charges of having once belonged to a communist organization. Photographs of her with one of her clients, the songwriter who had written "Brother Can You Spare a Dime," show a very beautiful, poised young woman who looked as if she were part of the entertainment industry rather than the lawyer representing it.

In 1949 the Abzugs' first daughter, Eve, was born. Contrary to the prevailing expectations of the time, Bella did not give up working. Her husband was the son and partner of an affluent shirt manufacturer, as well as an aspiring novelist. (He later became a successful stockbroker and author of two novels.) He also had highly evolved ideas about what women could do in the world and agreed they would hire a full-time housekeeper. "While I was at Columbia," Bella wrote, "my future husband Martin Abzug . . . courted me in an unconventional manner. He typed my term papers while I studied in the library." Before they married, they had long discussions about the responsibilities of each partner within marriage and decided that both of them would take equal responsibility for working and parenting. "[We] agreed that I would work at my legal career even after we had children. . . . we raised our two daughters together. . . . our informal understanding of respect for each other's work has endured throughout our marriage." No one should underestimate the accomplishment of creating marriage as a partnership in the postwar 1940s and 1950s. When Gloria Steinem was asked about the source of Bella Abzug's unusual courage and confidence in the political arena at a time when there were few models, she answered, "She had a mother who thought she should be President; and she married a man who thought she should be President." Martin encouraged Bella's ambitions and admired her vision. Friends agree that his loving support and unstinting generosity were crucial to her public life. He often said Bella was too good for the political arena; she said he made her public life possible, because she never experienced the conflict between home and profession that afflicted so many women. "He is the last non-neurotic man on the planet," she once said as Martin kept his equilibrium during a particularly overwhelming moment of media celebrity during her congressional career. It was a marriage of equals, a partnership that lasted throughout their lives; when Martin died unexpectedly of a heart attack in 1986, in the middle of Bella's fourth and last run for public office, she said it was the worst year of her life. Friends say she was never quite the same person after his death. "There's a whole emptiness," she said. "I think about how he would be reacting, the strength he would be giving me."

THE CASE OF WILLIE MCGEE

One of the most visible civil rights cases in the 1950s was that of Willie McGee in Mississippi. Culturally, Mississippi was a state essentially unchanged from the time of Reconstruction. Economically, it had the lowest per capita income in the country. African Americans, who made up more than 50 percent of the state's population, were mostly sharecroppers in a system that allowed them neither civil nor political rights. It was the least mechanized state in the South, with African American laborers providing the muscle for a one-crop cotton economy. Mississippi had many counties in which not one black citizen was registered to vote. War veterans like Medgar Evers, founder of the first Mississippi branch of the National Association for the Advancement of Colored People (NAACP) in 1954, came back from fighting the battle of Omaha Beach in World War II to a state where he could not vote, go to college, or get a white-collar job. He would be assassinated in 1963 on his doorstep for his efforts to bring voting rights to black Mississippians. The state was run by the big landowners of the Delta like Senator James Eastland and Congressman Jamie Whitten, who held their seats in Washington for decades and successfully blocked virtually every piece of civil rights legislation introduced in Congress. (They would still be there in 1970 when Bella arrived.) The tyranny of the Mississippi system was enforced by white supremacist organizations like the Ku Klux Klan, the White Knights, and White Citizens Councils, which were organized around a spurious Christianity that required racial purity and saw sexual contact between the races as satanic or communist—except for unlimited access of white men to black women.

Lynchings and random killings of black men were part of the landscape in 1949 when Willie McGee was arrested and tried for having sexual relations with a white woman. A Mississippi jury found him guilty of rape and sentenced him to death. The facts of the case showed he had had a consensual relationship with the woman for over three years, and it was believed that she had charged him with rape only after he told her the affair was over. His appeal was taken up by the NAACP and the National Lawyers Guild. The Mississippi system provided black defendants with white courthouse lawyers who, according to custom, theoretically "defended" their clients, but without raising any constitutional issues.

Bella Abzug was not quite thirty years old when the National Lawyers Guild asked her to go to Mississippi to develop a constitutional argument against Willie McGee's death sentence. She went and made a cogent argument for his appeal. First, since the "rape" was actually a consensual relationship of more than three years, McGee was not guilty of the crime for which he had been convicted.

Second, she argued that since Mississippi law allowed only whites on juries, McGee did not have a jury of his peers, as required by constitutional law. Third, since southern judges and juries never gave the death penalty to whites for rape, only to blacks, McGee's sentence clearly constituted cruel and unusual punishment.

She succeeded in getting Willie McGee a stay of execution, but it was only temporary. Six months later, in 1950, she was back in Jackson, Mississippi, to argue a second appeal. This time she was several months pregnant. No hotel in Jackson would give her a room. The hotel owners knew the Ku Klux Klan would be looking for her, and they did not want any trouble. It was part of the Klan's credo that outsiders who came from the North, particularly Jews, were all communists. Abzug did not realize how dangerous her situation was until a taxi driver offered to find her a place to stay fifteen miles out in the country. She decided to sit up all night in the ladies' room of the bus station. The next day she presented a six-hour argument for appeal. Despite worldwide publicity and protest marches in many cities, the appeal was denied. Back in New York, Abzug suffered a miscarriage. McGee eventually had three trials. After the last, which included several blacks on the jury, he was denied further appeal and executed in 1951.

This case had a profound influence on Abzug's awareness of the hidden structures of the American legal system. The execution of Willie McGee represented a legal lynching and exposed her to the rules and culture of the Deep South in a way that would not become widely known in America until the civil rights movement of the 1960s. As a Jewish woman highly aware of Nazi history, she was deeply affected by the McGee case. Without the inclusion of African Americans in the political process, there was no changing the system that legally executed Willie McGee. Abzug had seen firsthand what happened where power, not law, ruled. She knew what a power structure looked like, and she understood that changing structure required changing consciousness.

RUNNING FOR CONGRESS

Abzug was fifty years old when she decided to run for Congress. She had never before run for public office. Throughout the 1960s, Bella Abzug maintained her private law practice, worked as a national legislative director for Women's Strike for Peace, and participated in different local coalitions to end the war in Vietnam. The event that precipitated her run for Congress was a confrontation with Mayor John Lindsay of New York over the Taxpayers Campaign for Urban Priorities, a group she had organized to support him in the mayoral race of 1969. In the mid-1960s the Abzug family had moved from Westchester County to a townhouse on Bank Street in Greenwich Village. Bella became an active supporter of politicians who opposed the Vietnam War. Lindsay, a Republican-Liberal, was one.

Movie-star handsome and with the bearing of an elegant old-money patrician (which he really was not), Lindsay was trailing badly in his reelection campaign. To help create support for him Abzug organized a coalition of over a hundred community groups under the name of Taxpayers Campaign for Urban Priorities. As she demonstrated throughout her career, she was a magician when it came to coalitions and caucuses and publicity. The size and influence of the Taxpayers Campaign were magnified by signed full-page ads in the *New York Times* pointing out how more New York tax dollars went to pay for bombs in Vietnam than for repairs to New York's subway system. Emphasizing the imbalance in America's national priorities, the coalition applauded Lindsay's efforts to stop the Vietnam War and help the city. "[We] spelled out in shocking detail," Abzug wrote, "how more of our tax money was being used to kill people in Vietnam . . . than to help people in our city, which was beginning to fall apart at the seams."

Although Abzug supported Lindsay and his policies, she was impatient with him personally. Describing him in her autobiographical book of her first year in Congress, she wrote, "Lindsay . . . gets very uptight when you disagree with him. That must be his social background and temperament, which he would do well to get rid of. . . . Although I suppose . . . I can't expect him to act like a Russian Jew."

Her biggest disagreement came after Lindsay's reelection victory. She wanted him to keep the coalition together and appoint her as its head. He refused. Didn't she want to be a judge? Or maybe head of the housing department? No, she wanted to be head of the Taxpayers Campaign with an official title in city hall. Lindsay refused again. She became angry, but he didn't back down. "You're always so critical of politicians and government," he told her. "Why don't you try it yourself, and you'll find out how hard it is."

"Then and there I decided to run for Congress," she wrote later. "It was like a light switch being turned on in my brain, that 'click' which my friends at *Ms. Magazine* called the moment of recognition of a feminist truth. I had been working hard all those years to elect men who weren't any more qualified or able than I, and in some cases they were less so." She decided to run for the Nineteenth Congressional District of New York, where she now lived, for a seat that had been held for seven terms by a relatively undistinguished Democratic incumbent named Leonard Farbstein.

At the time she ran, there was no *Ms.* magazine; the women's movement, composed mainly of radical feminist cells in New York, Boston, and San Francisco, was still in its infancy; and Jane O'Reilly was at least three years away from writing her classic essay "Click! The Housewives' Moment of Truth," an article published in *Ms.* that named the epiphany many women experienced when they recognized for the first time the artificiality of the cultural constructions under which they lived. Abzug's epiphany was that she, too, could run for Congress. Who better to represent the district than herself? Why should Lenny Farbstein have an eighth term?

"This Woman's Place Is in the House—the House of Representatives" became her campaign slogan. The press, however, named her primary campaign "The Woman's Crusade." It is a measure of Abzug's native political gifts that in a mere nine years she had been able to educate a movement of apolitical housewives and mobilize them into an organized political force. The women of New York Women's Strike for Peace formed her political base. They raised money, conducted effective primary and district campaigns, and helped elect her to Congress in an upset election in 1970. Two hundred thirty-five volunteers from WSP worked in her headquarters throughout the campaign, dozens accompanied her on the streets every day, and hundreds canvassed door to door, dropping literature and telling voters about Bella Abzug the candidate. Across the country other WSP branches raised tens of thousands of dollars at local fund-raising events, distributed handbills, typed and stuffed envelopes of campaign literature, and raised the media's awareness of her campaign. Abzug ran on a platform of peace in Vietnam, a reordering of national priorities, and women's equality.

Women's Strike for Peace had grown and changed over the course of the decade. As the members moved from nuclear testing to opposing the war in Vietnam, they became more sophisticated politically. Abzug was an important leader in informing WSP members about military expenditures and war-related legislation and organizing trainloads of women from all over the country to go to Washington to lobby their congressmen. In less than ten years the war in Vietnam had grown from five hundred American advisers to over a million troops. Abzug had traveled throughout the country speaking to different women's groups about strategies and tactics to use with their congressmen. She had honed her speaking skills and her knowledge of public issues. In New York many of the women she had worked with over the years became dedicated campaign workers, even though they neither considered themselves feminists nor made the transition to the new women's rights movement. "Everytime I tried to show the historical perspective of the women's rights movement and the [transition] from abolition to suffrage to peace, as well as to labor, they thought I was irrelevant. They never understood their historic role as women [or] the . . . link of the peace issue with the feminist issue," Abzug told Swerdlow.

Her credentials as a lawyer and her years as the legislative chair of Women's Strike for Peace made Abzug a credible candidate. Her own articulateness and native drive made her a natural campaigner. She received support of youth groups, antiwar activists, civil rights groups, feminist organizations, neighborhood groups, lesbian and gay organizations, journalists, labor leaders, movie stars (Barbra Streisand campaigned with her), and dozens of New York celebrities. She put together the ultimate progressive coalition and defeated Lenny Farbstein in the Democratic primary and then beat the Republican candidate, a popular radio talk show host, in the general election. When she arrived in Washington in 1970, she was the first woman since Jeannette Rankin in 1916 to have run and been elected in a congressional campaign of peace and women's equality. She was also the first Jewish congresswoman.

She had two swearing-in ceremonies: one, the formal oath on the House floor; the second, on the Capitol steps in front of a thousand cheering supporters with Representative Shirley Chisholm (the first African American woman elected to Congress) performing the ceremony. They were two of thirteen women out of 435 representatives. There were two women in the Senate. As John Lindsay had warned, Abzug was going to find out how hard political life was.

NO ROOM FOR RADICALS

The operating principle for freshmen congressmen was to be seen and not heard. "To get along, go along," was the advice that older congressmen gave to freshmen. The seniority system ruled. Congress was culturally a men's club. It was also a southern men's club where elaborate courtesies, complex protocols, and poetic circumlocutions of speech were the custom. Institutionally, leadership went to those who endured years, even decades, of patient waiting. Southerners controlled the House through the seniority system and the resulting ability to dominate committee assignments, rule changes, information, and appropriations. The inner club made few concessions to newcomers, barely recognized the sprinkling of congresswomen, and retained power by means of obscure rules and procedures that took years to learn and were closed to question or debate. Although reform was a constant topic of discussion, the reformers—usually liberals from the East and West Coasts—were frequently voted out of office after a few terms, long before they could mobilize the necessary numbers to reorganize internal mechanisms. The House was a deeply ritualistic institution and largely insulated from change.

So when Congresswoman Abzug from New York arrived and on her first day in Congress introduced a resolution calling for a withdrawal of American troops from Vietnam, both establishment leaders and reformers alike shook their heads. Conservatives and liberals were equally uncomfortable with professional women, dealt with few women on their committees except as secretaries, and put all women viewing House proceedings into the "Ladies Gallery," even the rare female staff of other congresspeople.

When Bella asked for a seat on the Foreign Affairs Committee, she was given Public Works and Transportation and Government Operations. When she wanted to swim in the House swimming pool, she was told it was open to women only at five in the morning. When she arrived at the House to cast her vote, she was told she could not go on to the floor unless she removed her hat. No other woman member, the leadership told her, had ever complained. As an example they cited Martha Griffiths of Michigan, known as one of the House's most respected and capable legislators, who had not complained when she was given the chair of the House Beauty Committee to oversee the women's beauty salon. Abzug soon learned that no woman had ever chaired a full committee in Congress. (Even now in 2002 with thirteen women in the Senate and sixty women in the House, no woman has chaired a standing committee.)

It is easy to imagine her frustration after rallying her troops, educating women to the necessity of change through political power, successfully mounting a congressional campaign and arriving at her goal only to find that Congress was a men's club and she was shut out. Unlike the dozens of women who quit the British Parliament in 2001, publicly denouncing it as a late-night men's club, Bella was one of only a handful of women in Congress. Congress in 1970 held no critical mass of women to project an effective voice. (In 1997 over a hundred women were elected to the House of Commons in the Labor landslide of Prime Minister Tony Blair. Four years later dozens of them quit after they found that Parliament had a chess room but no day care center, that Parliament sold whiskey but no fax paper, that the working day began in the middle of the afternoon and votes were frequently taken at two in the morning by exhausted and drunk members. One MP called all woman members by the same name, Margaret. After the women objected loudly and to the press, many resigned in 2001.)

Because there were so few women in public life, Abzug became the subject of immense press attention. *Life* magazine did a feature. Her daughter Liz remembers that her high school graduation ceremony, held at Carnegie Hall, was overwhelmed by the presence of the *New York Times*, which cordoned off the first two rows in order to photograph Congresswoman Abzug at her daughter's graduation. Since Abzug was covered by an all-male press corps, there were few women political reporters to give a balanced description. The press corps presented a stereotyped image of Abzug, "the battleaxe," a modern-day temperance type with a voice, in Norman Mailer's words, "that could boil the fat off a cab driver's neck." Accurate portrayals of her intelligence, her sense of humor, her influence, and her understanding of House rules were all too rare.

As Abzug made her way without mentors or guides, she incurred huge personal costs. She worked irrational hours, tried to cover too much, compulsively overate, did not take care of her health until she collapsed and wound up in the hospital. Her tantrums were famous. She showed all the signs of extreme stress and psychological isolation. "Outside of Martin and the kids, I don't feel very related to most people at this point," she wrote about her first year in Congress. "I feel detached in social situations. I'm always thinking about other things, about Congress, about the issues, about the political coalition I'm trying to organize. It never leaves me."

On the positive side, she used her single-mindedness of purpose and her inexhaustible energy to learn all the arcane rules and procedures of the House. She came to her committee meetings famously well prepared, showed up for every Public Works meeting, and managed to get $6 billion in public works funding for New York's sewage treatment facilities and mass transit. She deliberately made policy by inserting amendments into obscure public works bills, requiring, for example, the hiring of women on federally funded public works projects.

On the Government Operations Committee she was able to draw upon her previous civil liberties experience to coauthor several groundbreaking pieces of legislation that included the Freedom of Information Act, the Government in the Sunshine Act, and the Right to Privacy Act. These bills allowed Congress to conduct inquiries into covert and illegal activities of the CIA, gave individual citizens a process by which they could obtain their files from the FBI and other intelligence agencies, and opened government agencies to public scrutiny. She was the first member of Congress to call for Nixon's impeachment after Watergate, and her legislation helped journalists and historians examine the FBI's massive infiltration of civil rights and antiwar groups in the 1960s and 1970s.

After Abzug's first term, the New York Democratic party responded to her visibility by redistricting her out of her seat. The political pros told her to run in Staten Island. "Staten Island is a place I like to visit," she retorted, "but it is not a place where I can win." Instead, she chose to run against popular, liberal congressman William Fitz Ryan on the Upper West Side of Manhattan. It was a painful decision that would have lifelong consequences and generate deep animosity within New York's notoriously fractious Democratic party. The race was further complicated by Ryan's illness from cancer, a medical reality denied by both him and his campaign staff. When Ryan died before the primary, the street gossip was that "she killed him." Had she been a man and a member of the club, the redistricting conflict might have been handled differently. Although Abzug won and was returned to the House, she made enemies who never forgave her.

Within the House leadership, however, she was respected for her brains and her knowledge. At a time when many new congressmen arrived in Washington and issued press releases in lieu of learning about institutional procedures, she studied structure, House dynamics, and the mechanics of the legislative process. Her knowledge of the rules made an impression. When a New Orleans reporter asked Eddie Hebert, chairman of the House Armed Services Committee, to comment about the outrageous and notorious congresswoman from New York, his answer surprised many: "I admire her. We're great friends. Not many realize she was once editor of the *Columbia Law Review*. . . . She is one of the most brilliant Congresswomen we have."

Tip O'Neill, then majority leader, later Speaker of the House, made Abzug one of his deputy whips and was photographed on the Capitol steps handing her a real whip. O'Neill knew she could rally the votes when he needed them. During her third term in Congress a *U.S. News & World Report* survey judged her to be one of the three most influential members of the House.

But the job did not get easier, and Abzug did not learn how to manage the stress. She complained about staff who overscheduled her, yelled at her friends, ripped up speeches that weren't to her liking, and demanded that everyone work the same eighteen-hour days she did. She worked her staff hard and then was hurt when they quit. At the same time, she was tremendously loyal, knew how to apologize, and had a sense of humor; once she connected with someone—even those she berated—she was a friend for life. "I love Bella," said a lifelong friend, "but I hated the way she talked to people. I used to hang up on her." John Lindsay was right. She did find out how hard it was.

Abzug was psychologically isolated, both because of being a woman in a men's club and because of the amount of publicity and celebrity surrounding her. When Spiro Agnew, President Nixon's vice president, told a Republican fund-raising audience that he was doing everything possible to make sure Bella Abzug (who was some fifty pounds overweight at that point) did not appear on the House floor in "hot pants" (short shorts), his remark made the evening news on every television network. Bella retorted, "I expect that hot pants and Agnew will soon be gone from the national scene." She was right on both counts.

Her response to her isolation in a hostile environment was creative and rooted in her early training in labor Zionism. Don't do it alone, was one of her lifetime mantras. Find allies. The first planning session for the National Women's Political Caucus—which called for equal numbers of women and men in elective and appointive office in both the Republican and the Democratic parties—was held in her congressional office in 1971. Among the members of the steering committee were Fannie Lou Hamer of Mississippi; Gloria Steinem, founding editor of *Ms.* magazine; Ann Lewis, later an aide to Senator Barbara Mikulski and White House director of communications during the Clinton administration; and Betty Friedan, author of *The Feminine Mystique* and founder of the National Organization for Women (NOW).

Within Congress Abzug was one of the key movers to organize a congressional caucus on women's issues. She gathered support for the first bills on comprehensive child care, domestic violence, family planning, abortion rights, and a law banning discrimination against women in obtaining credit. (Until that law passed, it was difficult for a woman to get credit or a mortgage without a male cosigner.) These bills were at least twenty years ahead of their time. Ann Lewis said Abzug was one of the very first in 1975 to propose civil rights legislation to prevent discrimination against gays.

Had Abzug stayed in the House, she could have held her seat forever. But like many others—including Lyndon Johnson, who endured the House for eleven years and left at the first opportunity to run for the Senate—she announced in 1976 that she was leaving. Senate seats opened up only once a decade, and it was the height of the women's movement. Women did think, in the words of the Helen Reddy song, they were invincible. Abzug had beaten the odds once; why couldn't she do it again? She was going to run for the Senate.

Viewed sociologically, however, rather than politically, the Senate posed an entirely different set of challenges. As the most exclusive club in the country, it was the preserve of white, male millionaires of middle age. Five of the eight standing committees were chaired by Southern senators. In 1976 there was not one woman member, and there had never been a woman senator who had not been a widow. (Until 1986 there would not be a woman senator who did not arrive as a widow of a deceased senator.) The only entry qualification Abzug possessed was that of age. She was fifty-six when she embarked on her campaign for the Senate. Politically, she faced the opposition of

New York's internecine Democratic party, the national foreign policy establishment that was familiar with her extensive FBI file, powerful southern senators who still remembered the Willie McGee trial, and liberal congressmen in the House for whom her primary struggle against popular Congressman Ryan was still bitterly remembered.

She lost, but just barely. In a remarkable campaign she lost the Democratic primary by less than *1 percent of the vote*. It was not easy to beat her: it took the candidacies of *two* male liberals siphoning off her vote, the eleventh-hour reversal of the *New York Times*'s editorial board, and some late-night voting tallies coming out of Queens. The *Times'* editorial board had voted eight to two to endorse Abzug when Arthur Ochs Sulzberger exercised his prerogative as owner and switched the endorsement to Daniel Patrick Moynihan. Moynihan was a conservative academic, nominally a Democrat, who had served in two Republican administrations. Once elected to the Senate, Moynihan stayed for the next twenty-four years. (His successor was Hillary Clinton.) He built his reputation, critics say, on soliloquies about Medicare, social security, health care, and education, but few substantive results for the state of New York.

Abzug would mount three more campaigns for public office but would never again win elective office. President Carter named her co-chair of his National Advisory Committee for Women, then fired her two years later because the committee protested the effect his 1978 federal budget cuts would have on women. The majority of the members resigned in protest, and Abzug said unapologetically, "I've got to find myself another big, nonpaying job." She tried again for elective office (mayor of New York City, two more campaigns for the House), but political winds shifted. America moved to the right, into a conservatism characterized by the values of individualism, welfare reform, privatization, and bottom-line corporate thinking. The causes of racial injustice, labor unions, housing, antimilitarism, economic justice, and women's rights were eclipsed by the conservatism of the Reagan and Bush presidencies.

THE WORLD ENVIRONMENTAL CRISIS

At some point in the mid-1980s Abzug turned her gaze to the United Nations and the international bodies dealing with global climate change, population, and food. Different international agencies held conferences that focused on different facets of the same question:

How were six billion people (up from three billion in 1960, soon to be nine billion in 2050) going to organize themselves to make sure every man, woman, and child got twelve hundred calories a day and clean water? What would be the global consequences of such massive population growth? Poor people depended most directly on natural resources such as land, wood, and water, yet they suffered the most from environmental degradation. Women in many countries had no basic medical care and were unable to control the number of children they had. Abzug noticed that the agendas for the international meetings dealing with these topics were set in preparatory conferences at which virtually no women participated.

While still a congresswoman, Abzug had served as a congressional adviser to the official U.S. delegation in Mexico City at the 1975 meeting for the United Nations Decade of Women. She had glimpsed the issues of women on an international scale and recognized that because men dominated governmental appointments and official national delegations, women did not have voice in some of the most crucial questions of international policy making. How can you discuss population control without women? How can you discuss world health without women? Why discuss agricultural trade when women were growing much of the food in developing countries and were often the traders in local markets? If women ruled the world, she said, these issues would be framed very differently. So in 1985, at a meeting in Nairobi, Kenya, she organized a panel called "What If Women Ruled the World?" Over a thousand women showed up from countries around the world. Many were active in nongovernmental organizations dealing with population, health, and agriculture. Seeing the response to her panel, she had another epiphany about the need for women's participation in world politics, even though she also knew that foreign policy is the most male-dominated arena in all governments.

Back in New York, now in a small office on Wall Street—with the "Bella Abzug, Attorney-at-Law" sign outside her door—Abzug and journalist Mim Kelber, a friend from high school, formed a foreign policy advocacy group called Women USA. Among its networking activities, Women USA compiled, published, and distributed a directory of women involved in foreign affairs, including the many nongovernmental organizations connected with the United Nations. Just as she had studied the rules of the House of Representatives, she studied the procedures of the United Nations and the rules governing world conferences and their preparatory meetings. Her question was this: How could women obtain input into the preparatory meetings?

She decided that women from many countries had to become involved in global politics, whether or not their governments allowed them an official role. Environmental problems did not respect national borders. Global warming was creating floods in Bangladesh, desertification in Africa, famines in Asia, and temperature increases in Athens and Chicago. The explosion at a nuclear power plant in Chernobyl, Russia, caused deaths and cancer from radiation exposure in all the countries along the North Sea. Now age seventy, Abzug embarked on a new adventure of institution building. In 1990 she cofounded and raised the money for the new Women's Environment and Development Organization (WEDO), based in New York City. WEDO's first action was to call for a World Women's Congress for a Healthy Planet. The purpose of this congress, which took place in Miami in 1991, was to create a women's agenda for the World Environmental Conference (popularly called the Earth Summit) to be held in Rio de Janeiro in 1992. Using the Women USA network to publicize the meeting, Abzug and the WEDO organizing committee succeeded in pulling together fifteen hundred women from eighty-three countries. The Healthy Planet Congress produced the Women's Action Agenda for the Twenty-first Century, a document still consulted for setting standards for women's political participation in developing countries. For the first time an international women's caucus had access and influence within the United Nations.

Many high officials of the United Nations agreed that it was Abzug who was the first to open up the UN to the participation of outside women's organizations. "All of us here today," said UN secretary Kofi Anann at Abzug's memorial service, "know about the 1991 Congress for a Healthy Planet convened by WEDO in Miami, Florida which . . . led to the creation of the international women's caucus. It was at Rio that the caucus carved out political space for non-governmental organizations within the United Nations and then seized that space. There has been no turning back since then. . . . I pledge to do my utmost to guarantee that those doors remain open from this day forth. Bella's legacy shall endure."

It was not easy to get her internationalist viewpoint across to the American public. The American press gives limited coverage to the

United Nations (only one national newspaper, the *New York Times*, assigns a full-time reporter to the UN), and the United States has proved to be famously reluctant to sign international environmental treaties. When the United Nations, for example, adopted the environmental Kyoto Accords 178 to 1, the United States cast the one negative vote. Abzug provided leadership for women's input into a series of United Nations conferences following the Rio environmental conference of 1992. These included the International Conference on Population in Cairo in 1994; the World Summit on Social Development in Copenhagen in 1995; the Fourth World Conference on Women in Beijing in 1995; and the series of meetings in 1998 on reproductive health and reproductive rights.

Abzug would not have been surprised by the demonstrations that erupted in 2000 and 2001 in Seattle and Genoa against the meetings of global economic institutions like the World Trade Organization and the International Monetary Fund. Long before these developments, she warned an international audience at the World Summit for Social Development that social development, health care, and universal education cannot emerge from global markets. Markets can only facilitate trade, she pointed out; they cannot build communities or institutions or legal systems.

> We are all in a dangerous and fragile transition to an integrated, global market economy dominated by resourcism—an ethic based on exploiting the planet's natural and human wealth for uncontrolled growth.... We must have the boldness to restructure the global institutions that have the power to shape our lives.... Who's watching this process? Who's watching the decisions that get made here? Of one thing I am certain. The women's movement has put women into movement everywhere. And women will be watching. We will continue to demand accountability and transparency—in the World Bank and the World Trade Organization, the IMF and the UN.... We will insist upon Codes of Conduct to regulate the behavior of these so-called "faceless" corporate bodies that consider only financial gain, not human pain.

Over the four decades of Bella's public life, one of her greatest contributions was her tireless—and fearless—promotion of women in public life. She believed politics was a team sport, not an individualist's game. She knew, and said, that the absence of women from policy councils around the world created such a great imbalance that it resulted in all nations placing emphasis on war-making as the primary function of governments. Many Americans attending international conferences often noticed that a woman delegate might introduce herself as the "Bella Abzug" of her country. Translated, this meant a woman who was willing to step forward to occupy public space, to speak loudly for what she believed in, and, in Bella's words, to never give in, never give up.

Abzug had extraordinary oratorical skills, and anyone who was in the audience for one of her major speeches realized there was a musical rhythm underneath the words, the cadence of her language following the beat of an invisible metronome. Her speaking skills were so singular that once she caught an audience, she could hold it spellbound or move it to tears. Her speechmaking seemed effortless, but she always worried about her talks, even to the most friendly audience. When she was a congresswoman, she worried about a speech she had to give to Women's Strike for Peace. "What am I going to tell them that they don't already know? Besides, it takes a lot out of me to speak to groups like WSP because they expect so much. They're never satisfied with a small, reasonable speech. They only want to be moved to tears and passion." She rarely gave a small speech; she frequently moved her audience to tears and passion. One observer said that the only time he had seen such mutuality and responsiveness was with African American preachers.

With failing health and in a wheelchair, Abzug insisted on attending a meeting at the United Nations in late February 1998. Upon completing her speech she went immediately to the hospital, where she subsequently underwent heart surgery and died of complications a month later.

Abzug was so fresh and so inventive right to the very end of her life, it seemed that the answer she gave to a reporter after her first year in Congress was the same answer she would have given at the end. Looking back, the reporter asked is there anything you would have done differently?

"No. If anything, I should have done more of it."

WOMEN AND
THE ENVIRONMENTAL
MOVEMENT

A point that has generally been overlooked by historians and analysts of political currents . . . is that historically environmental activism has been the work of women. Theory, philosophy and writing have been the handiwork of men such as Henry Thoreau and John Muir, but action—that is letter-writing campaigns, organization, boycotts, demonstrations, the willingness to lie down in front of bulldozers—has been the business of women.

JOHN MITCHELL, *Sanctuary*, 1996

Every new movement creates its own language. The actions of a few stand out among the many women who have helped to define the vocabulary of the science, history, and philosophy of the modern environmental movement. In this chapter I will look at the contributions of Harriet Hemenway, Rachel Carson, Marjorie Stoneman Douglas, Lois Gibb, and Roberta Blackgoat. At the turn of the twenty-first century a young environmental activist named Julia Butterfly Hill lived for 738 days in the canopy of an ancient redwood tree in California. Her goal was to make the world aware of the destructive effects of the logging of old-growth forests. With help from steelworkers and environmentalists, she was able to live 180 feet above ground, thereby preventing the cutting down of the thousand-year-old redwood. In the end she helped not only to protect the tree but also to negotiate a new vocabulary, one in which the decision-making process of corporate numbers had to include subjective information—linear board feet versus spiritual aspects of forests.

The radical thinking that underpinned the actions of Julia Hill was also the thinking of activists who demonstrated against the Word Trade Organization in Seattle in 1999 and in Genoa in 2001. Environmental thinking has become global, and it involves resisting an international system that tends to encompass only technology and markets while ignoring communities, environment, wildlife, habitat, and local concerns. Economist and futurist Hazel Henderson has observed that capitalism is a system in which the divine right of kings was replaced with the divine right of money. "I am certain of only one thing," observed author and former business school professor David Korten, "that business as we know it is destroying the Earth including all culture and living systems. Never before has there been a system so ubiquitous, so destructive and so well managed."

In America women have long been leaders and activists in environmental causes, although the term "environmentalist" was not coined until the 1960s. (The first published use of the term, according to the Oxford English Dictionary, was in the New Yorker in 1970.) Traditional environmentalism emphasized the protection of wilderness and wildlife. In the 1960s the new ecology movement began to focus on the fallout from specific technologies such as nuclear weapons testing, nuclear energy plants, supersonic transport, hydro-electricity drawn from dams on wild rivers, and pesticide-driven agriculture. "Each battle was fought as though it was isolated from the others," wrote Gerry Mander. "In fact we were opposing a para-digm: a system of logic and a set of assumptions that led to the prob-lems of dams, pesticides, nukes, growth, and the rest of it." That paradigm accepted the absolute beneficence of technology; it held that technology served progress, and that no one could stop progress. The idea that there was such a thing as bad science was still to evolve.

The first person to gain a national audience by posing hard ques-tions about technological decisions was Rachel Carson. In 1962 she published *Silent Spring*, which for the first time raised the issue of how decisions about new technologies are made and whether or not they are subject to democratic debate.

In the mid-1950s Rachel Carson received an outraged letter from Olga Owens Huckins of Massachusetts. Huckins, a resident of the coastal town of Duxbury who had turned her small property into a bird sanctuary, was agitated over the consequences of mosquito spray-ing. She told Carson that after the state had finished aerial spraying the community where she lived, she found hundreds of dead birds. For the first time in memory, birds that nested on her property year after year had not reappeared. Because of these unintended, but dev-astating, effects on birdlife, she requested Carson's help in locating the appropriate officials in Washington who might be able to regu-late the spraying of the pesticide DDT for mosquito control.

Carson, who had spent twenty-five years working as a publica-tions specialist in the Fish and Wildlife Service of the Department of the Interior, tried to find people to help her but in the end was unsuccessful. She put Huckins's letter, and its accompanying letter to the editor of a Boston newspaper, into her own file of pesticide-related incidents, a subject she had been concerned about for some time.

In that moment the seeds of the modern environmental move-ment were planted. It marked the confluence of a superb writer and investigative scientist with a larger nationwide organization whose very origins were rooted in creating an aroused citizenry. Carson was the writer-scientist; Huckins was the field agent and member of the Audubon Society, a national organization with branches in every state. This new movement marked a significant break with the preservation movements of the past because it would require the challenging of corporations and the U.S. government.

Today, almost fifty years after Carson began to examine the systematic development and delivery of pesticides, the environmental movement is epic in its scope and global in its implications. People speculate about the carrying capacity of the planet and the need for new thinking beyond the limits of economic growth. In 1955, however, it was the height of the cold war, and any challenge to America's beliefs about progress, technology, and scientific superiority was considered unpatriotic and subversive.

Huckins was one of those women whom many journalists loved to deride for their flat white tennis sneakers and nondescript clothing ornamented only by a pair of binoculars. She and her colleagues in the Audubon Society were not afraid to block bulldozers or stop road crews to protect bird habitat. They wrote letters to the editor, they lobbied, they camped out in the offices of any state official responsible for land, marsh, or water. At one point the Massachusetts Audubon Society had 118 chapters, 114 of which were headed by women.

The very idea of the Audubon Society had been conceived by Massachusetts women over a century ago. In fact, at the time of Huckins's letter to Carson, the organization's founder, Harriet Hemenway, was still alive. The activist culture she helped to create wove together several strands that would be crucial to the development of a modern environmental sensibility: a sense of geography unfettered by state or national borders, an understanding of bird migration routes and how seemingly unrelated lands thousands of miles apart constituted related bird sanctuaries, and a multigenerational sense of time.

Harriet Hemenway (1858–1960) founded the Audubon Society in 1896 in her outrage over the slaughter of birds to adorn women's hats.

By the 1890s the mark of a stylish woman was a large-brimmed hat, richly ornamented with sweeping plumes and feathers. To supply the market for feathers, bird hunters by the thousands went out into tropical lands to seek out the most brilliantly colored birds. By the 1890s five million birds a year were being killed for their feathers. The beautiful snow-white feathers of the egret, called *aigrette* by the French, were the most popular. Some hats even included an entire stuffed bird on the top. The richest source of birds was in Florida, where hunters went into the Everglades during nesting season. Since the birds would not leave their eggs even with the sound of gunfire around them, the hunters shot sitting birds, plucked the feathers, tossed the carcasses into a pile, and left the chirping babies to starve.

When Harriet Hemenway, a woman of considerable social standing in Boston, read an article describing the state of a heron rookery in Florida after the bird hunters departed, she was appalled. Never before had she made the connection between the beautiful hats she and her friends wore and the destructive reality that made them possible. What can we do about it? she asked her cousin Minna Hall, who lived across the street. Florida bird rookeries seem awfully far away from Boston's Marlborough Street, her cousin answered, but perhaps we could stop women from wearing feathered hats.

Never underestimate the importance of tea, Mrs. Hemenway decided. Together the two women invited a number of society women for afternoon tea, and over cucumber sandwiches they asked if Boston women would be willing to give up wearing their feathered hats to stop the slaughter of plumed birds. Hemenway, who proved to be a skilled strategist, also invited a number of well-known ornithologists to join them. Out of these teas emerged the Massachusetts Audubon Society, named after the great artist and naturalist James Audubon. Like the women who lead the contemporary campaign against fur coats to save fur-bearing animals from trappers and cruel farming practices, Hemenway began to instruct and energize her friends in environmental activism to halt what she saw as a needless slaughter of birds on behalf of women's vanity.

Since Mrs. Hemenway was a woman who knew how to use her social prominence, her guests agreed to stop wearing feathered hats and to pay hefty dues to support her new society. (Five dollars was a lot of money in 1896.) They "vowed to work to discourage the buying or wearing of feathers and to otherwise further the protection of native birds." By the end of the first year, the new society had nine hundred dues-paying members, mostly women. Hemenway urged them to call their cousins in Philadelphia, and within a year there was a Pennsylvania Audubon Society. Soon society women in Boston, Philadelphia, and New York were making a public show of refusing to wear feathered hats. Milliners protested that they would all be put out of business. The new activists asked their milliners to create fashionable hats without feathers. Within four years there were Audubon Society branches in Pennsylvania, New York, Maine, Colorado, and Washington, D.C.

A good tactician who understood the activists had to present a constructive program as well as a negative demand, Hemenway got a prominent ornithologist to chair the organization and persuaded family friends, like Senator George Hoar of Massachusetts, to introduce legislation to prohibit the shooting of nongame birds. In Washington Senator Hoar introduced a bill in the U.S. Senate to prohibit the sale and shipment of plumes within the United States and their export to other nations. Over the next ten years the Audubon Society succeeded in getting similar legislation introduced in state legislatures, including New York. (As a young man, Franklin Roosevelt introduced protective bird legislation in the New York legislature. On the other hand, his cousin Teddy, who was a great conservationist when it came to land, seemed to enjoy shooting any animal species that crossed his path.) Professional ornithologists joined the board of the Massachusetts Audubon Society, giving its efforts more credibility. Since women did not have the vote and had few platforms from which to conduct political activity, it was important that they have male figureheads.

Hemenway galvanized women to sponsor informational teas in their own communities, telling women that even though they did not have the vote, they could write letters and lobby for new legislation to outlaw the slaughter of birds. Soon they started a newsletter linking the branches, suggesting new organizing techniques, and giving news about the rare birds that members had spotted. Many members also belonged to suffrage organizations and used many of the same organizing techniques. ·

By 1905 fifteen other states had formed Audubon Societies, and many consolidated into the National Audubon Society. The Massachusetts group, however, remained independent, safeguarding its funding and the independent leadership roles of women in their branches. (Women were state officers in equal numbers with men.)

"Within a matter of a decade," John Mitchell wrote, "the little bird club had spawned what would be the most influential conservation movement in America up to that time."

When Hemenway died in 1960 at the age of 103, the movement she had initiated had become the training ground for many of the talented women and men who would take leadership roles in the new environmental movement of the 1960s. Unlike the conservation movement of the past, new environmentalists would question science and challenge the technological developments of corporations.

Rachel Carson (1907–64) was one of the rare women of her generation who was both a trained scientist and an immensely talented writer. Despite the prejudice against women in science, she had studied genetics and received a master's degree in zoology from Johns Hopkins University. Although her ambition was to be a writer, family obligations and financial need made it necessary for her to take a steady job. From 1930 to 1953 she worked at the Fish and Wildlife Service in Washington, D.C., as director of publications, one of the first women professionals hired by the service. During the week she wrote about national wildlife refuges and other federal programs and in the process set a new standard for the quality of government publications. On weekends she did her own writing.

Her first book, published in 1951, was *The Sea around Us*, a poetic book that captured the compelling world of nature, a microscopic world of the sea unseen by most nonscientists. Serialized in the *New Yorker*, it won the National Book Award, was published in thirty-two languages, and was so successful it enabled Carson to leave her job with the federal government to write full-time. Her next book, *The Edge of the Sea*, published in 1955, was the work of a gifted writer and another book on the ecology of ocean life. Neither book broke with any of the conventions of traditional nature writing. It was not until 1957, after the accumulation of reports of bird kills from aerial pesticide spraying and trucks spraying residential neighborhoods, that she decided her next book would be about pesticides, particularly DDT. The topic was a great departure from her previous writing and tapped a deep passion and lifelong concern for the direction science was taking.

Rachel Carson analyzed her research. Her thesis was that the indiscriminate use of pesticides, particularly DDT, over the long term would result in genetic damage to both animal life and humankind. "I shall be concerned," she wrote to her editor, ". . . with the slow, cumulative and hard-to-identify long-term effects. It is chiefly when life-span experiments are conducted with animals that the real damage shows up. No one now can honestly say what the effects of lifetime exposure in man will be, because not enough time has elapsed since these chemicals came into use."

DDT was considered a miracle substance when it was introduced in the late 1930s, and the Swiss scientist who invented it received the Nobel Prize for science in 1948. When sprayed in villages in South and Central America, DDT killed disease-carrying mosquitoes and had the beneficial effect of wiping out malaria. During World War II, the U.S. Army sprayed DDT in the Pacific theater to combat typhus and malaria. Closely related to nerve gas, DDT was considered a great scientific advance and was brilliantly effective when it came to killing mosquitoes. Some of the immediate side effects, however, were worrisome. In Egypt, for example, after a village near the Nile was sprayed with DDT, the walls of the adobe buildings began to crumble. And the mosquitoes that reappeared after DDT spraying were resistant to the pesticide.

The book that Rachel Carson published as *Silent Spring* had as its central metaphor a landscape without birdlife. If industrial societies continued in their rampant use of persistent pesticides like DDT, she warned, one day we would all wake up to find a silent spring in which no birds returned to sing or build nests or maintain the balance of nature. "It is ironic," she wrote in *Silent Spring*, "to think that man might determine his own future by something so seemingly trivial as the choice of an insect spray." She proposed that the long-lasting "persistent" chlorinated hydrocarbon pesticides be restricted and their use regulated. To combat agricultural pests, she proposed new techniques that today might be characterized as organic farming and integrated pest management.

When *Silent Spring* was published in 1962, reaction was immediate and virulent. Although Carson had not proposed the banning of all chlorinated hydrocarbon pesticides, only those that had longlasting residues and whose long-term impact on biological systems was still unknown, her stance was criticized as being uninformed, anecdotal, and unscientific. Chemical companies said she was not a chemist and thus lacked the expertise to evaluate the chemical composition of pesticides. They attacked her for being against science, against progress, against new technology. Where, her critics asked, were other scientists to support her? The Department of Agriculture, which had to approve all pesticides as "safe," dismissed Carson's analysis out of hand with attacks that were both personal and sexist. "I thought she was a spinster," said a member of the Federal Pest Review Board. "What's she so worried about genetics for?" Two chemical companies that manufactured DDT sued Houghton Mifflin, her publisher. The media reported all the chemical industries' claims but only a few of the rebuttals. Three out of five corporate sponsors canceled their support of a television documentary based on *Silent Spring*. Even so, the book went to the top of the best-seller lists and was translated into twelve languages.

Carson tried to keep her distance from the controversy. "I'm convinced," she wrote to a friend, "there is a psychological angle in all this, that people, especially professional men, are uncomfortable about coming out against something, especially if they haven't absolute proof that 'something' is wrong, but only a good suspicion. So they will go along with a program about which they privately have acute misgivings. So I think it is most important to build up the positive alternatives." She advocated managing insects through sterilizers, introducing natural predators, and eliminating monoculture, farming a single crop over vast areas of land, a practice that invites pest infestations and plant diseases. She recommended a variety of crop fields, cultivated in close proximity to one another.

Silent Spring—a brilliant work of synthesis, investigative reporting, and interdisciplinary investigation—became one of the most influential books of the twentieth century. It changed how people thought about the environment and science. As cancer rates in the United States and other industrial countries skyrocketed, people began to rethink the slogan of Dow Chemical, "Better living through chemistry." In 1969 Sweden was the first country to ban DDT after its scientists proved that milk given to children contained DDT residues. In the ensuing years scientists have shown that the long-term effects of chlorinated hydrocarbons are destructive to the reproductive systems of both humans and animals, particularly in utero. In the 1990s Rachel Carson's work was carried to its next stage by Dr. Theo Colborn (already in her late fifties and a grandmother when she obtained her Ph.D. in genetics), who published the "endocrine disruption hypothesis." After seven years of research she showed that at least fifty-one synthetic chemicals, especially those made from chlorinated hydrocarbons, were disturbing the endocrine systems of wildlife and humans by disrupting sex hormone functions during prenatal development. (Her work resulted in the book *Our Stolen Future*, co-authored with Dianne Dumanoski and John Myers.)

Rachel Carson died of cancer in 1964. She did not live to see the U.S. Congress pass the Environmental Protection Act, the Endangered Species Act, or the Clean Air and Clean Water Acts or create the Environmental Protection Agency and the President's Council on Environmental Quality. She did set out a thoroughly modern framework in which to think about nature and the interrelatedness of all species.

"In each of my books," she wrote,

"I have tried to say that all of the life of the planet is interrelated, that each species has its own ties to others, and that all are related to the earth. . . . We have already gone very far in our abuse of this planet. Some awareness of this problem has been in the air but the ideas had to be crystallized, the facts had to be brought together in one place. If I had not written [*Silent Spring*] I am sure the ideas would have found another outlet. But knowing the facts as I did, I could not rest until I had brought them to public attention."

The ability to bring all "the facts together in one place" was also the talent of Carson's contemporary **Marjory Stoneman Douglas (1890–1998)**, whose mission was saving the Florida Everglades. Because of her longevity—she lived to be 108—Douglas was able to make the transition from writer to environmental activist in the 1960s. Her subject was the ecology and history, both natural and human, of all of southern Florida, a topic still in the headlines. A recent editorial in the *New York Times*, "Two Bushes and the Everglades," decried the failure of President George W. Bush and his brother, Florida Governor Jeb Bush, to implement the $8 billion congressional legislation to restore the Kissimmee River and the Florida Everglades.

The hydrology of the Everglades was a subject that Marjory Douglas first brought to national attention in the 1940s when she was a reporter and writer. Her book *The Everglades: River of Grass* (1947) was the definitive work on Florida's natural environment. More than any other single person, Douglas was responsible for educating Americans and the world (the Everglades today is a United Nations World Heritage Site) about the unique and complex ecosystem of southern Florida and why it must not be destroyed by ranchers, developers, and sugar beet farmers. The environmental complexity that she captured in three words, "river of grass," reframed people's perception of the Everglades, a primal water landscape filled with sawgrass that covered over a third of southern Florida (it has since been reduced by half).

Rather than the snake-infested, mosquito-thick swamp that most native Floridians believed the Everglades to be, Douglas described a complex water landscape, a complicated system of rivers, lakes, and freshwater sloughs crucial to Florida's hydrology. Although the intricacy of the Everglades was well understood by the Miccosukee and Seminole Indians who lived within the region's borders, it was not valued by Florida's Anglo residents, who were bent on economic development. It was Douglas's genius that she was able to create a unique and accessible synthesis of Florida's human history, geography, weather patterns, geology, archaeology, and anthropology in a book that has remained in print over fifty years and has sold over a million copies.

Like Rachel Carson, Douglas became involved in her topic out of concern for birds. As the only woman reporter on the *Miami Herald* (a paper founded by her father), she had written a freelance article in the 1930s for the *Saturday Evening Post* about Everglades bird poachers who murdered a popular game warden hired by the National Audubon Society. In 1941 a New York editor asked her to write a book about Florida, although he wanted its focus be the Miami River. She proposed a larger subject. "I suggested it [the Miami River] connected to the Everglades." It would be her first nonfiction book, and the topic turned into a giant project, one that pulled together all her explorations and articles she had written about Florida over the previous twenty-five years. "I was hooked with the idea that would consume me for the rest of my life," Douglas wrote. "A great release of energy seemed to launch me into my most ambitious and important project. The Everglades book, no doubt my best writing, was a product of this personal renewal." Marjory Douglas had found the subject that would be her life's work.

Florida's geology is unique in the world. The entire state sits on a slab of limestone that juts some seven hundred miles out into the sea. Much of the state is only a few feet above sea level and is angled at a southern-sloping slant so that water drains from north to southwest. The land area, which has no mountains and few hills, is laced with lakes and streams, creeks and rivers. The resulting water ecology is key not just to the Everglades but to the weather system of the entire state. Seventy years of draining rivers and wetlands has resulted in pervasive cycles of drought that began in 1940 and currently produce the annual fires that rage in Florida during the dry season, closing highways, cutting off transportation across the state, and filling the air with choking smoke. Every year the watershed drained by the Kissimmee River flows south into the huge Lake Okeechobee. During the rainy months the lake overflows and sends a slow-moving wave of fresh water, no more than five inches deep, across the entire southern third of the state. This freshwater flush takes a year to complete and creates a delicate balance of fresh and salt water in the ground, with accompanying evaporation that produces rain clouds in the air overhead. This cycle is crucial to the timing of Florida's rainfall and the composition of fresh, brackish, and saltwater mix that determines the animal and plant life.

A Massachusetts native, Marjory Douglas went to Florida after her graduation from Wellesley College and a short, disastrous marriage to a man thirty years her senior. (He was an alcoholic and a forger of bad checks.) When her mother died, she decided to go meet the father her mother had divorced when she was six. In the twenty-year interval her father had settled in Florida, founded the *Miami Herald*, and was greatly criticized by developers, sugarcane farmers, and ranchers for his editorials opposing draining the Everglades and endangering Florida's economic future. Douglas stayed in Miami, joined the newspaper staff, and traveled all over the state, meeting some of its early settlers, getting to know some of the Indian population, and reporting on all aspects of Florida life. In the process she also became an accomplished writer. In her book on the Everglades she pulled all these elements together. When *The Everglades: River of Grass* came out in 1947, it was an original and fresh treatment of

natural and human history. Douglas described the natural phenome-
non of a shallow river seventy miles wide flowing several hundred
feet a day through the saw grass to the sea; she described a wildlife
habitat as rich as any on the North American continent; and she described the bloody clash between conquering whites and Florida's
Native Americans, who understood the complexities of ecology and
environmental systems. (One chapter about Indians is called "The
Free People.") That same year the Women's Association of Miami,
of which Douglas was a member, bought the first parcel of land to
create Everglades Park, now a national park and one of the jewels of
America's national park system.

By the 1960s Florida developers put several environmentally destructive new plans on the drawing boards. The first was a proposal
for a jet airport within the Everglades; the second was for an oil refinery on Key Biscayne; the third was a proposal to reclaim more
land from the Everglades for sugarcane farmers by straightening the
Kissimmee River. With public support growing for these misguided
projects, Marjory Stoneman Douglas became an activist. Writing a
book, she realized, was not enough. Now in her seventies, she
founded Friends of the Everglades to lobby, demonstrate, and create
a public campaign of opposition to the Kissimmee River plan. She
lectured to any group that was willing to listen. She had been a suffragist, a feminist, and a civil rights activist, and she understood the
possibilities of an aroused citizenry. She issued press releases, lobbied public officials, and gave talks to any group that pulled together
an audience. "Since 1972 I've been going around making speeches
on the Everglades all over the place. No matter how poor my eyes
are [she was losing her sight] I can still talk. I'll talk about the Everglades at the drop of a hat. Whoever wants me to talk, I'll come over
and tell them about the necessity of preserving the Everglades.
Sometimes I tell them more than they want to know."

By the 1980s ninety percent of the birds had disappeared from the
Everglades, one the most populous bird habitat in the world. Douglas
explained how runoff of chemicals and fertilizers from the sugarcane
production had polluted the entire ecosystem, including coastal wa-
terways and coral reefs, killing sea life. Seawater was leaching into
freshwater wells because of dropping groundwater levels. Within the
Everglades, the change in water was killing plant life, fish stocks,
and animals. Even worse, the U.S. Army Corps of Engineers was pro-

ceeding in its plan to straighten the curves of the Kissimmee River without a study of the environmental impacts on hydrology or animal life. The great oxbow curves of the river soon were eliminated and the river channeled into a straight concrete canal.

Although Friends of the Everglades were successful in stopping the jetport and the oil refinery, the straightening of the Kissimmee River could not be defeated. Congress passed legislation and appropriated federal money. Soon after the project was completed in the late 1960s, water temperatures in the river began to rise, wildlife disappeared, fish died, birds no longer nested because they could not find fish, and the entire southern third of the state began to experience drought because the annual freshwater flush from Lake Okeechobee had been cut off. It took another thirty years of citizen activism for the Corp of Engineers to admit it had made a mistake. Congress passed the Everglades Restoration Act to unstraighten the river—now costing $8 billion (the original project cost $32 million)—in the mid-1990s, but its execution has not yet begun. The *New York Times* warned in 2001, "The forces of regression in Florida—the developers and the sugar barons and all the others with a stake in business as usual—could well prevail."

In addition to working for the restoration of Lake Okeechobee and the Kissimmee River system and campaigning to preserve wetlands, birds, and mangroves, Marjory Stoneman Douglas took on the plight of the endangered Florida panther and the wood stork and worked to preserve the dying coral reefs of Key Largo (also linked to fertilizer runoff). Friends of the Everglades now boasts more than six thousand members, conducts environmental education programs, and trains citizens to be activists. On her ninety-fifth birthday Florida named its new Department of Natural Resources building in Tallahassee the Marjory Stoneman Douglas Building.

She believed in activism and gave this advice to people who asked: "But what can we do?"

> Join a local environmental society, but see to it that it does not waste time on superficial purposes. . . . Don't think it is enough to attend meetings and sit there like a lump. . . . It's better to address envelopes than to attend foolish meetings. It is better to study than act too quickly, but it is best to act intelligently when the appropriate opportunity arises. . . . Speak up.

Learn to talk clearly and forcefully in public. Speak simply and not too long at a time, without over-emotion, always from sound preparation and knowledge. *Be a nuisance where it counts, but don't be a bore at any time. . . . Do your part to inform and stimulate the public to join your action. Be depressed, discouraged and disappointed at failure and the disheartening effects of ignorance, greed, corruption and bad politics— but never give up.* (italics added)

Rachel Carson and Marjory Stoneman Douglas were both educated women who had known the suffragist and feminist movements of the 1920s. In the 1960s women from different backgrounds and experience came to the fore in the environmental movement. These were housewives like Lois Gibbs or working-class women like Karen Silkwood who had neither formal education nor social privilege to give them confidence that people would listen to them. Yet they encountered conditions so life-threatening that they overcame their lack of training and education to courageously speak out against bureaucratic and corporate crime: Gibbs on the realities of toxic chemical dumping at the Love Canal housing development in upper New York state, Silkwood about the unacknowledged and unpublicized hazards of handling radioactive materials at Kerr McGee nuclear processing plants in Oklahoma.

Lois Gibbs (1946–) was a housewife and a bricklayer's daughter who was in her midtwenties when she and her husband invested their life savings in a modest home adjacent to Love Canal near Niagra Falls. They soon found the neighborhood was not all they had hoped for. Named for the romantic theme that the city of Niagara promoted, Love Canal had been partially dug in the 1940s, then abandoned. A local company, Hooker Chemical Corporation, purchased the canal and used it to dump 21,800 tons of benzene, toluene, lindane, dioxin, PCBs, chloroform, and other toxic wastes. In 1953 Hooker Chemical filled in the canal and sold the sixteen-acre site to the municipal School Board of Niagara Falls for one dollar. The deed included a clause that exempted Hooker from any liability involving chemical wastes. The school board ignored the advice of its own attorney to have a chemical consultant investigate the site before taking ownership and proceeded to build a new school directly on top of the dump. The city sold the rest of the land parcel to a local builder, who designed a residential development called Love Canal that eventually provided housing for over a thousand families.

After a winter of heavy snows and rains, Gibbs and her neighbors noticed a choking stench and a sludge oozing out of the ground. Because of the rise in groundwater levels, chemicals began rising to the surface, and neighbors discovered rusted-out metal drums popping up in their backyards and on the school playground. In 1976 Gibbs wrote that a report by Calspan, a private research laboratory hired to test in the area,] "had stated that dangerous chemicals were leaking out of Love Canal. Calspan . . . had made numerous recommendations, but none had been followed."

In 1977 Gibbs's six-year-old son, Michael, started the first grade. After four months of attending the Love Canal school, he began suffering from asthma and having epilepsy attacks. Doctors also found that Michael had liver, urinary, and respiratory problems. When Lois Gibbs tried to get her son transferred to another school, the superintendent refused. It was then she decided to take matters into her own hands. "I was furious," Gibbs recalled. "Like many people I can be stubborn when I get angry. I decided to go door-to-door and see if the other parents in the neighborhood felt the same way." The petition she asked them to sign consisted of four lines demanding the school be closed.

At first she was afraid that people would slam doors in her face and she would be ostracized. Then she asked herself, "What's more important—what people think [of you] or your child's health? Either you're going to do something or you're going to have to admit you're a coward and not do it." She got a friend to help her—a friend who had had three miscarriages since living at Love Canal—and began ringing doorbells on her own street. Soon she had 161 signatures. Some neighbors accused her of ruining property values, and others gossiped about her, but by this time Gibbs had heard too many stories about the health problems of her neighborhood. Although she had been focused solely on the school, she realized the problem was far larger. "The more I heard, the more frightened I became. This problem involved much more than the 99th Street School. The entire community seemed to be sick!"

After meeting with a retired employee of Hooker who told her his disfigured face was the result of dioxin poisoning, Gibbs went to the Roswell Park Memorial Institute in Buffalo and got the help of Beverly Paigen, a biologist, geneticist, and cancer research scientist. Paigen helped Gibbs and other housewives design a research survey about the health problems in the community to present to the New York State Health Department. At first the health department refused to consider the information because it had been collected by housewives instead of epidemiologists, but finally it agreed to review the findings. In the spring of 1978 the department did its own inspection of Love Canal. It found that between 1958 and 1975, five out of every twenty-four children had been born with defects: deformed ears and teeth, deafness, cleft palates, mental retardation, as well as abnormalities of kidneys, heart, and pelvis. One woman had testified that her dog's nose had been burned after sniffing the ground, and a father said the soles of his little girl's feet had been burned when she ran outside barefoot. The Department of Environmental Conservation then conducted a house-to-house survey, tested the air and soil, took samples of residents' blood, and put monitoring equipment in some of the basements. Based on its findings, the health department warned residents to stay on the sidewalks, to not grow or eat vegetables grown in their own yards, and to stay out of their yards and basements. In August 1978 President Jimmy Carter declared Love Canal a federal disaster area. This is not to say that a remedy was readily apparent. The designation as a disaster area simply meant that the State of New York could apply for federal funds to study the problem.

That same month Gibbs presented her school-closing petition at a hearing in Albany. "I was intimidated by the meeting—me, Lois Gibbs, a housewife whose biggest decision up to then had been what color wallpaper to use in my kitchen." At the conclusion of the hearing, the health department ordered the elementary school closed and recommended that children under age two and pregnant women be temporarily evacuated. Gibbs stopped being intimidated. What about everybody else? she asked. She realized the state government had no plan to deal with the larger implications of Love Canal. Calling the health commissioner a murderer, she yelled at him, "If the dump will hurt pregnant women and children under two, what for God's sake is it going to do to the rest of us? We can't eat out of our garden. We can't go in our backyard. We can't have children under two. We can't be pregnant. You're telling us it's safe for the rest of us?"

Following that meeting, Love Canal reached the nation's headlines. Reporters began calling Lois Gibbs for statements. She had never had to deal with national media before. "It was all a new experience ... exciting but also frightening. ... I have a limited education and my vocabulary isn't that large. I didn't know quite what to write or say."

She admitted that in the beginning she did not even know what the initials "EPA" stood for. But she also knew that staying in the news was the only way Love Canal residents were going to get something concrete to happen; otherwise they would continue to be shunted from one state bureaucracy to another. At issue was who was going to assume financial responsibility. Their homes were worth nothing, and residents had no money to move elsewhere. Yet to stay was to risk toxic chemical poisoning. Gibbs suggested that her neighbors organize the Love Canal Homeowners Association. The organization staged rallies and media events, at one point delivering a child's coffin to the governor's office in Albany. Gibbs appeared twice on Phil Donahue's television talk show and once on NBC's *Today* show. She conducted press conferences and testified before Congress. She consulted *Robert's Rules of Order* to learn how to conduct a meeting. She ran the organization from an empty school building and raised money through donations, dues, raffles, bake sales, and speaking fees. Gibbs was not universally well liked, and many argued with her tactics and leadership, but she saw that persistence was the only thing that would see them through. Ladylike behavior was not going to break through bureaucratic red tape.

In the summer of 1978 the governor of New York announced that the state would purchase the homes of 237 families living closest to the dump site. The 710 families left behind, Gibbs included, were to endure the best they could. Mailmen wore gas masks when they came to deliver the mail. The Homeowners Association kept up the pressure. Gibbs was arresting for picketing; the group took two EPA officials hostage for five hours, telling the press they were "protecting" the officials from an angry mob of 250 persons outside. President Carter "sympathized" but did little. It would be another year before federal funds were provided to remove all residents. Finally, in 1980, the New York environmental authorities, on advice from scientists and assurance from Washington that they would get federal funds, announced they would buy the homes of any Love Canal resident who wished to relocate.

Lois Gibbs had learned how to deal with lawyers, scientists, and nationally known reporters. She learned about law, politics, engineering, and chemistry. She ceased to be intimidated by mayors, governors, senators, and the president of the United States. Largely because of Gibbs and the efforts of the Love Canal Homeowners Association, Congress passed legislation creating a federal Superfund to identify and clean up toxic dump sites around the country was introduced and passed in Congress.

After leaving Love Canal, Gibbs and her husband divorced. She moved to Arlington, Virginia, where she started the Center for Health, Environment and Justice, a group that provides grassroots environmental organizations with information and technical assistance. In 1990 Lois Gibbs was one of the recipients of the Goldman Environmental Foundation awards.

As this chapter is written in the winter of 2002, an epic battle is taking place in Congress over opening up the Arctic National Wildlife Refuge in Alaska to oil drilling. Since Alaska holds most of America's last true wilderness lands, the developmental drive reflects the shadow of the energy industry over environmental goals. President George Walker Bush, former owner of an oil company and admittedly sympathetic to the stated goals of the energy industry, has made the opening of the Arctic Wildlife Refuge to oil drilling a priority of his administration's energy policy. BP Amoco and Phillips Petroleum, which control 80 percent of the oil production in the Arctic region (including the Trans-Alaska Pipeline and the Prudhoe Bay complex), maintain that energy development in the Arctic Wildlife Refuge will have minimal environmental impact. In fact, biologists have warned that even without oil spills, millions of gallons of waste products from oil and gas production will be introduced into the subsurface or frozen into the permafrost, with significant long-term effects on plant and animal life.

In the passionate debate over the needless ruin of a unique and pristine wilderness for oil that the country does not need (but which will make a few people very rich), few realize that the very concept of wilderness and the preservation of this Arctic land were the lifework of a woman. If it had not been for the lifetime commitment of **Margaret Murie (1902–)**, begun with her husband, Olaus Murie, the Arctic Wildlife Refuge might never have been established in the first place.

Born in Seattle, Murie grew up in Fairbanks, Alaska, and was the first woman to graduate from the University of Alaska. In 1924 she was a young bride accompanying her husband, Olaus Murie, a renowned wildlife biologist, to the Brooks Range in northern Alaska to conduct studies on caribou for the U.S. Biological Survey (now the Fish and Wildlife Service). They were among the first modern white people to venture into this vast wilderness far above the Arctic Circle. The indigenous inhabitants, the Gwich'in in the interior and the Inuit on the coast, shared their knowledge of terrain, climate, and wildlife with the Muries. In her memoir, *Two in the Frozen North*, Mardy, as Murie is known, described going by dogsled up the Porcupine River: "An ideal day to hit the trail; twelve below, just right for mushing." She saw for the first time the Porcupine caribou herd, which migrates some eight hundred miles every year and numbers almost 130,000.

Home to polar bears, shaggy musk ox (survivors of the last Ice Age and a relative of the wooly mammoth), wolves, millions of migratory birds (snow geese, trumpeter swans, arctic terns), multiple herds of caribou, as well as 160 other bird species, the Arctic Wildlife Refuge is recognized as one of the last truly pristine places on the planet. Frequently called America's Serengeti, its nineteen million acres on the northern coast of Alaska far above the Arctic Circle enclose a vast, sweeping tundra laced by rivers and bordered by the towering mountains of the Brooks Range.

In 1927 Murie and her husband left Alaska to study elk in the Grand Tetons of Wyoming, where they established a permanent home. But year after year they returned to Alaska, traveling by river, even taking their two small sons with them. Then, as now, the only way to travel these Arctic lands was by river. Their son Martin, less than a year old, traveled in a little box they built for him on their boat, where "he sat or jumped up and down or slept. . . . he also wore a baby harness . . . hooked to a stout screw eye in the bottom corner of his box. The boat was open and the rushing relentless water was right there beside us."

In the 1930s, in the midst of the Depression, it was difficult to interest citizens of "the lower forty-eight" in Alaskan wilderness. It had also become obvious that the relentless threat of highways, resorts, dam construction, and oil and gas exploration would make it increasingly difficult to save unspoiled wilderness anywhere in the United States. In order to educate the larger American public about the value and integrity of wilderness lands, Murie, her husband, and two colleagues organized the Wilderness Society in 1935. Both Murie and her husband served in leadership roles. They mobilized thousands, including conservation leaders, sportsmen's groups, garden clubs, scientists, bird-watchers, and other individuals across the country who were concerned about America's unique wilderness areas. "My sense of wilderness is personal," Murie wrote. "It's the experience of being in wilderness that matters, the feeling of place."

"In this day and age," Murie wrote about their summers in the Arctic, "it is a rare experience to be able to live in an environment wholly nature's own, where the only sounds are those of the natural world. . . . Far across from us, we sometimes heard the indescribably haunting call of the arctic loons. . . . I have watched a band of fifty caribou feeding back and forth on a flat a quarter mile away; ptarmigan soaring and cluck-clucking." In 1956 a filmmaker accompanied Murie on a summer expedition to the Sheenjek River Valley in the Brooks Range, where the sun never sets. The resulting documentary, *Letter from Brooks Range*, captured on film the valley's spectacular wilderness and wildlife and became an important lobbying tool in support of the 1960 legislation creating the ten-million-acre Arctic Wildlife Range. After the bill passed, Mardy Murie said it was the only time she had ever seen her husband cry. The Arctic region was not declared a wilderness area because at the time there was no legal wilderness designation.

In 1964, after Congress finally passed the Wilderness Act, President Lyndon Johnson invited Murie to the Rose Garden signing ceremony. Olaus Murie had died in 1963, but Murie continued their work to protect wild lands from development by having them declared federally protected wilderness. She wrote letters, gave lectures, and promoted legislation. She regularly returned to Alaska and, with Celia Hunter, head of the Alaska Conservation Society, continued to monitor the region. They held off various development schemes such as a hydroelectric dam, a "wolf control" project, a natural gas pipeline, and a plan to use atomic explosions to create a deepwater port. In 1975 she and Hunter, who was copiloting the plane, crash-landed in a small floatplane while doing an aerial survey of a remote wilderness area. It was seventeen hours before a rescue helicopter found them. Murie was seventy-three. Two years later, appearing at congressional hearings held in Denver, she introduced herself and admitted she was "testifying as an emotional woman." She hoped that the United States was not so rich that it could afford to allow the Alaska wilderness to be lost, nor so poor that it could not afford to keep it. Her testimony created a spontaneous standing ovation.

The Alaska Lands Act passed in 1980. It gave something to everyone, oil lobbyists and environmentalists alike. After feverish lobbying by oil industry lobbyists (who had identified vast oil reserves on the north coast of Alaska), the bill denied a wilderness designation to the Arctic Wildlife Refuge. The environmentalists of the Alaska Coalition (an organization of fifty-five conservation groups) succeeded in adding ten million acres to the original lands of the Alaska Wildlife Range, now renamed the Arctic National Wildlife Refuge (ANWR). The loophole, however, was that although the refuge now included almost twenty million acres (the size of South Carolina), it was not designated a "wilderness" area. The oil industry had succeeded in confining the wilderness designation to only eight million acres in the interior; the remaining twelve million acres of the coastal plain remained legally open for energy development at some point in the future. In 2002 the Bush administration decided that the future had arrived and strongly supported legislation to open up ANWR, as it is called, to oil drilling.

The continuity and dedication that Mardy Murie brought to the wilderness movement and the preservation of the Arctic National Wildlife Refuge for more than sixty years have educated tens of thousands of people and three generations of Americans to the values of wilderness and the need to protect even remote lands from the never-ending pressures of development. Much of the environmental knowledge focused on the current battle over oil drilling in the Arctic Wildlife Refuge comes from studies and research she and her husband helped organize and promote at the earliest stages.

Although the big oil companies claim they can drill surgically without disturbing wildlife or plant life, history shows that oil spills in the Arctic are frequent and toxic. In the past decade, according to the Alaska Department of Environment and Conservation, oil fields in Prudhoe Bay (sixty miles west of the refuge) have seen 2,454 spills, sending over 1.5 million gallons of crude oil into the environment. In 1999 alone, Prudhoe Bay saw 293 spills, amounting to more than 45,000 gallons of oil. No one has forgotten the 10 million gallons of crude oil spilled by the *ExxonValdez* after it left Prudhoe Bay, nor that Exxon's guarantees of on-the-spot emergency cleanup procedures proved largely false. Sophisticated biological studies show that even a small amount of development has a ripple effect over ecosystems, and direct impacts like oil spills are compounded by indirect noise and air pollution that affect migratory patterns and reproduction cycles. The Porcupine River caribou herd that Margaret Murie first saw in 1924 has failed to reproduce at expected numbers. Reports by the U.S. Geological Survey have concluded that oil drilling would affect wildlife, particularly the Porcupine caribou.

During Senate debate over the Bush administration's proposal to open ANWR to oil development, Senator Dianne Feinstein made the most cogent argument against drilling. "If American automobile manufacturers would increase the fuel consumption of SUV's [sports utility vehicles] by three miles a gallon," she pointed out, "in ten years it would save the total amount of oil expected to be recovered from the Arctic Wildlife Refuge."

Murie, now in her nineties and living in Wyoming, was asked if she thought environmental activists could prevail. She answered, "I believe that the dedication of environmentalists in working for positive changes and putting pressure on decision makers will do it." She added, however, that Congress must be constantly watched.

Within the past decade, international environmental organizations have focused increasing attention and resources on the inability of indigenous peoples throughout the world to protect their lands and resources from transnational corporations which frequently operate in collusion with host governments. These conflicts raise questions of both environmental justice and human rights. Native peoples, who have deep knowledge of land and its ecology, are often displaced from their ancestral lands without being able to gain voice, publicity, or protection. While the dilemmas of the indigenous people in Ecuador (oil reserves) or Malaysia (timber) reached

American media, similar conflicts in the United States have remained largely invisible.

One person who has broken that media whiteout is Navajo elder **Roberta Blackgoat (1917–2002)**. In 1994 the National Woman's History Project awarded Blackgoat its "America's Unsung Woman" prize for her leadership in publicizing the environmental and human rights abuses that have accompanied massive strip-mining on Black Mesa, Arizona. In February 2000 the European Parliament noted those same Arizona lands when it passed a human rights resolution, introduced by Green party members, citing the United States for abuses in regard to "Native Americans in the U.S.—Dineh (Navajo)."

Black Mesa, where Roberta Blackgoat lives, is not black and is not a mesa. It is high, dry plateau-land of dry washes and canyons that descend to a ginger-colored desert. Encompassing a four-thousand-square-mile section of the Colorado Plateau, roughly the size of Connecticut, it contains the largest coal reserve in the United States, some twenty-one billion tons of low sulfur coal. Roberta has lived on Black Mesa her entire life, herding sheep, weaving rugs, and trading goods with the neighboring Hopi, whose eleven villages are approximately eighteen miles to the south of her sheep-herding camp. Over the years, while the Hopi and Navajo have had various boundary conflicts, largely attributable to inconsistent reservation policies pursued by the U.S. government, they have also traded goods (Hopi corn and vegetables for Navajo mutton), attended each other's social dances, and frequently intermarried.

In the mid-1960s, unknown to the larger tribal populations, both the Hopi and Navajo tribal councils secretly negotiated coal-mining leases with the Peabody Coal Company, the largest coal production company in the United States. (In 2001 Peabody Coal went public under the name Peabody Energy, Inc.) Neither tribal council held any vote or referendum over the pros and cons of mining, the effects it would have on the larger populations, the number of acres involved, the projected environmental impacts, or how long the strip-mining would last. Since America still gets 53 percent of its electricity from coal, the leases were projected to run until the year 2035. The traditional leaders of each tribe (not to be confused with the tribal council) were horrified when they saw the strip-mining equipment rumbling down Cactus Valley Road. The Hopi elders eventually sued their own tribal council, charging that the leases were illegal because they had been signed without a quorum. The Navajo tried to stop the mining by blocking the access roads with abandoned trucks. The elders of each tribe viewed land as a sacred trust and, like traditional Yankees for whom preservation of principal is an unquestioned value, they regarded destroying land for strip-mining as tantamount to spending the next generation's capital.

The coal, however, had been sold even before it came out of the ground. In 1970 the Mohave Generating Station went on line in Laughlin, Nevada, 273 miles away. Few realized that the coal to run it came from Black Mesa, because the coal was transported by pipeline, a prototype slurry system and the only operating coal slurry pipeline in the country. (In white communities slurrylines are always defeated because of the impact on groundwater levels. Black Mesa remains the only operating coal slurryline in America.) The water to run the slurryline came from pumping a billion gallons a year of scarce groundwater from Black Mesa's only aquifer. Even tribal council members did not realize they had sold precious water rights when they signed the coal leases. The coal-fired electricity was going to Los Angeles, Phoenix, and Las Vegas. The Navajo saw none of it.

Roberta noticed that the watering holes where she took her sheep were turning into mud holes and that her sheep often became ill after drinking. Lambs born in the spring died by fall. Within a few years her Hopi friends told her that their springs, the Hopi's sole water supply, were going dry. Problems soon worsened because a second mining site opened on Black Mesa, this one even larger than the first. Despite many good efforts, it was impossible to block the mining expansion. The new coal production had been pre-sold to another power plant under construction. The Navajo Generating Station—ironically named because fewer than 50 percent of Navajo families have electricity—near Page, Arizona, was the second largest electrical generating station in the country. Supplying additional electricity to the everexpanding cities of Las Vegas and Los Angeles, it also ran the pumps to send water from the Colorado River up over three mountain ranges into the desert cities of Phoenix and Tucson. Its largest owner was the U.S. government.

Soon a hundred-car coal train was thundering across the isolated high desert to the Navajo plant: coal dust in the air was causing asthma rates to soar; sheep were dying from the toxic runoff leaching into the groundwater; drag-lines used in the strip-mining obliterated whole valleys, including over a thousand ancient Anasazi ruins; the ecology of the entire region was changing rapidly. Plants didn't re-seed and vegetation soon disappeared. In an arid climate the stripped land could not be reclaimed with native plants. Because of dropping groundwater levels, rain clouds didn't form and a drought began. But the worst was still to come. In 1974, the same year the Navajo Generating Station opened, Congress passed a law mandating the removal of thousands of Navajos from family lands where many of them had lived their entire lives.

Congress transferred a land parcel the size of Rhode Island from the Navajo, who lived on it, to the Hopi, who did not. The law that passed in December 1974—called "Chinatown" by insiders but officially known as Public Law 93–541—represented the first time in American history that a land conflict between two Indian tribes had been settled by giving the land of one tribe to the other and by physically removing thousands of inhabitants. (To date over twelve thousand Navajos have been relocated, more than the entire population of the Hopi tribe.) Congress saw a parade of witnesses who testified that the land was largely uninhabited, that at most eight hundred nomadic Navajo sheepherders would have to be relocated, and that the removal would be similar to an eminent-domain proceeding for a new highway. One such expert witness, assistant secretary of the interior Harrison Loesch, soon became a vice president for Peabody Coal. As the relocation proceeded and thousands of Navajo families were caught up in the government's net and abandoned in border towns at the edge of the reservation without any support services, one environmental activist asked, "Do we really want to destroy one of America's last indigenous cultures in order to water twenty-six golf courses in Phoenix?"

Roberta, as she is widely known, was told she would have to move. At the time she was a fifty-eight-year-old widow still supporting five children. Among the residents of the Big Mountain area, she was one of the few who spoke English, the result of having been sent to the Keams Canyon Indian boarding school as a child. "I hated it," she recalled. "I ran away every chance I could." But she did learn English and, unlike most of her neighbors, who spoke only the Navajo language, she had the experience of knowing how important it was to understand and speak English if you had to deal with the U.S. government.

Ten years earlier her husband had been killed while changing a tire by the side of the road. The state of Arizona denied her welfare benefits. She protested the decision and with her lawyer, Martha Blue, an Indian-rights attorney based in Flagstaff, traveled to San Francisco to testify at a federal government welfare hearing. Martha Blue recalled that she was a great witness. "Roberta was different because she knew English. She was very Navajo, yet she was comfortable wherever she was. It was clear from the beginning she was a very articulate woman." Her testimony was clear and persuasive; she didn't get confused under cross-examination; the press gave her a lot of coverage (this occurred the same time as the Native American occupation of Alcatraz). Blackgoat won her case.

By the early 1980s, when it became clear that the Navajo tribal council could (or would) not help the thousands of Navajos who were being removed from their lands on Black Mesa, Blackgoat reprised her San Francisco experience. She began the life of an activist, speaker, marcher in demonstrations, writers of letters to the editor, and confronter of high government officials and corporate executives—roles she relinquished only with her death in April 2002. Her San Francisco experience exposed her to the mechanics of Anglo bureaucracies, showed her the power of publicity, and provided her with the rare experience (for an Indian) of winning. While many Navajo elders on Black Mesa, particularly the women elders, known collectively as the grandmothers, continued to speak out and resist the different phases of the government relocation effort, Roberta was the one who could get to the microphone because she spoke English and was willing to travel. For the next twenty-five years she journeyed to Washington, testified in Congress, spoke to hundreds of human rights and environmental groups, traveled to the United Nations, flew to Geneva to appear before the UN Working Group on Indigenous Peoples, participated in the Earth Summit in Rio de Janeiro, spoke at Peabody's corporate parent's stockholder meeting in London, and helped organize Black Mesa support groups in the United States, Europe, and Japan. "You Never Fail Until You Stop Trying," was a sign she hung prominently on her kitchen wall. Appearing before a group of Harvard students in 1992 she told them, "I am doing this for all of us. Your children and my children and their children." In London in 1998 for the annual stockholders meeting of Hanson's Limited, the most recent corporate parent of Peabody

Coal, she managed to get her picture in the newspapers after Lord Hanson berated her when she tried to take the microphone. "I only wanted to offer a prayer," she said disarmingly. Her accomplishment was to provide focus and continuity to three decades of resistance and to push a parallel story about Black Mesa's massive energy development into public consciousness. Although the American public was informed about "the most bitter and tortured land dispute between American Indian tribes in history," as the New York Times characterized Hopi Navajo relations, it did not know of the buildup on that same real estate of the most intensive energy infrastructure in the United States.

Viewed within a foreign policy framework, Blackgoat took America's closed system of Native American policy into the international arena of indigenous rights and environmental standards. Her persistence extended from an era when the ability to cheat Indians out of land and resources was considered good sport ("we're going to steal these lands fair and square," said one congressional staffer in the 1970s) into the era of the Internet and global environmental activism. It was out of this long history that the European Parliament, in 1999, led by Green Party delegates, first introduced the human rights and environmental resolution about America's Navajo on Black Mesa. The final resolution was sent to the American secretary of state and to the leaders in both the House and Senate. A new generation of activists questioned both the values of corporate governance and the capability of global capital markets to be socially or environmentally responsible. When the deadline for the final removal of the last of the twelve thousand Navajo arrived in February 2000, American embassies across Europe and in Japan saw crowds of demonstrators on their doorsteps asking about the treatment of Native Americans and the true costs of America's energy policies on Indian lands.

American media had dealt mainly with a boundary dispute between the Hopi and Navajo Indians that theoretically required the Navajo relocation for its resolution. The wider context of the story—massive energy development for the urban Southwest, more air conditioning for Los Angeles, more neon for Las Vegas, more water for Phoenix and Tucson, thirty years of strip-mining—was just beginning to be examined. Roberta Blackgoat was one of the people who helped make it part of the story.

EPILOGUE

The Legacy of the Radical Tradition

H istory is context. We choose our history by selecting certain events to include in the national narrative. Events take on meaning only in relation to other events. These narratives, or stories, make up the myths of American culture—myths that are changing all the time. The questions we ask of history change with each successive generation.

A radical sensibility embodies the notion that there are certain political, economic, and social values that a nation must stand for. Understanding the tradition of American radical women frees us to discard myths that no longer serve us well.

Radical movements have always been a minority position. What one generation takes for granted, another generation might have risked jail to attain. The generation of activists that is currently protesting the rule of international institutions like the World Bank and the World Trade Organization or that criticizes the social and political effects of "structural readjustment" is insisting that a world focused solely on corporate profits and global cheap labor can only result in a world without a fair and equitable distribution of resources.

Women radicals have always been a minority within a minority. It has been in the antislavery struggle, the labor movement, the antiwar movement, and the environmental movement that conceptual shifts have allowed women to be seen in a new light. Only in the tension of these movements for change have the contrary images of woman and radical been reconciled. "True costs" of development require the inclusion of the costs of environmental damage.

It takes great courage to act publicly in such a way that questions of social and economic policy are taken out of the dead language of bureaucracy and put in human terms so that everyone can understand them. It takes great lucidity to see the madness of customs that others take for granted.

Women have spoken out and questioned assumptions throughout American history. They· deserve our attention not only for the women's rights movement but also for their participation in the radical political movements that have fashioned the substance of America's growth and maturity.

Further Readings
and Individual Bibliographies

Selected Bibliography
on Women, Radicals,
and Historiography

Updated Bibliography

Index

FURTHER READINGS
AND INDIVIDUAL
BIBLIOGRAPHIES

———— ◆—◆◆◆—◆ ————

SARAH MOORE GRIMKÉ

Nothing has been written on Sarah Grimké as an individual. The most readable account of the lives of the two sisters is Gerda Lerner's *The Grimké Sisters from South Carolina: Rebels Against Slavery* (1967), which focuses on their roles in the abolitionist movement.

Catherine H. Birney's *Sarah and Angelina Grimké: The First American Women Advocates of Abolition and Woman's Rights* (1885) was written with Weld's presence in the background and carries a strong anti-Garrison viewpoint, but it does preserve some valuable incidents of Sarah Grimké's life and has an excellent, colorful account of the sisters' speaking tour in Massachusetts.

Letters on the Equality of the Sexes, written by Sarah Grimké in 1837, was reissued in 1970 and is one of the seminal books on the role of women in America.

Books

Barnes, Gilbert Hobbs. *The Antislavery Impulse, 1830–1844.* New York: D. Appleton-Century, 1933.

Barnes, Gilbert H., and Dumond, Dwight L., eds. *Letters of Theodore Dwight Weld, Angelina Grimké Weld, and Sarah Grimké, 1822–1844.* New York: D. Appleton-Century, 1934.

Birney, Catherine H. *Sarah and Angelina Grimké: The First American Women Advocates of Abolition and Woman's Rights.* Boston: Lee and Shepard, 1885. Reprint. St. Clair Shores, Michigan: Scholarly Press, 1970. Catherine Birney was the wife of William Birney, James Birney's son. She had gone to Eagleswood School, had resided in the Weld home, and had known both sisters. Weld gave her full access to correspondence and letters and was thoroughly involved in the preparation of the book.

Blackwell, Alice Stone. *Lucy Stone, Pioneer of Woman's Rights.* Boston: Little Brown & Co., 1930. Reprint. Detroit: Grand River Books, 1971.

Chesler, Phyllis. *Women and Madness.* New York: Doubleday, 1972.

Chestnut, Mary Boykin. *A Diary From Dixie.* Edited by Ben Ames Williams. Boston: Houghton Mifflin, 1949, 1961.

Child, Lydia Maria. *Letters of Lydia Maria Child.* Boston: Houghton Mifflin, 1883. Reprint. New York: Arno Press and The New York Times, 1969.

———. *History of Women.* 2 vols. *Brief History of the Condition of Women in Various Ages and Nations.* New York and Boston: C. S. Francis, 1835–54.

Culver, Elsie Thomas. *Women in the World of Religion.* New York: Doubleday, 1967.

Filler, Louis. *The Crusade Against Slavery, 1830–1860*. New York: Harper & Brothers, 1960.

Flexner, Eleanor. *Century of Struggle: The Woman's Rights Movement in the United States*. New York: Atheneum, 1968.

Fuller, Margaret. *Women in the Nineteenth Century*. 1855. Reprint. New York: W. W. Norton, 1971.

Garrison, Wendell P., and Francis, J. *William Lloyd Garrison, 1805–1879*. 4 vols. New York: The Century Company, 1885–89. Reprint. New York: Arno Press and The New York Times, 1969.

Graham, Abbie. *Ladies in Revolt*. New York: The Woman's Press, 1934.

Grimké, Angelina. *Appeal to the Christian Women of the South*. New York: American Anti–Slavery Society, 1836. Reprint. New York: Arno Press and The New York Times, 1969.

Grimké, Sarah. *Letters on the Equality of the Sexes and the Condition of Women*. Boston: Issac Knapp, 1838. Reprint. New York: Source Book Press, 1970.

Hunt, Harriet. *Glances and Glimpses*. Boston: John P. Jewett, 1856. Reprint. New York: Source Book Press, 1970.

Kraditor, Aileen S. *Means and Ends in American Abolitionism*. New York: Random House, Vintage Books, 1967.

Lerner, Gerda. *The Grimké Sisters from South Carolina: Rebels Against Slavery*. Boston: Houghton Mifflin, 1967.

Litwack, Leon F. "The Abolitionist Dilemma: The Antislavery Movement and the Northern Negro." In *Understanding Negro History*, edited by Dwight Hoover. Chicago: Quadrangle Books, 1968.

Lumpkin, Katherine DuPre. *The Emancipation of Angelina Grimké*. Chapel Hill: University of North Carolina Press, 1975.

Lutz, Alma. *Crusade For Freedom: Women of the Antislavery Movement*. Boston: Beacon Press, 1968.

Myrdal, Gunnar. *An American Dilemma: The Negro Problem and Modern Democracy*. Vol. 2, Appendix 5, "A Parallel to the Negro Problem." New York: Harper & Row, 1944–1962.

Sanger, William W., M.D. *The History of Prostitution: Its Extent, Causes and Effects throughout the World*. New York: Eugenics Publishing Co., 1937. Reprint. New York: Arno Press and The New York Times, 1972.

Scott, Anne Firor. *The Southern Lady: From Pedestal to Politics, 1830–1930*. Part I. *The Antebellum Lady*. Chicago: University of Chicago Press, 1970.

Sillen, Samuel. *Women Against Slavery*. New York: Masses and Mainstream, 1955.

Stanton, Elizabeth Cady, et al. *History of Woman Suffrage*. Vol. 1. New York: National Woman Suffrage Association, 1881. Reminiscence of Angelina Grimké, p. 393–406.

Thomas, Benjamin Platt. *Theodore Weld, Crusader for Freedom*. New Jersey: Rutgers University Press, 1950.

Violette, August Genevieve. *Economic Feminism in American Literature Prior to 1848*. New York: Burt Franklin, 1925. Reprint. New York: Lenox Hill Publishers, 1971.

Weld, Theodore Dwight. *In Memory: Angelina Grimké Weld. Sarah Grimké*. Printed for private circulation. Boston: Press of George H. Ellis, 1880.

Articles

Ruchames, Louis. "Race, Marriage and Abolition in Massachusetts." *Journal of Negro History* 40 (1955): 250–65.

Unpublished Sources

Boston, Massachusetts. Boston Public Library. Weld-Grimké Letters. Manuscript Collection.
Cambridge, Massachusetts. Schlesinger Library, Radcliffe College. Grimké Letters.
Washington, D.C. Library of Congress. Theodore Dwight Weld Papers. Grimké Papers. Stanton Papers.

HARRIET TUBMAN

The most readable study of Harriet Tubman's life is Earl Conrad's *Harriet Tubman* (1943), which details her work on the Underground Railroad, her life as a soldier in the South, and her work as an abolitionist. The basic source is still Sarah Bradford's *Harriet Tubman: The Moses of Her People* (1886 version expands on the sketch of 1869), which was reissued in paperback in 1961. It contains splendid anecdotes from Tubman about her life and excellent letters and documents about her activities. The article by Franklin Sanborn in Bradford's book is one of the best short biographical sketches ever written about her.

For younger readers Dorothy Sterling's *Freedom Train: The Story of Harriet Tubman* (1954) is an imaginative account of her work on the Underground Railroad. The moving story of what it was like to be a black soldier during the Civil War is to be found in a biography of Henry Singleton, *Contraband of War*, by Laurel Vlock and Joel Levitch (1970). Several excellent accounts of the lives of women in slavery are in *Root of Bitterness: Documents of Social History of American Women* (1972) by Nancy F. Cott. Marcy Heidish has written a dramatic novel based on Tubman's life, *A Woman Called Moses* (1976).

Books

Brackett, Jeffrey. *The Negro in Maryland: A Study in the Institution of Slavery.* Baltimore: Johns Hopkins University Press, 1889.
Bradford, Sarah E. *Harriet Tubman: The Moses of Her People.* 1886. Reprint. New York: Corinth Books, 1961.
Brawley, Benjamin. *Women of Achievement.* Chicago: Woman's American Baptist Home Mission Society, 1919. Harriet Tubman, pp. 27–39.
Conrad, Earl. *Harriet Tubman.* Washington, D.C.: Associated Publishers, 1943.
————. *Harriet Tubman: Negro Soldier and Abolitionist.* New York: International Publishers, 1942.
Cott, Nancy F. "The Trails of Girlhood by Linda Brent." In *Roots of Bitterness: Documents of the Social History of American Women.* New York: E. P. Dutton, 1972.
Dorson, Richard M. *American Negro Folktales.* Greenwich, Conn.: Fawcett Publications, 1967.
Eppse, Merl R. *The Negro Too in American History.* Nashville: National Publication Co., 1943.
Franklin, John Hope. *From Slavery to Freedom: A History of Negro Americans.* New York: Random House, Vintage Books, 1969.
Frederickson, George M. *The Inner Civil War: Northern Intellectuals and the Crisis of the Union.* New York: Harper & Row, 1965.
Frothingham, Octavius Brooks. *Gerrit Smith.* New York: G. P. Putnam's Sons, 1878.

Gaines, Ernest J. *The Autobiography of Miss Jane Pittman*. New York: Dial Press, 1971.

Genovese, Eugene D. *The Political Economy of Slavery: Studies in the Economy and Society of the Slave South*. New York: Random House, Vintage Books, 1967.

Heidish, Marcy. *A Woman Called Moses: A Novel Based on the Life of Harriet Tubman*. Boston: Houghton Mifflin, 1976.

Higginson, Thomas Wentworth. *Letters and Journals of Thomas Wentworth Higginson, 1846–1906*. Edited by Mary Thatcher Higginson. New York: Negro Universities Press, 1969.

Hoover, Dwight W., ed. *Understanding Negro History*. Chicago: Quadrangle Books, 1969.

Hughes, Langston. *Famous American Negroes*. New York: Dodd, Mead and Co., 1954.

Nelson, Truman. *The Old Man: John Brown at Harper's Ferry*. New York: Holt, Rinehart, and Winston, 1973.

Quarles, Benjamin. *Blacks on John Brown*. Urbana: University of Illinois Press, 1972.

———. *Black Abolitionists*. New York: Oxford University Press, 1969.

———. *Frederick Douglass*. Washington, D.C.: Associated Publishers, 1948.

———. *The Negro in the Civil War*. Boston: Little, Brown, 1953, 1969.

Redpath, James. *Echoes of Harper's Ferry*. New York: Arno Press and The New York Times, 1969.

Stampp, Kenneth M. *The Peculiar Institution: Slavery in the Anti-Bellum South*. New York: Random House, 1956.

Sterling, Dorothy. *Freedom Train: The Story of Harriet Tubman*. New York: Doubleday, 1954.

Still, William. *The Underground Railroad: A Record of Facts, Authentic Narratives, Letters Narrating the Hardships, Hair-breadth Escapes and Death Struggles of the Slaves in Their Efforts for Freedom, as Related by Themselves and Others, or Witnessed, by the Author; Together with Sketches of Some of the Largest Stockholders and Most Liberal Aiders and Advisers of the Road*. 1871. Reprint. Chicago: Johnson Publishing Company, 1970.

Stroyer, Jacob. *My Life in the South*. Salem, Mass.: Salem Observer Book and Job Print, 1889.

Villard, Oswald Garrison. *John Brown, 1800–1859: A Biography Fifty Years After*. Boston: Houghton Mifflin, 1910.

Vlock, Laurel F., and Levitch, Joel A., eds. *Contraband of War*. New York: Funk and Wagnalls, 1970.

Woodson, Carter G. *The Negro in Our History*. Washington, D. C.: Associated Publishers, 1922.

Articles

Bardolph, Richard. "Social Origins of Distinguished Negroes." *Journal of Negro History* 40 (1955): 211–38.

Conrad, Earl. "General Tubman at Troy." *The Crisis: A Record of the Darker Races* (Publication of the National Association for the Advancement of Colored People) 48 (1941).

Eggleston, G. K. "Relief Societies During the Civil War." *Journal of Negro History* 14 (1929): 272–90.

Frazier, E. Franklin. "The Negro Slave Family." *Journal of Negro History* 15 (1930): 198–224.

"Moses." *Freedman's Record,* (Publication of the New England Freedman's Aid Society) (1865): 34–38. Author unknown.

Wyman, Lillie B. Chace. "Harriet Tubman." *New England Magazine* 14 (1896): 110–18.

Unpublished Sources

Washington, D.C. Howard University, Moorland Collection.

ELIZABETH CADY STANTON

The most valuable source on Stanton is her autobiography, *Eighty Years and More, 1815–1897: Reminiscences of Elizabeth Cady Stanton* (1970). A short but excellent account of Stanton's life is *Elizabeth Cady Stanton* by Mary Ann Oakley (1972). The most complete biography is Alma Lutz's *Created Equal: A Biography of Elizabeth Cady Stanton* (1940). Alma Lutz, a feminist who knew many of the major figures of the feminist movement in the 1920s and 1930s, collaborated with Stanton's daughter, Harriet Blatch, in writing *Challenging Years: Memoirs of Harriet Stanton Blatch* (1940). Two of Stanton's children, Theodore Stanton and Harriet Stanton Blatch, edited *Elizabeth Cady Stanton as Revealed in Her Letters, Diary, and Reminiscences* (2 vols., 1969). The first two volumes of the *History of Woman Suffrage* (1969) give a history of the origins of the woman's movement and contain several fine sketches that Stanton wrote on Lucretia Mott, Angelina Grimké, and other early women leaders.

For younger readers Winifred E. Wise has written *Rebel in Petticoats: The Life of Elizabeth Cady Stanton* (1960), which emphasizes her early years.

Books

Blatch, Harriet Stanton, and Lutz, Alma. *Challenging Years: Memoirs of Harriet Stanton Blatch.* New York: G. P. Putnam's Sons, 1940. Excellent description of Margaret Livingston Cady, Stanton's mother.

Burnett, Constance Buel. *Five For Freedom.* New York: Greenwood Press, 1968. Includes portraits of Lucretia Mott, Elizabeth Cady Stanton, Lucy Stone, Susan B. Anthony, and Carrie Chapman Catt.

Catt, Carrie Chapman, and Shuler, Nettie Rogers. *Woman Suffrage and Politics: The Inner Story of the Suffrage Movement.* 1923. Reprint. Seattle: University of Washington Press, 1969.

Cromwell, Otelia. *Lucretia Mott.* Cambridge, Mass.: Harvard University Press, 1958.

Dorr, Rheta Childe. *Susan B. Anthony: The Woman Who Changed the Mind of a Nation.* New York: Frederick A. Stokes, 1928.

Flexner, Eleanor. *Century of Struggle: The Woman's Rights Movement in the United States.* New York: Atheneum, 1970.

Hallowell, Anna Davis. *James and Lucretia Mott: Lives and Letters.* Boston: Houghton Mifflin, 1884.

Hare, Lloyd, C. M. *The Greatest American Woman: Lucretia Mott.* New York: Negro Universities Press, 1970.

Kisner, Arlene, ed. *The Lives and Writings of the Notorious Victoria Woodhull and Her Sister Tennessee Claflin.* New York: Times Change Press, 1972.

Kraditor, Aileen S. *The Ideas of the Woman Suffrage Movement, 1890–1920.* New York: Doubleday, 1971.

Lutz, Alma. *Created Equal: A Biography of Elizabeth Cady Stanton.* 1940. Reprint. New York: Octagon Books, 1973.

———. *Crusade for Freedom: Women of the Antislavery Movement.* Boston: Beacon Press, 1968.

Mott, Lucretia. *Slavery and the Woman Question: Lucretia Mott's Diary of Her Visit to Great Britain to Attend the World Anti-Slavery Convention of 1840.* Edited by Frederick B. Tolles. Haverford, Pa.: Society of Friends Historical Association, 1958.

Oakley, Mary Ann. *Elizabeth Cady Stanton.* Maryland: The Feminist Press, 1972.

O'Neill, William R. "Feminism as a Radical Ideology." In *Dissent: Explorations in the History of American Radicalism,* edited by Alfred Young. DeKalb, Ill.: Northern Illinois University Press, 1968.

Rossi, Alice S. "Selections from the History of Woman Suffrage." In *The Feminist Papers: From Adams to Beauvoir.* New York: Columbia University Press, 1973. Bantam Paperback, 1974.

Schneir, Miriam. *Feminism: The Essential Historical Writings.* New York: Random House, Vintage Books, 1972. Declaration of Sentiments and Resolutions, Seneca Falls, p. 76. Frederick Douglass's editorial from *The North Star,* p. 83. Elizabeth Cady Stanton's address to the New York legislature, 1854, p. 110. Address to New York legislature, 1860, p. 117. "Solitude of Self," p. 157.

Seager, Allen. *They Worked For a Better World.* New York: Macmillan, 1939. Contains sketches of Thomas Paine, Ralph Waldo Emerson, Edward Bellamy, Elizabeth Cady Stanton.

Sinclair, Andrew. *The Emancipation of the American Woman.* New York: Harper & Row, 1966.

Sorin, Gerald. *The New York Abolitionists: A Case Study of Political Radicalism.* Westport, Conn.: Greenwood Publishing Co., 1971.

Stanton, Elizabeth Cady; Anthony, Susan B.; and Gage, Matilda Joslyn. *History of Woman Suffrage.* 6 vols. New York: Arno Press and The New York Times, 1969.

———. *The Woman's Bible.* 2 vols. New York: European Publishing Co., 1895. Reprint. New York: Arno Press, 1972.

Stanton, Elizabeth Cady; Anthony, Susan B.; and Gage Joslyn Matilda. Gage, *History of Woman Suffrage.* 6 vols. New York: Arno Press and The New York Times, 1969.

The first two volumes were published in 1881 and were written by Elizabeth Cady Stanton. Volume 1, pp. 407–40, contains her tribute to Lucretia Mott. Volume 3 was published in 1886. Volume 4 was edited by Susan B. Anthony and Ida Husted Harper and was published in 1902. Volumes 5 and 6 were edited by Ida Husted Harper and published in 1922.

Stanton, Elizabeth Cady; Anthony, Susan B.; and Pillsbury, Parker. *The Revolution.* Vols. 1 and 2. (1868–70). Westport, Conn.: Greenwood Press, 1970.

Stanton, Henry B. *Random Recollections.* New York: Harper and Brothers, 1887. Memoir by Elizabeth Cady Stanton's husband. Mentions her only once. Gives excellent detail on her father, Judge Cady.

Stanton, Theodore, and Blatch, Harriet Stanton, eds. *Elizabeth Cady Stanton as Revealed in Her Letters, Diary and Reminiscences.* Vol. 1 Reminiscences. Vol. 2 Letters and Diaries. New York: Arno Press and the *New York Times,* 1969.

Suhl, Yuri. *Ernestine L. Rose and the Battle for Human Rights.* New York: Reynal, 1959.

Tanner, Leslie B. *Voices from Women's Liberation.* New York: New American Library, 1971.

Wise, Winifred. *Rebel in Petticoats: The Life of Elizabeth Cady Stanton.* Philadelphia: Chilton, 1960.

Articles

"Personal Reminiscences of Lucretia Mott." *Harper's Weekly*, December 4, 1880.
Quarles, Benjamin. "Frederick Douglass and the Woman's Rights Movement." *Journal of Negro History* 25 (1940).

Unpublished Sources

Washington, D.C. Library of Congress. Elizabeth Cady Stanton Letters and Scrapbooks. Lucretia Mott Letters.
Cambridge, Massachusetts. Schlesinger Library, Harvard University. Mary Grew's Diary of London Convention of 1840.

CHARLOTTE PERKINS GILMAN

Charlotte Perkins Gilman's autobiography, *The Living of Charlotte Perkins Gilman* (1935), is the best source of information about her life and family, although she omits almost all reference to her second marriage, to Houghton Gilman. (The only source about her personal life is in her unpublished papers at the Schlesinger Library at Radcliffe College.) Elaine R. Hedges has written an excellent interpretive essay of Gilman's literary masterpiece "The Yellow Wallpaper," to be found in a recently published edition of *The Yellow Wallpaper* (1973).

Women and Economics (1898) is Gilman's best-known book, although not the easiest of her works to read. An excellent introductory essay by Carl Degler is in a recent paperback edition (1970). The books which were most influential on her, Lester Ward's *Dynamic Sociology* and Edward Bellamy's *Looking Backward*, are both available in recent editions (1966).

Books

Beard, Mary Ritter. *Women As a Force in History.* New York: Collier Books, 1971. First published 1946.
Bellamy, Edward. *Looking Backward.* 1888. Reprint. Boston: Houghton Mifflin, 1966.
Boston Women's Health Collective. "Postpartum Disturbances." In *Our Bodies, Ourselves.* New York: Simon and Schuster, 1973.
Bruere, Martha, and Beard, Mary. *Laughing Their Way: Women's Humor in America.* New York: Macmillan, 1934.
Chafe, William Henry. *The American Woman: Her Changing Social, Economic and Political Roles, 1920–1970.* New York: Oxford University Press, 1972.
Gilman, Charlotte Perkins. *Concerning Children.* Boston: Small & Maynard, 1900.
———. *The Forerunner.* Vols. 2, 3, 7 (1911, 1912, 1916). New York: Greenwood Reprint Corporation, 1968.
———. *The Home, Its Work and Influences.* 1903. Reprint. Introduction by William L. O'Neill. Urbana: University of Illinois Press, 1972.
———. *In This Our World and Other Poems.* San Francisco: James H. Barry and John H. Marble, 1895.
———. *His Religion and Hers: A Study of the Faith of Our Fathers and the Work of Our Mothers.* New York: The Century Company, 1923.
———. *The Living of Charlotte Perkins Gilman: An Autobiography.* 1935. Reprint. New York: Harper and Row, 1975.

———. *The Man-Made World, Or Our Androcentric Culture.* 1911. Reprint. New York: Source Book Press, 1970.

———. *Women and Economics: A Study of the Economic Relation between Men and Women as a Factor in Social Evolution.* 1898. Reprint. Edited by Carl N. Degler. New York: Harper and Row Torchbook, 1970.

———. *The Yellow Wallpaper.* New York: Feminist Press, 1973. The story originally appeared in *New England Magazine,* January 1892.

———. "Feminism and Social Progress." In *Problems of Civilization,* edited by Ellsworth Huntington. New York: D. Van Nostrand, 1929.

Lippmann, Walter. *Drift and Mastery.* 1914. Reprint. Englewood Cliffs, N.J.: Prentice-Hall, 1961.

Logan, Mrs. John A. *The Part Taken by Women in American History.* Wilmington, Delaware: Perry-Alle Publishing, 1912.

Rourke, Constance Mayfield. *Trumpets of Jubilee.* New York: Harcourt, Brace, 1927. Portraits of Henry Ward Beecher, Harriet Beecher Stowe, Lyman Beecher, Horace Greeley, P. T. Barnum.

Stowe, Lyman Beecher. *Saints, Sinners and Beechers.* Indianapolis: Bobbs-Merrill, 1935.

Veblen, Thorstein. *The Theory of the Leisure Class; An Economic Study in the Theory of Institutions.* 1899. Reprint. New York: The Viking Press, 1967.

Ward, Lester. *Lester Ward and the Welfare State.* Edited by Henry Steele Commager. Indianapolis: Bobbs-Merrill, 1967.

———. *Dynamic Sociology.* 1883. Reprint. New York: Johnson Reprint Corporation, 1966.

Articles

Bibring, Grete L. "Some Considerations of the Psychological Processes in Pregnancy." *The Psychoanalytic Study of the Child* 14 (1959): 113–21.

Bibring, Grete L., et al. "A Study of the Psychological Processes in Pregnancy and of the Earliest Mother-Child Relationship." *The Psychoanalytic Study of the Child* 16 (1961): 9–71.

Degler, Carl. "Charlotte Perkins Gilman on the Theory and Practice of Feminism." *American Quarterly,* Spring, 1956.

Gilman, Charlotte Perkins. "The Wisteria Vine." *New England Magazine,* May 1891.

Stein, Karen. "Reflections in a Jagged Mirror: Some Metaphors of Madness." *Aphra* 6 (1975): 2–11. Analysis of "The Yellow Wallpaper" p. 4–5.

Unpublished Sources

Cambridge, Massachusetts. Schlesinger Library of Women's History, Harvard University. Letters referred to in this chapter were written in the years from 1878–97 and include correspondence with Houghton Gilman, Edward Bellamy, Susan B. Anthony, Jane Addams. Newspaper clippings include her obituary in The New York Times, August 20, 1935; *Publishers Weekly,* August 24, 1935. Complete correspondence of Charlotte Perkins Gilman was received by the Schlesinger Library in 1972.

MOTHER JONES

The Autobiography of Mother Jones (1925), edited by Mary F. Parton, gives a real sense of Mother Jones's spirit and eloquence although its chronology is doubtful.

Dale Fetherling's recent biography, *Mother Jones, The Miner's Angel: A Portrait* (1974), gives a more complete historical account of her life, with dates and places filled in. For younger readers Irving Werstein's *Labor's Defiant Lady* (1969) is an excellent biography. Also for younger readers Irving Werstein's *Pie in the Sky, An American Struggle: The Wobblies and Their Times* (1969) gives a good account of the struggles of the period and the impulse that gave rise to the radical labor movement and the IWW. There are many excellent labor histories but they rarely mention women in general or Mother Jones in particular. One recent example is the otherwise splendid account of the epic Colorado mine struggles in *The Great Coalfield War* by George S. McGovern and Leonard Guttridge (1972).

Books

Brophy, John. *A Miner's Life*. Madison, Wisconsin: The University of Wisconsin Press, 1964.

Browne, Henry J. *The Catholic Church and the Knights of Labor*. Washington, D.C.: Catholic University of America Press, 1949.

Dubovsky, Melvyn. *We Shall Be All: A History of the Industrial Workers of the World*. Chicago: Quadrangle Books, 1969.

Dulles, Foster Rhea. *Labor in America*. New York: Thomas Y. Crowell, 1949.

Fetherling, Dale. *Mother Jones, The Miner's Angel: A Portrait*. Carbondale, Illinois: Southern Illinois University Press, 1974.

Fink, Walter H. *The Ludlow Massacre*. Washington, D.C.: United Mine Workers of America, 1914.

Finley, Joseph E. *The Corrupt Kingdom: The Rise and Fall of The United Mine Workers*. New York: Simon and Schuster, 1972.

Foner, Phillip. *History of the Labor Movement*. Vol. 3, 1900–1909. New York: International Publishers, 1964.

Gluck, Elsie. *John Mitchell: A Study of Leadership and Mass Movements*. New York: John Day, 1929.

Handlin, Oscar. *The Uprooted*. New York: Grosset & Dunlap, 1951.

Hennacy, Ammon. *The One-Man Revolution*. Salt Lake City, Utah: Ammon Hennacy Publications, 1970. Mother Jones pp. 112–30.

Jackson, T. A. *Ireland: Her Own*. New York: International Publishers, 1947.

Jenson, Vernon. *Heritage of Conflict: Labor Relations in the Nonferrous Metals Industry up to 1931*. New York: Greenwood Press, 1968.

Jones, Mary Harris. *The Autobiography of Mother Jones*. Edited by Mary Field Parton. Foreword by Clarence Darrow. 1926. Reprint. Chicago: Charles H. Kerr & Co., 1972. Excellent introduction and bibliography by Fred Thompson.

Lens, Sidney. *The Labor Wars: From the Molly Maguires to the Sitdowns*. New York: Doubleday, 1973.

McLean, Lois. "Looking Back at Mother Jones," address to West Virginia Historical Society. *Beckley Post-Herald* (Beckley, West Virginia), May 30, 1972. Forthcoming book; includes her personal interviews with West Virginia residents who remember Mother Jones.

Powderly, Terrence. *The Path I Trod*. New York: Columbia University Press, 1940.

———. *Thirty Years of Labor*, 1859–1889. Columbus, Ohio: Excelsior Publishing House, 1889.

Schnapper, M. P. *American Labor: A Pictorial Social History*. Washington, D.C.: Public Affairs Press, 1972. Mother Jones, pp. 242, 365, 427, 394.

Vorse, Mary Heaton. *A Footnote to Folly*. New York: Farrar & Rinehart, 1935. Chapter 19, "The Great Steel Strike," Mother Jones, p. 287–90.

Yellen, Samuel. *American Labor Struggles*. New York: Harcourt Brace, 1936. Chapter 7, "Bloody Ludlow," Mother Jones, p. 231

Werstein, Irving. *Labor's Defiant Lady: The Story of Mother Jones*. New York: Thomas Y. Crowell, 1969.

——. *Pie in the Sky, An American Struggle: The Wobblies and Their Times*. New York: Delacorte Press, 1969.

Articles

Federation News, May 7, 1932. "Mother Jones Birth Anniversary Issue." Official publication of the Chicago Federation of Labor, Chicago, Illinois.

"Rockefeller Greets Mother Jones."*New York World*, January 26, 1915, p. 1

"Mother Jones." *People's Appalachia*, Spring 1970, pp. 6–13.

Senate Document No. 415. 64th Congress, 1st Session, Vol. XI (1915–16). Testimony before U.S. Commission on Industrial Relations.

Steele, Edward. "Mother Jones in Farimont Field, 1902." *Journal of American History*, Sept. 1970: 290–307.

Struggle in Colorado for Industrial Freedom. August 17, 1914. "The Activities in Colorado of Mother Jones."

"About Mother Jones: Something Concerning the Woman before the Public in Connection with Labor Troubles." *Wilkes-Barre Record*, March 30, 1901.

Unpublished sources

Mother Jones's letters, newspaper clippings, photographs are in the department of manuscripts and archives at Catholic University, Washington, D.C.

Raffaele, Sister John Francis. *Mary Harris Jones and the United Mine Workers of America*. Unpublished dissertation, Catholic University of America, 1964.

ANNA LOUISE STRONG

The only book about Anna Louise Strong is her autobiography, *I Change Worlds: The Remaking of an American* (1935). It excludes the most interesting period of her life in China. She died before a second autobiography was completed. Her papers are at the University of Washington in Seattle.

Many of her books are not on library shelves (even the Library of Congress) and are available only in private collections.

Perhaps with the official reopening of relations with the People's Republic of China, new interest in the life of Anna Louise Strong will be generated.

Books

Strong, Anna Louise. *The Psychology of Prayer*. Chicago: University of Chicago Press, 1909. Published as Ph.D. thesis in 1908 by the University of Chicago under the title "A Consideration of Prayer from the Standpoint of Social Psychology."

——. *Biographical Studies in the Bible*. Vol. I, *Patriarchs and Pioneers*. Edited by Sydney Strong and Anna Louise Strong. New York: The Pilgrim Press, 1912.

——. *Child-Welfare Exhibits: Types and Preparations*. Washington, D.C.: Government Printing Office, 1915. Pamphlet prepared for the Children's Bureau, Julia Lathrop, Chief.

——. *The First Time in History: Two Years of Russia's New Life*. Preface by Leon Trotsky. New York: Boni and Liveright, 1924. Collected articles originally published in Hearst's International on topical questions concerning Russia during the period August 1921 through December 1923.

——. *China's Millions: The Revolutionary Struggles from 1927 to 1935*. Introduction by John Cournos. New York: Knight Publishing Co., 1935. Reprint. Plainview, N.Y.: Books for Libraries, 1973. Originally published in Russian, English, and German in 1928 as two separate books: *Mass Revolt in Central China* and *From Hankow to Moscow*. Includes her account of the great revolution in Wuhan in 1927 and her trip with Borodin across the Gobi Desert and Outer Mongolia. Edition published in 1935 includes brief chapter on events in China from 1928–35.

————. *Children of Revolution: Story of John Reed's Children's Colony on the Volga*. Seattle: Pigott Printing Concern, 1925.

————. *Red Star in Samarkand*. New York: Coward-McCann, 1929. Account of her travels through Soviet Turkestan, the emancipation of Moslem women, and the efforts to modernize.

————. *From Stalingrad to Kuzbas: Sketches of the Socialist Construction in the USSR*. New York: International Pamphlets, 1931.

————. *I Change Worlds: The Remaking of an American*. Introduction by Lincoln Steffens. New York: Henry Holt and Co., 1935. Her autobiography recounts her childhood, education, working life in America, her decision to go to Russia, and her life there up until the time the book was written.

————. *The New Soviet Constitution: A Study In Socialist Democracy*. New York: Henry Holt and Co., 1937.

————. *One Fifth of Mankind, History of China*. New York: Modern Age Books, 1938. Published in England by L. Drummond Co. in 1939 under the title, *China Fights for Freedom*.

————. *My Native Land*. New York: The Viking Press, 1940. Her account of touring America after the New Deal in 1938; visits to the TVA and Grand Coulee Dam, and her interviews with President Roosevelt and Eleanor Roosevelt.

————. *The Soviets Expected It*. New York: Dial Press, 1942.

————. *The Russians are People*. London: Cobbett Publishing Co., Ltd., 1943. Includes interview with Stalin.

————. *Peoples of the USSR*. New York: Macmillan, 1944.

————. *Inside Liberated Poland*. New York: The National Council of American-Soviet Friendship, 1945.

————. *I Saw the New Poland*. Boston: Little, Brown, 1946.

————. *Tomorrow's China*. New York: Committee for a Democratic Far Eastern Policy, 1948.

————. *The Chinese Conquer China*. New York: Doubleday & Co., Inc., 1949. During the truce of 1946 Strong traveled to Yenan and the liberated areas of China. This account of that period includes her "paper tiger" interview with Mao Tsetung in Yenan.

————. *The Rise of the Chinese People's Communes*. Peking: New World Press, 1959.

————. *China's Fight for Grain: Three Dates from a Diary in Late 1962*. Peking: New World Press, 1968.

————. *Cash and Violence in Laos and Vietnam*. New York: Mainstream Publishers, 1962.

————. *Letters from China*. Nos. 1–10. Peking: New World Press, 1963.

————. *Letters From China*. Nos. 21–30. Peking: New World Press, 1966.

Articles

Allee, Rewi. "Some Memories of Anna Louise Strong." *Eastern Horizon* 9 (1970): 7–19, 44–45.

"Une Garde Rouge Américaine." *Le Monde*, 31 March 1970, p. 3. Obituary.

"Lilly Red After All." *Newsweek*, 14 March 1955, p. 52.

"Soviet Clears Anna Louise Strong of '49 Spy Charge: Blames Beria." *New York Times*, 5 March 1955, p. 1. Account of her arrest, false charges against her, and subsequent clearance.

New York Times, 9 June 1955, p. 15.

"Anna Louise Strong Dies in Peking at 84." *New York Times*, 30 March 1970, p. 1.

Snow, Edgar. "Chinese Conquer China." *Saturday Review*, 19 November 1949, p. 18. Review of her book *Chinese Conquer China*.

The Guardian, 4 April 1970, p. 11. Obituary.

Time, 20 June 1955, p. 24. Account of her press conference announcing exoneration of spy charges by the Soviet Union.

Wales, Nym. [Helen Foster Snow.] "Anna Louise Strong: The Classic Fellow-Traveler." *The New Republic*, 25 April 1970, pp. 17–19.

DOROTHY DAY

Dorothy Day's autobiography, *The Long Loneliness*, is the story of the intertwining of the religious and political impulses of her life. Her other books, *Loaves and Fishes* (1963), *Houses of Hospitality* (1939), *On Pilgrimage* (1972), are on the major themes of the Catholic Worker movement. Most of her books on the Catholic Worker movement have recently been reissued in paperback. The best source about Dorothy Day is still Dwight Macdonald's profile for *The New Yorker* magazine written in 1952 and reprinted in *Politics Past* (1970).

A great deal has been published recently about the Catholic Worker movement and Dorothy Day. William D. Miller's *A Harsh and Dreadful Love: Dorothy Day and the Catholic Worker Movement* (1973) is a complete history of the movement. *A Spectacle Unto the World: The Catholic Worker Movement* (1973) by Robert Coles with photographs by Jon Erikson is a very good introduction to the movement and the people in it.

Books

Brice, C. P. *Teresa, John and Thérèse: A Family Portrait of Three Great Carmelites—Teresa of Avila, John of the Cross, Thérèse of Lisieux.* New York: Frederick Pustet & Co., 1946.

Catholic Worker, Vols. 1–28. Westport, Conn.: Greenwood Reprint Corporation, 1971.

Cogley, John. *Catholic America.* New York: Dial Press, 1973.

Coles, Robert. *A Spectacle Unto the World: The Catholic Worker Movement.* Photographs by Jon Erikson. New York: The Viking Press, 1973.

Cornell, Thomas and Forrest, James, eds. *A Penny a Copy: Readings from the Catholic Worker.* New York: Macmillan, 1968.

Cullen, Michael. *A Time to Dance.* Ohio: The Messenger Press, 1972.

Day, Dorothy. *From Union Square to Rome.* Silver Spring, Md.: Preservation of the Faith Press, 1938.

———. *Houses of Hospitality.* New York: Sheed and Ward, 1939.

———. *Loaves and Fishes.* New York: Harper & Row, 1963.

———. *The Long Loneliness.* New York: Harper, 1952.

———. *Thérèse.* Notre Dame, Indiana: Fides Publishers, 1960. Thérèse of Lisieux was a Carmelite nun who died the day Dorothy Day was born.

———. *On Pilgrimage in the Sixties.* New York: Curtis Paperback, 1972. Compilation of her columns "On Pilgrimage" written for the *Catholic Worker*.

Dickens, E. W. Trueman. *The Crucible of Love: A Study of the Mysticism of St. Teresa of Jesus and St. John of the Cross.* New York: Sheed and Ward, 1963.

Fairfield, Richard. *Utopia U.S.A.* San Francisco: Alternative Foundation, 1972.

Gray, Francine du Plessix. *Divine Disobedience: Profiles in Catholic Radicalism.* New York: Alfred A. Knopf, 1970.

Hennacy, Ammon. *The One-Man Revolution in America.* Salt Lake City, Utah: Ammon Hennacy Publications, 1970. Dorothy Day, p. 280–97. Hennacy was an editor of the *Catholic Worker* in the 1950s and a well-known Catholic anarchist.

James, William. *The Varieties of Religious Experience.* New York: University Books, 1902. Lectures on Natural Religion delivered at Edinburgh, 1901–1902.

Macdonald, Dwight. *Politics Past.* New York: The Viking Press, 1970. p. 349–68.

McCarthy, Abigail. *Public Places, Private Faces.* New York: Doubleday, 1972. Chapter I mentions Dorothy Day's work in the Catholic Worker movement.

Miller, William D. *A Harsh and Dreadful Love: Dorothy Day and the Catholic Worker Movement.* New York: Liveright, 1973.

Moore, Jenny. *The People on Second Street.* New York: William Morrow, 1968. Dorothy Day, pp. 31–32.

Sampson, Ronald V. *The Anarchist Basis of Pacifism.* London: Stuart Morris Memorial Fund, Peace Pledge Union, 1970.

Sheean, Vincent. *Personal History.* Boston: Houghton Mifflin, 1969. Originally published in 1934. Chapter on revolution describes Rayna Prohme, her death in Moscow, and the presence of Anna Louise Strong.

Sheehan, Arthur. *Peter Maurin: Gay Believer.* New York: Hanover House, 1959.

Articles

Cogley, John. "Dorothy Day, Comforter." *New York Times,* 8 November 1972.

Corry, John. "The Style of the Catholic Left." *Harper's,* September 1966, p. 58.

"Dorothy Day and the Catholic Worker Movement," *America,* November 11, 1972. Entire issue devoted to Dorothy Day.

Macdonald, Dwight. "Profile of Dorothy Day." *The New Yorker,* October 4, 1952 p. 37, and October 11, 1952, p. 37.

———. "Revisiting Dorothy Day," *New York Review of Books,* 28 January 1971, p. 12. The introduction to the Greenwood reprint of the *Catholic Worker.*

McCarthy, Colman. "The Pilgrimage of Dorothy Day." *Washington Post,* 19 January, 1971.

———. "The IRS, Dorothy Day and the Poor." *Washington Post,* 18 July 1972.

———. "Colman McCarthy on Dorothy Day." *The New Republic,* 24 February 1973.

Unpublished Sources

The files of Stanley Vichnewski at the Catholic Worker farm in Tivoli, New York, contain a great store of letters, newspaper clippings, books, and memorabilia of the Catholic Worker movement. The staff at the Catholic Worker farm and at the house in New York were extremely helpful in giving me information about the Catholic Worker movement and Dorothy Day. Much information came from interviews with Stanley Vichnewski, Walter Kerrell, Deana Mowrer, and Dorothy Day herself. Others who provided insight were Dwight Macdonald, Francine du Plessix Gray, Abigail McCarthy, Jenny Moore, Colman McCarthy.

A Bibliography on Peter Maurin, Dorothy Day, and the Catholic Worker by Alex Avitabile, S.J. Available from author, Fordham University, Bronx, New York 10458.

FANNIE LOU HAMER

Books

Belfrage, Sally. *Freedom Summer*. New York: Viking Press, 1965.

Branch, Taylor. *Parting the Waters: America in the King Years, 1954–63*. New York: Simon and Schuster, 1988.

———. *Pillar of Fire: America in the King Years, 1963–65*. New York: Simon & Schuster, 1998.

Davison, Chandler, and Bernard Grofman, eds. *Quiet Revolution in the South: The Impact of the Voting Rights Act, 1965–1990*. Princeton, N.J.: Princeton University Press, 1994.

Goodwin, Doris. *Lyndon Johnson and the American Dream*. New York: Harper and Row, 1976.

Kling, Susan. *Fannie Lou Hamer: A Biography*. Chicago: Women for Racial and Economic Equality, 1979.

Hampton, Henry, and Steve Fayer. *Voices of Freedom: An Oral History of the Civil Rights Movement from the 1950s through the 1980s*. New York: Bantam Books, 1990.

Lee, Chana Kai. *For Freedom's Sake: The Life of Fannie Lou Hamer*. Urbana: University of Illinois Press, 1999.

Lemann, Nicholas. *The Promised Land: The Great Black Migration and How It Changed America*. New York: Knopf, 1991.

Lerner, Gerda. *Black Women in White America: A Documentary History*. New York: Pantheon Books, 1972. Documents and writings by and about black women from slavery to the sit-ins.

McAdam, Doug. *Freedom Summer*. New York: Oxford University Press, 1988.

Mills, Kay. *This Little Light of Mine: The Life of Fannie Lou Hamer*. New York: Dutton, 1993.

Moody, Anne. *Coming of Age in Mississippi*. New York: Dell, 1968.

Walton, Anthony. *Mississippi: An American Journey*. New York: Knopf, 1996.

Williams, Juan. *Eyes on the Prize: America's Civil Rights Years, 1954–1965*. New York: Viking Penguin, 1987.

Articles

Baker, Ella. "Developing Community Leadership." Interview with Gerda Lerner. Reprinted in Lerner.

Black Women in America: An Historical Encyclopedia. Vol. 1. Brooklyn, N.Y.: Carlson Publishing, 1993.

DeMuth, Jerry. "Tired of Being Sick and Tired,." *The Nation*, June 1, 1964, p. 549.

Hamer, Lannie Lou. "It's in Your Hands. The Special Plight and Role of Black Women." Fannie Lou Hamer speech to NAACP Legal Defense Fund, May 7, 1971. Reprinted in Lerner.

Murray, Pauli. "The Negro Woman in the Quest for Equality," for *The Acorn*, publication of Lambda Kappa Mu Sorority, Inc. June 1964. Reprinted in Lerner.

Norton, Eleanor Holmes. "Woman Who Changed the South: Memory of Fannie Lou Hamer." *Ms.*, July 1977.

Videotapes and Recordings

Interview with Fannie Lou Hamer. Series of Interviews with Five Mississippi Women. Jackson, Miss.: Center for Educational Television, 1974.

"Mississippi: Is This America? 1962–64." Episode 5, *Eyes on the Prize*, a six-part series for PBS, 1987. Blackside, Inc. Henry Hampton, executive producer.
"Voices of the Civil Rights Movement: Black American Freedom Songs, 1960–66." Smithsonian Folkways Recordings, 1997. Side 1, three songs recorded with Fannie Lou Hamer.

Unpublished Sources

New Orleans, Louisiana. "Autobiography of Fannie Lou Hamer." Fannie Lou Hamer papers, Amistad Research Center.

BELLA ABZUG

Books

Abzug, Bella. *Bella! Ms. Abzug Goes to Washington.* Edited by Mel Ziegler. New York: Saturday Review Press, 1972.
Abzug, Bella, with Mim Kelber. *Gender Gap: Bella Abzug's Guide to Political Power for American Women.* Boston: Houghton Mifflin, 1984.
Antler, Joyce. *The Journey Home: Jewish Women and the American Century.* New York: Free Press, 1997. Chapter 9, "Feminist Liberations. First Mothers: Betty Friedan and Bella Abzug," pp. 259–79.
Breton, Malry Jo. *Women Pioneers for the Environment.* Boston: Northeastern University Press, 1998. Chapter 12, "Women and International Forums, Bella Abzug," pp. 281–84.
Donner, Frank J. *The Age of Surveillance: The Aims and Methods of America's Political Intelligence System.* New York: Random House, 1981. Bella Abzug, pp. 271, 273n.
Echols, Alice. *Daring to Be Bad: Radical Feminism in America, 1967–1975.* Minneapolis: University of Minnesota Press, 1989.
Glenn, Susan A. *Daughters of the Shtetl: Life and Labor in the Immigrant Generation.* Ithaca, N.Y.: Cornell University Press, 1990
Rosen, Ruth. *The World Split Open: How the Modern Women's Movement Changed America.* New York: Penguin Books, 2001
Swerdlow, Amy. *Women Strike for Peace: Traditional Motherhood and Radical Politics in the 1960s.* Chicago: University of Chicago Press, 1993. Chapter 7, "The Women's Vote Is the Peace Vote," about Abzug's early days in WSP.

Unpublished Sources

New York, New York. Columbia University, Manuscript Library, Bella Abzug Papers. Congressional materials, 1970–76. Material added in 1981 includes transcripts of oral history interviews.
Swerdlow, Amy, "The Impact of Bella Abzug's Youthful Commitment to Labor Zionism on Her Lifelong Political Theory and Practice." Unpublished paper.

Articles

Abzug, Bella. "In Her Own Words: A Sampling of Speeches by Bella S. Abzug." New York: Women's Environmental and Development Organization, 1998.
———. "Women and the Environment." In *Focus on Women: Looking Beyond 2000.* International Authors Series. New York: United Nations, 1995.
Collins, Gail. "When Politics Had Passion: Bella Abzug and Paul O'Dwyer." *New York Times Magazine,* January 3, 1999, p. 31.

Cook, Blanche Wiesen. *Jewish Women in America: An Historical Encyclopedia.* Vol. 1. New York: Routledge, 1998. Bella Abzug, pp. 5–10.

Echols, Alice. "'We Gotta Get Out of This Place': Notes toward a Remapping of the Sixties." In *Cultural Politics and Social Movements,* edited by Marcy Darnovsky, Barbara Epstein, and Richard Flacks. Philadelphia: Temple University Press, 1995, pp. 110–130.

Friedman, Leon. "How to Get Your File." *Ms.,* June 1977, p. 42.

Lyall, Sarah. "London Journal: With a Parting Swipe, Women of the House Exit." *New York Times,* May 18, 2001, p.A4.

Mansnerus, Laura. "Bella Abzug, 77, Congresswoman and a Founding Feminist, Is Dead." *New York Times,* April 1, 1998, p. 1.

Nagourney, Adam. "Recalling Bella Abzug's Politics and Passion." *New York Times,* April 3, 1998, 17.

Nies, Judith. "The Abzug Campaign: A Lesson in Politics." *Ms.,* February 1973, p. 76.

Pogrebin, Letty Cottin. "The FBI Was Watching You." *Ms.,* June,1977, 37–44, 69–76.

Interviews and Correspondence

Abzug, Liz. Interview with author. New York, March 16, 2001.

Holzer, Harold, former press secretary. Copies of remarks at memorial service. April 2, 1998.

Kelber, Mim. Interview with author. Brooklyn, New York, March 17, 2001.

Lewis, Ann. Telephone interview with author. February 4, 2001.

Steinem, Gloria. Telephone interview with author. February 10, 2001.

Swerdlow, Amy. Telephone interview with author. July 12, 2001.

Zeitlin, June. Interview with author, New York. March 16, 2001.

Videos

"Bella's Last Decade." Prudence Hill, producer. Video montage produced by Women's Environment and Development Organization. New York. April 24, 1998.

"Funeral Service." Filmed by Skip Blumberg, April 2, 1998. Women's Environment and Development Organization.

"Intimate Portrait: Bella Abzug." New York: International Digital Centre, date unknown.

United Nations Public Tribute. Filmed by Skip Blumberg and UNTV, April 24, 1998.

WOMEN IN THE ENVIRONMENTAL MOVEMENT

Books

Boulding, Elise. *The Underside of History.* Newbury Park, Calif.: Sage, 1992.

Breton, Mary Joy. *Women Pioneers for the Environment.* Boston: Northeastern University Press, 1998.

Brown, Lester, ed. *Vital Signs, 1997: The Environmental Trends That Are Shaping Our Future.* Washington, D.C.: World Watch Institute; New York: Norton, 1996.

Caldicott, Helen. *If You Love This Planet.* New York: Norton, 1992.

Carson, Rachel. *Silent Spring.* Boston: Houghton Mifflin, 1962.

Colburn, Theo, Dianne Dumanoski, and John Peterson Myers. *Our Stolen Future: Are We Threatening Our Fertility, Intelligence and Survival? A Scientific Detective Story.* New York: Dutton, 1996.

Cronon, William. *Uncommon Ground: Rethinking the Human Place in Nature.* New York: Norton, 1996.

Crosby, Alfred W. *The Columbian Exchange: Biological and Cultural Consequences of 1492.* Westport, Conn.: Greenwood Press, 1972.

Douglas, Marjory Stoneman. *The Everglades: River of Grass.* 1947. Reprint, Marietta, Ga.: Mockingbird Books, 1995.

Fox, Stephen. *The American Conservation Movement: John Muir and His Legacy.* Madison: University of Wisconsin Press, 1985.

Gibbs, Lois, as told to Murray Levine. *Love Canal: My Story.* Albany: State University of New York Press, 1982.

Gore, Al. *Earth in the Balance: Ecology and the Human Spirit.* New York: Penguin Books, 1993.

Hawken, Paul. *The Ecology of Commerce.* New York: HarperCollins, 1993.

Henderson, Hazel. *Creating Alternative Futures: The End of Economics.* New York: G. P. Putnam's Sons, 1978.

Kohn, Howard. *Who Killed Karen Silkwood?* New York: Simon and Schuster, 1981.

Korten, David. *When Corporations Rule the World.* West Hartford, Conn.: Kumarian Press; San Francisco: Berrett-Koehler Publishers, 1995.

Lyons, Oren R., and John C. Mohawk. *Exiled in the Land of the Free: Democracy, Indian Nations and the U.S. Constitution.* Preface by Senator Daniel K. Inouye. Forward by Peter Matthiessen. Santa Fe, N.M.: Clear Light Publishers, 1992.

Mander, Gerry. *In the Absence of the Sacred: The Failure of Technology and the Survival of Indian Nations.* San Francisco: Sierra Club Books, 1992.

Mander, Gerry, and Edward Goldsmith. *The Case against the Global Economy and for a Turn toward the Local.* San Francisco: Sierra Club Books, 1996.

Meadows, Donella. *The Limits to Growth: A Report for the Club of Rome's Project on the Predicament of Mankind.* New York: Universe Books, 1974.

Merchant, Carolyn. *The Death of Nature: Women, Ecology, and the Scientific Revolution.* San Francisco: HarperSanFrancisco, 1989.

———. *Ecological Revolutions: Nature, Gender and Science in New England.* Chapel Hill: University of North Carolina Press, 1989.

Murie, Margaret. *Two in the Far North.* New York: Knopf, 1962.

Reisner, Marc. *Cadillac Desert: The American West and Its Disappearing Water.* New York: Viking Penguin, 1986.

Thomas, Janet. *The Battle in Seattle: The Story behind and beyond the WTO Demonstrations.* Golden, Colo.: Fulcrum Publishing, 2000.

Thompson, William Irwin. *The American Replacement of Nature: The Everyday Acts and Outrageous Evolution of Economic Life.* New York: Doubleday Currency, 1991.

Wagner, Sally Roesch. *Sisters in Spirit: Iroquois Influence on Early American Feminists.* Summertown, TN: Native Voices Book Publishing Company, 2001.

Articles

"Corporate Futures: An Interview with Paul Hawken and David Korten." *Yes!,* summer, 1999, p.1.

Guignard, Lilace Mellin. "Mapping Wilderness: Preservation and Paradox in Nevada's Back Country." *Orion Afield,* winter 2001–2.

Mitchell, John. *Sanctuary,* magazine of Massachusetts Audubon Society, special 100th anniversary issue, 1996.

"Nature's Voice." Natural Resources Defense Council, January/February 2002.

Nies, Judith. "The Black Mesa Syndrome." *Orion,* summer 1998, pp. 18–29.

"Two Bushes and the Everglades," *New York Times,* editorial, November 23, 2001, A32.

Verhovek, Sam Howe. "Drilling Could Hurt Wildlife, Federal Study of Arctic Says." *New York Times*, March 30, 2002, p. A12.

Unpublished Sources

Price, Jennifer. "When Women Were Women, Men Were Men, and Birds Were Hats: Gender Roles and the Formation of the Audubon Societies at the Turn of the Century." Unpublished manuscript, January 8, 1989.

Interviews

Roberta Blackgoat, interviews with author Feb. 21–24, 1991.
Martha Blue, telephone interview with author, January 23, 2002.

SELECTED BIBLIOGRAPHY ON WOMEN, RADICALS, AND HISTORIOGRAPHY

Abcarian, Gilbert. *American Political Radicalism*. Waltham, Mass.: Xerox College Publishing, 1971.

Adams, Russell. *Great Negroes Past and Present*. Chicago: Afro-American Publishing Co., Inc., 1969.

Alinsky, Saul. *Rules for Radicals: A Pragmatic Primer for Realistic Radicals*. New York: Random House, Vintage Books, 1972.

Arendt, Hannah. *On Revolution*. New York: The Viking Press, 1965.

Ash, Roberta. *Social Movements in America*. Chicago: Markham Publishing Co., 1972.

Aya, Roderick, and Miller, Norman, eds. *The New American Revolution*. New York: The Free Press, 1971.

Barber, Benjamin R. *Superman and Common Men: Freedom, Anarchy and the Revolution*. New York: Praeger, 1971.

Bardwick, Judith. *Readings on the Psychology of Women*. New York: Harper & Row, 1972.

Berger, Peter L., and Neuhaus, Richard J. *Movement and Revolution*. New York: Doubleday, 1970.

Bernstein, Barton J. *Towards a New Past: Dissenting Essays in American History*. New York: Pantheon Books, 1968.

Blackwell, Sarah Ellen. *A Military Genius: Life of Anna Ella Carroll of Maryland*. Washington: Judd & Detweiler, 1891.

Block, Marc. *The Historian's Craft*. New York: Alfred A. Knopf, 1953.

Bolton, Sarah K. *Lives of Girls Who Became Famous*. New York: Thomas Y. Crowell, 1941.

Bottomore, T. B. *Critics of Society: Radical Thought in North America*. New York: Random House, Vintage Books, 1969.

Breckinridge, S. P. *Women in the Twentieth Century: A Study of Their Political, Social and Economic Activities*. New York: McGraw-Hill, 1933. Reprint. New York: Arno Press and The New York Times, 1969. A report of the President's Research Committee on Social Trends formed by Herbert Hoover in 1929 and funded by the Rockefeller Foundation.

Carr, Edward Hallett. *What is History?* New York: Alfred A. Knopf, 1967.

Chafe, William Henry. *The American Woman: Her Changing Social, Economic and Political Roles, 1920–1970*. New York: Oxford University Press, 1972.

Chamberlin, Hope. *A Minority of Members: Women in the U.S. Congress*. New York: Praeger, 1973.

Choisy, Maryse. *Psychoanalysis of the Prostitute*. New York, 1961.

Civics Society, Chicago, Illinois. *The Woman Citizen's Library*. 12 vols. Chicago:

Civics Society, 1913. A systematic course of reading in preparation for the larger citizenship. Vol. 9, *Why Women Are Concerned with the Larger Citizenship,* by Jane Addams.

Clarke, Ida Clyde. *American Women and the World War.* New York: D. Appleton, 1918.

Commager, Henry Steele. *The Era of Reform, 1830–1860.* Princeton, N.J.: Van Nostrand, 1960.

———. *The Search for a Usable Past.* New York: Alfred A. Knopf, 1967.

Davis, Elisabeth Logan. *Mothers of America.* London: Fleming H. Revell Co., 1954.

Diamond, Solomon. *A Study of the Influence of Political Radicalism on Personality Development.* New York: Columbia University Press, 1936.

Duberman, Martin. *The Uncompleted Past.* New York: Random House, 1971.

———. *The Antislavery Vanguard: New Essays on the Abolitionists.* Princeton, N.J.: Princeton University Press, 1965.

Ellet, Elizabeth. *The Women of the American Revolution.* Vol. 1. Philadelphia: George W. Jacobs, 1900.

Ellul, Jacques. *Violence: Reflections from a Christian Perspective.* London: SCM Press Ltd., 1970.

Epstein, Cynthia Fuchs. *Woman's Place: Options and Limits in Professional Careers.* Berkeley, Ca.: University of California Press, 1971.

Epstein, Cynthia Fuchs, and Goode, William J. *The Other Half: Roads to Women's Equality.* Englewood Cliffs, N.J.: Prentice-Hall, Inc., 1971.

Erikson, Erik. *Identity, Youth and Crisis.* New York: W. W. Norton, 1968.

Ferris, Helen Josephine. *When I Was a Girl.* New York: Macmillan, 1930. Autobiographical stories of childhood told by Marie Curie, Jane Addams, Eleanor Roosevelt, Ernestine Schumann-Heink, etc.

Firestone, Shulamith. *The Dialectic of Sex.* New York: Bantam, 1971.

Fuller, Margaret, ed. *The Dial.* 1840–1844. Microfilm, Library of Congress, Washington, D.C.

Goldberg, Harvey, ed. *American Radicals: Some Problems and Personalities.* New York: Monthly Review Press, 1957.

Goldman, Emma. *Living My Life.* 2 vols. 1931. Reprint. New York: DaCapo Press, 1970.

———. *My Disillusionment in Russia.* New York: Thomas Y. Crowell, 1970.

Gornick, Vivian, and Morgan, Barbara K. *Woman in Sexist Society: Studies in Power and Powerlessness.* New York: New American Library, 1971.

Griffin, Clifford, S. *Their Brothers' Keepers: Moral Stewardship in the United States, 1800–1865.* New Brunswick, N.J.: Rutgers University Press, 1960.

Hamalian, Leo, and Karl, Frederick R., eds. *The Radical Vision: Essays for the Seventies.* New York: Thomas Y. Crowell, 1970.

Hampden-Turner, Charles. *Radical Man: The Process of Psycho-Social Development.* Cambridge, Mass.: Schenkman Publishing Co., 1970.

Harrington, Michael. *Toward a Democratic Left.* New York: Macmillan, 1960.

———. *Socialism.* New York: Saturday Review Press, 1972.

Hecker, Eugene A. *A Short History of Women's Rights: From the Days of Augustus to the Present Time. With Special Reference to England and the United States.* New York: G. P. Putnam's Sons, 1914. Reprint. Westport, Conn.: Greenwood Press, 1971.

Herschberger, Ruth. *Adam's Rib.* New York: Harper & Row, 1970. First published 1948.

Hofstadter, Richard. *The Progressive Historians.* New York: Alfred A. Knopf, 1968.
———. *The American Political Tradition and the Men Who Made It.* New York: Alfred A. Knopf, 1948.
Hofstadter, Richard; Miller, William; and Aaron, Daniel. *The American Republic.* 2 vols. Englewood Cliffs, N.J.: Prentice-Hall, 1959.
Hole, Judith, and Levine, Ellen. *Rebirth of Feminism.* New York: Quadrangle Books, 1971.
Howe, Irving, ed. *The Radical Imagination.* New York: New American Library, 1967.
———. *The Radical Papers.* New York: Doubleday, 1966.
Huber, Joan, ed. *Changing Women in a Changing Society.* Chicago: University of Chicago Press, 1973.
Ingraham, Claire R. and Leonard W. *An Album of Women in American History.* New York: Franklin Watts, 1972.
Irwin, Inez Haynes. *Angels and Amazons: A Hundred Years of American Women.* New York: Doubleday, 1933.
Jacobs, Paul, and Landau, Saul. *The New Radicals.* New York: Random House, Vintage Books, 1965.
Janeway, Elizabeth. *Man's World, Woman's Place: A Study in Social Mythology.* New York: William Morrow & Co., 1972.
Kanowitz, Leo. *Women and the Law: The Unfinished Revolution.* Alburquerque: University of New Mexico Press, 1969.
Kempton, Murray. *Part of Our Time.* New York: Simon & Schuster, 1955.
Keniston, Kenneth. *Young Radicals: Notes on Committed Youth.* New York: Harcourt Brace & World, 1968.
Kennedy, Davis M. *Birth Control in America: The Career of Margaret Sanger.* New Haven: Yale University Press, 1970.
Kisner, Arlene, ed. *The Lives and Writings of the Notorious Victoria Woodhull and Her Sister Tennessee Claflin.* Washington, N.J.: Times Change Press, 1972.
Koedt, Anne; Levine, Ellen; and Rapone, Anita, eds. *Radical Feminism.* New York: Quadrangle Books, 1973.
Lasch, Christopher. *The Agony of the American Left.* New York: Alfred A. Knopf, 1969.
———. *The New Radicalism in America, 1889–1963: The Intellectual as a Social Type.* New York: Random House, Vintage Books, 1965.
Lens, Sidney. *Radicalism in America.* New York: Thomas Y. Crowell, 1969.
Lerner, Gerda. *The Woman in American History.* Reading, Mass.: Addison-Wesley Publishing Co., 1971.
Lifton, Robert Jay. *History and Human Survival.* New York: Random House, 1970.
———, ed. *The Woman in America.* Boston: Beacon Press, 1967. First issued as Spring 1964 issue of *Daedalus.*
Lindenfeld, Frank. *Radical Perspectives on Social Problems: Readings in Critical Sociology.* New York: Macmillan, 1968.
Lippmann, Walter. *Drift and Mastery.* New York: Mitchell Kennerley, 1914.
Lipset, Seymour, and Hofstadter, Richard, eds. *Sociology and History: Methods.* New York: Basic Books, 1968.
Logan, Mrs. John A. *The Part Taken by Women in American History.* Wilmington, Del.: Perry-Nalle Publishing Co., 1912.
Long, Priscilla. *The New Left: A Collection of Essays.* Boston: Porter Sargent, 1969.
Lynd, Staughton. *Intellectual Origins of American Radicalism.* New York: Random House, Vintage Books, 1969.

Madison, Charles A. *Critics and Crusaders: A Century of American Protest.* New York: Henry Holt & Co., 1947.

Massey, Mary Elizabeth. *Bonnet Brigades: Women in the Civil War.* New York: Alfred A. Knopf, 1966.

Miller, Perry. *The Life of the Mind in America: From the Revolution to the Civil War.* New York: Harcourt Brace & World, 1965.

Mitchell, Juliet. *Woman's Estate.* New York: Random House, Vintage Books, 1971.

Nevins, Allan, and Commager, Henry Steele. *A Short History of the United States.* New York: Alfred A. Knopf, 1966.

Notable American Women: A Biographical Dictionary. 3 vols. Cambridge, Mass.: Belknap Press of Harvard University, 1971.

Oglesby, Carl. *The New Left Reader.* New York: Grove Press, 1969.

O'Neill, William. *Coming Apart: An Informal History of America in the 1960's.* Chicago: Quadrangle Books, 1971.

———. *Everyone Was Brave: The Rise and Fall of Feminism in America.* Chicago: Quadrangle Books, 1969.

———. *The Woman Movement.* New York: Barnes & Noble, 1969.

Parker, Gail, ed. *The Oven Birds: American Women on Womanhood, 1820–1920.* New York: Doubleday, 1972.

Parkes, Henry Bamford. *The American Experience: An Interpretation of the History and Civilization of the American People.* New York: Random House, Vintage Books, 1959.

Randall, Mercedes Moritz. *Improper Bostonian: A Biography of Emily Greene Balch.* New York: Twayne Publishers, 1964.

Reigel, Robert. *American Woman: A Story of Social Change.* Rutherford, N.J.: Fairleigh Dickinson University Press, 1970.

Reisman, David. *Abundance For What: And Other Essays.* New York: Doubleday, 1964.

Rogers, Agnes. *Women Are Here to Stay: The Durable Sex in Its Infinite Variety through Half a Century of American Life.* New York: Harper & Brothers, 1949.

Rossi, Alice S., ed. *Essays on Sex Equality by John Stuart Mill and Harriet Taylor Mill.* Chicago: University of Chicago Press, 1970.

Rosenberg, Bernard, and Fliegel, Norris. *The Vanguard Artist: Portrait and Self-portrait.* Chicago: Quadrangle Books, 1965.

Sampson, Ronald Victor. *The Psychology of Power.* New York: Pantheon Books, 1966.

Scott, Anne Firor. *The American Woman: Who Was She?* Englewood Cliffs, N.J.: Prentice-Hall, 1971.

———. *The Southern Lady: From Pedestal to Politics, 1830–1930.* Chicago: University of Chicago Press, 1970.

Sillen, Samuel. *Women Against Slavery.* New York: Masses and Mainstream, 1955.

Sinclair, Andrew. *The Emancipation of the American Woman.* New York: Harper & Row, 1965.

Smith, Page. *Daughters of the Promised Land: Women in American History.* Boston: Little, Brown, 1970.

Steffens, Lincoln Joseph. *The Letters of Lincoln Steffens.* Vol. I, 1889–1919. Vol. II, 1920–1936. New York: Harcourt Brace, 1938.

———. *The Autobiography of Lincoln Steffens.* 2 vols. New York: Harcourt Brace & World, 1931.

Storr, Anthony. *The Dynamics of Creation.* New York: Atheneum, 1972.

Terrell, Mary Church. *A Colored Woman in a White World.* Washington, D.C.: Ransdell Publishers, 1940.

Tolstoy, Leo. *The Law of Love and the Law of Violence.* New York: Holt, Rinehart and Winston, 1970.

Wascow, Arthur I. *Running Riot.* New York: Herder and Herder, 1970.

Wieth-Knudsen, Knud Asbjorn. *Feminism: A Sociological Study of the Woman Question from Ancient Times to the Present Day.* London: Constable & Co., Ltd., 1928.

Williams, William Appleman. *The Contours of American History.* Cleveland & New York: World Publishing Co., 1961.

Winick, Charles. *The New People: Desexualization in American Life.* New York: Pegasus Press, 1968.

Wollstonecraft, Mary. *A Vindication of the Rights of Woman.* New York: W. W. Norton & Co., 1967.

UPDATED
BIBLIOGRAPHY

———————◆·▸◆◂·◆———————

Since the original bibliography was compiled, a new generation of writers and scholars has addressed the lives of many of these women. The following appended bibliography highlights a few of the current biographies or new editions of previous collections that incorporate explanatory introductions or interpretive essays.

SARAH GRIMKE

Bartlett, Elizabeth Ann. *Liberty, Equality, Sorority: The Origins and Interpretation of American Feminist Thought—Frances Wright, Sarah Grimke and Margaret Fuller.* Brooklyn, N.Y.: Carlson Publishers, 1994.

Bartlett, Elizabeth Ann, ed. *Letters on the Equality of the Sexes and Other Essays by Sarah Grimke.* New Haven: Yale University Press, 1988.

Lerner, Gerda. *The Feminist Thought of Sarah Grimke.* New York: Oxford University Press, 1998.

HARRIET TUBMAN

Bradford, Sarah. Introduction by Butler Jones. *Harriet Tubman: The Moses of Her People.* Secaucus, N.J.: Carol Publishing Group, 1997.

ELIZABETH CADY STANTON

Farrell, Michael P. *Collaborative Circles: Friendship Dynamics and Creative Work.* Chicago: University of Chicago Press, 2001.

Gordon, Ann D, ed. *The Selected Papers of Elizabeth Cady Stanton and Susan B. Anthony.* New Brunswick, N.J.: Rutgers University Press, 1997.

Griffith, Elisabeth. *In Her Own Right: The Life of Elizabeth Cady Stanton.* New York: Oxford University Press, 1984.

"Not For Ourselves Alone: The Story of Elizabeth Cady Stanton and Susan B. Anthony," a documentary film by Ken Burns and Paul Barnes. Burbank, California: PBS Home Video, 1999.

Waggenspack, Beth Marie. *The Search for Self-Sovereignty: The Oratory of Elizabeth Cady Stanton.* New York: Greenwood Press, 1989.

Ward, Geoffrey C. *Not For Ourselves Alone: The Story of Elizabeth Cady Stanton and Susan B. Anthony: An Illustrated History.* Based on the documentary film by Ken Burns. New York: Knopf, 1999.

CHARLOTTE PERKINS GILMAN

Gilman, Charlotte Perkins. *The Dress of Women: A Critical Introduction to the Symbolism and Sociology of Clothing*. With an introduction by Michael R. Hill and Mary Jo Deegan. Westport, Conn: Greenwood Press, 2002.

Gilman, Charlotte Perkins. *Women and Economics: A Study of the Economic Relations Between Men and Women as a Factor in Social Evolution*. Introduction by Michael Kimmel and Amy Aronson. Berkeley, Calif: University of California Press, 1998.

Hill, Mary Armfield. *Charlotte Perkins Gilman: The Making of a Radical Feminist, 1860–1896*. Philadelphia: Temple University Press, 1980.

Kessler, Carol Farley. *Charlotte Perkins Gilman: Her Progress Toward Utopia*. With selected writings. Syracuse, N.Y.: Syracuse University Press, 1995.

Knight, Denise, ed. *The Later Poetry of Charlotte Perkins Gilman*. London: Associated University Presses, 1996.

Knight, Denise, ed. *The Yellow Wallpaper and Selected Stories of Charlotte Perkins Gilman*. Newark: University of Delaware Press, 1994.

Lane, Ann J. *To Herland and Beyond: The Life and Work of Charlotte Perkins Gilman*. New York: Pantheon Books, 1990.

MOTHER JONES

Atkinson, Linda. *Mother Jones, the Most Dangerous Woman in America*. New York: Crown Publishers, 1978.

Foner, Philp S., ed. *Mother Jones Speaks: Collected Writings and Speeches*. New York: Monad Press, 1983.

Gorn, Elliott J. *Mother Jones: The Most Dangerous Woman in America*. New York: Hill and Wang, 2001.

Steel, Edward M., ed. *The Correspondence of Mother Jones*. Pittsburgh, Pa.: University of Pittsburgh Press, 1985.

Steel, Edward M., ed. *The Speeches and Writings of Mother Jones*. Pittsburgh, Pa.: University of Pittsburgh Press, 1988.

ANNA LOUISE STRONG

Strong, Tracy B. and Keyssar, Helene. *Right in Her Soul: The Life of Anna Louise Strong*. New York: Random House, 1983.

DOROTHY DAY

Klejment, Anne and Roberts, Nancy L, eds. *American Catholic Pacifism: The Influence of Dorothy Day and the Catholic Worker Movement*. Westport, Conn: Praeger, 1996.

Mass, Mark Stephen. *Catholics and American Culture: Fulton Sheen, Dorothy Day and the Notre Dame Football Team*. New York: Crossroad Publishing Co., 1999.

Merriman, Brigid O'Shea. *Searching for Christ: The Spirituality of Dorothy Day*. Notre Dame, Ind.: University of Notre Dame Press, 2001.

Miller, William D. *Dorothy Day: A Biography*. San Francisco: Harper & Row, 1982.

O'Connor, June. *The Moral Vision of Dorothy Day: A Feminist Perspective*. New York: Crossroad, 1991.

INDEX

BAKER & TAYLOR